JOURNAL FOR THE STUDY OF THE OLD TESTAMENT
SUPPLEMENT SERIES

60

Editors
David J A Clines
Philip R Davies

JSOT Press
Sheffield

HER PRICE IS BEYOND RUBIES

The Jewish Woman in Graeco-Roman Palestine

Léonie J. Archer

Journal for the Study of the Old Testament
Supplement Series 60

HQ
1172
.A7
1989

Published by JSOT Press
JSOT Press is an imprint of
Sheffield Academic Press Ltd
The University of Sheffield
343 Fulwood Road
Sheffield S10 3BP
England

Typeset by Sheffield Academic Press
and
Printed in Great Britain
by Billing & Sons Ltd
Worcester

British Library Cataloguing in Publication Data

Archer, Léonie J.
    Her price is beyond rubies: the Jewish
    woman in Graeco-Roman Palestine.
    (JSOT Supplement Series: ISSN 0309-0787; 60)
    1. Palestine. Jews, history
    I. Title   II. Series
    956.94'004 924

ISBN 1-85075-079-3

CONTENTS

PREFACE

This book springs directly from my doctoral thesis which was submitted to the University of London in 1983. Apart from some additional material in the form of supplementary notes and the inclusion of a chapter on death ritual, the text is unchanged from that of the original thesis. As in 1983, its focus is on uncovering a history, tracing the practicalities of a lifestyle, and bringing to light the wealth of previously untapped (from this perspective) source material. In this respect the work reflects a particular stage in my personal history vis-à-vis feminism. In 1983 I researched and wrote in response to the requirements of doing women's history. Were I to be writing now the emphasis would lie more with explicit analysis of social forms, language, gender construction, and so on—issues only implicit to the present text but of primary concern to feminist scholarship. Having said this, however, I believe this volume constitutes a significant and valuable starting point: it looks at a previously unaddressed history; demonstrates the need for an interdisciplinary approach to the subject; and reveals the considerable amount of source material available for a study of women in Graeco-Roman Palestine. The necessary spadework has been done for future study of this period which was so vital to the development of Judaism and changing attitudes vis-à-vis women.

Léonie J. Archer
Oxford, March 1989

ABBREVIATIONS

PRIMARY SOURCES

OLD TESTAMENT			
Chron.	Chronicles		
Dan.	Daniel		
Deut.	Deuteronomy		
Esth.	Esther		
Exod.	Exodus		
Ezr.	Ezra		
Ezek.	Ezekiel		
Gen.	Genesis		
Hos.	Hosea		
Isa.	Isaiah		
Jer.	Jeremiah		
Josh.	Joshua		
Judg.	Judges		
Kgs	Kings		
Koh.	Koheleth		
Lam.	Lamentations		
Lev.	Leviticus		
Mal.	Malachi		
Mic.	Micah		
Neh.	Nehemiah		
Num.	Numbers		
Prov.	Proverbs		
Ps.	Psalms		
Sam.	Samuel		

APOCRYPHA, PSEUDEPIGRAPHA	
Apoc. Mos.	*Apocalypse of Moses*
Sir.	Ben Sira
Ep. Jer.	*Epistle of Jeremy*
Jub.	*Jubilees*
Jdt.	Judith
Macc.	Maccabees
Ps. Sol.	*Psalms of Solomon*
Sib. Or.	*Sibylline Oracles*

T. Ben.	*Testament of Benjamin*
T. Jos.	*Testament of Joseph*
T. Levi	*Testament of Levi*
T. Reub.	*Testament of Reuben*
Tob.	Tobit

JOSEPHUS	
Ant.	*Antiquitates Judaicae* (Antiquities of the Jews)
BJ	*Bellum Judaicae* (Jewish War)
Con. Ap.	*Contra Apionem* (Against Apion)

PHILO	
Abr.	*De Abrahamo* (On Abraham)
Ebr.	*De Ebrietate* (on Drunkenness)
Fug.	*De Fuga et Inventione* (On Flight and Finding)
Jos.	*De Iosepho* (On Joseph)
Leg.	*De Legatione ad Gaium* (On the Embassy to Gaius)
Leg. All.	*Legum Allegoria* (Allegorical Interpretations)
Op. Mun.	*De Opificio Mundi* (On the Creation)

6   Her Price is Beyond Rubies

Sac.	De Sacrificio Abelis et Caini (on the Sacrifices of Abel and Cain)	M.K.	Moed Katan
		Naz.	Nazir
		Ned.	Nedarim
		Nidd.	Niddah
Spec. Leg.	De Specialibus Legibus (On the Special Laws)	Ohol.	Oholoth
		Pes.	Pesahim
		R.H.	Rosh ha-Shana
Virt.	De Virtutibus (On the Virtues)	Sanh.	Sanhedrin
		Shabb.	Shabbath
Vit. Cont.	De Vita Contemplativa (On the Contemplative Life)	Sem.	Semachoth
		Shek.	Shekalim
		Shev.	Shevuoth
		Sot.	Sotah
Vit. Mos.	De Vita Mosis (Moses)	Sukk.	Sukkah
		Taan.	Taanith
		Tem.	Temurah
QUMRAN		Ter.	Terumoth
CD	Damascus Document	Toh.	Tohoroth
		Yeb.	Yebamoth
DSS	Dead Sea Scrolls		
Gen. Apoc.	Genesis Apocryphon	t.	Tosefta
		y.	Yerushalmi

TALMUD		NEW TESTAMENT	
Arak.	Arakhin	Col.	Colossians
A.Z.	Abodah Zarah	Cor.	Corinthians
B.B.	Baba Bathra	Gal.	Galatians
B.K.	Baba Kamma	Jn	John
B.M.	Baba Metzia	Lk.	Luke
Ber.	Berakhoth	Mt.	Matthew
Bikk.	Bikkurim	Mk	Mark
Eduy.	Eduyoth	Pet.	Peter
Erub.	Erubin	Phil.	Philippians
Gitt.	Gittin	Rom.	Romans
Hag.	Hagigah	Tim.	Timothy
Hor.	Horayoth		
Hull.	Hullin	EUSEBIUS	
Kel.	Kelim	HE	Historia Ecclesiastica
Kerith.	Kerithoth		
Ket.	Kethuboth	Praep. Evan.	Praeparatio Evangelica
Kidd.	Kiddushin		
Kil.	Kilaim		
M. Sh.	Maaser Sheni	Deut. Rab.	Deuteronomy Rabbah
Makk.	Makkoth		
Meg.	Megillah	Gen. Rab.	Genesis Rabbah
Men.	Menahoth	Ps. Jon.	Pseudo-Jonathan
Midd.	Middoth		

SECONDARY SOURCES

AAJR	American Academy for Jewish Research
ALUOS	*Annual of the Leeds University Oriental Society*
BA	*Biblical Archaeologist*
BASOR	*Bulletin of the American Schools of Oriental Research*
C.	Cowley, *Aramaic Papyri of the Fifth Century B.C.*
CPJ	*Corpus Papyrorum Judaicarum*
DJD	*Discoveries in the Judaean Desert*, ed. Benoit, Milik, *et al.*
EJ	*Encyclopaedia Judaica*
HUCA	*Hebrew Union College Annual*
IEJ	*Israel Exploration Journal*
JOAS	*Journal of the American Oriental Society*
JBL	*Journal of Biblical Literature*
JE	*Jewish Encyclopaedia*
JJS	*Journal of Jewish Studies*
JPOS	*Journal of the Palestine Oriental Society*
JQR	*Jewish Quarterly Review*
JSS	*Journal of Semitic Studies*
K.	Kraeling, *The Brooklyn Museum Aramaic Papyri*
PAAJR	*Proceedings of the American Academy for Jewish Research*
PEQ	*Palestine Exploration Quarterly*
RB	*Revue Biblique*
RQ	*Revue de Qumran*

INTRODUCTION

The purpose of this volume is to examine the social and legal position of the Jewish woman in Palestine during the Graeco-Roman period—or, to use different chronological demarcation points, during the intertestamental period (so-called) and the Mishnaic period. The book will examine the attitude which Jewish society had towards its women, and will present the consequences of that attitude by surveying various aspects of the woman's daily existence (for example, domestic activity, duties as wife and mother, permitted movement in the public arena, dress, etc.) and significant (ritualized) transition points in her life (for example, marriage, divorce, death).

Although the focus of the survey will be on the Graeco-Roman period, it will also reach back in time to the Old Testament and in particular to the sixth-century BCE exile to Babylon—an event which has aptly been labelled a watershed in the history of Judaism. Its cut-off point at the other end of the scale will be c. 200 CE when the oldest extant code of Jewish law, the Mishnah, was edited. The survey will be restricted to life within Palestine and will cover that period which saw the beginnings of modern rabbinic Judaism, a complex religious and social system quite distinct from that of earlier Hebrew history and of profound significance for the determination of future Jewish development. These centuries were marked by additions to and completion of the Old Testament, a flourishing of extra-canonical writings, the rise of new theologies and philosophies and the production of a detailed oral law, committed to writing in the Mishnah.

In terms of political history, Palestine during this period was first under Persian domination; it then passed into the control of Hellenistic overlords, the Ptolemies and Seleucids (third to second centuries BCE). Following the struggles of the Maccabees in the second century the country enjoyed a brief period of independence under native Jewish rule (the Hasmonaeans) but then in the first century BCE was incorporated into the Roman empire. Finally, it was ruled by vassal princes (the Herodians) and then by Roman governors. The details of this history will not however be our concern here. Our focus will be on what may be termed internal Jewish development, with its shifts in social structure and moves towards becoming a law-bound, purity-conscious, monotheistic nation.

While some general studies have been made of Jewish women in antiquity, little if any work has been done specifically on the changes in attitude and position which occurred during this crucial period—changes which were to have far-reaching implications for women down through the centuries. Previous studies have also tended to be legalistic in character; have concentrated on particular issues rather than reviewing features of daily life; have drawn, usually without discrimination, upon diaspora and Palestinian source material; and have tended to combine material from sources as chronologically diverse as Bible, Talmud and Mediaeval commentary or have drawn solely on the evidence of Bible and/or Talmud without any attention to the intervening literature.

This survey will focus on material from the period in question (while also being aware of historical development from one period to the next), and in addition to looking at important transitional points in the woman's life, will endeavour to trace the reality of everyday experience. As that experience varied according to age and marital status, care will be taken to distinguish between the several legal categories occupied by the woman in the course of her life (again a feature rarely observed by present-day writers). The survey will treat in chronological order the lifestyles of the unbetrothed minor, the betrothed minor, the unbetrothed/unmarried adult, the married adult, the divorcee, the widow, and the dead woman (death also being treated, in line with the sources, in terms of the marital status and age of the woman at the time of her demise). Within this framework, the various subjects to be considered will include property rights, education, kinship law, incest, rape, religious/cultic activity, veiling, work, conjugal rights, maintenance entitlement, and the general legalized subordination of women to the divinely ordained authority of men. The survey will also consider such areas as the ascription of 'innate' gender characteristics to men and women and Jewish society's culturally constructed (male) fear of women (or 'woman'), together with the societal needs which such construction/ascription served. The concern of the review throughout will be with the lifestyle of the 'ordinary' or 'average' woman in Graeco-Roman Palestine. No attention, therefore, will be given to examining the special and peculiar lifestyles of individual personages or members of royal households as these are not representative of the 'average' woman. Notice will be taken— where the sources permit or where conjecture is reasonable— of the differences between urban and rural life. It must be said, however, that the literary material in the main derives from urban circles and consequently provides evidence primarily for life within those communities. In addition the literature, with its own dynamic and purpose, can only be taken as reflecting a possible reality, be that a possibility for the particular community or for society on a wider basis. These considerations must be borne in mind throughout the survey.

The sources utilized will be legalistic, literary, and documentary. They will include the Bible (both Old and New Testaments), the non-canonical books of the Apocrypha and Pseudepigrapha, the Dead Sea Scrolls and the Judaean Desert discoveries, the Talmud (especially Mishnah), and such ancient historians as Josephus and the Alexandrian writers Philo and Pseudo-Phocylides. This material will be supplemented by examination of other archaeological site findings from the period in question. The Alexandrian writings will not be used as independent witnesses but only to supplement or rather complement information gleaned from the Palestinian sources, that is, in those instances where correspondence can be established between the two bodies of literature or when it is apparent from examination of the Palestinian material that they reflect a fundamental of Hellenistic Jewish thought and practice which would have had application both within and outside of Palestine. Certain books of the New Testament will be used in a similar manner where appropriate.

The Old Testament, while technically removed (in the main) from the period under consideration, will of course be utilized, for its law pertained in the Graeco-Roman period and was the foundation for subsequent development. However, care will be taken to differentiate between the pre- and post-exilic strands, and emphasis will be placed on those books (or parts of books) which reflect the changes which occurred in the woman's position consequent v˙ ɔn the exile to Babylon. The reasons for those changes will be examined. As already mentioned, previous studies have tended either to focus on the Bible (taken as some kind of homogeneous whole) or to combine the evidence of chronologically disparate sources with the result that the woman's role and status are seen as static. One concern in this survey is to tease out and emphasize the *dynamic* of women's history. Close attention will therefore be paid to the possible dating of the biblical and extra-biblical texts and to their evidence regarding socio-economic development and structural shifts in Jewish society—a mutually revealing and reinforcing methodology. The traditional sigla J, E, D, and P will on occasion be used, and the continuing majority opinion of locating the Priestly material in the time of the exile and thereafter will be followed.

Central to the survey will be the 'intertestamental' writings which in their re-presentation of biblical law and narrative and in their own additional information bear invaluable witness to the attitudes and practices current within Graeco-Roman Palestine (or at least within certain circles, though probably on a wider level too). Within this body of literature particular attention will be paid to the work of the Jerusalemite Ben Sira (otherwise known as Ecclesiasticus) who had much to say on the position of women in his time. His writings, produced in Hebrew c. 190–175 BCE and later translated into Greek by his grandson, contain a multitude of rules of behaviour for all situations on the basis of ethical conviction, and they will provide the central pivot for the survey as a whole. Other writings which contain extensive, though from the original author's viewpoint largely incidental, information about women will include 1 Maccabees, composed in Palestine in the first decades of the first century BCE and describing the events of 175–135 BCE (the Maccabaean revolt down to the death of Simon); the more rhetorical 2 Maccabees, again written in Palestine (124 BCE) though based on the work of Jason of Cyrene and also telling (in polemical style) of the religious persecution under the Seleucids and the subsequent Maccabaean revolt; *3 Maccabees*, a work of very different character, deriving from Alexandria and written sometime between the second century BCE and the first CE which addresses, in the style of romantic fiction, the legendary and miraculous delivery of the Jews in the time of Ptolemy IV Philopator; *4 Maccabees*, a work in the genre of philosophical literature whose provenance is unknown though it may have been written in Antioch around the middle of the first century CE.

The survey will also draw extensively on the popular book of Tobit, an apocryphal story based on contemporary fables of the grateful dead, which was probably written in the third century BCE, though whether in Palestine or the diaspora remains a matter open to debate; *Ahikar*, another evidently popular work also in the realm of folklore which had its origins in non-Jewish circles but was Judaized in the fourth to third centuries BCE; *Jubilees*, an apocryphal book from Palestine commenting and embellishing in haggadic style on OT Patriarchal history and written, possibly from within pre-Essene hassidic circles, around the middle of the second century BCE; the *Testament of the Twelve Patriarchs*, again an haggadic-style book which was written in Palestine probably around the beginning of the second century BCE but which later suffered extensive interpolations at the hands of Christian scribes.

Works used less frequently in the survey (because they contain less information) will include the *Wisdom of Solomon* (written sometime between 200 BCE and mid-first century CE, possibly from Alexandria); the *Life of Adam and Eve* (a Jewish work surviving in Christian recensions, composed originally around the first or early second century CE); Judith (a quasi-fictional work set in the time of Nebuchadnezzar but written in the mid-second century BCE, possibly deriving from Antioch); the *Genesis Apocryphon* (from Palestine, composed in the second, possibly first, century BCE); and finally the *Sibylline Oracles* (a composite Jewish-Christian work of

which the oldest [Jewish] portions are to be found in Book 3
dated to the first or second century CE and possibly from
Alexandria, though a Judaean origin in part is possible). Texts
deriving specifically from the Qumran community (as
opposed to other material simply found on the Qumran site)
will be rarely used as they in the main provide direct evidence
only for the life of that particular sect. (Details regarding
provenance, character and general problems of these and
other sources used in the survey may conveniently be obtained
from Vols III.i and III.ii of the recently revised work by E.
Schürer, *A History of the Jewish People in the Age of Jesus
Christ*. Particular problems related to their use in the present
work will be discussed in the course of the survey.) Finally,
additional to these writings will be the works of the historian
Josephus (born Jerusalem, 37/38 CE) and the philosopher and
biblical exegete Philo (born Alexandria between 20 and 10
BCE).

   Of the rabbinic texts from the period, reference will be made
predominantly to the Mishnah, the oldest extant code of Jewish law which basically is a record of the decisions reached by
rabbinic scholars in the exegesis of biblical law and narrative
during the period 70–200 CE. The origin or traditional basis of
their decisions and recorded discussions may often be traced
further back in time than this, and the code preserves not only
the final majority opinion but in many cases the views of dis-
senting rabbis also. In this respect it is an invaluable source of
knowledge. (The Tosefta, a collection similar to the Mishnah
but one which never achieved the same status, will also on
occasion be used.) In treating the rabbinic legal material
emphasis will remain with this Tannaitic stratum of the Talmud, though at times it will be necessary to look to the
Amoraic material (essentially a commentary on the earlier
code) for clarification, explanation and occasionally additional
information. As far as possible this material will be used in
conjunction with the other sources, for, taken in isolation it is
difficult to determine the extent to which this complex of
sophisticated legislation had application in everyday life or the
extent to which the rabbis were simply engaging in academic
activity removed from the concerns of the people at large—
points which will be discussed more fully in the course of the

survey. It was only later that the intricate weave of Mishnaic law came to be regarded as normative and orthodox. For the period under consideration, when there was no normative Judaism as such, no one source may legitimately be taken to reflect a broad and general social reality.

The survey will also draw upon such documentary evidence as is available. Unfortunately, this is both limited and fragmentary, and is restricted (from our point of view) almost exclusively to a few marriage contracts and divorce writs from the first and second centuries CE discovered in the Judaean Desert region. (Even more unfortunate is the fact that at the time of writing this book the thirty-five apparently well-preserved documents, dated to 93/94–132 CE and dealing with various law suits and matters of property to do with the Jewish woman Babatha and her family, are still unpublished despite their discovery some thirty-five years ago.) In addition to analysis of such documentary evidence as exists, the survey will also draw upon other discoveries from the realm of archaeology, particularly in the chapter on death ritual where tomb types, funerary inscriptions and grave goods will be discussed.

Throughout the work an, as it were, holistic approach to the evidence and subject matter will be pursued. The impulses, discoveries and models of the methodologically differentiated but without doubt compatible and complementary disciplines of history, sociology and anthropology will be drawn together, and the period's shifts in religious behaviour and thought (the concern of history and theology) will be viewed as aspects of the changes which occurred in the wider network of social, economic and power relations (sociology) together with their ritual manifestations, other societal structures and symbolic forms (anthropology, folklore). On occasion anthropological fieldwork in twentieth-century Palestine will be introduced, not as representative of a continuation of ancient practice but more by way of illustration where the ancient and modern customs seem similar. In the main no cross-cultural analysis or comparative material will be presented.

Without both male and female children the world could not exist, but blessed is he whose children are male, and woe to him whose children are female.

(*Baba Bathra,* 16b)

Chapter 1

EARLY YEARS:
THE LIFE OF THE GIRL WHILE
A MINOR (PRE-12 YEARS)

A. *Attitude toward the Birth of a Daughter*

From the beginning of the literary record of the Hebrews, through the intertestamental literature, the works of Jewish philosophers, historians and sectarians, to the rabbinic writings at the close of the period under consideration, the birth of a son but not that of a daughter was recorded as an occasion of particular significance. Old Testament passages too numerous to cite bear witness to the tremendous desire for male children, record the lengths to which individuals would go to obtain such offspring, and reflect the great joy which surrounded the birth of a boy. Indeed, a son was regarded as a special blessing from above, more often than not the direct result of divine intervention in a couple's life. Thus, for example, Eve, having given birth to the first child to come from a human union (significantly a boy), could triumphantly declare:

> I have gotten a man with the help of the Lord (Gen. 4.1).

while Abraham, having despaired of Sarah's sterility, was informed by God:

> And I will bless her, and moreover I will give thee a son of her; yea, I will bless her and she shall be a mother of nations (Gen. 17.15).

Similarly, in Gen. 30.21-24 we learn that:

> God remembered Rachel and God hearkened to her and opened her womb. And she conceived and bore a son, and said 'God hath taken away my reproach'.

The passage finishes with Rachel's plea for more sons:

And she called his name Joseph, saying 'The Lord add to me
another son'.[1]

So important were sons that barren women sometimes
resorted to the legal fiction of having children by their hand-
maids (Gen. 16.2; 30.3), and in the earliest strands of the Old
Testament even incest (in the later sense of the word, see
below) was condoned if it were to produce male offspring. So,
in Gen. 19.31-38, we are told of how the daughters of Lot, in
the absence of other men, contrived to lie with their father in
order to preserve his seed, and by their union succeeded in
having two sons, Moab and Ben-ammi.[2]

Even where there is no mention of a blessing from above or
of special joy, the birth of a boy, and his name, in the Old Testament was carefully recorded and the formula 'N. son of N.'
formed the basis of all genealogical lists. The birth of a daughter, on the other hand, by no means created such a sensation.
If noted at all, such an occasion received but cursory mention,
often with the omission of the girl's personal name. Indeed, a
detailed analysis of the genealogical tables and general narrative of the Old Testament would indicated a startling disparity
in the ratio of male:female births, a disparity which can in no
way reflect a demographic reality. It does, however, reflect the
ancients' attitude toward the birth of a daughter.

In their re-presentation of Old Testament narratives, the
intertestamental writers continued to emphasize the importance of sons, at times elaborating the original stories in a
revealing way. Thus, for example, in recounting the trials and
tribulations of Joseph with the wife of Potiphar (Gen. 39.7f.),
the author of the *Testament of Joseph* chose to give as the reason for the Egyptian woman's behaviour not sexual frustra-
tion or dissatisfaction with her husband, but rather the fact

---

1   Verse 23b derives the name Joseph from אסף, to take away, but v. 24 more naturally
    has it coming from יסף, to add. Note that in the Old Testament barrenness usually
    denoted absence of male offspring, and infertility was seen as only occurring in
    women, a tradition which continued through the centuries.
2   For the use of concubines and handmaidens in this early period and the legiti-
    macy of offspring from such unions, see Archer, 'The Virgin and the Harlot in
    the Writings of Formative Judaism', *History Workshop Journal* 24 (Autumn
    1987), p. 4. Regarding changes in the attitude toward and definition of incest in
    Hebrew/Jewish society, see *ibid.*, pp. 4-7 and below pp. 133ff.

that she had had no male child, a 'fact' by no means even implied in the biblical story. Under this writer's pen Joseph is claimed to have said:

> And because she had no male child she pretended to regard me as a son, so I prayed to the Lord and she bore a male child (3.7).

Other Jewish thinkers of the Graeco-Roman period also reflect this obsession with the birth of sons rather than daughters. The Alexandrian Philo declared on one occasion that the virtue of midwives lay specifically (and exclusively?) in 'bringing the males to birth' (*Leg. All.* 3.3, on the basis of Exod. 1.17-21). More particularly, the historian Josephus witnesses to the Judaeans' belief that a woman mistakenly suspected of adultery, having undergone the trial of bitter waters (Num. 5.14f.), would bear a son ten months after her ordeal as compensation for her suffering (*Ant.* 3.271).[1] The biblical text merely suggests the possibility of conception, with no reference to the sex of the child.[2]

Turning now to the rabbinic writings, we learn that the strictly traditional School of Shammai regarded the command to 'Be fruitful and multiply' (Gen. 1.28) as fulfilled once two sons had been sired; the School makes no mention of daughters (*Yeb.* 6.6).[3] Other Mishnaic passages offer further proof of society's negative attitude toward daughters. For example, *Naz.* 2.7 speaks of a man vowing to become a Nazirite if a son was born to him; *Naz.* 2.9 has a man vowing to become a

---

1 For the same view from a slightly later date, cf. *Ps. Jon.* Num. 5.28; *Sifre ad loc.*; *Ber.* 31b; *Sot.* 26a.

2 Num. 5.28, 'shall conceive seed'; *Ant.* 3.271, 'shall give birth to a male child'. We might note that Josephus, *Ant.* 1.52, and *Jub.* 4.1 both contain legendary accretions to the biblical story of Adam and Eve, stating that this union produced female offspring as well as sons. However, this should not be taken as indicative of any change in attitude regarding daughters. The addition to the Old Testament narrative was dictated simply by considerations of logic: how could the newly created human race have propagated itself without women?

3 The School of Hillel, which followed the oral as well as the written tradition, admitted that the command was fulfilled with the birth of a son and a daughter, declaring, 'for it is written "male and female created He them" (Gen. 5.6)' (*Yeb.* 6.6). It should be remembered, however, that the views of this School were often more lenient and 'progressive' than those of the School of Shammai, which continued to represent the more traditional views of society.

Nazirite if 'a child' is born, with the disparaging additional comment that he will fulfil his vow 'even if a daughter' is born. In another passage we learn of how the rabbis denied the efficacy of a man praying for male offspring from his already pregnant wife, a rabbinic decision revealing a fundamental truth about the attitude toward sons (*Ber.* 9.3). Nowhere is there a parallel passage expressing the futility of praying for a daughter. Such a prayer needed no denial for it would never have been uttered.

But, to return to the intertestamental literature, it is the second-century wisdom writer Ben Sira who most clearly and emphatically states the attitude prevalent among the Jews of Graeco-Roman Palestine, expressing what others in their praise of sons had left implicit. Before describing in glowing terms the benefits to be gained from the birth of a son, he delivers us one bare sentence regarding that of a girl:

> a daughter is born to his [the father's] loss (22.3).

It is a bold, unequivocal declaration of dissatisfaction with the siring of daughters. Subsequent passages in his book of wisdom elaborate this idea, and show a startling contrast in the attitudes manifested toward sons and daughters. Regarding the former Ben Sira wrote:

> He that loveth his son will continue (to lay) strokes on him,
> That he may rejoice over him at the last.
> He that disciplineth his son shall have satisfaction of him,
> And among his acquaintance glory in him.
> He that teacheth his son maketh his enemy jealous,
> And in the presence of friends, exulteth in him (30.1-3).

What concerns us in this passage is the way in which a son was viewed as bringing much joy and satisfaction, even glory, to his father. The task of bringing the child up may have been onerous, but the reward was certainly great. Some twelve chapters later Ben Sira turned his attention to the problem of daughters:

A daughter is to a father a treasure of sleeplessness,[1]
And the care of her banisheth slumber...
Over thy daughter keep a strict watch,
Lest she make thee a name of evil odour,
A byword in the city and accursed of the people,
And shame thee in the assembly of the gate (42.9, 11).

The whole tenor of this passage is in marked contrast to the one above. Here the rearing of the child has one aim: to avert the daughter's assumed natural propensity to bring shame to her father by her indecent behaviour.[2] Correct training of a son allows a father to exult and glory in him amongst his friends; strict observation of a daughter might possibly prevent his being put to shame among his associates. One passage vibrates with potential joy, the other with warnings and despondency.

Why was a daughter so poorly regarded, or conversely, why was the birth of a son considered so important? The reasons for the strikingly different attitudes are many and varied, but all spring directly or indirectly from one root cause: the rigid patriarchy which had structured and organized the lives of the Jewish people from the beginning of their recorded history.[3] Under such a social system, economic control and all positions of leadership (in government, religious life, tribe and family) lay in the hands of men and passed along the male line. Men were full and independent participants in all aspects of life, while women's involvement, as will be demonstrated in the course of this book, was severely restricted by the social

---

1 Translated from the Greek: ἀπόκρυφος ἀγρυπνία. The Hebrew of MS B reads: מטמן שקר, 'a deceptive treasure'. The Massada scroll is defective at this point, but could be restored שק[ר] on the basis of the Greek.
2 The assumption that women by their very nature were inclined toward evil will be treated more fully in Chapter 1 §E.
3 In the early biblical period there were systems of social organization (e.g. with regard to the structuring of kinship networks, the arrangement of marriage, etc.) which gave considerable significance to women, but these may not be taken as indicative of any matriarchy. They too functioned under the rule of men and in the course of the centuries shifted into what may now be seen as the more familiar patriarchal pattern (so, e.g., the centrality of *mother's* brother in early kinship and marriage shifted to *father's* brother; husband travelling to wife's family home changed to transfer of the woman to his home, etc.). For details of these early institutions, of which only traces remain in the OT, see Archer, *op. cit.*, and Cross, *The Hebrew Family*, Chapter 1.

structure, its custom, and law. For a family to have at least one son was therefore of paramount importance: once he had reached the age of majority and become a fully-fledged member of society, with none of the grave legal disabilities which women suffered, he could provide his parents with valuable support and assistance.[1] More importantly, he was the means by which the family's future was secured. Regarding this, Ben Sira captures for us the ordinary man's feelings regarding his son, the hopes that could not rest with a daughter in a society whose ordering and continuity depended upon men:

> When his father dieth, he dieth not altogether
> For he hath left one behind him like himself.
> In his life he saw and rejoiced
> And in death he hath not been grieved (30.4-5).

In a patriarchal society a son enabled the father to die with the knowledge (or at least the hope) that his name and the family line would not come to an abrupt end. Daughters, who at marriage were transferred to another family group, could not act in this capacity, a fact nicely demonstrated by the biblical tale of Lot and his daughters.[2] Closely associated with this but on a less practical, quasi-religious level, a man's natural desire for personal immortality was, in a sense, also fulfilled by having a male child, for he could view himself as living on in his son, in his son's son, and so on.[3] More immediate comfort rested in the knowledge that he would receive all the necessary atten-

---

1 According to the Tannaim, a boy attained majority at the age of thirteen years and one day (*Nidd.* 5.6). Pre-mishnaic literature does not specify an age, but presumably he was deemed an adult once the signs of puberty were evident. For the girl's passage to adulthood, see Chapter 1 §C.

2 Gen. 19.31-38. The express purpose of the girls' incestuous union with Lot was the attainment of sons for their father: 'Come, let us make our father drink wine, and we will lie with him, in order that we may preserve the seed of our father' (v. 32). For the woman's transfer on marriage, and for the way in which it was rare for women to remain unmarried, see Chapter 2.

3 There was at this time no clear conception of a life hereafter. At best a mere shadowy existence beyond the grave was considered, but usually it was simply a case of seeing human fate as resting with the worms. Cf. Sir. 17.28 for the non-existence of an afterlife, and 39.9 for the consolation offered: 'His memory shall not cease, and his name shall live from generation to generation'. Later various notions of personal immortality did come into play (see Chapter 4 below), but these seem not to have altered the basic sentiment here presented.

tion at death with regard to burial and funeral rites—matters which were of primary importance to the ancients (as indeed to us today)—for this was a duty incumbent only upon sons, as was maintenance of parents in their old age (women would also look to sons or male relatives for comfort in this respect).[1] Thus in the book of *Ahikar* we read:

> But I ask of thee, O God, that I may have a male child, so that when I shall die, he may cast dust on my eyes (1.4-5; cf. Tob. 6.15).[2]

Still looking to the future, another consideration of very great importance was that of inheritance, and here again the law gave preference to males.[3] By having a son, a man had the assurance that his property and goods would remain within his immediate family, preserving the economic strength and integrity of that social unit, and profiting his direct male descendants and their dependents. In the absence of sons, a daughter could inherit (Num. 27.1f.; 36.1f.), but this involved the removal of the inheritance from her father's house to that of her husband, for on marriage she and her property became a part of the latter's family group to be used and then inherited by its male members.[4] In the eventuality of there

---

1 For women's inability to perform the various religious duties, including those associated with death, see Archer, 'The Role of Jewish Women in the Religion, Ritual and Cult of Graeco-Roman Palestine', in Cameron and Kuhrt, *Images of Women in Antiquity*, pp. 273-87.

2 Although a non-Jewish work, the book of *Ahikar* was popular in Jewish circles and clearly contained the type of general Near Eastern sentiment with which the Jews of Graeco-Roman Palestine would have readily identified. As a point of comparison, see M. Burrows, 'The Ancient Oriental Background of Hebrew Levirate Marriage', *BASOR* 77 (1940), p. 2, who quotes in connection with the water-libation offered for the dead by the Babylonians the following malediction: 'May he [the god Ninurta] deprive him of his son, the water-pourer . . . May he destroy his name, his seed, his offspring, his descendants from the mouth of men, and may he not let him have a son and a pourer of water'.

3 See note below, and *B.B.* 8.1.

4 *B.B.* 8.2, on the basis of Num. 27.8, states: '. . . the son precedes the daughter, and all the son's offspring precede the daughter; the daughter precedes the brother [of the deceased] and the daughter's offspring precede the brothers; brothers [of the deceased] precede the father's brothers and the brother's offspring precede the father's brothers. This is the general rule: whosoever has precedence in inheritance, his offspring have also precedence. The father has precedence over all his offspring [if none of these is the direct offspring of the deceased].'

being no children the same dispersal of family wealth occurred, for then more distant male kin inherited the property. Absolute security, therefore, was to be found only with a son.

Finally, in a line which by centring upon male offspring again highlights the full legal and social competence of men as opposed to the severely restricted lifestyle of women, Ben Sira furnishes us with another reason as to why sons were favourably regarded:

> Against enemies he [the father] hath left behind an avenger,
> And to friends one that requiteth favour (30.6).

As one who enjoyed full and independent participation in society, a son could, as it were, take over where his father left off. A daughter, in consequence of her removal at a relatively early age to her husband's house, could never be regarded as a permanent member of the family into which she was born and could not, therefore, bear any of the responsibilities outlined above. Society's attitude toward the birth of daughters was necessarily dictated by such considerations.

In addition to her inability to act in these essential roles, there were other considerations which would temper parental response to the birth of a daughter. As will be shown in more detail below, a father was obliged to maintain his daughter until such time as she enjoyed the support of a husband. He was also responsible for furnishing her with a suitable dowry. Although he did profit from her labour and received the monies of her bride-price (see Chapter 1 §C), in the main he had the expensive task of rearing a child from whom he would later derive no benefit, for when married she and her services could only profit her husband's family.[1] As the Talmud declared:

> When a male comes into the world, his provision comes with him . . . A female comes with nothing (*Nidd.* 31b).

In the unlikely event of a daughter not marrying, she would

---

1   There could of course be indirect benefit: cousin-marriage (see below, Chapter 2 §A) would strengthen the bonds within the extended family unit; new alliances could be created; the bride-price acquired could be of practical assistance in marrying off sons who had to furnish their father-in-law with a similar sum.

remain a burden on the family resources. At least with a son, as has been indicated above, a father could expect some return for those years spent supporting the child.

Finally, there was one worry peculiar to the raising of daughters which parents, given the preoccupations and dictates of society, had to concern themselves with, and that was the preservation of their sexual purity.[1] In a passage already quoted (Sir. 42.9-11), a girl's potential to bring shame to her father was underlined. It was assumed that unless a daughter was strictly watched over she would engage in illicit relations, thereby disgracing her father's good name and bringing additional problems to the family.[2] Various measures, which we shall examine in detail later in this chapter, had to be taken to ensure that she remained a virgin until she was married. If she were defiled (either willingly or forcibly) and the fact were known, her father would have great difficulty securing a husband for her (unless action could be taken against the offender, see pp. 51-54). He would also not have the benefit of receiving the higher bride-price demanded for a virgin.[3] If, on the other hand, a daughter's defilement had gone undetected and a marriage had been negotiated on the basis of her being a virgin bride, an enraged husband could involve her parents in a virginity suit (Deut. 22.13f.). If the tokens of the girl's virginity could not be provided then:

> they shall bring out the damsel to the door of her father's house, and the men of the city shall stone her with stones that she die; because she hath wrought a wanton deed... to

---

1 The same concern did not attach to boys. The reasons for it and the evolution of society's belief in the innate evil (especially sexual) of females will be treated in more detail in subsequent sections. Additionally see Archer, 'The Virgin and the Harlot in the Writings of Formative Judaism', *History Workshop Journal* 24 (Autumn 1987), pp. 1-16.

2 Of a daughter's proclivity for illicit sexual relations Ben Sira wrote, 'As a thirsty traveller that openeth his mouth and drinketh of any water that is near, so she sitteth down at every post and openeth her quiver to every arrow' (26.11-12). On this see Chapter 1 §E below.

3 According to the Mishnah, a virgin received twice the amount stipulated for a non-virgin (*Ket.* 1.2). For this, and for the way in which the bride-price in fact gradually evolved into a form of deferred payment or divorce penalty, see Chapter 2 §B.

play the harlot in her father's house (Deut. 22.21).[1]

Thus Ben Sira declared one of the main concerns of a father in the upbringing of his daughter to be:

> in her virginity lest she be defiled (42.10a).[2]

Intimately connected with this was the fear

> in her father's house lest she become pregnant (42.10b).[3]

Even if none of these problems arose and a girl was safely married, her father's worries were not at an end. Ben Sira expressed the parents' fear in these words:

> by her husband lest she prove unfaithful...
> At her husband's lest she become barren (42.10a-b).[4]

Since the earliest times adultery had been regarded as a crime deserving of the severest penalty (Lev. 20.10; Deut. 22.22; cf. Exod. 20.14). Originally it was seen primarily as an infringement of a husband's property rights, the punishment of death acting as a deterrent to would-be offenders (see Chapter 1 §E). Gradually, however, and in keeping with a general evolution in ideas concerning sexual purity, the act came to be viewed as an evil in itself, as an offence against the moral sensibilities (and structural concerns) of the society at large.[5] For a daughter to commit adultery was therefore an extremely

---

1 For the way in which 'playing the harlot in her father's house' was not only a crime against the moral order ('morality' being the product or label for a complex weave of pragmatic, and here patriarchal, concerns) but also one against the authority of the *pater familias*, analogous to the case of the rebellious son (Deut. 21.18f.), see Chapter 1 §E and Archer, *op. cit.*

2 Reading from the Massada scroll: [lit. 'pierced'] בבתוליה פן תחל חחל פן בתוליה = Gk. ἐν παρθενείᾳ μή ποτε βεβηλωθῇ ['polluted']. B text· תפותה ['be seduced'], B marg. תתפתה. Cf. *Sanh.* 100b.

3 Reading from the Massada scroll: [lit. 'be sown'] בית אביה פן חזריע = Gk. καὶ ἐν τοῖς πατρικοῖς αὐτῆς ἔγκυος γένηται. The proposed restoration of תזנה, 'fornicate', does not fit into the passage's character of idea-correspondence and contrast. Note the plausibility of the scroll with regard to the parallelism of Cols. A and B, correcting the verse order of the Greek (see Y. Yadin, *The Ben Sira Scroll from Massada*, p. 25).

4 Reading from the Massada scroll: ['go astray'] חשטה [פן] ועל אישה = Gk. μετὰ ἀνδρὸς οὖσα μή ποτε παραβῇ ['transgress']. Working from the corrected verse order of the Greek text, the defective Hebrew of v. 10b can be restored: καὶ συνῳκηκυῖα μή ποτε στειριώσῃ = [ר] ובעלה פן תע[צ]לה (B Text: צר[פן תע] ה[וביתי א[יש]).

5 For this evolution see Archer, *op. cit.*, and subsequent sections below.

serious matter, not only for her but also—and perhaps more importantly, to judge by the sources—because her action reflected poorly on her father:

> she that bringeth shame is a grief to him that begat her. She that is bold bringeth shame on father and husband, and she is despised of both (Sir. 22.4b-5).[1]

The final worry in Ben Sira's list of paternal fears regarding a daughter was the question of her possible sterility in marriage (42.10b). If a woman did prove barren then her husband had every right to divorce her, procreation being the purpose of their union.[2] In the event of a divorce taking place, the woman, having lost the protection and maintenance provided by her husband, would return to her father's house and his protection. There she would once again become a burden on the family resources, a prospect which a father would hardly find attractive. He could but hope that such a curse would not descend upon his daughter.

The practical advantages in having a son, therefore, were many and obvious. In a society ordered along strictly patriarchal lines his existence was essential. A woman was simply not competent legally to shoulder his responsibilities. In addition to this, as we have seen, a woman was viewed as presenting other problems peculiar to her sex, 'problems' which again stemmed from the all-embracing patriarchy and which will be discussed in greater depth together with other points touched upon in this introductory section as we go through the book. In the light of these facts we can appreciate the two very different attitudes manifested at the birth of a child, returning with some comprehension to Ben Sira's statement that 'a daughter is born to his [the father's] loss'. Indeed, this writer felt so strongly about daughters and the onerous burden they represented, that his only consolation to fathers having sired

---

1 Note that here, as with the case of the unmarried girl engaging in illicit sexual relations, it is primarily the father's (and husband's) good name that is affected. This reveals much about the ordering and concerns of the society and will be treated in greater detail below.

2 Note that this verse parallels what we earlier learned of the way in which infertility was seen as a peculiarly female problem (p. 18 n. 1). See *Gitt.* 4.8; *Yeb.* 6.6.

such offspring was: 'Marry thy daughter and sorrow will
depart' (7.25).[1]

Although daughters were manifestly not regarded as a welcome addition to the family, it should be said that the practice
of exposing unwanted infants common to many peoples of the
ancient world was not found among the Jews of the Graeco-
Roman period, a fact commented upon by Tacitus in his
Histories.[2] Placing infanticide in the general category of mur-
der, both Josephus and Philo declared it to be biblically prohibited, stating that

The Law orders all the offspring to be brought up.[3]

and a line from the Jewish *Sibylline Oracles*, probably written
in Egypt in the middle of the second century BCE, warned
against adopting the practice of other nations:

Rear thy offspring and slay it not: for the Eternal will surely
be wroth with him who commits these sins (3.765-66).[4]

These words, directed here at a community living at a distance from its ancestral home and within a community which
practised infanticide, and being therefore more susceptible to
the influence of alien practice, reflect a universal Jewish sentiment.[5] It would seem, therefore, that in whatever low

1 Though, as we have seen, a father's worries regarding his daughter did not necessarily come to an end at her marriage. For the close connections which continued
between a married woman and her family, see below, Chapter 2 §B.
2 5.3: '. . . they take thought to increase their numbers; for they regard it as a crime
to kill any late-born child'.
3 *Con. Ap.* 2.202; *Spec. Leg.* 3.110f. In fact the exposure of children is nowhere
expressly forbidden in the Law, though it is evident that such practice was quite
alien to Jewish tradition by this period. Both authors base their condemnation of
infanticide upon Exod. 21.22-23 which deals with assault upon a pregnant
woman. See also *Vit. Mos.* 1.11 where Philo writes of the Jews' horror at having to
expose the infant Moses. It would seem from both the cultural and literary context
that both male and female children are included in the prohibition.
4 See Charles, *Apocrypha and Pseudepigrapha of the Old Testament*, II, p. 368 for
the authorship of the *Sibylline Oracles* as a whole, and pp. 371-72 for his view that
these lines were '. . . either composed or incorporated by a Jew, probably living in
Egypt about 140 BC'. On this see also Schürer, *The History of the Jewish People in
the Age of Jesus Christ*, III.i, pp. 618-54, and especially pp. 632-41 in reference to
the authorship and provenance of Book 3.
5 See, however, *CPJ*, II, No. 421, a document from the first century CE concerned
with the Jewish tax in Arsinoe (the Fayûm) to be extracted from men, women and
children over the age of three years. The relative paucity of children recorded in
the document has led the editors to wonder whether the Jews had in fact adopted the
practice of their neighbours (notes, p. 205). In this respect they also point to the
existence of 'foundlings' in Talmudic law (אסופים); see below, p. 137. It should be
noted, however, that while the number of children is small, there is equal representation of male and female children in the document, and with regard to אסופים

esteem a baby girl might be held, her life was sacred and she could not be disposed of at the convenience of her parents.[1]

B. *Rites/Ceremonies at the Birth of a Daughter*

In the preceding section there were outlined some of the fundamental ways in which women occupied a position of secondary importance with regard to the fulfilment of certain socio-legal obligations. In the course of this book many aspects of the woman's life will be examined, and from this examination one essential fact will emerge: her subordination to and dependence upon men in virtually every sphere of activity. The way in which a woman in a sense never attained full and individuated membership of the society in which she lived is most clearly reflected—and restated—in the rites and ceremonies which took place early on in the child's life. Many of these, being based in biblical law, are by no means peculiar to the Hellenistic period. Discussion of their significance is nevertheless incumbent upon us in consequence both of their being performed by the Jews of that time and of the new significances which were attached to them during that period. Here again, it is by reviewing those rites surrounding a boy that we can best appreciate the position of the girl.

> Great is circumcision whereby the covenant was made thirteen times[2]... Great is circumcision which overrides the

there are many possible reasons for the existence of foundlings in a society over and above any culturally endorsed system of abandonment/infanticide.

1 We might note that abortion was similarly condemned by the Jews of our period. Thus Josephus: 'The Law... forbids women either to cause abortion or to make away with the foetus; a woman convicted of this is regarded as an infanticide, because she destroys a soul and diminishes the race' (*Con. Ap.* 2.202); and rather more colourfully, Ps.-Phocylides: 'A woman should not destroy the unborn babe in her belly, nor after its birth throw it before the dogs and the vultures of prey' (ll. 184-85). (For Ps.-Phocylides being an Alexandrian Jew who lived around the turn of the eras, see van der Horst, *The Sentences of Pseudo-Phocylides*, especially pp. 81-83).

2 'Covenant' is repeated thirteen times in Genesis 17.

> rigour of the Sabbath[1] ... Great is circumcision: but for it the
> Holy One, blessed is He, had not created His world, as it is
> written, 'Thus saith the Lord, but for my covenant day and
> night I had not set forth the ordinances of heaven and earth'
> (Jer. 33.25) (*Ned.* 3.11).

Thus did the rabbis of the second century CE declare the all-important place which the rite of circumcision had in the lives of the Jewish people.

By the time the Tannaim were expressing their thoughts on the subject, circumcision was regarded as it is today, that is, as the special mark of the Jew, the sign of God's eternal covenant with his chosen people, Israel. Historically, however, such was not always the case: the first mention of the covenantal aspect of circumcision is to be found in Gen. 17.10f., verses which belong to the Priestly (P) strand of the Bible, that is, to that section written or revised in and beyond the Babylonian exile (see Introduction). Although it is not our concern here to trace in detail the evolution of ideas pertaining to the rite, some notes will be necessary to enable us to appreciate more fully the significance which was attached to circumcision in the Graeco-Roman period. For it must be remembered that this was a time when Jewish philosophy and theology were still being worked out; it was a world in which superstitious belief abounded; it was also a time, with regard to the practice of circumcision, when, in consequence of its relative chronological proximity to the work of the P redactors, older ideas about the rite still persisted, encouraged by the social and religious state already indicated and by the characteristic tenacity of systems of ritual and superstition. By acquiring a fuller understanding of the various significances circumcision held for the Hellenistic Jew, we shall be able to appreciate the social, religious and legal implications the absence of any comparable or substitute ceremony had for the life of the Jewish woman.

The origin of the rite in antiquity would seem to have been that of an act of redemption. The first seven days of an infant's life were commonly believed to be especially threatened by evil

---

1 Cf. *Shabb.* 19.1.

spirits:[1] propitiatory sacrifice of a part of the tabooed person redeemed him from the power of the spirit or deity and he was then able to enter into non-tabooed life. Circumcision was performed at the close of the period of danger, on the eighth day after birth.[2] The operation could not take place any earlier because during the first seven days the child was regarded as being in some kind of dangerous transitional state. The only precautions that could be taken were, first, a statement that the necessary sacrifice would be performed (a sacrifice which could also be regarded as some kind of thanksgiving at the close of the period of danger), and secondly, guarding the child day and night to prevent the spirits gaining control over the as yet uncircumcised infant.[3] Ritualistic remnants of this superstition have survived even to this day, as evidenced by the continuing observance of the so-called 'watch-night' among certain orthodox circles on the eve of a boy's circumcision, that is, the time when the child's life was perhaps most threatened as

1 For the way in which the number seven was generally regarded as unlucky in the ancient Near East, even to the extent of avoiding its mention when counting, see J. Morgenstern, *Rites of Birth, Marriage, Death and Kindred Occasions among the Semites*, pp. 24-26; *EJ*, I, cols. 1053-54. Note the occurrence of the seven day period in various contexts of ritual impurity/danger in the laws of Num. and Lev.; in marriage ceremony (see Chapter 2 §D); mourning ritual (see Chapter 4), etc.

2 See J.B. Segal, *The Hebrew Passover from the Earliest Times to AD 70*, and Morgenstern, *op. cit.*, pp. 73-80 for the theory that circumcision was first practised on a communal basis on adult males at the feast of Passover both as a ritual of redemption and as a mark of rejuvenation and fertility in keeping with the feast's original significance. Following various cultural shifts, performance of the rite was moved to the close of the seven day period of danger, i.e. the eighth day after birth.

3 Additionally, as Morgenstern notes regarding performance of the rite on the eighth rather than on what one would assume to be the more significant seventh day, 'Both the seventh and eighth days seem to be indiscriminately called... "the seven" or "the day of the seven". It is clear from this that there is actually no distinction between seventh and eighth days and that the former merely marks the closing moment of a peculiar state of being... while the latter is the first day of the new state... Logically one day is quite as appropriate as the other for the performance of these rites...' (p. 26). It could also be that the operation was performed specifically on the eighth day in consequence of the *mother's* week-long period of post-natal impurity, i.e. circumcision acted as a rite of separation as well as of initiation. On this, see pp. 36-37 below.

then was the spirits' last chance to gain control.[1] It is to be assumed that this redemptive characteristic was felt more keenly by those living in the Graeco-Roman world where, as already stated, superstitious belief and practice were rife. One might wonder, therefore, why there was no parallel rite of redemption among the Jews for a girl.[2] Was she not also considered as standing in peculiar relation to the deity? Apparently not.

The next stage in the changing thought process regarding circumcision and a consequence of its primary character was that it served as a rite of initiation into the tribe. In addition to his having entered into ordinary, profane existence, a boy was henceforth considered a full, public and potentially active member of society. The logical corollary of there being no initiation ceremony for the girl was that she would not be thus considered. She was in a sense but an associate of the tribe through her father or brothers. Such a state of affairs could only have a profound effect upon her competence to act within that group.

It was the final step, however, which was to have the most far reaching implications for the woman and her role in society. With the establishment in the exile and beyond of circumcision as a sign of Yahweh's covenant with his people (Gen. 17.10ff., P), the act became the official rite of initiation into

1 For this belief and details of the ritual of the Watch-Night, see conveniently Morgenstern, *op. cit.*, pp. 18-19. See also pp. 58ff. for the close relation between the *Akikah* rites on the eighth day in the Arab world and circumcision (the *Akikah* ceremony consisting of the sacrifice of a substitute animal and the cutting off of the child's first hair). Morgenstern also makes the interesting point that the modern Arabic term *tahhara*, 'to circumcise', literally means 'to purify, to render clean, to remove taboo' (p. 62).

2 Strabo is certainly incorrect in his view that the Jews circumcised both male and female children (*Geographica*, XVI, 2.37; 4.9; XVII, 2.5). An appropriate substitute ceremony for the girl could have been the cutting off of her first hair, hair being considered a living and important part of the body and something which was commonly dedicated or offered by way of redemptive sacrifice to the deity, the part substituting for the whole. So, for example, the significance of hair in priestly circles, mourning ritual, the Nazirite vow and marriage ceremonial, all of which will be touched upon in greater detail below. See also Robertson Smith, *Religion of the Semites*, pp. 323ff., and Morgenstern, *op. cit.*, Chapter 12. Alternatively, a substitute sacrifice could have been offered, with an animal being ritually slaughtered and its blood shed on her behalf and for her redemption.

Judaism and all that that meant. By the Graeco-Roman period this had become the dominant aspect of circumcision, although earlier ideas, for reasons already mentioned, persisted to a certain degree. An entire chapter in the second-century BCE book *Jubilees* is devoted to this institution, emphasizing its special significance to the holy people, and elaborating the simpler biblical message. The author warns:

> And everyone that is born, the flesh of whose foreskin is not circumcised on the eighth day, belongs not to the children of the covenant... but to the children of destruction; nor is there, moreover, any sign on him that he is the Lord's, but (he is destined) to be destroyed and slain from the earth, and to be rooted out... for he has broken the covenant of the Lord our God (15.26).[1]

Circumcision, therefore, was now unquestionably the mark of the Jew. It was in consequence of this that when Antiochus Epiphanes sought to destroy the religion of the Jews in the second century BCE he prohibited circumcision of their male children (1 Macc. 1.48). Similarly, those members of the hellenizing party in Jerusalem who wished to absorb themselves completely in the new world underwent a painful operation to hide this physical token of their Jewishness (1 Macc. 1.15). Non-Jewish writers of this period also witness to the importance of circumcision for, although knowing little else about Jews and Judaism, they were aware of two great institutions which characterized this strangely aloof people: the sabbath and circumcision.[2] What they were unaware of was the fact, already noted, that according to the oral law the latter had precedence even over the sanctity of the seventh day (*Ned.* 3.11; *Shabb.* 19.1; Jn 7.22, 23). Circumcision was thus an, if not the, essential mark of the Jew in the Hellenistic period.

The occasion of a boy's circumcision thus had two funda-

---

1 Cf. *Ant.* 1.192, where Josephus claims that circumcision originated in a desire to prevent Abraham's posterity mingling with other nations.
2 On the Sabbath, for example, Pompeius Trogus, in Justinus, *Historiae Philippicae* XXXVI, Epitoma, 2.14; Apion, *Aegyptiaca*, in *Con. Ap.* 2.20-21; Seneca, *De Superstitione*, in Augustine, *De Civitate Dei* 6,11; Tacitus, *Historiae*, 4.3-4. On circumcision, for example, Diodorus Siculus, *Bibliotheca Historia*, I, 28.3; 55.5; Strabo, *Historica Hypomnemata*, in *Ant.* 13.319; *Geographica* 16, 2.37; Apion, *Aegyptiaca*, in *Con. Ap.* 2.137; Tacitus, *Historiae*, 5.2.

mental effects upon his life. Henceforth he was considered a member of the Jewish nation and as one upon whom that nation's religious law was incumbent. Regarding the latter aspect, the apostle Paul, when writing to his pagan converts, had these words to say:

> I warn every man that gets himself circumcised that he is under obligation to fulfil the whole law (Gal. 5.3).

The fact that to be a Jew in the full sense of the title necessitated circumcision is underlined by various ancient writers who when speaking of God-fearers and converts characterized the former—who were not under an obligation to fulfill the whole Law—as 'the uncircumcised' (see Schürer, *op. cit.*, III.ii, pp. 165ff.).

I have dwelt at some length on the character of the rite of circumcision in an endeavour to direct our thinking to an appreciation of one point: the absence of any comparable ceremony for a girl. The eighth day of her life passed without any special recognition; she was accorded no official initiation into the society or religion of her people. The implications of such an omission are obvious. Although considered a Jew by birth,[1] she was to remain in a sense an outsider to her own society, the full participants of which were men.[2] Circumcision, then, as established with Abraham and his male descendants, was a divine contract with practical consequences. In the absence of any parallel rite for daughters, circumcision reflected, restated and reinforced a woman's position of secondary importance in a society ordered along strictly patriarchal lines. The scene was set, as it were, early on in her life.[3]

1 Indeed, with regard to the question of Jewish identity, we should note that at least by Talmudic times the (ethnic) status of the child was determined by that of his or her mother and not by the father. So *Kidd.* 68b, 'Thy son by an Israelite woman is called thy son, thy son by a Gentile woman is not called thy son'. According to *EJ*, X, cols. 54-55, such halakhic definition of Jewish identity had already been reached in Hasmonaean times, though more research needs to be done regarding exactly when this understanding of ethnic transmission was introduced.

2 Significantly, one of the objections to circumcision among the leaders of the nineteenth century Reform Movement in Frankfurt was precisely the fact that there was no initiation for daughters into Judaism.

3 For a more detailed survey of the significance and evolution of circumcision, see Archer, 'Bound by Blood: The Link between Circumcision and Menstrual Taboo in Post-Exilic Judaism' in J. Martin-Soskice (ed.), *Women and Judaeo-Christian Tradition* (Marshall Pickering, 1990) and 'In Thy Blood Live: Gender and Ritual in Judaeo-Christian Tradition', in Alison Joseph (ed.), *Through the Devil's Gateway* (Channel 4 Publications, 1990). These papers explore the way in which covenantal circumcision stood as an act of cultural rebirth for men, ritualistically separating the male from the female and establishing a

Another ceremony whose character had close association with the original significance of the rite of circumcision, and which also applied only to boys, was that of Redemption of the firstborn. Again the original belief was that all life was taboo to the deity, that is, stood in precarious relation to the lord of creation who bestowed life and could equally reclaim it. In popular consciousness, sacrifice of the first issue—that is, of the first fulfilment of the potential of fertility—was considered a particularly efficacious way to satisfy the demands of a deity and thereby redeem or secure the safety of subsequent offspring. Consequently, the earliest aspect of the rite demanded actual human sacrifice, as evidenced by the early narrative and law of the Old Testament.[1] With the evolution of Hebrew society and culture, human sacrifice became unacceptable and it was replaced with a symbolic act by which the *bekhor* (first-born) was redeemed through the payment of five shekels to the priests of the Temple when the boy was thirty one days old (Num. 3.40f.; 18.15-16). Explanation for this revision in practice was linked to the tradition of Yahweh striking down the first-born of the Egyptians but sparing those of the Hebrews (Exod. 13.13f.; Num. 3.13).

Our concern with regard to this ceremony is to pose the question why the rite pertained only to the male who 'openeth the womb'—patently a female was also a part of creation, a part of the life-giving force of the deity. The reason lay in the people's desire to offer (or later redeem) the most acceptable

---

brotherhood of blood which was bound by special duties and mutual obligations. Significantly, in the later post-exilic period of the rite's evolution, only men were allowed to perform the operation.

1 So Exod. 22.28, and the narrative of Genesis 22. Although prohibited in Exod. 34.19f., it is evident that human sacrifice continued (or revived) in pre-exilic times. So 2 Kgs 3.27; 16.3; 17.17; 21.6; 23.10; Isa. 57.5; Jer. 7.31; 19.5; 32.35; Ezek. 16.20f.; 20.26, 31. It was not until after the exile that the practice was eradicated completely. Of these fourteen passages, eight speak only of sons, four embrace both sons and daughters, and one has simply ילדים (children). Passages on the substitution of redemption for sacrifice, with explicit reference to the first-born, refer exclusively to males.

sacrifice. The first-born male fulfilled this desire on two counts, first through the simple fact that he was male,[1] and second, on account of primogeniture, that is, the special rights accorded to the first-born male with regard to inheritance and other socio-legal requirements. Within these terms of reference the *bekhor* was literally the best that society had to offer the deity.[2]

The fact that it was not considered necessary to redeem the first-born daughters, or to evolve an eighth-day ceremony in substitute for a boy's circumcision, or indeed to devise a ritual peculiar to the girl, is of great significance in the light it sheds on the attitude toward and position of women in Graeco-Roman Palestine.

Finally, a word should be said regarding the laws of purification following childbirth, for although these affected only the life of the mother (and to a lesser degree those with whom she came in contact), they again reveal something of the attitude towards female children. According to the book of Leviticus, a woman was unclean for seven days following the delivery of a boy. During this time the same restrictive rules or taboos applied as at the time of her menstruation. Also, as long as the Temple stood, a further thirty-three days were allotted during which the mother was to 'continue in the blood of purification' and was allowed to touch 'no hallowed thing nor come into the sanctuary'. If, however, she had given birth to a female child, she was to remain in a state of *niddah* ('uncleanness') for fourteen days, that is, double the length of time prescribed for a male birth. Similarly, she was to continue in the 'blood of purification' for an extended period of sixty-six days. At the end of her period of uncleanness (whether of forty or of eighty days), the woman was to offer a sacrifice at the sanctuary whereby she was restored to her

---

1 See above, Chapter 1 §A. See also Lev. 27.1-8 where a male's personal vow of valuation to God, reckoned in monetary terms, was deemed to be roughly double that of
a female at all periods of their life (e.g., a boy under the age of five years was valued at five shekels, a girl of the same age at three shekels).

2 See 2 Kgs 3.27; Mic. 6.7 for the benefits believed to accrue from sacrifice of the
first-born son. Note also that with regard to animal sacrifice the male victim was
valued more highly than the female, being offered on more prestigious ocasions
than was the case for the latter. See *Spec. Leg.* 1.198f.

normal state of existence (Lev. 12.2f.).[1]

It is not our concern here to enter into a rationalization or explanation of this blood taboo. Much could be said regarding this culturally constructed fear of 'female' blood (both menstrual and following childbirth); concerning the fact that detailed legislation for the taboo emerged at the same time as the rules for covenantal circumcision which also involved a flow of blood, though in that instance positively valued;[2] the fact that one set of rituals involved exclusion from cult, the other inclusion; and so forth.[3] For our immediate purposes interest must lie with the stipulation that there should be two differing lengths of time for the mother's purification, dependent upon the sex of her child.

As with the number seven, special importance was attached to the number forty and hence to the fortieth day after the birth of a child.[4] Rites or ceremonies intended to remove taboo from the child or to purify the mother were (and still are) performed on this day.[5] Given this widely attested belief in the power of the fortieth day, why did the Hebrews see fit to add a further forty days consequent on the birth of a female

1   See Archer, 'The Virgin and the Harlot...' and 'Bound by Blood...' for details of the emergence of these purity laws and for my argument that their emergence was a consequence of societal restructuring following the exile to Babylon.
2   In this respect we should remember that circumcision occurred on the eighth day, i.e. immediately following the seven-day period of uncleanness, and so could be regarded as a rite of separation as well as of initiation. Note the wording of Lev. 12.2ff. where circumcision intrudes in the text, interrupting both the period of the woman's pollution and the account of that pollution: circumcision separates the boy from his mother and joins him to the male community. Note also the way in which the woman is finally cleansed of her impurity through the blood of sacrifice as administered by a circumcised male.
3   See Archer, 'Bound by Blood...'.
4   Instances of the significant number forty may be found, for example, in the story of Jesus' temptation when the power of the devil was deemed to have automatically ceased at the close of a forty-day period (Mt. 4.1-11; Mk 1.13; Lk. 4.1-13). Similarly, in *The Life of Adam and Eve*, Adam is said to have stood up to his neck in the river Jordan for forty days in order that the evil of his former acts be washed from him (I.3-8). See Morgenstern, *op. cit.*, pp. 27-30, 81-82, 149ff., for examples from the Semitic world generally of this belief in the power of the forty-day period.
5   So, for example, rituals of baptism, salting, naming, cutting off of first hair and tattooing of children among various Semitic peoples occur on the fortieth day, i.e. at the close of the second stage of the power of the evil spirits. For this, and various superstitions regarding the danger presented by women during this period, see Morgenstern, *op. cit.*, Chapters 5 and 11.

child to the mother's period of impurity? The only possible
explanation for this revision of the original superstition is that
a daughter was regarded in some sense as inflicting 'double
impurity' on her mother, first (as with a son) on account of the
blood of her birth (the original taboo = forty days impurity),
and secondly on account of her being female (additional taboo
= extra forty days impurity). The extended period of impurity
would therefore have been a result or aspect of the complex of
ideas which combined to create the lowly position of the
woman. So, for example, according to *Jub.* 3.8ff. the levitical
laws were to be explained by a reworking of the Genesis
tradition: Adam was created at the close of the first week and
did not enter the Garden of Eden (equated with the Temple
sanctuary) until an additional thirty-three days had elapsed,
hence the forty days' impurity following the birth of a son;
Eve, on the other hand, was not created until the end of the
second week and was not brought into the Garden for a
further sixty-six days, hence the eighty days' impurity after
the birth of a daughter. According to this Hellenistic Jewish
author, the extended period of impurity was in consequence of
the belief that woman was created after man and was, therefore, regarded as an inferior and in some way suspect being.[1]
Thus greater stringency in the mother's purification following
the birth of a daughter was required.

A custom associated with this blood taboo was that of salting
a newly born infant. Unlike other rituals, this was performed
for male and female children alike. Although there is no mention of the custom in the intertestamental literature, there is
no reason to assume that the practice referred to in Ezekiel
(see below) did not persist throughout the Graeco-Roman
period and even beyond. Indeed, the salting of infants has
remained a common feature of the Middle East up until this
century,[2] and the Talmud recognized its importance by allow-
ing salting to take place on the sabbath (*Shabb.* 129b). The
custom did not acquire the same religious significance as

1 On this, see subsequent sections, especially Chapter 2 §D and Chapter 3 §C.
2 See Morgenstern, *op. cit.*, pp. 8-9 for examples from Moslem Palestine and Syria
in the 1920s where salting regularly occurred as soon as the child was born and
for forty days after its birth.

those rituals already described, but it was nevertheless important from the standpoint of folk-lore. According to a study of Palestinian Arab practices in the first half of the present century, the belief was that salting the child 'strengthens the skin and enables it to resist external forces. A common belief insists that non-salted children have a weak and silly character.'[1] The same author adds that 'The greatest disgrace for anyone is to be called an *Ibn haram* or *banduq*, bastard. Only a *banduq* is neglected and not salted after birth.'[2] The same sentiment is expressed by Ezekiel who in an allegory of Jerusalem wrote of her early history in the following terms:

> And as for thy nativity, in the day thou wast born thy navel was not cut, neither wast thou washed... thou wast not salted at all. No eye pitied thee to do any of these unto thee; but thou wast cast out in the open field (16.4-5).[3]

Sprinkling the child with a substance known to have the property of preserving things was believed to strengthen the child and bestow longevity on him or her.[4]

Salt was also considered to have magical properties in that it could repel evil spirits or avert evil influences, a common superstition still amongst groups of Jews (and others) in parts of the world today,[5] such spirits, as we have seen, being regarded as especially threatening during the early days of a person's life. Salt was also a means of purification: to purify the bad waters of Jericho, Elisha cast salt into the springs (2 Kgs

1 T. Canaan, 'The Child in Palestinian Arab Superstition', *JPOS* 7 (1927), p. 163.
2 Canaan, 'The Curse in Palestinian Folk-Lore', *JPOS* 15 (1935), p. 257.
3 The last line presumably refers to the practice of infanticide. It is evident, however, from the tenor of the passage as a whole, that non-Jewish practice is meant, a point stressed in v. 3: 'Thy birth and thy nativity is of the land of Canaan; thy father was an Amorite, and thy mother a Hittite'. The first part of the allegory refers to Jerusalem before the Covenant was established.
4 In this respect one should note the obligatory use of salt in all sacrifices to symbolize permanence; honey and leaven, symbolic of fermentation and subsequent decay, are specifically prohibited (Lev. 2.13). Cf. Mt. 5.13 where the term 'salt' is applied to the disciples who are to delay the day of decay; *Nidd.* 31a where salt is used as a metaphor for the soul, the preserver of the human body.
5 See *JE*, X, p. 661; Morgenstern, *op. cit.*, pp. 196-98 n. 27; and for medieval examples, J. Trachtenberg, *Jewish Magic and Superstition. A Study in Folk Religion*, Chapter 11. Cf. Chapter 2 §D below for the use of salt in wedding crowns to protect bridal couples from demonic attack.

2.20-21; cf. Mk 9.49). It was the agent used in the process of koshering meat to draw off the blood whose consumption was taboo (*Hull.* 113a; cf. 97b). Possibly, therefore, the salting of an infant had connection with the blood taboo which lay behind the purification laws after childbirth. Here, however, it would have been in respect of the child itself rather than the mother. Washing the child with water would clean it, but sprinkling it with salt would ensure the complete removal of the blood of its birth, and render it ritually pure. With regard to this possible interpretation, it is interesting to note that Ezekiel continues his description of the unsalted Jerusalem as follows:

> but thou wast cast out in the open field in the loathsomeness of thy person, in the day thou wast born. And when I [the Lord] passed by thee and saw thee wallowing in thy blood, I said unto thee: In thy blood live... (16.5-6).

Whether the original concept behind the salting of infants was that of purification, or whether it arose from a combination of the superstitious beliefs outlined above, the fact of interest for us is that here was one ritual—of some significance at least in popular consciousness—which was performed for children irrespective of their sex. By their salting, daughters as well as sons were purified, strengthened, preserved, and protected from evil spirits. It should be noted, however, that the one ritual in which females were included remained simply an expression of superstitious belief (despite its recognition by the Talmud), a part of the folk-lore and, unlike other ritualistic practices, it never evolved to become a part of the Law, a concern of Judaism proper.

Another ceremony or ritual which must be considered in this examination of the early days in a child's life is that of name-giving. With the bestowal of a distinguishing title, society accorded the infant status as a full human being, and henceforth regarded the child as having an identity of its own.[1] For the individual, the name, being an integral part of

---

1   It is interesting to note that among certain groups of modern Bedouin, the un-named child, possessing as yet no identity, is referred to simply as 'the excre-menter'. In our own society the impersonal term 'baby', together with the neuter pronoun 'it', is used.

the person, was a fundamental aspect of his or her self-image. Even in modern so-called sophisticated societies, the significance of the personal name has never been lost: much thought is expended in choosing a proper name for the child; the name-giving ceremony is usually an occasion of note; and significantly, in circumstances which demand a denial of self and the obliteration of past life (such as entering religious orders), the practice continues of discarding the individual's original name and adopting a new one. In the Bible, the changing of names was equally symbolic of a new status or destiny (e.g. Abraham in Gen. 17.5, Jacob in Gen. 32.38, and Joshua in Num. 13.16), and the Talmud declared it to be one of the 'four things that cancel the doom of man' (*RH* 16b). To the ancients a name also had a certain magical quality, of importance to its bearer. Each name conveyed a special meaning and was chosen either to reflect circumstances peculiar to the child's birth or in the belief that a specific name imparted a certain characteristic or virtue (implied in the name) to the infant.[1]

In consequence of the concept that the giving of a name marked the passage of the child from unreal, impersonal existence to personal, human, and individual life, the infant—in the case of a boy—could not receive its name until it had survived the dangerous first seven days of life and undergone the rituals necessary to remove taboo. For a boy, therefore, the obvious and most appropriate occasion for the name-giving was the day of his circumcision.[2] Support for this is to be found in the New Testament:

> And at the end of eight days, when he was circumcised, he was called Jesus (Lk. 2.21).

and,

> And on the eighth day they came to circumcise the child; and they would have named him Zechariah... but his

---

1 See, for example, Gen. 21.6; 30.6, 8, 11, 13, 24; Exod. 6.23; Num. 13.6; 2 Kgs 22.14; Esth. 2.7.

2 Note that in the Arab world, the naming of the child normally accompanied the ceremony of *Akikah*. For the close affinity between the character of circumcision and that of the *Akikah* ceremony, see p. 32 n. 1 above.

mother said, 'Not so; he shall be called John' (Lk. 1.59).

However, as has already been noted, the eighth day in a girl's life passed without any special recognition. There was no ceremony to mark her passage from profane to non-profane existence, nothing to indicate that Jewish society believed a daughter was threatened in the same way as a son during the first week of life, or that therefore she stood in need of redemption. Bestowal of a name for a boy had particular significance because it, together with the redemptive rite of circumcision, heralded his entry into full non-tabooed life. The two were intimately connected. In consequence of there being no demarcation point in the girl's life, her name-giving could not have had the same significance in the eyes of society. The silence of the sources, therefore, with regard to the existence of a specific day on which a girl was to receive her name is not only revealing but also expected. There was no special day set aside for the naming of a daughter, and no ceremony or particular significance (in the sense of a public or formal rite of passage) attached to the moment when her name was announced.

To conclude this survey of the rites and ceremonies attending the birth of a child, consideration must be given to whether there was any village celebration of a general kind to mark the safe arrival of the new addition to the community. There are two passages which may indicate the existence of such communal festivites. In *4 Ezra* 9.45, personified Zion, depicted as a woman, speaks in the first person of her newly-born 'son':

> And I rejoiced in him greatly, I and my husband and all my fellow townsfolk.

The second reference is provided by the evangelist Luke who, writing of the birth of John the Baptist, recorded the following:

> Now the time came for Elizabeth to be delivered and she gave birth to a son. And her neighbours and kinsfolk... rejoiced with her (Lk. 1.57-58).

The point of interest is that both authors specifically note the involvement of neighbours in some kind of celebration for the newborn infant.

However, even without these two possible references to the

custom, it is extremely likely that village festivities did take place in Graeco-Roman Palestine, for the occurrence of such post-natal celebrations in societies where the safe delivery of a child was by no means assured is widely attested.[1] The only question would be, Did formal rejoicing occur in honour of daughters? Given the patriarchal tenor of Jewish society and the unfavourable attitude toward the birth of girls, it is unlikely that a daughter's birth occasioned any particular celebration, let alone a village feast. It is perhaps significant, therefore, that in both the passages quoted above, a son is the cause for rejoicing.[2]

Finally, brief mention should be made of a reference in the book of *Jubilees* to another occasion for celebration. The work records how 'in the first year of the fourth week Isaac was weaned in this Jubilee, and Abraham made a great banquet in the third month, on the day that his son Isaac was weaned' (17.1; cf. Gen. 21.8-21). Although this one reference does not allow us to conclude that celebrating a child's weaning was the general practice in Graeco-Roman Palestine, it is possible that such was the case, for again, festivities of this type were common amongst other peoples. In the light of what has been said in this and the preceding section regarding daughters, the fact that our one reference to celebrations at the time of weaning centres upon a son may be more than mere coincidence.

C. *Patria Potestas—Maintenance*

> The Sages spoke in a parable about woman: she is like an unripe fig, or a ripening fig, or a fully ripe fig: 'an unripe fig' while she is yet a child; and 'a ripening fig'—these are the days of her girlhood... ; and 'a fully ripe fig'—after she is past her girlhood (*Nidd.* 5.7).

Thus did the Tannaim divide the life of a girl with regard to her legal competence.[3] Until the age of twelve she was

1   See Granqvist, *Birth and Childhood among the Arabs*, Chapter 3.
2   See Granqvist, *op. cit.*, for the way in which up to at least the 1920s (the time when Granqvist's field work was conducted), Moslem Arab peasants in Palestine celebrated only the birth of sons. The birth of a daughter was not even announced for 'she is deficient' (Fellahin saying, quoted on p. 77).
3   It is interesting to note that the rabbis chose to liken the female to a fig (symbolic of fertility). Their choice of image reveals much of the way in which women were viewed primarily as physical/sexual beings whose main purpose was procreation and motherhood, points which have been touched on earlier in this book and will be explored in greater detail in Chapter 3.

regarded as a minor (*qetanah*) and *in aliena potestate*; from
twelve to twelve and a half years as having some degree of
independence (*na'arah*); and at twelve and a half years as
having attained her majority (*bogereth*) (cf. *Ket.* 3.8). In this
section we shall examine the legal position of the girl before
she became a *bogereth* and later discuss the parental maintenance which was her due during the years of her minority. To
obtain a reasonably detailed picture of a girl's life while a
minor it is necessary to concentrate primarily on material
gleaned from the Mishnah, as the other sources from the
period do not provide sufficient information on the subject.
Although the analysis will therefore follow the division into
age groups as defined by the Mishnah (pre-12 years; 12 years
and 1 day to 12 and a half years; 12 and a half years plus), it is
doubtful whether the Jews of the Hellenistic period observed
these rigid specifications regarding the changing status of
their daughters. There is no explicit mention of the three categories in pre-Mishnaic literature, and the Old Testament does
not state a specific age at which a minor passed into adulthood
(the word *bogereth* not occurring in the Old Testament). The
likelihood is that a girl was considered a minor until she
departed from her father's house,[1] and that the laws described
below applied to varying degrees throughout this period of her
life. Indeed, the Mishnah, despite having stated that a girl
obtained independence at the age of twelve and a half years,
declares elsewhere that a daughter

> continues within the control of the father until she enters
> into the control of the husband at marriage (*Ket.* 4.5).

This is probably closer to reality, reflecting older and more
persistent tradition than the rabbinic divisions laid down in
Nidd. 5.7. The likelihood in any case was that by the age of

---

1 Cf. *B.M.* 12b where, with regard to a father's right to any object found by his minor
son, it is written, '[By] MAJOR [we do] not [mean one who is] legally a major, nor
[do we mean by] MINOR [one who is] legally a minor, but a major who is maintained by his father is regarded as a minor, and a minor who is not maintained
by his father is regarded as a major'.

twelve and a half a girl was already under the authority of a husband and her passage to adulthood, in respect of independent action and according to the rabbinic categorization, was a mere technicality.[1]

1. *Patria Potestas*

If my father orders, 'Give me a drink of water' and my mother does likewise, which takes precedence?

The response to this question, addressed to R. Eliezer, was:

Leave your mother's honour and fulfil the honour due to your father... for both you and your mother are bound to honour your father (*Kidd.* 31a; cf. *Kerith* 6.9).

Thus did later thinkers qualify the biblical injunction to 'honour thy father and thy mother', and by so doing they reaffirmed the all-important position in a patriarchal society of the father within the family unit. Although deserving of honour, the mother, legally, had little or no say in the upbringing of her children. Authority was vested in the father, and obedience to his dictates was enjoined on minor children and their mother alike.[2] Until such time as a daughter attained her majority or entered into marriage,[3] she remained within the control of her father, to a greater or lesser extent,

---

1 See below, pp. 151-53, for the early age of marriage. For the authority of a husband over his wife, see Chapter 3 §A. In the unlikely event of a girl not marrying (below, p. 125), it is to be assumed that she remained to some extent under the authority (and protection) of her father or other male relatives. We have, however, little evidence regarding such a situation.

2 For further details about the honour due a mother, and her lack of authority, see below, Chapter 3 §A.

3 However brief her passage into the marital state might be, as a widow or divorcee she remained legally independent of her father (*Ned.* 11.10; *Ket.* 49a). On a practical level, however, there did remain the problem of a single woman functioning in a male oriented and controlled society. The widow or divorcee might well return to her father's house or seek protection from other male relatives. Note that אלמנה (usually translated 'widow') denotes someone without the means of financial support rather than simply a woman whose husband is dead (= *almattu* in the Middle Assyrian Laws, 'a woman without male support'); see *EJ*, XVI, cols. 487-96. With regard to her functioning independently, there is limited evidence (except for the Babatha archive, see Chapter 2 §C and Chapter 3 §A), presumably because it was such an anomaly.

dependent upon whether she was a *qetanah* or a *na'arah*.

One of the fundamental expressions of this *patria potestas* was the way in which a father was fully entitled to sell his daughter into bondage (Exod. 21.7). In consequence of the absence in the Old Testament of any division into age-groups according to legal competence, the ruling in Exodus simply records his right to sell 'his daughter' (בתו). The law was subsequently limited by the Tannaim to refer to a father's power over his minor daughter. According to their interpretation he was only allowed so to dispose of her until she reached the age of twelve years. Over a *na'arah* he possessed no right of sale (*Ket.* 3.8). A man could take such action in respect of his minor children because they were regarded as his possession,[1] or, to use the Mishnaic term, 'because their hand is like his hand' (מפני שידן כידו)—a term comparable to the use of *manus* in Roman law[2] and one suggested by the earlier rule that a chattel be acquired by putting it into the hand (cf. Lev. 25.14). The ability so to control the destiny of his children demonstrates the far-reaching authority a father had. This, however, was the fullest extent of his power. Jewish law by the Hellenistic period did not allow him the right of life or death over his offspring.[3]

From the fact that the phrase 'their hand is like his hand' described the status of minors regardless of their sex, it would be natural to conclude that a father could exercise the full extent of his power over both sons and daughters. Signifi-

---

1 Regarded as the father's property, children could, at least in biblical times, be seized by creditors in payment for debt (see 2 Kgs 4.1, and p. 47 n. 1 below).
2 In Roman sources *manus* was used to designate the power of the *pater familias* over his wife, children or slaves; Mishnaic 'for their hand is like his hand' is applied only with reference to children and slaves. For an interesting comparison of the two terms, see B. Cohen, *Jewish and Roman Law, a Comparative Study*, pp. 240f.
3 In early Hebrew history a father did have the power of life or death over his children (see, for example, the sacrifice of Isaac in Gen. 22, the death of Jephthah's daughter in Judg. 11), but this was later limited by the Deuteronomic legislators to the case of a stubborn and rebellious son (Deut. 21.18-21), and then to prevent arbitrary decision by the parents, the boy's trial and execution were conducted before the city elders. Such control was doubtless exercised also in the event of a child smiting or cursing his parents, the penalty for which was death (Exod. 21.15, 17; Lev. 20.9).

cantly, however, such was not the case. While making provision for a father to sell his daughter into servitude, the Law remains silent concerning the sale of sons. Oral tradition later specifically denied the father this power over his son: only a daughter could be sold (t. *Sot.* 2.9).[1]

Another manifestation of *patria potestas* was the way in which a father could annul any vows made by his children. Here again biblical law referred only to the power he had over the vows of a daughter and made no provision for a similar arbitrary authority over male children. The chapter in Numbers which deals with this issue concentrates solely on the vows of females: as children under the power of their fathers, as wives under the authority of their husbands, and as widows and divorcees under the control of no man (Num. 31).[2]

In his amplification of the somewhat bald biblical text, Philo wrote:

> Virgins... are not allowed full control of their vows by the Law... that is surely reasonable for... owing to their youth they do not know the value of their oaths, so that they need others to judge for them (*Spec. Leg.* 2.24-25).

If the origin of this law truly lay in the desire to protect young people from rashly making promises whose full import they did not have the maturity to appreciate, then one would expect it to apply equally to boys and girls. Thus, although finding no foundation in biblical law, the Tannaim (presumably basing themselves on this obvious reasoning) would seem to have

1 Neh. 5.5 (time of the returned community, fifth to fourth centuries BCE) would appear to indicate that in practice sons could also be sold (though such action was not supported by the Law), for there is recorded the people's cry that 'Lo, we bring into bondage our sons and our daughters to be servants'. However, three points should be noted concerning this passage: (a) it was patently a time when the Law was not being observed; (b) it was a period of terrible deprivation and social abuse for the people of Judah such as could force them to take this step; (c) although forced to contemplate selling their sons, the passage's continuation 'and some of our daughters are brought into bondage already' shows that even in these dire times they tried to avoid selling sons by disposing of their daughters first.
2 For an analysis of the introduction and significance of this piece of legislation in terms of changing Hebrew social structure and erosion of female independence, see Archer, 'The Virgin and the Harlot in the Writings of Formative Judaism', *History Workshop Journal* 24 (1987), pp. 1-16. Regarding the vows of wives, widows and divorcees, see further below and Chapter 3 §A.

extended the original ruling to include minor boys, that is, those not yet thirteen years and one day old (*Nidd.* 5.6). However, the question of whether it was the biblical law or its modification in the oral tradition which pertained in the intertestamental period is open to speculation. If the former were the case—with its application only to daughters not yet of age—then it would underline the position of secondary importance occupied by females at all periods of their lives.

Finally, note should be taken of the fact that although some limitation was placed upon the power of the husband to revoke his wife's vows (he could only do so if they were considered as 'afflicting the soul'; Num. 30.14; *Ned.* 11.1-2; cf. 10.7), a father's authority over his young daughter was absolute and no attention was paid to the particular nature of her vows (cf. *Ned.* 10.4).[1]

In its regulation of this law the book of Numbers merely stated that a father had control over a daughter's vows only so long as she remained in her father's house and was in her youth (בבית אביה בנעריה, Num. 30.4, 17).[2] It then considered the position of the woman in relation to her husband. The Mishnah elaborated upon this code, presenting far more complex and rigid definitions to the application of a father's power. First, the expression 'in her youth' was limited to mean until such time as the girl attained her majority, that is, until she became a *bogereth* at twelve and a half years of age (*Nidd.* 5.7; *Ket.* 4.4; *Ned.* 10.2). If her father died whilst she was still a minor she became responsible for her own vows (*Ned.* 10.2). His authority did not pass to other male adults in the family group and a mother had no right to revoke or impose her children's vows (*Ket.* 43a-43b; *Sot.* 3.8). She also gained premature independence from her father by marrying (at which

---

1 See below, Chapter 3 §A. Though note that for those sectarians responsible for the writings contained in the Damascus Document, there would seem to have been some limitation placed upon the father. Such is implicit in CD's interpretation of Num. 30.9: 'no husband shall cancel an oath without knowing whether it should be kept or not. Should it be such as to lead to transgression of the Covenant, he shall cancel it and shall not let it be kept. The rule for her father is likewise' (CD 16; G. Vermes, *The Dead Sea Scrolls in English*, p. 109).

2 Compare the wording of this with that of the crime of playing the harlot in her father's house, above pp. 25-26 and below p. 121.

point she entered into the control of her husband). Should she be both married and divorced while still a minor, although she would in all probability return to the protection of her father's house she was technically deemed 'an orphan in her father's lifetime' (יתומה בחיי האב), that is, she no longer counted as within his control (*Yeb.* 13.6; *Ned.* 11.10). In the event of a young girl being betrothed, her father was obliged to share his authority with her husband. Neither one acting separately had the power to revoke her vows (*Ned.* 10.1). Should her husband die while the contract was still one of betrothal and she still a minor, the father regained full and sole rights over his daughter.[1]

The detailed analysis made by the rabbis of the laws regarding a daughter's vows is in marked contrast to the lack of elaboration on the control exercised over a boy. The Tannaim simply stated that his vows were to be examined (as to whether or not he knew their real nature), until he reached adulthood and from that time (thirteen years and one day) his vows were valid (*Nidd.* 5.6). He obtained his independence earlier if his father died. No further complication of the law was necessary in his case for he, unlike a daughter, did not pass from one man's control into another's: the only period in his life—according to the Tannaim—when he was subject to another person's authority was during his minority.[2]

Finally, the Mishnah provides us with a passage which, by being a report of actual practice, most clearly demonstrates the absolute power a father had over his daughter's vows. *Ned.* 10.4 recalls how,

Among the disciples of the Sages, before the daughter of one

---

1 The use of the term *na'arah* in this mishnah should be read as including that period when a girl was considered a *qetanah*, that is, the ruling is not limited to daughters between the ages of 12 years and 1 day and 12 and a half years. The reference here is to exclude a *bogereth*.

2 Should he enter upon either betrothal or marriage while still a minor, the fact that he then controls the vows of his wife would suggest his own independence from paternal authority. The Mishnah, however, is silent on this matter, possibly because the likelihood of a boy marrying at such a young age was remote. Note that the period allowed by the rabbis between formal betrothal and actual marriage was only twelve months (*Ket.* 5.2). See Chapter 2 §A for the recommended age of marriage for boys and girls.

> of them left his control, the custom was for him to say to her,
> 'Let every vow that thou hast vowed in my house be
> revoked'.[1]

Included in the general statement of *patria potestas* contained in *Ket.* 4.4 is the fact that

> The father has control over his daughter as touching her
> betrothal whether it is effected by money, by writ or by inter-
> course.

Although the act and state of betrothal will be treated fully in the next chapter (§B), some notes are necessary at this juncture in respect of a minor, for the negotiation of her betrothal is another aspect or example of the power exercised by the *pater familias*. The character of betrothal during this period must also be borne in mind if we are to appreciate the full significance of a minor's inability to contract her own betrothal. It was not the open-ended affair of our present day 'secularized' Jewish engagements (as influenced by Western practices) but rather a definite, legally binding contract equal to the state of marriage in all respects bar that of cohabitation.[2] To break the contract required an official act of divorce or the death of one of the parties. It was this very important phase in a girl's life which—in the case of a minor—was controlled by someone other than herself.

In the passage quoted above from m. *Kethuboth*, the girl was referred to simply as בתו, suggesting that a father had control over his daughter regardless of her age. *Kidd.* 2.1 qualifies this statement, however, by declaring that such was the case only 'while she is in her girlhood', that is, a *na'arah*. After the age of twelve and a half years, the validity of the betrothal was dependent upon her consent (*Kidd.* 2b, 44a).[3] If

---

1 Such action was in fact contrary to biblical law which clearly stated that a father could disallow her vows only 'in the day that he heareth [them]' (Num. 30.6). See *Ned.* 72b for the way in which the rabbis of a later period attempted to explain this transgression.

2 Plus the fact already noted that if the betrothed woman was a minor then the husband was obliged to share his authority over her with her father. Such would not be the case if they were fully married.

3 Though the betrothal itself was doubtless negotiated by others. Also see pp. 153-55 for the fact that consent, while legally required, could in fact be little more than a formality.

she were betrothed or married and was then divorced or widowed whilst still in her minority, she was regarded as an independent agent and no longer under the father's authority (*Yeb.* 13.6). In effect, therefore, he only had control over the first betrothal of a minor daughter.

The only time during her minority when a girl was legally entitled to refuse a betrothal was if her father was dead. Her betrothal/marriage was then arranged by her mother or brothers (she having not reached the age of legal competence), but as they did not inherit the authority possessed by the father (cf. *Sot.* 3.8), they had no right to enforce the betrothal. She could abjure the contract before three judges (*Sanh.* 1.2) and be set free without the need of a bill of divorce (*Yeb.* 13.1-2, 3-4). According to the School of Hillel, she could exercise this Right of Refusal as many times as necessary during her minority, but the School of Shammai advised that having refused once she should then accept the next husband or wait until she came of age (*Yeb.* 13.1). As her consent was required when she became an adult, her right to refuse automatically lapsed once the signs of the onset of puberty were evident (*Nidd.* 6.11).

Before leaving the question of a minor daughter's betrothal a few notes on the subject of rape and seduction are necessary, for here too the law took into consideration the rights of a father. The Covenant Code decreed that

> If a man entice a virgin that is not betrothed and lie with her, he shall surely pay a *mohar*[1] for her to be his wife (Exod. 22.15).

The book of Deuteronomy repeats the ruling but with the added prescription that

> because he hath humbled her, he may not put her away all his days (22.29).[2]

---

1 Bride-price paid to father. See further below.
2 Although the Talmud makes a distinction between seduction and rape based upon the different phraseology in Exodus and Deuteronomy, it is doubtful whether such distinctions were appreciated or observed in the biblical or intertestamental era. The girl is free from guilt in both cases and the only question is the loss of property to the father. Philo and Josephus treat rape and seduction without any legal difference. Cf. L. Epstein, *Sex Laws and Customs in Judaism*, pp. 181-83.

Thus far it would appear to be simply a case of punitive compulsory marriage—the offender being obliged to make restitution to the girl (or perhaps rather her father, see p. 25) for the damage done by marrying her with no prospect of future divorce. However, given the tradition of paternal control of a young daughter's betrothal, the legislators could not deny the father his rights in this instance. They therefore subjected the 'compulsory' marriage to the consent of the father: should he refuse, then the offender was still obliged to deliver him the *mohar*, but nuptials did not take place. Thus the continuation of Exod. 22.15 reads:

> If her father utterly refuses to give her unto him, he shall
> pay money according to the *mohar* of virgins (v. 16).

The fact that the later Deuteronomic code failed to mention the role of the father is not indicative of a change in the law. Some scholars have seen in this omission a conscious revision of the earlier law by the Deuteronomic legislators: the crime of rape in Exodus, a civil offence against a father's 'property', was henceforth a moral crime which demanded a marriage over which a father had no say. Such an interpretation of the passage is, however, totally contrary to the social and legal system of the day in which a father's authority was extensive and firmly entrenched. To deny him the power of intervention in the marriage of his young daughter would be inconceivable. Deut. 22.29 was written as a supplement to and not a revision of Exod. 22.15, and as such there was no necessity to repeat the provisions contained in the earlier ruling. That the two texts were treated as one law, the later merely supplementing the earlier, is shown by Philo's understanding of biblical legislation on rape. Happily combining material from the two texts, he wrote:

> if the victim of the violation has a father he must consider
> the question of espousing her to the author of her ruin...

(= father's right of refusal in Exodus)

> ... if the father consents to the union, he must marry her
> without delay... he must not be at liberty to draw back or

make difficulties.[1]

(= marriage compulsory on the offender in Exodus and Deuteronomy)

> ...giving the girl the consolation of a wedlock so firmly established that nothing but death will undo it. (*Spec. Leg.* 3.70).

(= no divorce clause in Deuteronomy).

Thus, even in the instance of rape/seduction, a father retained his rights to control the betrothal/marriage of his daughter.[2] Here again, though, his authority applied only so long as the girl was a minor (cf. *Ket.* 3.8; note the use of נער בתולה in Deut. 22.28) and unbetrothed. In the event of the seduction or rape of a virgin who was already betrothed, a father had no say in the matter, for in this case the law prescribed death for one or both parties (dependent upon the circumstances) and marriage was out of the question (Deut. 22.23f.; *Spec. Leg.* 3.72f.; cf. Jos. *Con. Ap.* 2.201).[3] Should a girl's father die while she was still a minor and she be raped/seduced, then, according to Philo, who regrettably is our only source on this particular question, she herself must be asked whether she wishes to consort with the man or not (*Spec. Leg.* 3.71). In the event of an unbetrothed *bogereth* being violated, the obligation of marriage did not apply, as Pentateuchal law (and consequently rabbinic too) in laying down liability to punishment, spoke only of the *na'arah*. The fact that there

---

1   Or perhaps to 'dismiss her'. Cf. examples of παραιτεῖσθαι = 'divorce' in Liddell and Scott. The clause would then parallel the no-divorce clause in Deuteronomy and complement Philo's statement in the next sentence that only death would end their union.

2   In its treatment of rape, the Mishnah makes no specific mention of a father's right of consent/refusal. A clause to that effect was not necessary as it would merely have been a restatement of the paternal control of a minor's betrothal legislated for elsewhere. The Mishnah qualifies the no-divorce clause of Deut. 22.29 to apply only to the violator and not the seducer. If the ravished woman proved 'not fit to be taken in marriage by an Israelite', that is, if marriage between them were prohibited by pentateuchal or rabbinic law then even a violator was allowed to put her away.

3   If the event took place in the countryside, the girl was assumed to be innocent, the theory being that she had cried for help but no one had heard her; if it occurred in the city, the reverse applied and she was executed. In either case the man was killed.

was no consideration taken for the rape of an unbetrothed adult and apparently no punishment for her violator reveals much about the attitude toward rape and the principal concerns of the legislators.[1] In context of the present survey, however, it should be remembered that very few girls in the intertestamental period would not have been betrothed by the age of twelve and a half years, and as already noted, different rules (comparable to those for adultery) came into effect for the violation of betrothed virgins. In their case the offence was against the husband rather than the parent.[2] As long as the daughter remained unbetrothed and in her minority, a father could exercise the same control regarding marriage with her violator as he did over her betrothal generally. Legally, his was the decision in all cases of betrothal of a minor.

Just as a father had the right to contract his daughter's betrothal, so did he receive her bill of divorce should her betrothed husband decide to put her away during her minority (*Ket.* 4.4). He was only entitled to accept her *get* so long as she was a minor and had only been betrothed. If the divorce was to terminate a full marriage then she herself, although a minor, took the *get*, for by marriage paternal control lapsed. As a *bogereth*, of course, the question of her father holding the bill of divorce did not arise.[3]

1   The legal codes do not treat of rape or seduction of widows or divorcees (following full marriage), that is, of those women independent of any male control and assumed non-virgins, or indeed of any adult woman who had never married. Legislation was only considered where male honour and authority were involved, and outrage to the woman was not a central concern. The Alexandrian Philo did feel that violence to such women should have redress of some sort, but his was a lone voice without biblical authority (*Spec. Leg.* 3.64).

2   See below, Chapter 2 §B and Chapter 3 §A.

3   The ruling that a father should receive the *get* is found in *Ket.* 4.4 which is a general statement of the rights held by a father over his daughter not yet 12 and a half years of age. It should be noted, however, that *Gitt.* 6.2 maintained that in the case of a *na'arah*, who enjoyed a greater degree of independence/competence than a *qetanah*, either she or her father could receive the *get* (cf. *Kidd.* 43b-44a for further explanation of this mishnah). R. Judah objected to this ruling on the grounds that a *na'arah* is still under her father's authority and as such 'her own hand counts as nothing' (*Gitt.* 64b). His view is in character with what we have already learnt of the exercise of paternal control, and it, together with *Ket.* 4.4 is more likely to reflect actual practice than the statement of *Gitt.* 6.2.

In addition to receiving the *get*, the *kethubah*[1] of the divorced girl also fell to him—and considering the age of the girl here (that is, younger than twelve and a half) this probably amounted to the larger sum prescribed for virgins (a minimum of 200 *zuzin, Ket.* 1.2). Should she be widowed following a contract of betrothal, her *kethubah* again fell to him, but if she had been married it passed to her. The same occurred if she were divorced following marriage, for

> After her father has given her in marriage he has no claim to her (*Ket.* 4.2).[2]

The fact of a father rather than the girl herself being entitled to receive the *kethubah* leads to the broader question of whether or not a minor could at any time hold property or earnings independent of him. Regarding a daughter not yet twelve and a half years old, *Ket.* 4.4 states that the father

> has the right to aught found by her and to the work of her hands (cf. *Nidd.* 5.7).

According to *B.M.* 1.5 this duty to deposit anything found with the father (there being no legal obligation to return lost goods to the original owner) was incumbent upon minor sons as well as daughters.[3] With regard to the second clause, however, on a father's right to his daughter's handiwork, there is no parallel passage in Tannaitic sources about the earnings of a minor son. Presumably, therefore, unlike a daughter, he was permitted to profit by his work and what he earned belonged to himself. This assumption is substantiated by the Gemara to *Ket.* 4.4 which ponders:

> Whence is it deduced that a daughter's handiwork belongs to her father?

---

1 That is, the bride-price. The word *kethubah*, originally used for a written instrument (here the marriage contract), came to be applied also to the monies of marriage, synonymous with the earlier *mohar* already referred to. For the history of this evolution, see pp. 158-64.
2 For the woman's entitlement to the bride-price monies in the event of widowhood and, with certain exceptions, divorce, and the problems sometimes experienced securing payment, see Chapter 2 §C and Chapter 3 §A.
3 Though see *B.M.* 12a-b where the rabbis conceded to the son the right to take possession of what he gathered as a gleaner after his father. Although a wife is also accorded this right, no mention is made in this context of a minor daughter.

and concludes:

> From Scripture where it is said, 'And if a man sell his
> daughter to be a maidservant';[1] as the handiwork of a maid-
> servant belongs to her master so does the handiwork of a
> daughter belong to her father (*Ket.* 46b).

The fact that a boy could not be sold placed him and his earnings in a different category to that of a girl. A son had a further
advantage over a daughter in that should his father die, the
boy, even as a minor, henceforth took possession of anything
that he found (and of course continued to benefit from his
earnings). A girl, however, was in these circumstances obliged
to give to her brothers anything she had found or earned while
her father was still alive but which had not been handed to
him, for what had been regarded as the father's property was
subject to the laws of inheritance (*Ket.* 4.1). Anything she
found or earned subsequent to her father's death, however,
was hers to keep even if still in her minority, for

> A man may not transmit his authority over his daughter to
> his son (*Ket.* 43a-43b).

It was also the father's right to receive any fines incurred by
violence to his daughter by another person. In the event of her
rape or seduction the Old Testament demanded a fifty shekel
fine from her ravisher (lit. 'fifty of silver', חמשים כסף), payable to
the father as remuneration for the theft of his daughter's virginity.[2]D Post-biblical law imposed further payments: both
seducer and rapist had to pay the fixed sum of fifty shekels
regardless of whether the violated woman had been from
among the 'greatest of the priestly stock or the least in Israel'
(*Arak.* 4.4), plus compensation for indignity and blemish (*Ket.*
3.4). The fine for indignity varied according to

> the condition of life of him who inflicts and her that suffers

---

1 Exod. 21.7. According to the rabbis, since 'daughter' and 'maidservant' appear
   here in juxtaposition, an analogy between them may be drawn.
2 Regarding compensation to the father and the difficulty of marrying off a non-
   virgin, see Chapter 1 §A above. The fine was probably equal to the sum normally
   demanded as a virgin's bride-price (compare Deut. 22.29, which required the fifty
   shekel fine, later 200 *zuzim*, with the earlier passage in Exod. 22.15 which
   demanded simply payment of a *mohar*. On this see further below, Chapter 2 §B.

the indignity.

while that for blemish was determined by assessing the value of the girl before and after the event:

> She is looked upon as if she was to be sold: how much was she worth before? and how much is she worth now? (*Ket.* 3.7).

Such re-evaluation was the normal procedure in all damages suits (cf. *B.K.* 8.1), though, of course, valuation according to virginity was something peculiar to women. Unlike the seducer, a violator was also obliged to pay a fine for having inflicted pain. According to *Ket.* 4.1 all these fines were to be paid to the girl's father if her case was tried while she was still in her girlhood. Should he die before the case came to trial or if she were violated after his death, then all compensations fell to her even if still a *na'arah*. However, if he died once legal action had been started, any payment ordered by the court passed to the girl's brothers for, as was the case with her earnings, the amount in question was considered the property of the father and was therefore inherited by the sons. If the girl became an 'orphan in her father's lifetime' (cf. *Yeb.* 13.6), then any compensation owed fell to her and not to her father (*Ket.* 3.3). Such at least was the view of R. Akiba, but his ruling was later objected to on grounds that

> Since her father is entitled to have the money of her betrothal he is also entitled to have the money of her fine. As the money of her betrothal belongs to her father even after she has been betrothed and divorced, so also the money of her fine should belong to her father even after she had been betrothed and divorced (*Ket.* 38a).

The reasoning behind this objection indicates why it was the father who received her fine and reveals much of the way in which rape/seduction was viewed by the society and its legislators. In the same mishnah and working from the premise that a *bogereth* could not lay claim to a fine for violation (*Ket.* 3.8), R. Jose the Galilaean concluded that a divorced *na'arah*—similar to a *bogereth* in having gained independence from paternal control—was not entitled to receive any fine. Rape of a woman removed from the authority of either father or husband was not considered a punishable offence (see p. 53).

With respect to compensation for other injuries which might be inflicted on minors the Old Testament is silent, but the Mishnah declared the offender culpable and liable to make restitution (*B.K.* 8.4). It did not, however, state to whom the damages were to be paid. This point was subsequently subject to debate, some declaring that the compensation owed should be placed in a fund for use by the injured party, male or female, on attaining adulthood, and others stating that in the case of a daughter the money was to go directly to her father (*B.K.* 87a-88a). The fact that part of the payment was intended as compensation for any loss of time incurred (*B.K.* 8.4) lends suppport to the latter view, for just as a father enjoyed the fruits of his daughter's labour so should it be he who received recompense for any decrease in income due to her inability to work. The other counts on which compensation was demanded were the same as those itemized for violation, and these, as we have seen, were payable to the father. Any injury or blemish which caused a decrease in her pecuniary value—whether it be the blemish of loss of virginity or that of any other wound[1]—was treated as a loss to the father (*B.K.* 88a).

For injury to a daughter's good name, the prescribed fine again fell to her father. Such was the case with a virginity suit (Deut. 22.13-21): should her husband accuse her of not having been a virgin when they married (that is, of having lost her virginity to another man during the period of their betrothal, (*Ket.* 1.6), this having been the condition upon which he had taken her to wife and paid the higher bride price, he was entitled to lay charges against her before a court of twenty-three judges (*Sanh.* 1.1) on account of her deceit and the fact that 'his bargain was a bargain made in error' (*Ket.* 1.6; 7.8). If it were proven that the girl had indeed 'played the harlot in her father's house' she was put to death.[2] If, however, her hus-

---

1   According to R. Jose b. Hanina, 'We suppose the wound to have been made to her face, thus causing her pecuniary value to be decreased' (*B.K.* 88a).
2   By stoning, Deut. 22.21. If, however, she were the daughter of a priest, to whom special laws of purity attached, she was burned to death (Lev. 22.9; cf. *Ant.* 4.248). On this, see below Chapter 2 §A. For this being an offence rather against the father's good name and his authority, see above p. 25 and below pp. 106ff.

band's accusation proved false, then he was fined one hundred silver pieces for having 'brought up an evil name upon a virgin of Israel' and was ordered never to divorce her.[1] This payment was given to the slandered girl's father as his was the responsibility to preserve her virginity and the accusation was a slight to his authority.[2] Such a suit could only be brought if the girl had had illicit sexual intercourse while still in her girlhood, the term *na'arah* being used throughout the biblical passage (cf. *Ket.* 45b). The amount payable for slander was twice that for rape of an unbetrothed virgin and equal to the *kethubah* of a virgin (200 *zuzin* = 100 shekels). The same sum applied whether the woman concerned was 'from among the greatest of the priestly stock or... the least in Israel' (*Arak.* 3.5).

Although a daughter during her minority was not entitled to keep the earnings from her work, or any articles found by her, or compensatory fines for damages, we might ask whether she was otherwise entitled to hold and own property/goods independent of her father, enjoy the fruits thereof, and engage in business transactions. That persons *in aliena potestate* could possess property in their own right is indicated by various rulings in the Mishnah, such as *Shek.* 1.5 which deals with the shekel contribution of a minor to the Temple, *B.K.* 4.4 which treats of damages caused by the ox of a minor, *Sheb.* 6.4 concerning claims against the property of a minor, *Gitt.* 5.4 about tithing the property of a minor, and so forth. A minor

1 Although neither Scripture nor the Mishnah accorded the woman choice as to whether or not she remained with her slanderer, Philo stated that '... the law permits the wives to stay or separate as they wish, but deprives the husband of any choice either way as punishment for their slanderous accusations' (*Spec. Leg.* 3.82). It is difficult to tell, however, whether Philo was reflecting reality or was simply confusing the liberty accorded the seduced fatherless girl (*Spec. Leg.* 3.71; see above p. 53) with the case of the slandered virgin. A woman herself could not institute a divorce: it had to come from the husband (see pp. 217ff.).

2 The Hebrew does not name a coin but simply demands a fine of 'a hundred of silver' (מאה כסף, Deut. 22.19). The LXX qualifies this by declaring the amount to be 100 shekels (ἑκατὸν σίκλους); similarly the Dead Sea Scrolls (*Commentary on Biblical Laws* II) have 2 *minas* = 100 shekels. Josephus, however, believed it to be only 50 shekels (πεντήκοντα σίκλους, *Ant.* 4.248), whilst the Mishnah has 100 *selas* (מאה סלע) = 200 common/100 sacred shekels, *Arak.* 3.5). Philo does not specify (χρημάτων ζημίας, *Spec. Leg.* 3.82).

could receive property/goods through gift (e.g. *Ket.* 6.7: a father depositing money to buy his daughter a gift, perhaps a field), or through inheritance (cf. *B.B.* 8.1f. for the place of daughters in the normal order of inheritance), or through special disposition in contemplation of death (cf. *B.B.* 131b where opinion varied as to whether property assigned a daughter was actually acquired by her if she had brothers).

In the light of what we have already learnt of the rights accorded a father over his daughter's income (from whatever source) the question automatically arises as to whether he was also entitled to derive any benefit from her property. On this the Mishnah is emphatic in its denial of any such paternal right, stating categorically that

> he has not the use of her property during her lifetime (אינו
> אוכל פרות בחייה) (*Ket.* 4.4).

In consequence of her tender years it is probable that the father did in fact administer his daughter's estate, but because he could not enjoy the fruits thereof, his administration was purely on her behalf and for her future benefit when she became a competent adult. Similarly, if a guardian had been appointed over an orphan, he was obliged to take an oath that he had not impaired the property (*Gitt.* 5.4). If, however, the girl were married, the right not accorded her father was possessed by her husband, for as *Ket.* 4.4 records:

> When she is married the husband exceeds the father in that
> he has the use of her property during her lifetime.[1]

The difference was due to the fact that a husband was legally obliged to provide maintenance for his wife (see below, Chapter 3 §A) whereas, as we shall see, no such duty was incumbent upon a father toward his daughter (*Ket.* 4.4, 6). Property inherited by a betrothed woman was hers to sell (*Ket.* 8.1).

Having seen that a minor daughter could (i) possess prop-

---

1 This ruling suggests that a husband had usufruct of *all* his wife's property, a view followed by many present-day scholars. I hope to demonstrate later on (below, Chapter 3 §A) that a wife could in fact hold separate, additional property over which he had no such right. This belief does not of course invalidate the point being made in the present discussion, for in the main the ruling would have had application.

erty in her own right, and (ii) be the sole beneficiary from that property so long as she remained unmarried, we can now turn to the final question of whether or not she was considered legally competent to engage in conveyancing, that is, could she dispose of her property by gift or sale or indeed increase her estate by buying new goods. *Gitt.* 5.7 clearly states that

> In matters concerned with movable property a purchase or sale effected by children is valid.

The word here translated as 'children' is פעוטות, an unusual word explained in the Gemara as meaning minors above the age of six years who demonstrate sufficient intelligence and understanding as to warrant faith in their powers of judgment when consenting to the purchase, sale, or gift of personal property (*Gitt.* 59a, 65a).[1] The reason why such young persons were permitted to engage in these transactions was

> in order that they may procure the ordinary necessities (lit. 'for the provision of his livelihood')

and here we should remember that a father was not legally obliged to provide maintenance for his children (although under a moral obligation till the children reached the age of six; see below under *Maintenance*, p. 63). Children who had not reached the required level of understanding could acquire only through the agency of others (cf. *B.B.* 9.7). This freedom to deal with their movable property was enjoyed by all competent minors over the age of six excepting one category of children: if an orphan had had appointed over him or her a guardian or trustee (*Gitt.* 5.4; *Ket.* 6.7) then the Talmud declared invalid any purchase or sale conducted by the child (*Ket.* 70a). It does not expressly say when the guardian was to hand the property over to the minor's control, but presumably this took place when the latter reached puberty.[2] After

---

1 Cf. *JE*, IV, p. 231: 'A rational or voluntary concurrence of the parties is necessary in all cases involving a legal act of contract'. Concurrence is defined as 'A voluntary yielding of the will, judgment or inclination to what is proposed or desired by another'.

2 Either then or possibly at a time fixed by the father in his appointment of a guardian. Such was the view of Paul who wrote that the heir 'is under guardians and trustees until the date set by the father' (Gal. 4.2).

minors had reached the age of maturity they were permitted to dispose of real estate also, but only so long as the property came into their possession by purchase or gift. The sale of inherited immovable property was not considered valid until the person reached the age of twenty or, according to some rabbis, eighteen (*B.B.* 155a-156). This rule was designed to protect one 'susceptible to the temptations of money' from making a rash sale on account of his or her inexperience and youth. However, there could be exceptions to this rule, for the rabbis, basing themselves on the same reasoning as to why a minor was competent to sell, did permit persons younger than the stipulated age to sell even inherited real estate if they demonstrated sufficient business acumen (see *B.B.* 155b, a baraitha in which the transactions of a girl aged fourteen years were deemed valid: 'If she understands how to carry on a business, her purchase is [legal] purchase and her sale is [legal] sale'. Disposal of inherited immovables by gift was allowed for it was assumed that such young persons needed no legal protection for they would not have considered donating their own goods if they had not received some considerable benefit in return (*B.B.* 156a).

Before closing this discussion on a minor's rights *vis-à-vis* her earnings and property, emphasis must be placed upon the fact that the sources used have been predominantly Talmudic, that is, the review has been based upon that complex of sophisticated legislation which was defined and redefined by generations of scholars within and outside Palestine. There is no way of determining to what extent these rulings reflect the reality of everyday life in Hellenistic Palestine. We have no means of knowing what proportion of the nation adhered to or were even aware of the intricate weave of Mishnaic law which only later came to be regarded as normative and orthodox. As was stated in the Introduction, in the period under consideration we have to be constantly aware of the fact that there was no normative Judaism as such and therefore no one source may legitimately be taken as reflecting a broad and general social reality. In addition to the differences which existed between schools of thought, sects and indeed individuals of the time, there would have been variation in custom consequent upon region, upon whether people were urban dwellers or village folk, upon their level of education, development and concern, and so on. If material for this discussion of the property rights of the minor could have been gleaned from the Old Testament or indeed from intertestamental literature, it is probable that our analysis would have approximated more closely to Hellenistic practice, for as was already mentioned above, it is questionable to what extent the Jews of that period observed or even were familiar with the Mishnah's rigid and detailed categorization according to age upon which its rules of ownership were based: pre-Mishnaic literature did not even entertain the concept of legal minority and majority.[1] Certainly some of the laws here discussed would have had application in that they did not derive from a vacuum, but we have no means of gauging how many and to what extent. The matter remains open to speculation.

2. *Maintenance*

Having looked at the various ways in which a father controlled his daughter's life, we can now turn to an examination of whether a daughter in turn could expect or was legally entitled to maintenance by him while under his authority. In the light of two facts which have already been mentioned— that a father had no use of his daughter's property but a husband, who was liable for his wife's maintenance, ransom and burial, did enjoy the right of usufruct, and that minors were permitted to sell movable property in order to procure the necessities of life—it comes as no surprise to read in *Ket.* 4.6 that 'The father is not liable for his daughter's maintenance' (אינו חיב במזונות בתו האב). Similarly, he was under no legal obligation to provide for his male children (*ibid.*).

Explicit though this ruling is, however, it is obvious that it could not have had real application, and neither can it be

---

1 There are no provisions made regarding the property of children in the Old Testament. Presumably they were subject to the all-embracing *potestas* of their father until his death or their marriage. The question of their holding property independent of him was either considered irrelevant by the legislators or left to the discretion of each family. Regarding the latter, cf. B. Cohen, *op. cit.*, on the custom in the pre-Tannaitic era of vesting the woman, slave or minor with property rights which enabled them to form a private fund of their own known as *segullah* which corresponds to the Roman *peculium*.

taken as reflecting actual practice. The Amoraim, therefore, in treating of this mishnah, reasoned that as it only exempted the father from a *legal* obligation he was by inference subject to a *moral* duty (*Ket.* 49a). *Ket.* 49b records how at the rabbinic synod held at Usha in Galilee in the mid-second century CE it was ordained that a man had to maintain his sons and daughters 'while they are young',[1] and a leading halakhic Amora of the late third century was of the opinion that

> Although it was said 'A man is under no obligation to maintain his sons and daughters when they are minors', he must maintain them while they are very young (lit. 'the small of the small') (*ibid.*).

His term 'the small of the small' was further defined as meaning children not yet six years of age (*Ket.* 65b). (Here we should recall that the youngest age at which children [פעוטות] were allowed to sell property to gain a livelihood was six years.) Because the man was under no legal obligation, the court had no power to force him to maintain his children (except possibly in the case of a very wealthy man, *Ket.* 49b), but it did recommend that censure should be heaped upon one guilty of neglect so that public opinion would ensure he fulfilled his moral duty.

The only time at which a daughter was legally entitled to maintenance was after her father's death when she was supported from his estate. Speaking in the context of a father's non-liability during his lifetime, R. Eleazar b. Azariah explained that

> Like as the sons inherit only after the death of their father, so the daughters receive maintenance only after the death of their father (*Ket.* 4.6).

The right of a daughter to be supported out of the father's estate was recognized by an early decision delivered at Jerusalem by Admon, c. 40 CE, and his decision was approved by Rabban Gamaliel. Moreover, Admon's decision included the provision that if the property was small, then the daughter's maintenance had priority and the sons went without their

---

1   According to Rashi, under the age of puberty.

inheritance (*Ket.* 13.3; *B.B.* 9.1). A daughter, however, had no right to demand maintenance from her mother's estate, presumably because a mother was neither legally nor morally obliged to support her children (*B.B.* 8.4).[1] If there was more than one daughter in the family, then they each received maintenance on an equal basis, the elder not being entitled to take a greater share than the younger, unlike the inheritance rights of sons where the institution of primogeniture applied (*B.B.* 8.8).[2]

Although the law could not force a man to maintain his children during his lifetime, it would seem that the moral obligation decreed by the rabbis was often translated into a legally binding duty by the insertion, at the wishes of the private parties, of a clause to that effect in the marriage contracts of the time. In the three marriage contracts discovered at Wadi Murabba'at (*P. Mur.* 20, 21 and 116) and the one contract of remarriage also found there (*P. Mur.* 115), the husband undertook to provide for any daughters from the union.[3] In

1 Note that the word יתום, 'orphan', literally means 'fatherless' and may be classed with the אלמנה, i.e. someone without financial support (above p. 45 n. 3). See Brown, Driver, and Briggs, *A Hebrew and English Lexicon of the Old Testament*, p. 450, for OT examples and parallels. On the man's death the mother too was reliant upon his estate, either for her *kethubah* payment or, in lieu of that, for maintenance by the heirs. Any additional private property which she held children had no claim to except in the event of her death when the normal order of inheritance was followed. See Chapter 2 §C and Chapter 3 §A.

2 Such rulings of course assume the existence of estates large enough to provide maintenance. However, the frequent references to the plight of orphans and their recommendation to public charity show that all too often family funds were not available or sufficient to support the children. We might also note that according to Philo, writing from the milieu of Alexandrian Jewry, daughters received a share in the paternal estate only if their father had failed to settle a dowry on them prior to his death. With regard to their general maintenance, he placed them in the charge of the chief magistrate (*Spec. Leg.* 2.125).

3 *DJD*, II, no. 20 is in a poor state of preservation, but on the basis of what has survived, and particularly noting the presence of ל בעלין at the start of line 9, the text at lines 7-8 can safely be assumed to have dealt with the question of daughters' maintenance up to their marriage. The relevant section of no. 21 (lines 10-12), although fragmentary, is better preserved and its meaning is quite clear. That it is concerned with the maintenance of female children can again be inferred from the presence of לבעלין. The pertinent clause in no. 115, although broken in the middle, clearly speaks of feeding and clothing children from the union. In line 4 of no. 116 there has survived an echo of the maintenance clause. See Appendix I for the text and translation of these documents.

the light of *Ket.* 4.6, 11 it is automatically assumed that this clause refers to maintenance after the father's death, which, as we have learnt, was the only time a daughter was legally entitled to support. However, we may wonder whether this easy interpretation is indeed the correct one. Could the clause not be taken as referring to the maintenance of children *during* the father's lifetime, that is, precisely because there was no legal obligation, parties to the contract decided to include a clause which would make the children's maintenance binding upon the father? A fact which may support such an interpretation is the position of the clause in relation to the other obligations laid down in the *kethubah*. The order of the obligations varies from document to document, but in one respect they are all alike: in all the Murabba'at contracts the clause dealing with the maintenance of daughters *precedes* that concerned with the death of the father and the provisions for his widow. The editors of *DJD* II in the commentary to *P. Mur.* 20 (to which the reader is referred for the other marriage contracts) confuse the issue by being inexact in the description of the document's clauses: 'les ll. 4-6 parlent de la dot [= *kethubah*, see pp. 177ff. below] et du divorce possible de la femme. Puis viennent les clauses envisageant le décès, de la femme d'abord (ll. 7-9), ensuite du mari (ll. 9-11), avec les précisions sur l'héritage des fils, la situation des filles et de la veuve.'[1] More specifically, the maintenance clause in *P. Mur.* 21 actually refers to the death of the father in a revealing way:

> And if there be children[2] to you by me legitimately, they are to live at my house and be nourished from my possessions... up to marriage or after me (i.e. my death) along with you (ll. 10-12).[3]

P. Mur. 115, a contract of remarriage, interestingly makes

---

1 *DJD*, II, p. 110.
2 The editor's translation at this point is inexact: the word מן (and there is no reason to doubt this restoration) should be rendered 'daughters' rather than 'children'. Even if 'children' was a correct translation, the presence of לבעלין would indicate that it did in fact refer to daughters and not to sons or children generally.
3 Translation by Fitzmyer and Harrington, *A Manual of Palestinian Aramaic Texts*, p. 143.

provision for the maintenance of both the children which the couple had prior to their divorce and those yet to be born from their renewed union. Again, the implication is that the clause refers to maintenance during the father's lifetime. Unusually this contract also makes specific mention of the sons of the marriage who are to receive maintenance alongside the daughters (l. 9).

Another possible indication that the maintenance clause in these marriage contracts might refer to maintenance during the father's lifetime may be derived from the Mishnah. *Ket.* 4.7-12 lists six duties incumbent upon the husband and necessary for a valid marriage. The fulfilment of any one of these duties was required whether or not it had been written in the *kethubah*, for

> If he had not written for her... [a condition]... he is still liable so to do since that is a condition enjoined by the court.

One of these obligations which to be binding needed no specific mention in the marriage contract was the duty of a husband to redeem his wife if she had been taken captive and again have her as his wife, or if he were a priest, return her to her father's house as she was then considered unfit to be his wife (*Ket.* 4.8). In the Murabba'at contracts there is no clause which treats of this obligation, not even in *P. Mur.* 20 which deals with the marriage of a priest. It was an understood condition of marriage. Another condition of this type was one which entitled a girl to support from the paternal estate:

> If he had not written for her, 'Female children which thou shalt have by me shall dwell in my house and receive maintenance from my goods until they marry husbands', he is still liable [thereto] since this is a condition enjoined by the court (*Ket.* 4.11).

It is this condition, which caters for the maintenance of daughters after the father's death, which has been equated with the clause under discussion in the Murabba'at *kethubah*. However, in the light of what we have already learnt of this maintenance clause in the context of the documents themselves, plus the fact that the rabbinic condition did not need to be included in the contract for it to be binding upon the husband, we may indeed question the truth of the conclusion that

they are one and the same. It is possible that as a girl's right to
support after her father's death was understood, a statement
to that effect was redundant, and therefore the clause we find
in the marriage contracts from Wadi Murabba'at was in fact
a distinct and separate contractual agreement between the
parties to the document inserted to ensure that the father was
legally obliged to fulfil what was regarded only as a moral
duty, that is, the maintenance of his female children during
his lifetime.

A final indication that (a) the practice of the day, despite the
express ruling of *Ket.* 4.6, was to provide for daughters until
they passed into the control of their husbands, and (b) that the
moral duty encouraged by the rabbis was commonly (perhaps
usually) translated into a legal obligation by contractual
agreement, is furnished by a ruling contained in *Ket.* 12.1. The
mishnah deserves to be quoted in full:

> If a man married a woman and she stipulated that he
> should maintain her daughter [from a previous marriage]
> for five years, he is bound to maintain her for five years. If
> she was [afterward] married to another and she stipulated to
> him also that he should maintain her daughter for five
> years, he, too, is bound to maintain her for five years. The
> first husband may not say, 'If she comes to my house I will
> maintain her', but he must send her her maintenance to the
> place where her mother is. So, too, the two husbands may
> not say, 'We will maintain her jointly', but the one must
> maintain her and the other must give her the cost of her
> maintenance.

Here it is clear that the daughter was to receive maintenance
during the lifetime of her step-father(s), and that this was
made a legally binding duty on the husband at the stipulation
of his wife-to-be. If maintenance as a pre-condition of marriage could be asked of a stepfather, how much more so could
it be expected, even demanded of the children's natural father,
a clause to that effect being inserted in the woman's *kethubah*.

Finally, it should be noted if a child continued to receive
maintenance from her father after attaining her majority,
she forfeited the right she would normally have had of keeping her earnings or any object which she had found, for by a
rabbinic decision designed to prevent ill-feeling between par-

ent and child, it was ordained that 'a major who is maintained by his father is regarded as a minor and minor who is not maintained by his father is regarded as a major' (*B.M.* 12b).

In addition to maintaining his daughters (if he could) a father was obliged to provide a suitable dowry, or, to use the words of the Talmud, to ensure that she was 'dowered, clothed and adorned that men shall eagerly desire her' [lit. 'spring upon her'] (*Ket.* 30b). He could assign her as much as he chose or his means allowed, but he was not permitted to give less than fifty *zuzin* (*Ket.* 6.5). Philo encouraged wealthy folk to

> help parents without the means to marry their daughters and provide them with an ample dowry (*Fug.* 29).

If a father died before his daughter's marriage, then she was entitled to receive her dowry from his estate, and if there was more than one daughter, then, as was the case with their maintenance, the elder was not permitted to take a larger amount at the expense of her sisters (*B.B.* 8.8). Should the estate be insufficient to furnish a suitable dowry, then the girl was assigned not less than fifty *zuzin* from the poor funds, and 'if there was more in the poor funds, they should provide for her according to the honour due her' (*Ket.* 6.5). Similarly, members of that sect which adhered to the ordinances of the Damascus Document set up a special fund from their earnings out of which 'the virgin with no kin, and the maid for whom no man cares' were to receive aid.[1]

It is apparent, therefore, from this review that in theory at least a father was under a social pressure to support his daughters during his lifetime; under legal obligation to make his estate available for their maintenance after his death; and under both social and legal pressure to provide a dowry both appropriate to her status and sufficient to secure a suitable husband. The nature of the dowry and its fate within marriage will be discussed more fully in the next two chapters.

D. *Education—Domestic Duties*

Another question which should be raised in this survey of the

---

1 CD 13, G. Vermes, *op. cit.*, p. 116.

young girl's life is that of education: did she receive an education, either by informal or formal instruction, and if so, how
did it compare with that received by a boy in the same period?
In order to gain the fullest appreciation of the relative position
of the woman in this respect, some space must first be dedicated to an appraisal of the general nature and state of education operating within Hellenistic Palestine. What was taught
and with what purpose in mind? (For this question it should be
remembered that education is a process of cultural transmission. If it is restricted to knowledge of one's own culture it
becomes a primary means of reinforcing national consciousness and religious and ethnic identity.) What were the means
by which selected knowledge was transmitted? Was there a
system of formal schooling, and if so, was it universal? Finally,
what importance did society attach to the acquisition of an
education? In consequence of the paucity of clear-cut evidence
in the Hellenistic sources themselves about specific aspects of
educational programmes and systems, it will be necessary to
look at material from other periods, trace the development of
education in Hebrew history, and thereby reach some understanding of the situation prevailing in Graeco-Roman
Palestine.

From early in the recorded history of the Hebrews, knowledge of the Torah, that is, of the nation's history, traditions,
customs and law, was required of the people by divine commandment. After delivering the Torah to the people, Moses is
said to have instructed the children to

> Remember the days of old,
> Consider the years of many generations;
> Ask thy father and he will declare unto thee,
> Thine elders and they will tell thee (Deut. 32.7)

and parents to 'make them [the statutes and ordinances]
known unto thy children and thy children's children' (Deut.
4.9).[1] Children were never to forget that their people, Israel,

---

1 Note in fact that these words are from the book of Deuteronomy whose 'discovery'
   (2 Kgs 22.8ff.) and content formed part of the great nationalistic reform of the
   reign of Josiah in the late seventh century BCE. For the religious state of affairs
   prior to this time and the people's ignorance and non-observance of Torah, see

stood in peculiar relation to God and had a special destiny and mission to fulfil. The duty of training children to an appreciation of these facts was placed firmly upon the parents' shoulders, knowledge being passed orally from generation to generation. As we shall see, although more formal systems of schooling evolved, instruction by parents within the home was to continue and indeed form the backbone of Jewish education, at least at a primary level, throughout the ages.

Another vehicle by which children gained knowledge of their nation's history and law was through the various festivals and ceremonies which occurred during the year. Observance of the simple family sabbath, involvement in larger communal festivities, or trips to the Temple on special high holidays were all part of the educational process, and indeed were consciously employed for that purpose. For example, at the Feast of Weeks, the book of Deuteronomy instructs:

> And thou shalt rejoice before the Lord thy God, thou and thy son, and thy daughter... And thou shalt remember that thou wast a bondman in Egypt (16.11-12).

Or again, the Passover ritual, instituted at the very inception of Israel's national history, made express provision for questions on the history and meaning of the service to be asked by the children of their parents (Exod. 12.25; 13.14-15; cf. Deut. 6.20).

In addition to home instruction, there was also instituted at a date prior to our period the custom of publicly reading the law once every seven years to those who had come up to Jerusalem to celebrate the feast of Tabernacles. The Temple custodians and elders of the nation were commanded to

> Assemble the people, the men and the women, and the little ones... that they may hear, and that they may learn, and fear the Lord your God, and observe to do all the words of this law; and that their children, who have not known, may hear and learn to fear the Lord your God (Deut. 31.12-13).

With regard to the same period mention should also be made of the existence of itinerant prophets who took upon them-

Archer, 'The Role of Jewish Women in the Religion, Ritual and Cult of Graeco-Roman Palestine', in Cameron and Kuhrt, *Images of Women in Antiquity*, pp. 273-75. Regarding the Deuteronomic reform, see J. Bright, *A History of Israel*.

selves the task of bringing the law to the people in general.[1]

Fresh impetus was given to the programme of Jewish education by the traumatic events of the sixth and fifth centuries BCE. The destruction of the Temple, the exile to Babylonia, and the return of a 'remnant' to an impoverished land riddled with syncretistic practices,[2] shocked part of the nation out of their earlier complacency and occasioned a fundamental rethinking of the position of the people *vis-à-vis* their God and his covenantal law.[3] The recognition by the returned community that the only way of making the law a living force in the land (which patently had not been the case in the pre-exilic years), and creating a people conscious of their identity, destiny and mission, was through a common knowledge of Torah, heralded the beginnings of a system of formal education. Under the leadership of men like Ezra and Nehemiah whose whole endeavour was directed to preserving the nation's racial, cultural and religious integrity, preliminary steps were taken to bring the Law to the people. From this period forward, education was no longer deemed

1   It would seem that a system evolved at an early date whereby certain days of the year were set aside for these holy men to receive and teach the people. Such is suggested by a passage in 2 Kings which records how when the Shunammite woman, distraught at the death of her son, wanted to seek the help of the prophet Elisha, her husband said, 'Wherefore wilt thou go to him today? It is neither new moon or sabbath' (4.23). Note again that the command to assemble is from the book of Deuteronomy and therefore most likely a part of the Deuteronomic reform (above, p. 70 n. 1). The prophets first came on the scene in the mid-eighth century and were a vociferous group of Yahweh supporters who struggled to return the people to worship of the One God.

2   Only the elite of the nation had been taken into exile by Nebuchadnezzar, leaving behind 'vinedressers, husbandmen, and the poorest sort of the people of the land (ודלת עם־הארץ)' (2 Kgs 24.14; 25.12). As is evident from the account of Ezra, only a portion of the exiles returned to rebuild the Temple and separate themselves from the *'am ha-'aretz* who had stayed on the land continuing the old syncretistic practices. For the threat presented by this group to the returned community, see Ezr. 3.3; 9.1, 11; 10.2; Neh. 10.29, 31-32. For a history of the *'am ha-'aretz* and the later pejorative use of the term in Pharisaic Judaism, see *EJ*, II, cols. 833-36 and *JE*, I, pp. 484-85, and further below.

3   That the people, despite the Deuteronomic reform, were still not observing the Law and worship of the One God right up until the eve of the exile is evidenced by the narratives of Kings and Chronicles. For this, the impact of the exile, and the role of the prophets in the re-thinking, see Archer, 'The Role of Jewish Women . . . ', and Bright, *op. cit.* For the fact that only a portion of the people concerned themselves with reform, see n. 2 above.

the responsibility of parents alone. There arose a class of professional teachers who acquired authority and respectability through no prophetic vision or zeal, but simply because they were informed bearers of the Law.[1] At this stage in Jewish history, it was predominantly the Levites who performed this vital duty, for with the establishment of the one legitimate sanctuary at Jerusalem and the consequent abolition of all the rural shrines which had abounded in preexilic times, the beginning of the Second Temple period saw the removal of many of the Levites from strictly priestly functions. They therefore turned their attention in new directions and developed into a body of instructors and interpreters of the Law.[2] Indeed, in a verse which belongs to that section of the book of Deuteronomy which was reworked in the exile and beyond, the teaching role of the Levites was made into the fulfilment of a divine commandment: 'They shall teach Jacob thine ordinances, and Israel thy Law' (33.10). Thus in the biblical account of the assembly which Ezra called for a public reading of the Law, it is reported that:

> He [Ezra] read... from early morning till midday in the presence of the men and the women... and the Levites caused the people to understand the Law. And they read in the book, in the Law of God distinctly; and they gave the sense and caused them to understand the reading (8.3-8).

And in Neh. 8.9 is found a clear reference to the complementary duties of those who preserved and those who transmitted the Law in its recently revised form,[3] for the verse speaks of הכהן הספר והלוים המבינים ('the priest, the scribe and the Levites

---

1 That the importance and necessity of public teachers was recognized from the very outset of the period is indicated by the fact that when Ezra was gathering people to make a return to the Land, he made a particular point of finding teachers who were willing to return. And in the biblical report of his endeavours, not only are the teachers (מבינים) specifically mentioned, but they are referred to together with the 'chief men' (ראשים) and *before* the 'ministers of the temple' (Ezr. 8.16-17).

2 For the history of this transitional period and the changing role of the Levites, see J. Bright, *op. cit.*, and R. de Vaux, *Ancient Israel, Its Life and Institutions*.

3 During the time in Babylonia, a group of the exiles had not only zealously preserved all records of their nation's past but had also inserted new material and revised and codified the whole in the light of newly developed concepts and attitudes. It was this revised book of the Law which Ezra brought with him to Palestine.

who taught'). To bring the Law to the greatest number of people, however, the Levites could not limit their teaching to those occasions when a general public reading took place. A passage in the post-exilic work of 2 Chronicles indicates that in fact their practice was to tour the land teaching in the cities and villages:

> they taught in Judah, having the book of the Law of the Lord with them; and they went throughout all the cities of Judah and taught among the people (17.7-9).[1]

In addition to the emergence of a body of professional teachers, the early post-exilic period also saw the beginnings of an institution which was to develop in the Hellenistic period into a central feature of the Jewish educational system: the synagogue. Although it cannot be stated with certainty, it seems likely that this institution, whose primary function was the exposition and interpretation of Scripture, gradually evolved from the time of Ezra and Nehemiah, that is, from the time when the nation's leadership was striving to make the Law a living force in the land and when Israel was making moves to become an education-centred people.[2] Certainly by the late Second Temple period it was such a well-established and widespread institution that the Jews of that time were of the opinion that it dated from the time of Moses. Thus the author of the Acts of the Apostles could write: 'For from early generations Moses has had in every city those who preach him, for

---

1 Although the author ascribes this activity to the reign of King Jehoshaphat, it is probable that he is in fact reflecting the practice of his own day when a class of professional teachers first emerged. Significantly, the account of the same king's reign in the earliest book of 2 Kings (D) makes no mention of the teaching role of the Levites or of their touring the land. See also 2 Chron. 15.3 which speaks of the teaching priest (כהן מורה) and 1 Chron. 25.8 which mentions the teacher-scholar relationship (מבין עם תלמיד).

2 Certainly later generations believed that the system of synagogue instruction dated from the time of Ezra. The rabbis declared that it was he who ordained that public readings of the Law should take place on Mondays, Thursdays and most importantly on sabbaths for those workers unable to attend weekday services (*B.K.* 82a). It is possible that the synagogue's origin goes back even to the exile itself (cf. Ezek. 8.16; 14.1; 20.1 and especially 11.6). For the history of the institution and evidence for it over the centuries, see *EJ*, XV, cols. 579-83 and Schürer, *The History of the Jewish People in the Age of Jesus Christ*, II, pp. 424-47.

he is read every sabbath in the synagogue' (15.21).[1]

From the Gospel accounts we learn of synagogues in Nazareth, Capernaum, and the Galilee in general (Mt. 4.23; 13.54; Mk 1.21; 5.2; 6.2; Lk. 4.16, 31, 44; 6.6; 7.5; 8.41; 13.10; Jn 6.59), and from Josephus of ones in Tiberias, Dor, and Caesarea Maritima (*Vita* 277; *Ant.* 19.300; *BJ* 2.285), while the Talmud speaks of there being a multitude of synagogues in Jerusalem itself (b. *Ket.* 105a; y. *Meg.* 3.1, 73d). Indeed, it is more than possible that every Jewish settlement of any importance had its own synagogue, at least in the last two or three hundred years of the Second Commonwealth.

The primary purpose of the synogogue was to serve as a place for the public reading of Torah. The main day upon which people assembled to hear the Law was the sabbath,[2] but readings also took place, according to Tannaitic sources, on Mondays and Thursdays, and of course on special feast days (*Meg.* 3.3-6; 4.1-2). As the Scripture readings, which followed a cyclical sequence (*ibid.*), were intended to be instructive rather than merely devotional,[3] they were accompanied both by an interpretative translation from the Hebrew (*Meg.* 4.4, 6, 10) and by a sermon.[4] In one passage Philo encapsulates for us the purpose and the method of the synagogue readings, and witnesses to the contemporary belief in the antiquity of the institution:

---

1 Similarly Josephus, *Con. Ap.* 2.175; and Philo, *Vit. Mos.* 2.216; *Spec. Leg.* 2.62.

2 Note the use of the term σαββατεῖov to describe the synagogue in Augustus' edict (*Ant.* 16.164); whenever a day of the week is mentioned in the Gospels for Jesus' attendance at the synagogue it is always the sabbath, and the same is the case with Paul's trips as described in Acts. Note also that Philo speaks of the Therapeutae as meeting only once a week (*Vit. Cont.* 30-32).

3 For the instructional purpose of the synagogue, see for example *Con. Ap.* 2.175 (people gather 'to listen to the law and learn it accurately'), *Vit. Mos.* 2.216 (synagogues called schools, διδασκαλία), and numerous passages in the NT where διδάσκειν figures as the main activity (Mt. 4.23; Mk 1.21; 6.2; Lk. 4.15, 31; 6.6; 13.10; Jn 6.59; 18.20).

4 The rendering verse by verse into Aramaic was probably established practice by the first century CE, with the translation being conveyed orally from generation to generation. The first reference to its being read from a written *Targum* comes from the fourth century CE. See Schürer, *op. cit.*, II, pp. 452-53. For the structure and content of the sermon in the first century CE, see conveniently S. Safrai, 'The Synagogue', in *Compendia Rerum Iudaicarum ad Novum Testamentum*, II, p. 932.

the Lawgiver [i.e. Moses] thought it necessary... that they
should... be well acquainted with their ancestral laws and
customs. What then did he do on these seventh days? He
required them to assemble in the same place, and to sit
down... and listen to the laws in order that none might be
ignorant of them... and some priest who is present, or one
of the old men reads to them the holy laws, and explains
each separately till nearly eventide, and after that they are
allowed to depart with a knowledge of their holy laws, and
with great improvement in piety.[1]

Thus, by the time we reach the Hellenistic period the principle of universal education in both oral and the written law was
firmly established, and indeed many of the means by which
such knowledge was to be acquired were in existence. Both
these facts are amply attested for the start of the period in the
book of Proverbs (though note that knowledge is here usually
termed חכמה, 'wisdom'; see further below), and as we have
seen the writers of the Hellenistic period continued to lay great
emphasis upon the importance of acquiring an education,
declaring knowledge of and adherence to the Law the
fulfilment of divine commandment and the people's *raison
d'être*. Ben Sira described the ideal scholar as one who

applieth himself to the fear of God
[And sets] his mind upon the Law of the Most High;
Who searcheth out the wisdom of all the ancients,
And is occupied with the prophets of old;
Who heedeth the discourses of the men of renown,
And entereth into the deep things of parables;
Searcheth out the hidden meaning of proverbs,
And is conversant with the dark sayings of parables (39.1-3).

The child was equipped with the necessary tools for tackling
such higher studies by the instruction he initially received at
home, for at this stage, that is the middle of the Second Temple
period, primary education continued to be the responsibility of
parents. Thus the author of *2 Baruch* (first century CE)
exhorted parents to

deliver ye... the traditions of the law to your sons after you,
as also your fathers delivered them to you (84.9).

1   Philo, *Hypothetica*, in Eusebius, *Praep. Evan.*, trans. Gifford, §§359-60.

And the *Testament of Levi* (between the second century BCE and the second century CE) instructs:

> do ye also teach your children letters, that they may have understanding all their life, reading unceasingly the law of God (13.2; cf. 9.1, 6-9; *1 Enoch* 68.7; Sir. 8.9; *Jub.* 7.38-39; 10.8),

while the second-century BCE book of *Jubilees* records how fathers taught their children the art of writing (8.2; 11.16; 47.9).[1] A chapter in *4 Maccabees* (first century CE) furnishes us with valuable information about the type of instruction children could expect to receive in the home at that time.[2] The passage deserves to be quoted in full by virtue of its vivid portrayal of Hellenistic family life. A mother is speaking to her sons about their dead father:

> He taught you the Law and the Prophets. He read to us of Abel who was slain by Cain and Isaac who was offered as a burnt offering and of Joseph in the prison. And he spoke to us of Phineas, the zealous priest, and he taught you the song of Ananias, Azarias, and Mishael in the fire. And he glorified also Daniel in the den of lions... and he called to your minds the sayings of Isaiah... he sang to us the words of David the psalmist... he quoted to us the proverb of Solomon... he confirmed the words of Ezekiel... For he forgot not the song that Moses taught (18.11f.).[3]

Having been provided with a certain degree of knowledge by his parents, the young person could continue his education by attending to 'the utterance of the prudent... in the assembly' (Sir. 21.17; cf. 6.34; 15.5). The word 'assembly' (קהל,

---

1 The dates of these sources range from the second century BCE to the second century CE and in fact evidence the continuing importance of home instruction even after more formal means of schooling had been introduced. See further below.

2 Although *4 Maccabees* is probably not a Palestinian work, its words complement what we have already learned from our other sources and so may with justification be used as illustrative of the education process in Palestine. For its provenance and use in the present survey see the Introduction above.

3 The setting for the mother's words was the imminent martydom of her sons at the hands of the Greeks. She therefore concentrated on reminding the boys of what they had learnt about the trials and tribulations of worthy Jews of the past. Despite the passage's obvious bias toward certain biblical stories, it does indicate the nature and scope of education within the home.

ἐκκλησία) probably refers either to the regular synagogue meetings or to the scholarly gatherings which took place around the Temple precincts (cf. Lk. 2.46). By the middle of the Graeco-Roman period, however, the acquisition of a higher education was not confined to synagogue or Temple instruction. This period also saw the emergence of a system of public schooling which supplemented the teaching given in the home, synagogue, Temple and at the feasts, and concentrated on imparting higher wisdom to those able and willing to learn. This new institution was called the *beth midrash* and is first mentioned in Ben Sira:

> Turn in unto me, ye unlearned,
> And lodge in my house of instruction (בבית מדרשי)...
> acquire wisdom for yourselves and without money (51.23, 25).

By speaking of this institution as a 'school' we should not be tempted to imagine the existence of actual school buildings, regular clases, organized and controlled curricula, or professional, paid teachers. Such schooling as existed was as yet non-uniform and unstructured. Individuals renowned for their learning or simply eager to impart knowledge of the Law, both oral and written, would gather to themselves students and disciples desirous of further knowledge. Any location could serve as a meeting place for these scholars and their audiences: the home of the master, market-places, courtyards, gatehouses of private buildings, fields, vineyards, or simply under the shade of an olive tree.[1] Indeed, outdoor teaching continued to be the norm in Palestine for centuries (witness the Gospel account of Jesus' teaching).[2] The informality of the system of higher education is highlighted by a passage in Proverbs which probably refers to the beginning of such 'schools of instruction':

> Wisdom crieth aloud in the streets,

---

1 Cf. A. Büchler, 'Learning and Teaching in the Open Air in Palestine', *JQR* n.s. 4 (1913-14), pp. 485-91; S. Krauss, 'Outdoor Teaching in Talmudic Times', *JJS* 1 (1948-49), pp. 82-84.
2 Cf. *ibid.* for Krauss' argument that the many Talmudic references to the famous vineyard of Yabneh are not, as many scholars have assumed, metaphorical allusions to an Academy but are in fact literal references to open-air gatherings of scholars, seated in an actual vineyard.

She uttereth her voice in the broad places;
She calleth at the head of the noisy street,
At the entrance of the gates, in the city
She uttereth her words (1.20-22),

and by the advice which Ben Sira gave to the eager student:
'Look for him who is wise, and seek him out earnestly' (6.36).
Having been accepted by the master of his choice, the student
simply sat at his feet and attended to the lesson.[1]

Finally, it should be remembered that there was no stan-
dardized or normative corpus of biblical interpretation in existence at this time which could be taught in the schools, for
although the various sects and movements which flourished
in the Second Temple period all accepted the Torah, they each
developed their own ways of interpreting the Law and passed
these traditions on to their students.[2]

In Ben Sira's day there would seem to have been no school
which catered for education at a primary level. As we have
seen, such instruction was regarded as the parents' responsibility. Talmudic tradition ascribes the development of public
schools for elementary education to the first century BCE. The
Palestinian Talmud states that one of the three things which
Shimon ben Shetah (a leading Pharisee at the time of Alexander Jannaeus and Queen Salome Alexandra, fl. 90–70 BCE)
instituted was '...that the children should go to school (שיהו

---

1 For the usual practice of students and disciples sitting on the ground at the feet of
   their masters even at later times when school buildings were utilized, cf. M.
   Aberbach, 'Educational Institutions and Problems in the Talmudic Age. Sect. 2:
   Seating Arrangements in the Palestinian and Babylonian Academies during the
   Talmudic Age', *HUCA* 36 (1966), pp. 111-20. It is in the light of this common practice that a line in Ben Sira is to be understood. After calling upon people to attend
   his *beth midrash*, he then wrote, 'May my soul delight in my *yeshibah*' (51.30). It
   has often been assumed that the term *yeshibah* used in this passage refers to an
   actual academy, the like of which was common in the Talmudic period and
   beyond. It is doubtful, however, if at this stage it had developed from its basic
   meaning of 'sitting' (that is, studying). Cf. D. Goodblatt, *Rabbinic Instruction in
   Sasanian Babylonia*, pp. 64f., for the use of *yeshibah* (= sitting) in Tannaitic
   sources.
2 See, for example, Josephus who, in describing his own education in the mid-first
   century CE, boasts of the way in which he did not limit himself to knowledge of one
   school but 'determined to gain personal experience of the several sects into which
   our nation is divided' and having dedicated some years to gaining such experience, decided to 'govern my life by the rules of the Pharisees' (*Vita*, 10-12).

(התינוקות הלכין לבית הספר) (*Ket.* 8.11, 32c). Although no further
details are furnished, the way in which the 'school' is termed a
בית ספר (*beth sefer*) and its pupils תינוקות ('little ones') would
indicate that the passage referred to an institution for elementary education. In the Babylonian Talmud we find a more
explicit statement regarding formal instruction for children
which pertains to the last days of the Second Commonwealth:

> Verily the name of that man is to be blessed, to wit Joshua
> ben Gamala,[1] for but for him the Torah would have been for-
> gotten from Israel. For at first, if a child had a father, his
> father taught him, and if he did not have a father, he did not
> learn at all... They then made an ordinance that teachers of
> children should be appointed in Jerusalem[2] ...Even so,
> however, if a child had a father, the father would take him
> up to Jerusalem and have him taught there, and if not, he
> would not go up to learn there. They therefore ordained that
> teachers should be appointed in each prefecture and that
> boys should enter school at the age of 16 or 17[3]...At length
> Joshua ben Gamala came and ordained that teachers of
> young children [מלמדי תינוקות] should be appointed in each dis-
> trict and each town, and that children should enter school at
> the age of 6 or 7 (*B.B.* 21a).

Many scholars have dismissed the evidence of this tradition
on the grounds that the years immediately preceding the
destruction of the Temple were ones of violent social and political upheaval and therefore hardly the most suitable moment
for a reform of elementary education on a wide scale.
However, as S. Safrai has pointed out, in the first place the
tradition was related by Rav, a Babylonian Amora who lived
for many years in Palestine and brought back with him many
reliable traditions, and in the second place, the Talmud does
not often attribute creditable achievements to the high priests
of the last days of the Second Commonwealth.[4] Although pre-

---

1 High priest, c. 63 CE.
2 Referring to the work of Shimon ben Shetah?
3 Formalizing the system of בתי מדרשות which was initiated in Ben Sira's day?
4 S. Safrai, 'Elementary Education: its Religious and Social Significance in the
  Talmudic Period', *Cahiers d'histoire mondiale* 11 (1968), p. 150; cf. his paper,
  'Education and the Study of Torah' in *Compendia Rerum Iudaicarum ad Novum
  Testamentum*, II, p. 948.

cise details cannot be determined, it seems certain that the two centuries around the turn of the era saw both the introduction and expansion of obligatory elementary education. Certainly, in the years which followed the destruction of the Temple, schools were counted among the essential institutions which a town was obliged to provide (see *Sanh.* 17b, which lists ten such obligatory institutions. That this list was formulated at a relatively early date is indicated by the way in which Rabbi Akiba, who died c. 135 CE, added a detail to it).[1] The syllabus of the *beth sefer* (primary education) and the *beth talmud* (secondary education) is indicated by a passage in *Pirke Aboth* (first century CE):

> At five years old one is fit for the Scriptures, at ten years for the Mishnah (5.21).

According to the later Talmudic source of *Ket.* 50a, attendance at the schools was compulsory until the age of twelve.[2] Following this, if the student showed aptitude or willingness, he could continue his education by 'sitting at the feet of the wise' in his spare time, or by dedicating some years to attending one of the established 'academies', that is, a *beth midrash*, which specialized in detailed Talmudic discussions.[3]

By the turn of the third century CE, the Jewish educational system was deemed so successful and widespread that Abaye declared that the only child who could remain ignorant of his nation's oral and written traditions was one who had been

---

1 The establishment of primary schools did not mark the end of the teaching role of parents. The simple advice offered by R. Akiba that 'when you teach your son, teach him from a corrected scroll' (*Pes.* 112a) shows that home instruction continued to constitute an important part of Jewish education (see p. 77 n. 1 above).

2 Such a ruling, however, might only reflect a rabbinic ideal or later reality. It is likely that for our period at least there would have been some rural-urban and rich-poor divides (bracketed to some extent by the notion of the *'am-ha-'aretz*—see below) which would doubtless have prevented some from making full use of the education programme.

3 It seems that a school for higher learning could also be called a בית אולפנא, for the Targumim use both בית מדרשא and בית אולפנא to designate the same institution. See also the conclusions Aberbach reaches about the בית אולפנא being a school for adult education in 'Educational Institutions and Problems during the Talmudic Age', *HUCA* 37 (1966), pp. 107-20. His discussion centres upon the later misunderstanding of 2 Kgs 22.14 (יושבת בירושלם במשנה [Hulda] והיא) in the translation of *Ps. Jon.* (והיא יתבא בירושלם בבית אולפנא).

taken into captivity among gentiles (*Shev.* 5a). It should be appreciated, however, that Abaye's comment applied only to children of that section of the people who made Torah observance central to their daily life, who saw themselves as the continuation of the 'remnant' of Ezra's day rather than the descendants (literally and metaphorically) of those who during the Babylonian exile had remained on the land observing syncretistic practices (see above, p. 72 n. 2). This latter group was termed *ha-'am ha-'aretz* and was characterized in the Talmud as 'Anyone who has sons and does not bring them up to the study of Torah... is an *'am ha-'aretz*' (*Ber.* 47b). Should the son of an *'am ha-'aretz* raise himself from illiteracy and become a scholar, his achievement was considered so unusual as to warrant particular attention (*B.M.* 85b). The sources make clear the contempt with which these people were viewed by the educated members of the society, and the gulf which existed between the two groups is indicated by the way in which the rabbis constantly exhorted the good Jew not to associate with the *'am ha-'aretz* for fear of contamination.[1] The Mishnah emphatically declared that

> He that has no knowledge of Scripture and Mishnah and right conduct has no part in the habitable world (*Kidd.* 1.10).

By the close of the period under consideration, therefore, Israel had without doubt developed into an education-centred people. Indeed, so elevated was the study of Torah held to be, that scholastic endeavour following the destruction of the Temple in 70 CE came to be equated with devotional duty or cultic service. Thus *Men.* 110a stated that:

> Whosoever occupies himself with the study of Torah [it] is as though he were offering a burnt-offering, a meal-offering, a sin-offering, and a guilt-offering.

---

1   Contamination in this respect concerned the laws of ritual purity. In the centuries following the Jews' return from exile the social concept of the *'am ha-'aretz* developed in two directions within the terms of reference of Pharisaic Judaism. It was applied either to those who failed to observe the commandments regarding tithed produce and ritual purity, and/or to those who were untutored in Torah (note that the term did not constitute a social class *per se*). Up until the destruction of the Temple, principal concern lay with the former and after CE 70 the emphasis shifted to study of Torah with the term coming to mean 'ignoramus'.

R. Meir was of the opinion that one who studied Torah, even an idolator or heathen, was equal to the High Priest (*A.Z.* 3a). Leadership no longer went with birth or, as so often in the past, even with inspiration, but with distinction in scholarship. The nation's future lay with the educated man: 'Since the day when the Temple was destroyed prophecy has been taken from the prophets and given to the wise' (*B.B.* 12a).

Before turning our attention, finally, to examining the position of women *vis-à-vis* education, a few further points need to be emphasized regarding the nature and purpose of education in general and Jewish education in particular. Regarding the latter, three characteristics distinguished Jewish education from systems pertaining in other societies of the time. First, the comprehensive system of schooling which developed in the course of the Hellenistic period functioned democratically, that is, it was designed to embrace rich and poor, aristocrat and ordinary citizen without discrimination (with the caveats noted above). Secondly, Jewish education operated on a very restricted level with regard to content. It consisted solely of instruction in the nation's own history, traditions, customs, and holy law, and did not seek to embrace other cultures or branches of knowledge.[1] It therefore served as a primary means of reinforcing national consciousness and religious and ethnic identity. Thirdly, education was an integral part of the Jewish religious system in that the command to instruct and learn did not come from any secular authority but was believed to have been given along with the other commandments to Moses at Mount Sinai by Yahweh himself. To study, therefore, was to fulfil a vital *mitzwah* and perform a devotional duty for the glorification of God. Thus, for those people in Graeco-Roman Palestine who availed themselves of the rapidly developing system of education—and, as we have seen, it was precisely that period with which we are concerned

---

1 Other subjects such as natural history (*Hull.* 62, 63; *Men.* 69a; *B.K.* 19b; *Sanh.* 108; etc.), anatomy (*Hull.* 45a), medicine, geometry, and astronomy (*Shabb.* 75a) and possibly also divination and augury (cf. *Jub.* 10.8) were studied. These, how-ever, were only to be found in the schools of higher learning and were peripheral to the main concern of the education programme. Greek language and culture were also studied in Palestine but only within the narrow aristocratic circles or by men aspring to high positions of civil leadership.

which saw the most significant progress in this respect—there was generated a feeling of social and spiritual equality regardless of birth, a heightened awareness of identity and destiny, and a sense of real involvement in the national religion. And, of course, participation in an education programme whose express purpose was the transmission of the governing rules of society meant much more than the mere acquisition of knowledge. Familiarity with the written and oral traditions gave access to certain public and religious activities and to positions of civil and spiritual leadership, in other words, knowledge was the prerequisite for meaningful participation in the functioning of society. Regarding the nature of education in general, two characteristics closely associated with this last point need to be mentioned. To use the words of Y. Cohen, a present-day scholar concerned with the anthropology of education,

> the modes of upbringing in a society—the means by which the mind is shaped—are to be regarded as mechanisms that are designed to create the kind of person who is going to be able to meet the imperatives of the culture in which he is going to participate as a mature adult.

Cohen goes on to outline the second characteristic:

> All educational systems are discriminatory to some extent, whether by sex, social class, caste, ethnic or religious membership or the like. These differentials in education are not only unequal distributions of privilege with respect to education but they are also preparations for differences in access to participation in the political apparatus. Educational differentials not only perpetuate systems of social stratification but are also affirmations of the relative political statuses of the groups making up a social system.[1]

These several points on the nature and purpose of Jewish education and education generally must be borne in mind as we examine the position of women.

As we have seen, the means by which knowledge was

---

1 Y.A. Cohen, 'The Shaping of Men's Minds: Adaptations to Imperatives of Culture', in *Anthropological Perspectives on Education*, ed. M. Wax, S. Diamond, and F. Gearing, pp. 21, 45-46.

acquired in Graeco-Roman Palestine was through home instruction, festival participation, synagogue attendance and formal schooling. We shall examine the involvement of women in each of these four areas.

In the earlier books of the Bible there seems to have been some equality between men and women both as teachers and as students of the law (as it then existed). Mother and father alike were charged with the duty of instructing their children whilst the command to learn apparently applied to both sons and daughters (see, for example, Deut. 29.10ff.; 31.12; Josh. 8.35). However, with the upheavals of the sixth century and the consequent internal reappraisal noted above, a number of changes came about which greatly affected the lives of Jewish women.

Some of these changes had already been in motion before the sixth century, but they were accelerated and refined by the experience of the exile. For a couple of centuries prior to the sixth century there had been a gradual move away from the extended family unit toward the nucleated one, a movement encouraged by the country's increasing urbanization and the development of more complex economic systems to those which had pertained in the earlier rural and semi-nomadic days of Hebrew history.[1] With the exile the process was completed. Concerned to guard against the dangers of assimilation and idolatrous practice, the exiles—and subsequently the community of returnees—consciously set about strengthening their inner bonding by reinforcing the basic social unit of the family. To this end they revised, tightened and elaborated the family-related laws which had already been developing in the earlier period, with the result that the extended family system finally collapsed. In one sense, the emergence of the nuclear family did much to enhance the position of the woman in terms of the respect accorded her. The command to 'Honour thy father and thy mother', which had been a fun-

---

1 These socio-economic developments may be seen clearly in the books of Kings, Chronicles and Deuteronomy, especially when compared with the narrative and law of earlier books of the Bible. For details of this evidence, and the evolution of the nuclear family, see Archer, 'The Virgin and the Harlot in the Writings of Formative Judaism', *History Workshop Journal* 24 (1987), pp. 3-7.

damental principle of Judaism since the earliest days, received special attention in the exilic and post-exilic writings, and an examination of the frequency with which the community in these later works was reminded of this holy duty speaks volumes for the rapidly developing social consciousness of the time. But that respect was mono-directional, and indeed served to bolster the new social order, for with the rise of the nuclear family there developed an increasing rigidity in the attitude toward and definition of function within the family group: the woman's role was placed firmly in the private sphere of activity as wife, mother and homemaker, while that of the man was located in the public sphere as worker/family supporter and active participant in social, religious, and political affairs.[1] This sharp differentiation of function according to gender is most clearly seen in the post-exilic book of Proverbs, the final chapter of which depicts the ordering of a nuclear family. There the woman is described as tending to the needs of her husband and children, labouring day and night at her distaff and spindle, and rising before dawn to prepare their food. In brief:

> She looketh well to the ways of her household
> And eateth not the bread of idleness (31.27).

In sharp contrast the activities of the man are described in the following way:

> Her husband is known in the gates
> When he sitteth among the elders of the land (31.23).

This move toward very separate and distinct male-female social functions, combined with the emergence of a more rigorously and exclusively male dominated/oriented religious system,[2] brought in its wake a change in attitude regarding the education of children. Henceforth, it was not deemed necessary to instruct girls in Torah as such knowledge would

---

1 The domestication of women might also have been encouraged by the rules of ritual cleanness which did much to constrain women's movements and were also a part of the exilic legislation. On this see further below.
2 For this development see Archer, 'The Role of Jewish Women in the Religion, Ritual and Cult of Graeco-Roman Palestine', in Cameron and Kuhrt, *Images of Women in Antiquity*, pp. 273-87.

serve no useful purpose for their future roles as homemakers. Instead, their education consisted of learning such domestic skills as cooking, spinning, sewing and the like, and in acquiring rudimentary knowledge of those laws which especially affected the lives of women (for example, the laws of purity). More than this was not required.[1] Thus in the later books of the Bible we find reference only to the obligation of boys to study the oral and written traditions.

Although at this stage it was still considered the duty of both parents to instruct their children, it is easy to see that if it were only sons who received an education, the situation would quickly arise wherein only fathers were qualified to teach. By the Hellenistic period such was the case. The intertestamental writings speak only of the teaching role of fathers and the education of sons (see, for example, 2 *Bar.* 84.9; *Jub.* 7.38-39; 8.2; 10.8; *T. Levi* 9.1, 6-9; 13.2; Sir. 30.3; *4 Macc.* 18.11f.).

Only one step remained and that was for society to view women's lack of Torah education as the result of divine will. This step was taken when the rabbis interpreted the biblical words 'and ye shall teach them [the statutes and ordinances] to your children' (Deut. 11.19) to mean that only men—now the only full participants in and officiants of the nation's religion and cult—were obliged to study and to teach Torah.[2] Thus the Mishnah declares that 'All the obligations of a father toward his son enjoined in the Law are incumbent on men but not on women' (*Kidd.* 1.7) and the Gemara comments,

> We thus learnt [here] what our rabbis taught: The father is
> bound in respect of his son to circumcise, redeem, teach him

---

1 Doubtless in the earlier (pre-exilic) biblical period, domestic tasks were also primarily the concern of women—but it would seem that they were not their exclusive activity. In the early OT narratives we see women out and about in the streets and countryside, engaged to some extent in political and cultic activites (see, for example, Exod. 15.20-21; Deut. 29.9f.; 31.12-13; Judg. 4–5; 21.21; 2 Sam. 20.16; 2 Kgs 22.14f.; Jer. 31.4; Ps. 68.12, 26-27). Now they were excluded.

2 In the course of the Graeco-Roman period the religious leaders declared women exempt from the need to fulfil many of the commandments, including those regarding education in Torah, i.e. the bedrock of the whole system. For this development, the types of commands from which women were exempt, and the way in which that exemption gradually came to be viewed in terms of actual exclusion, see further below and Archer, 'The Role of Jewish Women...', pp. 277-78.

Torah, take a wife for him and teach him a craft... 'To teach him Torah': how do we know it?—Because it is written, 'And ye shall teach them your sons'. And if his father did not teach him, he must teach himself for it is written, 'and ye shall study' (Deut. 5.1) (*Kidd.* 29a-b).[1]

With respect to the non-obligation of mothers to teach and of daughters to learn, the Gemara continues:

How do we know that she [the mother] has no duty [to teach her children]?—Because it is written, *welimaddetem* [and ye shall teach], [which also reads] *ulemadetem* [and ye shall study]: [hence] whoever is commanded to study is commanded to teach; whoever is not commanded to study is not commanded to teach (*Kidd.* 29b).[2]

Neither was a girl under any obligation to teach herself:

And how do we know that she is not bound to teach herself?—Because... the one whom others are commanded to teach is commanded to teach oneself; and the one whom others are not commanded to teach is not commanded to teach oneself (*ibid.*).

And, to cover all educational contingencies, the Gemara concludes:

How then do we know that others are not commanded to teach her?—Because it is written 'And ye shall teach them your sons' but not your daughters (*ibid.*; cf. *Naz.* 29a; *Erub.* 27a).

The low level of learning among women at precisely the time when education was becoming more and more important to the Jewish nation had far-reaching consequences in that there was fostered a belief that women were by their very nature inferior to men. This belief was encouraged and coloured by the contact Hellenistic Palestine had with the Greek world where women were regarded as inferior beings or at best necessary evils in a male-oriented society.[3] One

---

1　תנינא להא דח"ר האב ח"ב בבנו למולו ולפדיחו וללמדו תורה ולהשיאו אשה וללמדו אומנות ללמדו תורה.
מגלן דכתיב ולמדחם אותם את בניכם והיכא דלא אנמריה אבוה מיחייב איהר למיגמר נפשיה דכתיב ולמדתם.

2　איהי מגלן דלא מיחייבא דכתיב ולימדחם ולמדחם כל שמצווה ללמד מצווה ללמד וכל שאינו מצווה ללמד אינו
מצווה ללמד.

3　For the innate inferiority of women and male attitudes in general, see below, Chapter 3, §A.

aspect of this negative attitude was the belief that women were naturally light-minded and irresponsible.[1] They therefore were deemed intellectually incapable of coping with the demands of an education in Torah and unable to treat such a study with the necessary degree of seriousness. The Jewish woman was thus trapped in a vicious circle with regard to gaining access to education: at first excluded for practical reasons, her non-involvement quickly passed into the realm of exemption on religious grounds when halakhic decision released her from any obligation to study; her ignorance was then interpreted in terms of innate inferiority and she was considered capable of dealing only with domestic duties—for which no education was required. Thus, just as the words of Deuteronomy had been interpreted by the rabbis to exempt women from the obligation to study, so Scriptural authority was found to support the view that women were inherently incapable of deriving any benefit from an education and should therefore concentrate on household affairs:

> There is no wisdom in woman except with the distaff. Thus also does Scripture say: 'And all the women that were wise-hearted did spin with their hands' (Exod. 35.25) (*Yoma* 66b).

According to the Law, therefore, daughters had no place in the programme of home-instruction—instruction which continued to form the backbone of Jewish education even after the establishment of formal schooling. Whether they did in reality and despite the rabbinic rulings join their brothers in the informal tuition offered by parents is a matter which, given the legalistic character of our sources, must unfortunately remain open to speculation. But, in the light of what we have learnt of the Hellenistic Jews' attitude toward women

---

1 For this see especially the views of Philo who in his allegories frequently contrasted male (= strong rational reason) with female (= weak irrational sense perception, unable to apprehend any mental conception): *Leg. All.* 2.19f., 38, 50; 3.49-50; *Op. Mun.* 165f.; *Ebr.* 54-55; *Fug.* 127-28; *Abr.* 205-206; *Spec. Leg.* 1.198f.; *Leg.* 319-20. Philo explained the apparent exception to his rule—the female gender of personified Wisdom—in the following way: 'For that which comes after God, even though it were the chiefest of all other things, occupies a second place, and therefore was termed feminine to express its contrast with the Maker of the Universe who is masculine... For pre-eminence always pertains to the masculine, and the feminine always comes short of and is lesser than it' (*Fug.* 51-52).

and bearing in mind that the designated function of women was that of closeted homemaker, it seems reasonable to assume that daughters could never aspire to the high level of education enjoyed by sons.[1]

As we have seen from the outline above, another means by which children became acquainted with their nation's history and law was through their involvement in the various festivals which took place in the course of the year. Remembering that these festivals were consciously employed for the education of children, we must seek to ascertain whether girls enjoyed the same degree of involvement as boys, and so learn whether in this particular educational process they were on an equal footing with their male counterparts.

Although women and girls were by no means excluded from involving themselves in these occasions, it was the active participation of males which the Law demanded and encouraged, for, without them, the Jewish religion and cult, which was structured along strictly patriarchal lines, could not function. Thus, for example, according to Torah only men were under a religious obligation to observe the three major feasts of the year—those of unleavened bread, weeks, and Tabernacles (Deut. 16.16; Exod. 23.17).[2] In the halakhah women were usually coupled with slaves and minors as far as religious ceremonial was concerned, and they were also declared exempt from all (or nearly all) of the positive precepts whose observance depended upon a specific time of the day or year (see p. 87 n. 2 above).

Of course, exemption did not necessarily lead to total exclusion—witness Lk. 2.41 which reports how Mary accompanied Joseph each year when he went up to Jerusalem to fulfil the commandment 'to appear before the Lord' at the feast of Passover. But even if women did escape their domestic duties

---

1   We might also note that if girls on reaching adulthood did seek to acquire education in Torah, in terms of piety it benefited them nothing for the rabbis placed them in the category of 'one who is not commanded and fulfils', a Talmudic expression meaning the action was without value (*Sot.* 21a).

2   Interestingly, Philo saw the exemption of females from these three feasts to be the result of the Lawgiver's appreciation of the innate differences between men and women ('manly reasoning schooled in fortitude' vs. 'weak feminine passion of sense perception') and the consequent inferiority of the latter (*Leg. All.* 3.11).

(which were a primary cause of their exemption) and join with their menfolk in celebrating these feasts, their role in the main was one of passive onlooker rather than active participant. The same was true for the relative involvement of children. While a girl—like her mother—was under no legal obligation to attend these three feasts, the rabbis considered the future role of male children and decreed that a boy, although legally exempt until he reached his majority, must accompany his father to the Temple of Jerusalem and there be trained in the observance of those commandments whose fulfilment would be his responsibility on reaching adulthood (*Hag.* 1.1; *Sukk.* 2.8). And not only was the boy obliged to attend the feasts, he was also encouraged to engage actively in the ceremonial. An example of this real involvement of boys is to be found in the description of the Passover ritual. The Bible made express provision for questions on the history and meaning of the service to be asked by children of their parents (Exod. 12.25): significantly this duty fell to sons and not to daughters (Exod. 13.14-15; Deut. 6.20). That the child was here participating in a programme of education is emphasized in the Mishnah's description of the Seder ritual:

> They then mix him the second cup. And here the son asks his father (and if the son has not enough understanding his father instructs him [how to ask]), 'Why is this night different from other nights?... And according to the understanding of the son his father instructs him. He begins with the disgrace and ends with the glory; and he expounds from 'a wandering Aramean was my father...' until he finishes the whole section (Deut. 26.5f.) (*Pes.* 10.4).

Obviously, if a girl were present she too would learn from the biblical reading. The difference was, however, that for a boy it was intended to be a direct educational process, made especially meaningful by virtue of real involvement in the ritual. It must also be remembered that these feasts for a boy were but a complement to the instruction he received at home. For a girl excluded from that instruction, the holidays were one of her only means of gaining knowledge of the Scriptures. To be exempt from religious obligation and excluded from active participation in the feasts was, therefore, a real loss in educational terms.

The difference between the types of involvement of males and females is clearly seen in the Talmudic account of the public reading of the Law which took place every seventh year at the feast of Tabernacles. Despite the way in which the biblical commandment explicitly included both men and women (Deut. 31.12), the rabbis, by making an analogy between 'appear' in Exod. 23.14 and Deut. 16.16 and 'assemble' in Deut. 31.10-13, decreed women exempt from attending this sabbatical assembly (*Hag.* 3a; cf. 4a for their exemption on the grounds of it being a positive precept dependent on a specific time). Regarding the educational purpose of the feast and women's participation if they did join the gathering, the rabbis had this to say: 'If the men came to learn, the women came to hear' (*Hag.* 3a). The difference in phraseology highlights the way in which society was primarily concerned with the education of its male members. A festival which was originally intended to bring the law to the people as a whole thus developed into an occasion where emphasis was firmly placed on the instruction of men. As we have seen, the festivals were one of the few channels open to women for obtaining Scriptural knowledge. This fact was recognized by Josephus, who also perceived the way in which women's legal exemption could lead to their practical exclusion. Both considerations are reflected in the following exhortation by the historian:

> every seven years at the season of the Feast of Tabernacles let the high priest... recite the laws to the whole assembly; and let neither woman nor child be excluded from this audience ...Thus will they be kept from sin, being unable to plead ignorance (*Ant.* 4.209).

So, although the attendance of women was not to be hindered,[1] they were nevertheless accorded no real involvement in a feast whose express purpose was the people's education. If eager to avail themselves of this rare opportunity to learn, the most they could do was to sit and quietly listen to the readings and discussion as conducted by the assembled men.[2]

1   Indeed, the septennial reading took place in the most public area of the Temple—the Court of Women—so that none were barred access (*Sot.* 41b).

2   For the possible further removal of women from the ceremonial of the feast through the erection of a special gallery on this occasion, see Archer, 'The Role of Jewish Women in the Religion, Ritual and Cult... ', pp. 279-80. See *ibid.*, pp. 278-79 for their non-involvement generally in the main activity of the Temple, that is, sacrifice, which was conducted in the inner courts to which only males had access.

Of much greater importance than these infrequent public gatherings were the readings and instructional sermons which took place on a regular weekly basis in the synagogues of Graeco-Roman Palestine. As was the case with the festivals, no obligation was placed upon women to attend the synagogue. Indeed, their presence was not even required, for only men could make up the quorum of ten necessary for a service and only they could publicly read from the Torah scroll (*Meg.* 4.3, 23a). Once again the woman's role was one of passive onlooker rather than active participant. An order issued by Paul to disciples in Corinth bears witness to the attitude current among the Jews of the first century CE.[1] He writes:

> As in all the churches of the saints, the women should keep silence in the churches. For they are not permitted to speak, but should be subordinate, as even the Law says. If there is anything they desire to know, let them ask their husbands at home. For it is shameful for a woman to speak in church (1 Cor. 14.34-36; cf. 1 Tim. 2.11-14).

It is likely that domestic duties, in particular the care of young children, whose welfare was mainly the women's concern, frequently prevented regular synagogue attendance. Here it should be remembered that the law—in theory at least—did not allow mothers to carry their infants outside the privacy of the home on the sabbath (*Shabb.* 18.2). A consequence of this ruling, if it were applied, would be that all too often women were housebound on precisely the day when the main assembly and exposition of the Law took place (though here, as ever, we have no means of gauging the extent to which this law was either known or applied; the likelihood remains, however, that small children were not welcome (or allowed) in synagogue and so mothers too were not present).

A passage from Josephus' *Contra Apionem* may be used to illustrate some basic points about the educational function of

---

1 For the use of NT material as evidence for Jewish attitude and practice, see Introduction.

the synagogue. The historian wrote of the lawgiver Moses as follows:

> For ignorance he left no pretext. He appointed the Law to be the most excellent and necessary form of instruction, ordaining not that it should be heard once for all or twice or on several occasions, but every week men should desert their other occupations and assemble to listen to the Law and to obtain a thorough and accurate knowledge of it (2.175).

The passage underlines the way in which the synagogue was viewed primarily as a place of learning rather than as a house of worship. According to Josephus, the lawgiver apparently made no provision for the inclusion of women in this learning process. This significant omission may indicate more than the mere fact of women's legal exemption. It may also reflect a reality of Josephus' own day regarding synagogue attendance. No mention was made simply because women did not impinge upon the consciousness of their male counterparts in this respect, their attendance at the synagogue being both infrequent and irregular, while their participation in the main activity of the meeting was negligible.[1] If such were the case for adult Jewish women, it was probably even more so for young girls. As with the feasts, however, boys would probably have accompanied their fathers to the sabbath meetings in order to start their training and preparation for full membership of the male religious community.

The final area which we have to look at is that of formal schooling and women's position in relation to the *beth sefer*, *beth talmud* and *beth midrash*. An examination of the rabbinic

---

1　With regard to women's involvement if they did attend, we might note that given the taboos which developed in the course of our period regarding free mingling of the sexes (to be examined in the next section), it is likely that women sat apart from men in the synagogue and so in some way were physically distanced from the meetings' activities. Unfortunately, from the evidence so far available, it is not possible to say exactly what form this probable segregation took. Many modern scholars have argued for the existence of special women's galleries or lattice-work screens, but their conclusions rest heavily upon meagre evidence imaginatively manipulated in the light of present day (post-mediaeval) orthodox Jewish practice. For the Graeco-Roman period there is no clear evidence as to the means of segregation, though the likelihood that there was a separation remains. See Archer, 'The Role of Jewish Women in the Religion, Ritual and Cult . . . ', pp. 281-82.

sources does not reveal a single categorical statement, negative or positive, on the question of school attendance by females. Nevertheless, in the light of what we have already learnt of society's attitude toward the education of its womenfolk, and remembering that the designated role of the woman was that of wife and homemaker, it seems reasonable to assume that females had no place in the system of formal schooling which blossomed during the Hellenistic period. This assumption is substantiated by various Talmudic sayings. For example, Rabbi Simeon b. Eleazar was of the opinion that a boy matured more quickly than a girl in consequence of the intellectual stimulation he received at the house of his teacher (*Nidd.* 45b). The obvious inference from his comment is that the girl remained at home, presumably giving all her energy to domestic tasks. Another example is to be found in a Talmudic passage concerned with the question of Gentiles preparing food for Jews. Here the rabbis ruled that arrangements could be made by a man if he intended to go to the house of study, and by a woman if she needed to go to the bathhouse (*A.Z.* 38a-b). No mention was made of the woman attending the house of study. Similarly, a man was allowed even on the sabbath to negotiate for a teacher for his son's elementary education: the only talk about his daughter on the same sabbath centred upon arrangements for her betrothal (*Shabb.* 150a).

Indeed, any opportunity a girl may have had to acquire a formal education was further hampered by the custom of early marriage (see Chapter 2). The Jewish woman was usually married by the time she was twelve years old. Should she reach that age without a suitable partner having been found, her father was advised to provide a husband by manumitting one of his slaves (*Pes.* 118a). The woman was thus certainly unable to attend the *beth midrash* whose programme of higher learning began just as she was entering upon the responsibilities of wifehood. And, with regard to elementary education, society could dismiss the question of female participation in the *beth sefer* and *beth talmud* as the instruction provided by those schools could not avail a person who was shortly to enter into marriage. Men, on the other hand, were encouraged to study first and marry later so that their studies would not suffer on account of family responsibilities, and the average age recommended for them for marriage by the rabbis was twenty (*Kidd.* 29b-30a).

Another factor which contributed to women's exclusion from formal education was the restriction which society placed upon the free mingling of the sexes. As the concept of public and private domain and the question of the seclusion of women will be treated in the next section (see also Chapter 3, §B), we need not here enter into a detailed discussion of the subject as a whole. For the purpose of the present discussion we need only be aware of two facts: that there were very definite restrictions placed upon the movement of the woman at all stages of her life, and that these restrictions affected her access, both as a girl and as an adult, to the schooling system. With regard to her attendance at a *beth midrash*, it should be recalled that advanced instruction tended to be in the open air, in vineyards, market places, on street corners, and the like. For a woman to frequent such public places and thereby attend the scholarly gatherings was unthinkable in a society which had explicit, if often unwritten, rules about the proper behaviour of its womenfolk. Her designated place lay within the privacy of the home where she could lead the life of quiet modesty expected of a respectable woman.[1] Should the meetings take place in the house of the master rather than in the open air, the woman was then barred access on account of society's negative attitude toward the free mingling of the sexes. The same problem applied to girls' attendance at the *beth sefer* and *beth talmud*, whose classes were usually held in the local synagogue or an adjoining building. When speaking of these elementary schools the Talmud refers only to the participation of boys and nowhere alludes to the existence of female pupils. It contains no discussion on segregation of the sexes in the schools because the problem of mixed classes had not arisen: girls simply were not present. And, of course, as instruction in the oral and written traditions was at this stage considered a male prerogative, the idea of setting up separate

---

1   With regard to those women who are recorded as joining with the crowds listening to Jesus' teaching, it should be remembered that the Gospel accounts frequently cast doubt upon their respectability. See next section and Chapter 3 §B.

educational establishments for girls was not even entertained.

Thus, despite the absence of any explicit rabbinic statement on the subject, it seems certain that women were in fact excluded from the system of formal education. Only men enjoyed the privilege of sitting at the feet of a great master, of joining with

> the disciples of the wise, who sit in manifold assemblies and occupy themselves with the Torah, some pronouncing unclean and others pronouncing clean, some prohibiting and others permitting, some disqualifying and others declaring fit (*Hag.* 3b).

Finally a word needs to be said about the woman Beruriah, daughter of R. Hananiah and wife of R. Meir. From the various sayings and deeds attributed in the Talmud to Beruriah, many modern scholars have assumed that she achieved a high level of learning, and from this assumption have inferred that many women enjoyed the same advanced education. It is highly unlikely, however, that either the assumption or the inference are correct, at least as far as Palestine in the second century CE was concerned (the time of the historic Beruriah). First, let us consider those passages which deal specifically with her educational achievements, for an examination of the type of learning displayed will indicate the level of her education.

In *Erub.* 53b Beruriah explicitly cites a rabbinic dictum ('Engage not in much talk with women'; cf. *Aboth* 1.5; *Ned.* 20a). Knowledge of specific maxims was normally only acquired by attendance at one of the rabbinic schools, and hence it has been assumed that Beruriah enjoyed that level of education. However, if we consider the subject matter of this particular dictum (incidentally, the only one Beruriah evinces knowledge of), we see that it ceases to provide any real proof that Beruriah was unusually learned or possessed a formal education. It is concerned with the common code of conduct between men and women in rabbinic society, and as such would be well known outside of academic circles.[1]

In t. *Kel. B.M.* 1.6 Beruriah exhibits knowledge of a rule

---

1 It is moreover a strange dictum to be found in the mouth of a woman, and says much for the likelihood of male authorship, on which more below.

about the purification of kitchen ovens. At first glance this passage could be seen as portraying a woman with extensive
knowledge of the finer details of rabbinic law. In fact it need
not indicate any formal education at all. Girls, especially those
of a rabbinic household as Beruriah was, would be trained by
their mothers in those purity laws relating to the kitchen. As
we have seen, the woman's life revolved around the home. It is
to be expected, therefore, that she would be more than familiar
with those rules which pertained to her own domestic sphere
of activity.[1]

The knowledge displayed by Beruriah in the remaining
passages cannot, however, be so readily dismissed. *Ber.* 10a
and *Erub.* 53b-54a both refer to her acquaintance with rabbinic exegesis on specific scriptural verses, whilst *Pes.* 62b
speaks of her learning the *Book of Genealogies* (a commentary on Chronicles). Such knowledge could only be gained
through formal instruction, and instruction at an advanced
level. It would seem, then, that these sources offer definite evidence of the possibility of *a* woman (and here it should be
remembered that at best Beruriah can only be regarded as an
exception to the rule, for the sources make no reference to
other 'learned' women) attaining a high level of education.
However, in the light of what we have already learnt of the
attitude toward women and education, we may with some
justification pause to question the validity of this conclusion, at
least with regard to Graeco-Roman Palestine.

As the evidence of these passages will relate to the time and
place in which they originated, we must determine their
provenance. Significantly, all four passages are from the
Babylonian Amoraic stratum of Talmudic literature and are
unparalleled in other rabbinic literature. For example, in the
Palestinian Talmud's version of the anecdote about the *Book
of Genealogies*, no mention is made of Beruriah (y. *Pes.* 5.3,
32a-b). Thus, all the anecdotes which portray Beruriah as
possessing an advanced education are of Babylonian Amoraic
origin. This fact led D. Goodblatt to conclude that 'the

---

1 Rabbinic literature refers to several women who possessed detailed knowledge of
   this type. See t. *Kel. B.K.* 4.17; y. *Shabb.* 4, 6d; y. *Pes.* 4.4, 62c.

historical situation they reflect is not of second century Palestine, that is the time and place of the historical Beruriah, but Sassanian Babylonia', probably in the fifth centry CE.[1] In other words, what we have preserved in these four passages is a Babylonian reworking of earlier traditions and the attachment of those traditions to the name Beruriah[2]— possibly from some perceived need, for reasons now lost to us, to bolster the status of the wife of a famous rabbi. They do not provide evidence for the historic Beruriah, and neither do they witness to the educational opportunities for women in the Tannaitic period. They *may* say something about extra-Palestinian society of a later period, but even here it should be remembered that 'Beruriah' is an isolated instance of a 'learned woman'.

At the close of this survey on education, therefore, we may return with fuller comprehension to the words of Y. Cohen:

> the modes of upbringing in a society are... designed to create the kind of person who is going to be able to meet the imperatives of the culture in which he [sic] is going to participate as a mature adult.

For boys, who would grow to enjoy full participation and even leadership, secular and religious, in a society ordered along strictly patriarchal lines, instruction in the nation's oral and written traditions was provided and, at least at an elementary level, made compulsory. For girls, however, who were destined to lead a life of secluded modesty, tending to the needs of their husbands and children, such knowledge was not deemed necessary and they were consequently excluded from the education programme. Their 'education' lay in the home and was the responsibility of mothers.

Of course, it is not to be assumed that women lived lives in total ignorance of the Law. That would have been impossible in a society whose every effort was aimed at making the Torah a living force throughout the land. They would, one way or another, have acquired a rudimentary knowledge of the Scriptures, and were, moreover, expected to be familiar

---

1 D. Goodblatt, 'The Beruriah Traditions', in W.S. Green (ed.), *Persons and Institutions in Early Rabbinic Judaism* (Brown Judaic Studies, 3), p. 228.

2 See *ibid.* for details of this reworking and the reasons for it.

with those laws which especially affected the lives of women
(presumably to be learnt from their mothers). The level and
type of knowledge expected of the Hellenistic Jewess is indicated in the following Mishnaic passage:

> These are they that are put away without their *kethubah*: a
> wife that transgresses the Law of Moses and Jewish custom.
> What [conduct is such that transgresses] the Law of Moses?
> If she gives her husband untithed food, or has connection
> with him in her uncleanness, or does not set apart Dough-
> offering, or utters a vow and does not fulfil it. And what
> [conduct is such that transgresses] Jewish custom? If she
> goes out with her hair unbound, or spins in the street, or
> speaks with any man (*Ket.* 7.6).

Similarly, the rabbis declared that women who failed to
observe the laws of the menstruant, the Dough-offering, and
the lighting of the Sabbath lamp would be punished by dying in
childbirth (*Shabb.* 2.6). One scholar, Ben Azzai, urged fathers
to instruct their daughters in the details of the trial by Bitter
Waters (Num. 5.12-31, used for cases of suspected adultery;
Sot. 3.4),[1] while Josephus declared that 'Even our womenfolk
and dependants would tell you that piety must be the motive of
all our occupations in life' (*Con. Ap.* 2.181). Nevertheless,
there is some truth in the following rather sweeping remark
made by a twentieth-century scholar:

> [the woman's] exclusion from the school carried with it also
> the exclusion from every form of public activity and her
> reduction to the position of a subservient and inarticulate
> partner in Jewish life. She was coupled with the illiterate as
> a matter of course.[2]

Here we should remember that *all* males had access to a formal education at a time when it was becoming more and
more highly valued.

Finally, with regard to women being taught by their hus-

---

1   It was in response to Ben Azzai's recommendation to teach the laws of the sus-
    pected adulteress that the now famous words of R. Eliezer were spoken, 'If any
    man gives his daughter knowledge of the law it is as though he taught her
    lechery', at which R. Joshua continued, 'A woman has more pleasure in one kab
    with lechery than in nine kabs with modesty' (*Sot.* 3.4).
2   N. Morris, *The Jewish School*, p. 31.

bands—the course of action recommended by St Paul to those who wished to learn (1 Cor. 14.34-36; above, p. 93)—there were two problems. First, the women had to have a husband who was willing to teach her, and secondly, she would in any case often have little time to spare from her domestic duties to sit and learn. With respect to this second point, a verse in the New Testament is revealing. Lk. 10.39-40 tells how the woman Martha wished to sit at Jesus' feet and listen to his teaching. She was, however, unable to do this as she was 'distracted with much serving'. Moreover, as should be remembered throughout this survey, women were exempt from the command to study. As we have seen, if a girl or a woman did try to acquire a greater knowledge of Torah than that required of her, in religious terms her efforts were deemed totally valueless for she was placed in the category of 'one who is not commanded and fulfils' (*Sot.* 21a), a rabbinic expression meaning that the action was null and void, perhaps even of negative consequence. Women earned their merit by being supportive of men's spirituality and education, or, to use the words of the Talmud:

> by making their children go to the synagogue to learn Scrip-
> ture and their husbands to the *beth midrash* to learn Mish-
> nah, and by waiting for their husbands till they return from
> the *beth midrash* (*Ber.* 17a).

This was the lesson that was to be learnt by daughters.

E. *Seclusion of the Young Girl*

In this final section of our survey of the life of the Jewish woman while a minor we shall examine a feature of life which had its origin in the upheavals of the sixth century, developed into established practice during the Hellenistic period, and had a profound effect upon women's involvement in any activity beyond the domestic sphere. That feature was the enforced seclusion of women within the home.

In the course of the period under consideration, a complex of restrictive rules was brought to bear upon the freedom of movement and general conduct of women at all periods of their lives. However, in our examination of these various rules we must be careful not to treat women as one uniform body of persons for whom all the laws had equal force all the time. In line with our sources care must be taken to distinguish between the several legal categories which women occupied in the course of their lives, for the attitude of society and its legislators varied according to the woman's age and marital status. Modern scholars have, unfortunately, tended to confuse the issue by failing to observe these distinctions in their discussions on the subject. All too often the various codes of social conduct are presented as if they applied to all women regardless of their age and marital status. On other occasions scholars have simply been inexact in their use of the sources. Thus, for example, one present-day writer states that the young unmarried woman in Palestine was not imprisoned in her house or courtyard. Not only was she free to wander through the market places, but she might even find employment in shops and other concerns. The mishnah the author cites to prove this latter point is *Ket.* 9.4 which in fact refers not to a young girl but to a married woman.[1]

A more careful examination of the sources clearly shows that the ancient writers and legislators differentiated between the various categories of women when laying down the rules of social conduct. For example, far greater freedom of movement was accorded to married women than those yet to enter the bridal chamber. In this section we shall examine only the lifestyle of the non-betrothed virgin, and shall reserve discussion on other categories of women (betrothed, married, divorced and widowed) for a later chapter. The fact that girls seldom remained unmarried (or unbetrothed) much beyond the onset of puberty[2] means that we shall also be dealing with the lifestyle of a minor, that is, of a daughter not yet twelve and a half years old and consequently still under the control of her father. This discussion will conclude our survey of the life of the girl while a minor.

A controlling factor in the formulation of any code of sex

---

1 S. Safrai in *Compendia Rerum Iudaicarum ad Novum Testamentum*, II, p. 752 n. 3.

2 For women of pre-menstrual age being married, see *Nidd.* 1.4; 10.1; *Yeb.* 62a. See below, Chapter 2 §B.

morality and conduct is the position of woman in society. An appreciation of this fact is particularly important when one is dealing with regulations which are the product of a strictly patriarchal society. If such a society feels the need to place limits on the free mingling of the sexes, it is the woman who suffers restrictions on her freedom of movement and not the man whose role, as we have seen, was situated firmly in the public arena. With regard to the degree of restriction, Epstein writes:

> The more dependent she is on her father or husband or guardian, the greater the limits set on her freedom of movement and the more likely she is to be excluded from the company of men; conversely, the more independence she gains the greater is her freedom to mingle with men in innocent social contact.[1]

When we recall the absolute power a father possessed over the life and destiny of a daughter, we may with justification expect to find that very severe restrictions were imposed upon the movement of young girls. In the course of this discussion we shall see that such was indeed the case.

Before turning our attention to an examination of the rules and regulations which governed the young girl's life, however, we must first look at the reasons which lay behind society's decision to seclude its virgins. For this we must review in general the standard of sexual morality which pertained in Graeco-Roman Palestine, and in particular the attitude society had toward pre-marital chastity.

As has already been noted in the preceding section, the traumatic events of the sixth and fifth centuries BCE marked a watershed in the history of Judaism. Interpreted in the light of earlier doom prophecies, the exile to Babylon was viewed as the result of God's righteous wrath at his people's waywardness. To regain his favour, it was imperative that Israel make a return to the Law and rid itself of all perceived impurity. To this end all records of the past were zealously preserved, and older legal traditions extensively reworked. Particular attention was paid to those laws concerned with ritual purity, fam-

1   L. Epstein, *Sex Laws and Customs in Judaism*, p. 68.

ily life, and sexual relations. In sum, the effect of the exile was
to quicken and then firmly entrench the societal and particularly familial restructuring which had been slowly developing
in the preceding centuries (*viz.* attitude and law regarding
marriage, divorce, monogamy, the nuclear family, incest,
property, and the sexual division of labour), and to place the
whole on a new and elevated platform of moral behaviour
worthy of God's chosen.[1]

Of particular significance and far-reaching consequence to
the lives of women was the exilic legislators' obsession with
ritual cleanness. The blood taboo which lay behind so many of
the Hebrews' ideas about purity led to women being declared
unclean for a large part of their lives in consequence of the
blood of child birth and of the menstrual cycle (see above,
pp. 36f.).[2] The Priestly Code dealt in detail with the pollution
which resulted from contact with the woman during these
periods and prescribed vital purification rituals to avert danger. Further precautions were taken by severely restricting
the movement of women during their times of uncleanness.

A natural development from this legislation was for women
to be regarded as a constant stumbling block to man's improvement. How could he hope to maintain the required standard of personal purity when the world abounded in impurity
in the female form? One fourth-century writer despaired of
ever finding a solution to the problem:

> Man that is born of woman is of few days and full of trou-
> ble...
> Who can bring a clean thing out of an unclean?
> What is man that he should be clean?
> And he that is born of woman that he should be righteous?
> (Job 14.1, 3; 15.4).

An easy step from this type of attitude was to regard women
as the source of all evil in the world. There thus developed in

---

1 Note the point made in p. 26 n. 1 above that 'morality' is in essence the product of
   pragmatic concerns to do with the ordering and preservation of society, and not
   some abstract entity.
2 See Stephen F. Bigger, 'The Family Laws of Leviticus 18 in their Setting', *JBL* 98
   (1979), pp. 187-203; also see H.M. Kamsler, 'Hebrew Menstrual Taboos', in the
   Journal of American Folk Law 51 (1940), pp. 76-82.

the exile and beyond, the concept of the Evil Woman, of Wickedness personified in the female form.[1] The imagery employed in the post-exilic writings indicates the way in which this new belief quickly made inroads into the popular imagination, and preachers of the period repeatedly warned against the dangers of womankind, urging men not to associate too closely with women or fall foul of female snares.[2] By the Hellenistic period belief in the essential evil of woman was a fundamental feature of Jewish religious thought and became a theme to be constantly elaborated upon by the writers of that time. Thus Ben Sira, after cataloguing the various characteristics of the wicked woman, declared:

> From a woman did sin originate
> And because of her we all must die (25.24).

But it was not only the laws of ritual purity which generated a belief in the evil of women. The increasingly overt patriarchal tenor of Jewish society gave rise to a culturally constructed fear of women which manifested itself in the belief that women's assumed 'natural' propensity for evil had its outlet in luring men into liaisons which directly contravened the day's standards of sexual morality (and therefore threatened the gender-based power dynamic of society and its new restructuring):

> Since they have no power or strength over man, they use wiles by outward attraction, that they may draw him into themselves. And when they cannot bewitch by outward attractions, him they overcome by craft. For... women are overcome by the spirit of fornication more than men, and in their heart they plot against men; and by means of their adornment they deceive first the minds, and by the glance of the eye instil the poison and then through the accomplished act they take them captive (*T. Reub.* 5.1-3).

As men were deemed helpless in the face of such sexual

---

1 See, for example, Zech. 5.8 where an angel reveals 'a woman sitting in the midst of the measure' and declares to the prophet that 'this is Wickedness'. For details of this development see Archer, 'The Virgin and the Harlot in the Writings of Formative Judaism', *History Workshop Journal* 24 (1987), pp. 1-16.
2 This development and the supposed dangers of womankind will be treated more fully below and in Chapter 3 §D.

allurement and women were considered incapable of controlling their lust for pleasure, any innocent social contact between the sexes came to be regarded with suspicion. To ensure a proper level of 'moral' behaviour, therefore, the legislators placed great restrictions upon the free mingling of men and women, paying particular attention to the movements of the latter. Thus, the code of behaviour which had been conceived in response to the exile developed in the course of the Second Commonwealth into an all-embracing morbidity where sex relations were concerned. This morbidity and the rigorous code of conduct which resulted from it dominated Jewish life in Graeco-Roman Palestine, reflecting and reinforcing the new social order and structure.

The same desire for purity and moral behaviour (= proper order) manifested itself in the post-exilic community's changed attitude towards pre-marital chastity. Virginity came to be regarded as a virtue in its own right, while loss of virginity outside of marriage was viewed as a pollution of the individual and of the community at large.[1] A glance at the books of the Bible in their chronological context reveals much of society's new and developing concerns regarding virgins and virginity. In the earliest writings, that is, in those which preceded the Deuteronomic legislation of the immediate pre-exilic period and the prophetic writings deriving from roughly the same time, the word בתולה appears only twice (Gen. 24.16; Exod. 22.16),[2] and 'virginity' (בתולים) is never mentioned. The only legislation about loss of virginity prior to marriage deals with the rape of an unbetrothed girl (Exod. 22.15-16) and the law is presented briefly and pragmatically. Its explicit terms of reference are the infringement of a father's property rights and breach of his authority (see above, pp. 51ff.).

With the Deuteronomic reform and the societal and reli-

---

1 For an argument that the new concern for virginity—which was paralleled by a tightening of the laws regarding adultery, incest, etc.—reflected the growth of the nuclear family and concern for the appropriate transmission of property, see Archer, *op. cit.*

2 Moreover, in one of the passages *bethulah* is further qualified by the expression 'and neither had any man known her', and may therefore have been simply a female counterpart to *na'ar* ('youth'), i.e. indicative of age rather than of a *virgo intacta* and therefore without moral overtones.

gious developments noted above (pp. 85-86), slightly greater
attention was paid to the purity of daughters, with some six-
teen verses being dedicated to the penalties incurred through
enjoyment of illicit sexual intercourse with a virgin (Deut.
22.13ff.). However, while the language of these laws is somewhat more overtly 'moralistic' than that of the early legislation,[1] the concern of the legislators is still presented in a fairly
pragmatic way—at least when compared to the later literature. The penalty prescribed for the violation of a betrothed
virgin was death,[2] for the man had used his neighbour's wife
(Deut. 22.23f.), while the earlier legislation about the rape of
an unbetrothed girl was restated.[3] The same may be said
regarding a new piece of legislation which embodied the interests of both father and husband. According to Deut. 22.13f. a
man was entitled to lodge a virginity suit with the elders of a
city if he discovered his bride to have been a non-virgin at
marriage, despite the fact that he had paid her father the
higher price demanded for virgins. Should his accusation be
proven true, or, to use a later Mishnaic phrase which underlines the commercial aspect of virginity, if his bargain was
deemed to have been 'a bargain made in error' (*Ket.* 1.6), the
woman was condemned to death. Significantly, the charge
could only be brought if the girl were a *na'arah* who had had
sexual relations with another man while in her father's house

1 Thus, for example, Deut. 22.29 refers to the violated girl as one who has been
'humbled'. No mention of this aspect is to be found in Exod. 22.15-16. Similarly, a
man who falsely accused his bride with having been a non-virgin at marriage
was punished for having brought an evil name upon a virgin of Israel (Deut.
22.19).
2 That this law was not included in the pre-Deuteronomic legal codes is probably
due to the fact that in the earlier period there was no period of betrothal.
3 See above, pp. 51ff. for the fact that there was no development in thought between
the two rulings on the rape of an unbetrothed virgin. Note that there was no
penalty for the rape of a girl who had attained her majority and had passed out of
the control of her father.

(vv. 20-21).[1]

In startling contrast to the pre-exilic material, the later books of the Bible abound with references to בתולה (virgin) and בתולים (virginity).[2] And not only do the terms appear with greater frequency, they also appear with strong accompanying language and in the context of moral and righteous behaviour. The word בתולה is employed figuratively to depict the purity and innocence of Israel, while its opposite is used to represent the sins of the nation. (So, when writers wished to depict Israel behaving itself and obeying the law, they characterized it as the virgin daughter of Zion betrothed to God and deserving of blessing and reward; when misbehaving itself, they employed the image of a backsliding daughter, unfaithful to God and engaged in all sorts of sexual antics for which dire punishment would be meted out.) The movement toward such imagery started with the earlier prophets and their attempts to return the people to the One God, but it reached its peak in the exile with Ezekiel's description of the idolatry of Jerusalem and Samaria which he personified as two wicked women (23.5ff.). Writers of the later biblical books and of the so-called intertestamental literature then continued with the theme, paying particular attention to those dimensions of the image as purity *vs* impurity, passivity *vs* activity, obedience *vs* disobedience, private *vs* public, and so on.

Significantly, this imagery emerged at the same time as Jewish society was beginning to make moves toward a changed religious and social ordering (i.e. seventh century onwards, and especially post-587 BCE), and it is evident from the choice of image that a notion of woman was central to that restructuring. Initially the virgin image reflected the community's concern for its purity and physical integrity. It then

---

1   The full significance of the phrase 'to play the harlot in her father's house' and of the fact that the death penalty was not executed in the normal place outside the city gates but rather 'at the door of her father's house' will be considered below. Note the later rabbinic ruling that no virginity suit could be lodged in Judaea in consequence of the way in which couples there were permitted to meet without witnesses during their period of betrothal (*Ket.* 1.5; *Yeb.* 4.10). This ruling reflects the way in which marriage and betrothal customs varied from region to region and will be treated in Chapter 2 §§B and D.

2   בתולה appears in some thirty-four passages, בתולים in three.

served to promote non-ambiguous male-female social roles (the emphasis being upon the proper behaviour of women) within the new ordering of the nucleated family (issues central to its emergence being the desire for purity of heritage, non-ambivalent paternity, and appropriate transmission of property).[1] As with the earlier biblical passages on virginity, therefore, these later verses also had as their foundation issues of practicality and patriarchal authority. These issues were, however, compounded by the religious thinking of the time and so were placed on a new and overtly 'moralistic' platform. The stated concern of the passages is to create a community conscious of its purity and worthy of being God's chosen people. The impact of the writings, of the legislation about ritual purity, and of the social restructuring was enormous, and together they moulded a changed attitude toward pre-marital chastity. Virgins came to be cherished as 'tender and delicate' beings (Isa. 47.1) whose purity had to be preserved at all costs. Any girl who did 'play the harlot' was condemned outright by society for having sinned against the moral order of the day, defiled her personal purity, blighted the good name of her family, and polluted the community as a whole. The new respect which was accorded virginity is perhaps most clearly seen in an exilic ruling regarding the categories of women forbidden to the nation's high priests. Special attention was obviously given to maintaining a particularly high degree of ritual purity among this body of men for they alone of the people were anointed of God, and upon their shoulders rested the holy task of directing and leading the nation's cult and religious affairs. Thus the exilic legislators responsible for the so-called 'Holiness Code' ruled:

> And he shall take a wife in her virginity. A widow or one divorced, or a profaned woman, or a harlot, these he shall not take; but a virgin of his own people shall he take to wife (Lev. 21.13-14).[2]

---

1 For details of this argument, see Archer, *op. cit.*

2 In his fervour for ritual purity, Ezekiel placed the obligation to marry virgins upon all priests (44.22). The purity of priests' daughters was also hedged about with special laws. Any harlotry on their part was punishable by burning rather than the normal method of stoning. Thus Lev. 22.9, 'And the daughter of any priest if she profane herself by playing the harlot, she profaneth her father: she shall be burnt with fire'. Cf. *Ant.* 4.248.

By the start of the Hellenistic period, belief in the need to
maintain absolute purity among the daughters of Israel had
reached such a height that even to gaze upon a virgin was
considered an offence to public morality. The fourth-century
author of the book of Job thus included in the catalogue of the
hero's righteous behaviour the following report:

> I made a covenant with mine eyes;
> How then should I look upon a maid [בתולה]?
> For what would be the portion from God above,
> And the heritage of the Almighty from on high? (31.1-2)

Similarly, at the close of the period under consideration, the
Talmud tells the story of a man who was wasting away on
account of the passion he entertained for a certain young girl.
Doctors, fearing for his life, recommended that he be allowed
to have his way with the girl or at least be permitted to gaze
upon her. The rabbis, however, ruled that on no account was
the purity of a virgin to be sullied even by a glance, and so
allowed the man to die (*Sanh.* 75a; cf. *A.Z.* 20a). It is manifest
from this decision that society's attitude toward virgins and
virginity had indeed come a long way from the earlier years of
Hebrew history when virgins could be used to appease the
frenzy of the mob or to comfort ageing kings (see, e.g. Gen.
19.8; Judg. 19.24; 1 Kgs 1.1f.). Philo boasts of the high standard
of sexual morality which prevailed among the young people of
his day, declaring that Jewish girls entered their nuptials in
complete innocence and purity. He also boasts that men
entered the bridal chambers as innocent as their brides:

> We children of the Hebrews follow laws and customs which
> are especially our own. Other nations are permitted after the
> fourteenth year to deal without interference with harlots and
> strumpets and all those who make a traffic of their bodies,
> but with us a courtesan is not even permitted to live and
> death is the penalty appointed for women who ply this trade.
> Before the lawful union we know no mating with other
> women, but come as virgin men to virgin maidens (*Jos.* 42-
> 43).[1]

---

1 Philo's inclusion here of virgin men with virgin women is exceptional. Other
writers focus exclusively on the purity of women. The tremendous importance
which was attached to the bride being a virgin at marriage is highlighted by the
following Talmudic account: 'There was a certain family in Jerusalem that had
large steps whereby their virginity was destroyed. So they made them leg sus-
penders and placed a chain between them that their virginity was not destroyed'
(*Shabb.* 63b).

In sharp contrast to the nuptials of widows, divorcees, and defiled women, therefore, the marriage of a virgin was an occasion of great rejoicing and special ceremonial.[1] She was carried from her father's house in a special virgin's litter to the accompaniment of bride song. Dried corn was distributed to children, games were played, and wine flowed for the seven festive days of the celebration. Society also marked its approval of the virgin-bride by awarding her a *kethubah* which was twice the value of that granted other women (*Ket.* 1.2).

By the Graeco-Roman period, therefore, the purity of women had without doubt been placed centre stage, with virginity being viewed in terms of a morality overtly far removed from the philosophy of earlier years.

How was this ideal to be made a living reality? Society's belief in the essential evil of womankind precluded the girl from being responsible for her own innocence, for it was believed that given the slightest opportunity she would happily engage in illicit sexual relations. Such was the considered opinion of Ben Sira who bitterly warned fathers not to be surprised if their daughters sinned, for

> As a thirsty traveller that openeth his mouth
> And drinketh of any water that is near,
> So she sitteth down at every post
> And openeth her quiver to every arrow (26.11-12).

Preservation of her purity was therefore seen as the responsibility of the father.[2]

As we have already seen, a father was directly concerned with the virginity of his daughter. If she was defiled (whether willingly or forcibly) and the fact were known, he might have great difficulty securing a husband for her, and would also lose the benefit of receiving the higher bride-price demanded for

---

1   For details of the marriage ceremony, see below, Chapter 2 §D.
2   Cf. Ps. Phocylides, 'The beauty of children is hard for their parents to guard' (1. 217).

virgins.[1] If, on the other hand, a daughter's defilement went
undetected and a marriage was negotiated on the basis of her
being a virgin bride, he could be involved in the public embar-
rassment of a virginity suit. With the evolution of ideas, loss of
virginity also brought in its wake the pollution of his good
name, for not only did unchaste behaviour bring an evil name
to the girl, it also, and more importantly, sullied her father's
reputation and the purity of his house. It was a direct breach
of paternal authority and an upset to the general order of the
day. Thus, of the seriousness of the virginity suit, Philo wrote:

> the danger affects not only the daughters whose bodily
> chastity is impugned but also their guardians, against
> whom the charge is brought not only that they failed to
> watch over them at the most critical period of adolescence,
> but that the brides they had given as virgins had been
> dishonoured by other men, and thereby the bridegrooms
> were cheated and deceived (*Spec. Leg.* 3.81).

So it was that Ben Sira listed as one of the principal worries for
a father in the rearing of his daughter as:

> In her virginity lest she be defiled...
> In her father's house lest she become pregnant (42.10a,
> 10b).[2]

To guard against these dangers Ben Sira had the following
repeated advice to give:

> Hast thou daughters, keep their bodies[3]
> And show them not a pleasant countenance...
> Upon a headstrong daughter keep strict watch,
> Lest finding liberty she use it for herself...
> Over thy daughter keep a strict watch (7.24; 26.10; 42.11).

---

1 That is, unless the rapist/seducer were known to the family, in which case the
father had the right to oblige him to marry the girl and to pay the *mohar* (Exod.
22.15-16; Deut. 22.29; above, pp. 51ff. In this instance, though, the father lost out on
any hoped for alliances through marriage with other families (see next Chapter).
Should he chose not to marry her to her offender, although he still received the
mohar by way of a fine, he would still be in the position of having to find a husband
for his now non-virginal daughter.
2 See above, p. 26 nn. 2, 3.
3 Gk. πρόσεχε (pay attention to, be mindful of) τῷ σώματι αὐτῶν; Massada Scroll:
שארם (preserve, guard) נצור.

If a strict watch was not maintained, then fathers could be assured that the girl's natural propensity for sin would rear its head:

> Lest she make thee a name of evil odour—
> A byword in the city and accursed of the people—
> And shame thee in the assembly of the gate (42.11).

Thus, the girl who could not declare like Raguel's daughter Sarah,

> I am pure from all uncleanness with man... I never polluted my name nor the name of my father (Tob. 3.14).

was in truth despised by both father and husband[1] as 'the disgraceful daughter [who] poureth forth disgrace' (Sir. 42.14).

But how exactly was the father to guard against the loss of his daughter's virginity? In the earlier agricultural days of small, close-knit village communities, this was not much of a problem. And in any case there had not as yet developed that sexual morbidity so characteristic of the Second Temple period. Thus young women in the Old Testament seem to have moved about freely and still were able to declare that they 'had not known man'.[2] The new social ordering and moral consciousness of the Second Commonwealth rendered the preservation of the girl's virginity a matter of utmost importance, but the period's increased urbanization, with its possibilities for increased sexual laxity, presented grave problems as to how exactly the required degree of purity was to be attained.

The rapidly developing view of women as domestic beings with no part to play in the public life of the state (above, pp. 85-86) provided the purists with the solution to their problem: women would simply be kept in seclusion within the home ordering their household affairs. With the source of all temp-

---

1 Sir. 22.4-5: 'She that bringeth shame is a grief to him that begat her. She that is bold bringeth shame on father and husband, and she is despised of both.' This quotation, along with many other passages in the intertestamental literature, clearly demonstrates the way in which society's primary concern was not with the 'evil name' of the girl *per se* (Deuteronomy), but with the impact upon the male authority figures.

2 See, for example, the biblical accounts of the meetings at the well of Isaac and Rebekah, 'a damsel (who) was very fair to look upon, a virgin, neither had any man known her', and of Jacob and Rachel (Gen. 24.16; 29.9f.).

tation removed from view, the danger of men and women indulging in illicit affairs would be considerably diminished. With regard to the different social functions of the sexes and the seclusion of females, Philo had this to say:

> Market places and council halls and law courts and gatherings and meetings where a large number of people are assembled and open-air life with the full scope for discussion and action—all these are suitable to men both in war and peace. The women are best suited to the indoor life which never strays from the house... A woman, then, should not be a busybody, meddling with matters outside her household concerns, but should seek a life of seclusion (*Spec. Leg.* 3.169).

And with specific reference to virginal daughters, Ben Sira had this advice to offer their guardians:

> Let her not show her beauty to any male...
> For from the garment issueth the moth
> And from a woman a woman's wickedness (42.12-13).

But simply restricting women to the home did not solve the problem in its entirety. Chance meetings between the sexes could still occur in consequence of the way in which private homes (as we learnt in the previous section) were often used to accommodate scholarly gatherings of men. Further problems arose through the rabbinic prohibition of all unwitnessed meetings between close relatives of the opposite sex, many of whom would in all likelihood be members of the same household (*Kidd.* 81a). It was therefore necessary that women not only be restricted to the home, but that they be secluded in special quarters away from all possible contact with men. Finally, and in addition to the worry of sexual misbehaviour, consideration had to be taken of the way in which women transmitted ritual impurity during their periods of menstrual uncleanness.

A variety of sources bear witness to the existence of separate women's quarters in the houses of Graeco-Roman Palestine: *Gitt.* 8.1 and *Shabb.* 6.5 make a clear distinction between the areas occupied by men and those occupied by women by referring to 'her courtyard and her house' and 'his courtyard and his house'; Tob. 2.13 speaks of a woman coming from her loom

into the house of her husband; *Kidd.* 81a describes how a group
of visiting women were lodged in the upper room and the ladder beneath them removed for fear of defilement; *B.B.* 6.4
refers to the building of a 'widow house' for the daughter who
returned to her father's home following the death of her husband; and *Nidd.* 7.4 deemed all bloodstains ritually clean
except those found within the walls of chambers used by men-
struating women (בחורים ובסביבות בית הטמאות, lit. 'a house of
unclean women').[1] Finally, it would seem to have been the
custom for men and women to dine in separate areas of the
house. Thus Tob. 7.9f. records how the three men Raguel,
Raphael and Tobias 'bathed... washed... and laid them down
to dine': only when it was necessary for the host Raguel to conclude the marriage arranged with his kinsman Tobias was his
daughter Sarah summoned from the women's quarters. The
fact that Ben Sira made no mention of women when describing the rules of proper conduct to be observed at banquets, and
only had words of warning for 'elders' and 'young men', also
indicates the absence of females from such gatherings (32.1-
13).[2] Thus it would seem certain that there were separate
quarters for men and women in the houses of Graeco-Roman
Palestine.[3]

The relative positions of these separate quarters within the
house provided further safeguards against the occurrence of
chance or planned meetings between men and women whose
union was prohibited in the Torah. The men's apartments
were situated on the public side of the house while those of the
women were in the interior and were inaccessible from the
courtyard except by way of the men's quarters (*Erub.* 68a; cf.

---

1 Note also that according to a later source, *RH* 26a, the term applied to a menstruat-
ing woman was *galmudah*, 'segregated'.
2 Cf. Mk 6.21 for an account of the birthday banquet which Herod held for 'his
courtiers and officers and the leading men of Galilee'. Female members of the
royal household were not present: Herodias' daughter 'came in' (εἰσελθούσης)
and danced before the guests and then retired (ἐξελθοῦσα) to rejoin her mother.
3 It is to be assumed that the practices here described applied predominantly to certain sections of the urban community and to the wealthier strata of society. They
could not have had the same application for the poor, those in one-room dwellings,
etc. We have, however, no way of calculating what proportion of society was able
to implement the rules of domestic sexual segregation.

Kidd. 81a). By this arrangement the women's movement could be strictly monitored, for in order to leave the house they would have to pass through the men's quarters. Similarly, any male visitor or relative who hoped for a clandestine meeting with a woman would have his plans thwarted.

In addition to these arrangements, and of specific interest in this discussion of the lifestyle of a minor, there would seem to have been special boundaries laid down for virgins. With regard to the seclusion of daughters, Ben Sira wrote:

> In the place where she lodgeth let there be no lattice,
> Or spot overlooking the entrance round about.
> Let her not show her beauty to any male,
> And among wives let her not converse (42.11-12).[1]

The fact that is was considered inadvisable for young girls to mix on familiar terms with married women[2] would suggest that there were special virgin quarters within the women's area of the house, whilst Ben Sira's advice that there be 'no lattice or spot overlooking the entrance round about' indicates that preference was given to placing virgins deep in the interior of the house where they would be removed from all temptation and the possibility of sin.

Further evidence for the segregation of men and women within the home and for the existence of special inner chambers beyond which virgins could not pass, is provided by Philo.

---

1 Verse 11e is incomprehensible in the Massada Scroll and so the reading is from MS B: מקם תקור אל יהי (אשגב) ובית מבים מבוא סביב (the Greek is missing). The copyist presumably forgot to transcribe the last word of col. A. Segal suggests with Smend that מבים might be a double corruption of מבוא, that is to say, do not let there be an entrance or approach to her room in a place from which you cannot see strangers entering. Verse 12, col. A, from the Massada Scroll: לכל זכר אל תבן תאר. According to Yadin the scroll reading of תבן—to be understood from the root בין, in the sense of 'exposing', 'showing', 'revealing'—is preferable to B text תתן and also overcomes the textual difficulties of the Greek (see p. 26 for details). Col. B, from MS B: ובית נשים אל תסחויד. Gk: παντὶ ἀνθρώπῳ μὴ ἔμβλεπε ἐν κάλλει καὶ ἐν μέσῳ γυναικῶν μὴ συνέδρευε.

2 The reason is that by listening to the conversations of wives, sexual impulses and desires would be stirred in the young women which would lead to sin: 'for from a garment issueth the moth and from a woman a woman's wickedness' (Sir. 42.13). The strength of the word תסחויד in the line ובית נשים אל תסחויד is to talk secretly, to take counsel (Gk: συνέδρευε), a word which says much about an alternative and perceived female power base and male fear of it.

We may with justification draw upon the writings of the
Alexandrian, for although he obviously refers to the customs
of his own city, his writings without doubt reflect a
fundamental of Hellenistic Jewish thought and practice
which had application both within and outside of Palestine.[1]
That conditions within the Jewish community of Alexandria
were in fact close to those in Palestine—at least in respect of
the seclusion of women—is demonstrated by the striking
similarity in thought between the Judaean Ben Sira and the
Alexandrian Jew Pseudo-Phocylides: the latter's advice to
'guard a virgin in firmly locked rooms, and let her not be seen
before the house until her wedding day' (ll. 215-16) parallels
what we have already learnt of Ben Sira's views on the subject
(cf. especially 26.10; 42.11). Philo's attitude toward pre-
marital chastity and his descriptions of the steps taken to
ensure chaste behaviour also mirror Ben Sira. The
Alexandrian's usefulness lies in the fact that where the
Palestinian sources only implied or assumed the existence of
certain practices, he explicitly stated and described them.
Thus, with regard to the existence of separate quarters for
men and women (a fact already inferred from the Palestinian
material), Philo declared the properly constructed house to be
one which incorporated 'a gateway, colonnades, men's
quarters, women's quarters and other buildings' (*Leg. All.*
3.98). In respect of the relative positions of these quarters and
the practice of situating the men's rooms on the public side of
the house, he describes how 'in our houses the women's
apartments have the men's quarters outside them' (*Leg. All.*
3.40); and with regard to the banishment of virgins to the
innermost part of the house, removed even from the company
of married women, he wrote that

> Women are best suited to the indoor life which never strays
> from the house, within which the middle door is taken by the
> maidens as their boundary, and the outer door by those who
> have reached full womanhood (*Spec. Leg.* 3.169).[2]

---

1 See S. Belkin, *Philo and the Oral Law*, and I. Heinemann, *Philons griechische
  und jüdische Bildung*, pp. 233-35. For a view contrary to that expressed here, see
  Tcherikover, *CPJ*, I, Introduction, and Goodenough, *Jewish Jurisprudence in
  Egypt*, pp. 130f.
2 ... θηλείαις δὲ οἰκουρία καὶ ἡ ἔνδον μονὴ παρθένοις μὲν εἴσω κλισιάδων
  τὴν μέσαυλον ὅρου πεποιημέναις τελείαις δὲ ἤδη γυναιξὶ τὴν αὔλειον.

That the state of affairs here outlined by Philo was not simply
the product of the writer's own philosophy and outlook on life,
a hoped-for ideal removed from the reality of his day, is
demonstrated by certain historical details which were
included in his account of the troubles in Alexandria under
Flaccus—a work of very different character to those we have
so far drawn upon. In his *In Flaccum* Philo reflects the
outraged horror felt by the Jewish community when
Alexandrian soldiers invaded the privacy of their homes in
search of weapons. Of particular concern to the Jews was the
fact that

> Their women, kept in seclusion, never even approaching the
> outer doors, and their maidens confined to the inner cham-
> bers, who for modesty's sake avoided the sight of men, even
> of their closest relatives,[1] were displayed to eyes not merely
> unfamiliar but terrorizing through the fear of military vio-
> lence (§89).[2]

This clear description of the Hellenistic Jewish practice of
banishing virgins to the innermost reaches of the house both
complements Sir. 42.11-12 and confirms our interpretation of
that passage.

Without doubt, therefore, seclusion was the only acceptable
standard of modesty for young girls in Graeco-Roman
Palestine. It was with this in mind that the author of *4
Maccabees* gave the righteous mother of seven sons, who was
the heroine of his story, these words of self-praise to say concerning her youth[3]:

> I was a pure maiden and I strayed not from my father's
> house, and I kept guard over the rib that was builded [into
> Eve]. No seducer of the desert, no deceiver of the field cor-
> rupted me; nor did the false, beguiling serpent sully the

---

1 Here Philo complements Sir. 42.11, 'Let her not show her beauty to any male'; see
   above, p. 114.
2 ὅτι γύναια κατάκλειστα μηδὲ τὴν αὔλειον προερχόμενα καὶ θαλαμευόμεναι
   παρθένοι δι᾽ αἰδῶ τὰ ἀνδρῶν ὄψεις καὶ τῶν οἰκειοταντων ἐκτρεπόμεναι τοτε
   οὐ μόνου ἀσυνήθεσιν ἀλλὰ καὶ στρατιωτικόν... (μέσαυλον in *Spec. Leg.*
   3.169 = θαλαμενόμεναι here).
3 Although not a Palestinian source (see Introduction), *4 Maccabees* here complements what we have learned from the Palestinian material and so with justification may be quoted.

purity of my maidenhood (18.7-8).[1]

Further evidence for the custom of secluding unbetrothed girls within the privacy of the home may be gleaned from the way in which Jews of the period greatly esteemed the white-skinned beauty of virgins. Thus in the *Genesis Apocryphon* the beauty of Abraham's wife Sarah is compared to that of virgins and her unblemished skin is specifically commented upon:

> How lovely is her breast and how beautiful is all her white-ness... There are no virgins or brides who enter a bride chamber more beautiful than she (20.4, 6).

Elsewhere also a Jewish writer of the first century CE referred to the way in which a virgin 'guards her person from the sun' in preparation for her nuptials (*Assumption of Moses* 11.12).

Final proof of the way in which seclusion was interpreted as the only proper standard of modesty for girls may be found in the Hebrew word צניעות. The primary meaning of this term is 'secrecy' or 'retirement'; its secondary definition is 'chastity', 'piety', or 'decency'.[2] We might also note that the common word for a harlot was the Aramaic expression נפקת ברא (or simply נפקא), which means literally 'she who goes outside'.[3]

So strictly guarded were young women in Palestine that it was only at times of national disaster when the smooth ordering of daily life was disrupted that they saw beyond the narrow confines of their secluded quarters. Thus the author of *3 Maccabees* depicts the citizens of Jerusalem rushing forth in confusion on learning of Ptolemy Philopator's plan to invade

---

1 Here obviously the woman refers both to the human seducer and the non-human one. The Gospel accounts bear witness on many occasions to the Jewish belief in desert demons. Cf. *2 Bar.* 10.8 which speaks of 'Sirens... from the sea, ... Lilin... from the desert, and... Shedim and dragons from the forests'. For the way in which demons were believed to compete with men for the first sexual intercourse with a virgin, see Chapter 2, §D.

2 See Jastrow, pp. 1291a-1292b.

3 See *ibid.*, p. 926a. 'To go outside' was not only to risk sexual advances and a bad reputation, but also to break with the designated role of passive home-maker and to enter the male public arena. Contrast Prov. 31 with Prov. 7.10-23, the one describing the woman of virtue engaged in domestic tasks, the other depicting the 'riotous and rebellious' woman whose 'feet abide not in her house'.

the Holy of Holies.[1] Such was the people's consternation at Philopator's proposal that the normal code of conduct was momentarily forgotten and

> the virgins who had been shut up in their chambers rushed forth with their mothers and covering their hair with dust and ashes, filled the streets with groanings and lamentations (1.18).[2]

Another affront to the Jews' religious sensibilities was furnished in the reign of Seleucus IV (187–175 BCE) when the king's minister Heliodorus attempted to remove the Temple treasures. On this occasion a certain degree of decorum among the young girls of Jerusalem was maintained, for according to the report of 2 Maccabees, although they left their apartments they did remain indoors:

> the maidens who were kept in ward (κατάκλειστοι) ran together, some to the porticoes, others to the walls,[3] and others to look out at the windows (2 Macc. 3.19).[4]

Apart from these rare occasions, therefore, virgins did remain within their quarters removed from all contact with men.[5] Indeed, so secluded were they that marriages were

---

1   An event supposed to have taken place around 217 BCE. The account of *3 Macc.* regarding Philopator's persecution of the Jews and their miraculous delivery conflates various legends and is largely romantic fiction (though certain elements may reflect genuine problems of Alexandrian Jews under Philopator, 222-204 BCE). For our purposes, though, the author's choice of image to depict the Jews' distress remains significant and as we shall see is confirmed by other more 'historical' evidence.

2   Note that even in such dire circumstances as those here imagined by the author of *3 Macc.*, the Jews may well have observed some degree of decorum by gathering in sexually segregated groups. Thus Philo, in a somewhat more 'historical' account, records that when the Judaeans gathered to protest to Petronius about the proposed erection by Caligula of the statue in the Temple in 39/40 CE, they divided themselves into six companies, 'old men, young men, and boys, and again in their turn, old women, grown women and maidens' (*Leg.* 227).

3   The fact that the maidens are here described as being in an imprisoned state (κατάκλειστοι) means that the porticoes and walls here referred to are in fact the gate-houses and boundaries of private buildings rather than those of the city walls.

4   In this context see also the reference to 'tender deep girdled women (βαθυζώνους τε γυναῖκας), snatched from their chambers and with delicate feet falling forward' in the *Sib. Or.* 3.526.

5   The custom of the virgins of Jerusalem going forth to dance in the vineyards on 15 Ab and Yom Kippur was no longer practised in our period (Judg. 21.19f.; *Taan.* 4.8, 31a).

often arranged without the prospective bride and groom even meeting each other, agents commonly being employed to conduct the negotiations. The inherent dangers of this system, however, were recognized (from the male view point at least) by the rabbis, and they ordained that

> A man may not betroth a woman before he sees her, lest he (subsequently) see something repulsive in her and she become loathsome to him (*Kidd.* 41a).

The couple were not, of course, allowed to meet each other privately but had to have other parties present to ensure their proper behaviour (*Sanh.* 21a-b; *Kidd.* 4.12-14, 80b). According to the rabbis the punishment for unchaperoned meetings between a man and an unmarried woman was flagellation (*Kidd.* 81a).[1]

At the start of this section it was pointed out that the terms 'unbetrothed virgin' and 'minor daughter' were in fact synonymous in consequence of the way in which Jewish girls seldom remained unmarried (or unbetrothed) much beyond the onset of puberty. The seclusion of unbetrothed virgins, therefore, is to be viewed not only as an inevitable fact of life in a society ordered along strictly patriarchal lines and one obsessed with sexual purity, but also as another manifestation of *patria potestas*. A father controlled the movement of his virginal daughter not only because society judged her, as a sinful female, incapable of guarding her own chastity, but also because it was his right as a father to dictate the lifestyle of a minor daughter. Should he decide to protect her purity by secluding her within the home—and society demanded that he indeed take such action—then any unchaste behaviour on her part was condemned not only on moral grounds but also because she had defied her father's authority. Indeed, the Deuteronomic legislation made it absolutely clear that a daughter could only be condemned to death if she had indulged in pre-marital sex whilst still a minor. Thus Deut. 22.14f. speaks only of the *na'arah* and describes her crime not simply as one of having played the harlot but rather of having

---

1 Though see above, p. 108 n. 1.

played the harlot 'in her father's house'. The law, therefore, dealt with the female counterpart of the 'rebellious son', whose defiance also met with death (Deut. 21.18f.). The fact that Biblical law nowhere prescribed capital punishment (or indeed any punishment) for ordinary cases of harlotry[1] underlines the way in which the girl was here being penalized for rebellion against parental authority rather than for sexual misdemeanour. No legal action could be taken once she reached the age of twelve and a half and passed out of her father's control. Similarly, no action could be taken with regard to the harlotry of an orphan girl (*Ket.* 44b). As we have seen, the intertestamental writers continued to place emphasis upon male authority and female rebellion when treating virginity and non-virginity.

In the course of the Talmudic period, married women came to enjoy a degree of freedom in respect of their movement beyond the home. For virgins, however, the philosophy of 'All glorious is the king's daughter within the palace' (Ps. 45.14) continued unabated and their strict seclusion within the home remained a feature of Jewish life. A late Babylonian text confirms the way in which seclusion continued to be rigorously enforced in order to ensure that no charge of unchaste behaviour could ever be levelled against a virgin:

> a bride keeps herself secluded all the time she is in her father's house and only makes herself known when she goes out [that is, when she leaves her father's house for the wedding ceremony] [as if] to say: 'Anyone who can testify anything against me [against my virtue] let him come and testify' (*Derek Eretz Zuta* 7.2).[2]

In other words, the girl's first public appearance occurred on the occasion of her passing from the control of her father into the control of her husband.

---

1 In their puritanical fervour, Philo and the author of the book of *Jubilees* both state that death was the punishment for fornication (*Jos.* 43; *Jub.* 20.4), but for this they had no biblical or rabbinic authority.

2 Although completed after the Talmud and standing outside of that canon, *Derek Eretz Zuta* contains some early (Tannaitic) material and evinces some knowledge of the Talmudic corpus. In this instance it simply parallels what we have already learned from earlier sources.

Chapter 2

MARRIAGE (TECHNICALITIES)

In her survey of life among Moslem villagers of Palestine in
the 1920s, Hilma Granqvist recalls how the birth of a boy was
greeted with the words, 'Blessed be the bridegroom'. Similarly,
the birth of a girl heralded the cry, 'Blessed be the bride'.[1] This
choice of greeting by the Fellahin highlights one fundamental
characteristic of Near Eastern society: the tremendous
emphasis placed by that society (as with other societies) upon
marriage and the continuation of the family line. But this
emphasis is by no means confined to the modern oriental
world. In the ancient Near East marriage was regarded with
the same degree of seriousness and occupied a central position
in the lives and thoughts of all peoples, the Jews included.
Indeed, a blessing similar to that of the Fellahin could well
have been uttered by the Jews of Graeco-Roman Palestine
over their newly born infants. Certainly the same sentiment
would have been felt even if it were not formally expressed.

Celibacy was never considered a virtue in Jewish thought.
The commandment to 'be fruitful and multiply' (Gen. 1.28)
precluded the possibility of such a notion.[2] Marriage and the
raising of a family were regarded as holy duties to be fulfilled
as early in a person's adult life as possible.[3] The sources for

---

1 *Birth and Childhood Among the Arabs*, p. 89.
2 The celebrated celibacy of a section of the Essenes was due to their need to be in a
   state of constant ritual purity in consequence of their belief that a Holy War was
   imminent. According to the Bible (Deut. 23.10f.; cf. Exod. 19.15), soldiers had to
   remove themselves from all contact with women on the eve of battle. On this, see
   Buchanan, 'The Role of Purity in the Structure of the Essene Sect', *RQ* 4/3 (1963),
   pp. 397-406; Kohler, 'Essenes and Apocalyptic Literature', *JQR* 11 (1920), p. 145;
   Robertson Smith, *Religion of the Semites*, p. 455.
3 For the age of marriage recommended for men, see above, pp. 95-96; for the usual
   age for women, see next section. Note that fulfilment of this commandment, as
   with many others (see p. 87 n. 2), applied only to men, though obviously it directly
   embraced women.

our period (written by and predominantly for men) abound
with references to the joy that could be found in a life shared
with a well-matched partner, and equally warn of the
miserable, meaningless existence endured by the celibate. For
example, Ben Sira wrote:

> He that getteth a wife (getteth) the choicest possession,
> A help-meet for him and a pillar of support.
> Without a hedge the vineyard is laid waste
> And without a wife (a man is) a wanderer and homeless.
> Who trusteth an armed band that rusheth from city to city?
> So is the man that hath no nest,[1]
> Who resteth where evening befalls him (36.24-26).

In rabbinic literature the unmarried man was seen as living
without joy, blessing or good, without Torah, a wall or peace
(*Yeb.* 62b). In fact, he was 'in want of all things' (*Ned.* 41a).

The divinely ordained purpose of marriage was
procreation, and it was essentially for this rather than for the
possible joys of married life that men were urged to take
wives.[2] The concern of the ancients for children and the
continuation of the family line was succinctly expressed by
Pseudo-Phocylides in the following way:

> Remain not unmarried, lest you die nameless.
> Give nature her due: beget in turn as you were begotten (ll.
> 175-76).

So important was the duty to 'be fruitful and multiply' that the
rabbis declared: 'He who does not engage in propagation of the
race is as though he sheds blood... as though he has diminished the Divine Image' (*Yeb.* 63b). In their opinion such a
man would have to account for his action in the world to come
(*Shabb.* 31a). On a more popular level, the man who lacked
the security of a family was viewed as 'contemptible before his
enemies'. He was 'like unto a tree by the roadside from which
every passer-by plucketh and every beast of the weald teareth

---

1 Note the use of 'nest' (קן/νοσσία) here to mean 'wife'. Cf. Jastrow, p. 168, for the use of בית and ביתו to mean 'wife', and below, Chapter 3 §A for the significance of the term.

2 Note that a woman's barrenness could be grounds for divorce and that priests were not allowed to marry sterile women (*Gitt.* 4.8; *Yeb.* 6.5, 6). See pp. 18ff., 27 above for the way in which infertility was perceived to be an exclusively female problem.

down its leafage'.[1]

One fact emerges clearly from these writings: although marriage was a central feature of Jewish life, the choice whether to marry or not rested with the individual—for it was only in the context of choice that these exhortations to marry could have arisen and had meaning.[2] The fact that in all these passages the ancient writers addressed themselves to men and never to women is therefore significant. An unmarried man might be regarded as something of an oddity, but his decision to remain celibate did not affect his capacity to function in society. Such, however, was not the case for a woman. Where marriage was concerned she had no choice. She simply could not afford to be without a male provider/protector in a society which was ordered along strictly patriarchal lines.[3] The woman's lack of choice and the man's freedom in respect of marriage were neatly contrasted by Ben Sira in the following way:

> A woman will receive any man,
> Yet is one woman more pleasant than another (36.21).

The rabbis declared that a woman would tolerate an unhappy marriage rather than remain alone (*Yeb.* 113a; *Kidd.* 7a), and even advised parents to manumit a slave for the purpose of marriage if their daughter had reached adulthood without having secured a husband (*Pes.* 113a). Thus the words used by Westermark to describe oriental society in the first quarter of this century may be applied with equal validity to the community of women in Graeco-Roman Palestine. He observed

---

1   *Ahikar* 2.28 (Syr.). Although a non-Jewish work, the book of *Ahikar* was popular in Jewish circles and clearly contained the type of general Near Eastern sentiment with which the Jews of Hellenistic Palestine would have readily identified. Note the imagery employed in Isa. 56.3 of the eunuch who could have no children: 'Behold, I am a dry tree'. On the protection afforded by children, see Ps. 127.4-5, 'As arrows in the hand of the mighty men, so are the children of one's youth. Happy is the man that hath his quiver full of them; they shall not be put to shame when they speak with their enemies in the gate.'

2   Thus, for example, we learn of how the celebrated first-century scholar Simeon b. Azzai chose not to marry 'because my soul lusts for the Torah' (*Yeb.* 63b). A person could also decide not to marry because of economic difficulties. See *Ket.* 13.5, and below pp. 160-62.

3   In this context, note the repeated biblical references to the plight of the widowed woman.

that

> nothing is more rarely to be met with in the East than a
> woman unmarried after a certain time of life. She will
> rather marry a poor man, or become a second wife to a man
> already married, than remain in a state of celibacy.[1]

Marriage was the only real security for the adult Jewish
woman.

In this chapter we shall examine what I have termed the
'technicalities' of marriage. Sections B and C will deal respectively with betrothal and the *kethubah* and section D will be
devoted to an examination of the marriage ceremony. Questions pertaining to daily life within marriage have been
reserved for Chapter 3. Before embarking on a discussion of
any of these subjects, however, we must first look at the fundamental question of whom to marry.

A. *Whom to Marry?*

In line with the emphasis upon urging men to marry, discussion in our sources as to the choice of partner is mainly
couched in terms of permitted/preferred wife and not of per-
mitted/preferred husband. For example, while we have
detailed information regarding the categories of women permitted to priests, little is directly stated regarding the choice of
husband for a priest's daughter. Similarly, while the sources
offer detailed advice to men as to the qualities possessed by the
ideal wife,[2] there is scant reference to the qualities to be looked
for in husbands. The secondary literature simply tends to
reproduce this bias. In this examination, therefore, we shall
endeavour to discover and state the woman's viewpoint. In
order to do this, it will be necessary both to read between the
lines and to invert the familiar order within the biblical and
extra-biblical writings. Thus, for example, for the purposes of
the present discussion, the prohibition not to marry one's
father's sister (male viewpoint) will be stated as a prohibition

---

1 *The History of Human Marriage*, I, p. 378. See also Bauer, *Volksleben im Lande
der Bibel*, p. 84: 'Ganz "sitzen" bleibt kein Fellachenmädchen, es müsste denn
mit irgend einem Gebrechen behaftet sein, was selten der Fall ist; aber selbst ein
einäugiges Mädchen findet einen Mann'.
2 See Chapter 3, especially §C.

on marrying one's brother's son (female viewpoint). Throughout the examination we shall discuss only those rules and social considerations which applied to the marriage of a virgin, that is first marriage. We shall not look at the special and additional considerations which surrounded remarriage and the levirate or discuss the question of polygamy (though many of the rules described below applied in these instances also).[1]

In our analysis of the factors which governed the choice of husband, we shall examine firstly those partners who were biblically or rabbinically forbidden to the woman, secondly those permitted but not favoured, and finally those both allowed and preferred. At the outset of our discussion one fact must be both appreciated and stressed. In consequence of the Jews' belief in their special destiny as God's chosen people, tremendous emphasis was placed upon the need to maintain racial purity. Only Israelites of legitimate, unblemished ancestry could be a part of God's eternal covenant and only they could be assured of the promised messianic salvation. To ensure that the holy seed did not become polluted, a mass of restrictive, detailed legislation developed concerning prohibited unions and the status of the offspring of such unions, and the entire population was rigidly classified according to purity of descent. The dominance of this desire for racial purity in the lives and thought of the Jewish people must be constantly borne in mind as we examine the question of whom the woman (or the father, on her behalf) chose as a marriage partner.

The first consideration for the woman was for her not to enter into marriage with a non-Jew. The Pentateuch

---

1 Polygamy would appear not to have been common practice in the Second Commonwealth: monogamous unions are generally assumed in the literature of the period and economic difficulties often delayed a man in taking a first wife, let alone several (see below, pp. 160-62). On this see R. Loewe, *The Position of the Woman in Judaism*, p. 22; Safrai and Stern, *Compendia*, II, pp. 749f.; R. de Vaux, *Ancient Israel*, p. 25 and Archer, 'The Virgin and the Harlot in the Writings of Formative Judaism', *History Workshop Journal* 24 (1987), pp. 1-16. The institution of the levirate would also seem to have been less generally practised in postbiblical times, and its demise—together with that of polygamy—is to be linked among other things with the rise of the nuclear family. On this see Archer, *op. cit.* With regard to non-levirate remarriage, this subject will be treated *en passant* in our discussion of the provisions of the marriage contract (Chapter 3 §C). In the main, however, the focus throughout this book will be on first marriage.

expressly forbade marriage alliances with any of the seven nations who had occupied the promised land in the pre-Israelite period, declaring that such liaisons would cause the Hebrews to follow false gods (Exod. 34.11f.; Deut. 7.2-4; cf. Num. 25.1f.; Deut. 23.4; also Josh. 23.11f.). The legislators' fear was well founded for, as the Old Testament narratives and doom prophecies of the pre-exilic and exilic period clearly show, the nation quickly forgot this early ruling and mingled with their neighbours with the result that syncretistic practices abounded throughout the land. The prohibition against intermarriage had therefore to be rigorously repromulgated in the days of the restored community (Ezr. 9.10; Neh. 10.13). At that time a significant development in the nature of the biblical prohibition occurred. While the earlier legislation had only been concerned with the practicalities of averting the danger of religious assimilation, the emphasis of the post-exilic community was on purity in absolute terms. Intermarriage in the fifth century was condemned not only for 'religious' reasons but also because of the resultant 'racial' impurity, that is, pollution of the holy seed (the two of course are inextricably linked in the later Jewish system of thought and notion of self-identity/definition; they are here separated for the purpose of tracing the evolution in thought and for ease of discussion). Thus, when Ezra and Nehemiah ordered the removal of all foreign spouses, their decision was based both on the way in which marriages had been made 'with the peoples that do these [religious] abominations' (Ezr. 9.14; cf. Mal. 2.11-12, and above p. 72) and also on the fact that 'the holy seed have mingled themselves with the peoples of the lands' (Ezr. 9.2), with the result that the offspring of these unions were unable to speak 'in the Jews' language, but according to the language of each people' (Neh. 13.24). The new emphasis upon purity, racial and religious, is most clearly demonstrated by the words used by Ezra in his restatement of the original intermarriage prohibition. God's commandment regarding the seven nations in Exodus and Deuteronomy was recast by the post-exilic reformer in the following way:

> The land unto which ye go to possess, it is an unclean land (ארץ נדה) through the uncleanness of the peoples of the lands (היא נדת עמי הארצות)... Now therefore give not your daughters

unto their sons, neither take their daughters unto your sons
(9.11-12).

By the time we reach the Hellenistic period, therefore,
intermarriage was viewed primarily in terms of *niddah*, that
is, pollution or ritual impurity, to the individual and the community at large. This overriding concern for absolute purity
resulted in a logical extension of the biblical law in the period
under consideration. The intertestamental writers did not
restrict themselves to the original prohibition against marriage with the seven nations, but expanded the law to include
all gentiles.[1] Thus the author of the *Testament of Levi* urged
Jews to marry 'while yet thou art young, but not of the race of
strange nations' (9.11; cf. 14.6), and members of the Hellenizing party in Jerusalem at the time of Antiochus Epiphanes
were castigated by the author of *1 Macc.* for having 'joined
themselves to the gentiles and sold themselves to do evil'
(1.15). This more general interpretation of the biblical
prohibition was also upheld by Philo, who wrote: 'he [Moses]
says, Do not enter into partnership of marriage with a
member of a foreign nation' (*Spec. Leg.* 3.29)[2].

The author of *Jubilees* endeavoured to find biblical foundation for the belief that marriage with all gentiles was prohibited in a reinterpretation of Lev. 20.2 (cf. 18.21), declaring: 'the
man who has defiled his daughter [by giving her in marriage
to a gentile] shall be rooted out in the midst of all Israel *because
he has given of his seed to Moloch,* and wrought impiously so
as to defile it' (30.10).[3] Indeed, so condemnatory was this
writer of intermarriage that, again on the basis of Lev. 20.2
(though in fact without any real scriptural authority), he rec-

1   An earlier extension of the Pentateuchal law may be seen in Ezr. 10.11, where
    Ezra urges the Jews to 'separate yourselves from the peoples of the land (itemized
    in 9.1 as the seven nations) *and from the foreign women*' (מעמי הארץ ומן הנשים
    הנכריות).

2   Interestingly, Philo did not view intermarriage in terms of *niddah*, but rather in
    the traditional biblical light of the dangers of religious assimilation. This was
    presumably because of the fact that he was a diaspora Jew addressing a diaspora
    community which daily faced the problem of mingling with and absorbing Gen-
    tile customs.

3   See also *Ps. Jon.* on Lev. 18.21: 'and of your seed you shall not give in sexual
    intercourse at the side of a daughter of the nations to pass over to a foreign cult'.
    Also *Meg.* 4.9, which objected to this interpretation of Lev. 20.1.

ommended death for all Jews who arranged or engaged in
these polluting unions:

> And if there is any man who wishes in Israel to give his
> daughter or his sister to any man who is of the seed of the
> gentiles he shall surely die and they shall stone him with
> stones... and they shall burn the woman with fire (30.7).

According to him,

> Israel will not be free from this uncleanness if it has
> ... given its daughters to a man who is of any of the gentiles
> (30.14).

In other words, his concern lay solely with maintaining the
holy people's ritual purity. So deep-rooted was this aversion to
mixed marriage that one of the intertestamental writers even
went so far as to urge women to choose spinsterhood in preference to marriage with the heathen:

> happy is the barren that is undefiled,
> She who hath not conceived in transgression...
> Better than this is childlessness with virtue (Wis. 3.13; 4.1).

In his view, 'the multiplying brood of the ungodly shall be of no
profit, and with bastard slips they shall not strike deep root,
nor shall they establish a sure hold' (4.3; cf. vv. 4-6).[1]

In the later Tannaitic period there was some disagreement
as to whether intermarriage was in fact biblically prohibited.
The general opinion, however, was that it was not forbidden
and not therefore a punishable offence (*Meg.* 4.9; *Sanh.* 9.6;
A.Z. 36b). However, the question of prohibition did not affect
the fundamental issue of the validity of these marriages, and
the Tannaim were unanimous in declaring such unions
invalid. In their eyes, the union of an Israelite with a gentile
was mere concubinage,[2] and the offspring of such an

---

1 Compare this with the advice offered to men by Ben Sira: 'give not thy strength to
   strangers. Having found a portion of good soil... sow it with thy own
   seed... Thus will thine offspring flourish, and, having confidence in their
   noble descent will become great' (26.19-21).
2 That is, concubinage in the later rabbinic sense of the word, not in terms of the
   institution as practised in the Patriarchal period. For the way in which the rabbis
   had little or no understanding of the biblical *pilegesh* and in fact used Greek and
   Roman notions of concubinage in their thinking on the subject, see Epstein, *Marriage Laws*, pp. 62-71.

alliance were deemed non-Jews, inferior even to bastards (*Kidd.* 68b; *Yeb.* 17a, 22b; *Tem.* 29b).[1]

Throughout the Graeco-Roman period, therefore, marriage with a gentile was most vigorously condemned. Although such unions did occur (as evidenced by such passages as 1 Macc. 1.15 and the repeated exhortations not to intermarry), they never concerned more than a small percentage of the population (usually within the top echelons of society). In the main the Jews did not consider marriage outside of their circle of co-religionists, and their exclusiveness was the cause of much contempt among the pagan authors of the time who accused them of μισοξενία or ἀμιξία (hatred of strangers, unsociableness).[2] Indeed, the concern of the Jews of Graeco-Roman Palestine to see their women married to fellow Jews is perhaps most clearly indicated by a line in the divorce deed which was discovered at Wadi Murabba'at (*P. Mur.* 29).[3] The clause in question is a statement of the divorced woman's freedom to remarry, and it differs in one fundamental respect from the formula laid down in the Mishnah. It reads:

> you are free for your part to go and become the wife of any
> *Jewish* man that you wish (ll. 5-7) את רשיא בנפשכי למהך ולמהי
> .(אנת לכל זכר יהודי די תצבין)

The significant point about this clause is the insertion of the specification יהודי into the traditional Mishnaic formula, 'Lo, thou art free to marry any man' (*Gitt.* 9.3).

Thus, from the material we have examined, it would seem certain that Gentiles stood at the head of the list of partners forbidden to or spurned by the Jewish woman.

---

1 Philo called the children of intermarriage νόθοι (*Leg. All.* 2.94; *Virt.* 224; *Mos.* 2.193. Cf. Wisd. of Sol. quoted above which also has νόθοι, Lat. *spuria vitulamina*), a term for which there is no equivalent in rabbinic literature. His use of this term indicates that he was aware that these offspring were of lower status than bastards (Heb. *mamzerim*). See Belkin, *Philo and the Oral Law*, pp. 233-35, and Heinemann, *Philons griechische und jüdische Bildung*, pp. 313-14. The word 'bastard' (*mamzer*) in Hebrew (and rabbinic) usage applies to the offspring of a father and mother between whom there could in law be no binding betrothal (e.g. on grounds of adultery, incest, etc.), rather than to those born out of wedlock as in English usage.

2 See, for example, Diodorus Siculus 34.1; 40.3; Justinus 36.2, 15; Molon, in *Con. Ap.* 2.14; Lysimachus, in *Con. Ap.* 1.34. See also *Ant.* 13.83.

3 According to Yadin, this document may be dated to 71 CE. For text and translation of deed, see Appendix I.

The exclusion of Gentiles, however, did not imply that all Jews were possible or suitable candidates for marriage, for within the Jewish nation itself, further constraints were placed upon the woman in respect of her choice of husband. In particular, she was not allowed to enter into marriage with any man who lay within the forbidden degrees of kinship. Thus, according to the Law of Holiness, she was not to be taken in marriage by her brother or half-brother (maternal or paternal) (Lev. 18.9, 11; 20.17),[1] by the son of her brother or sister (prohibited aunt-nephew relationship) (Lev. 18.12-13; 20.19),[2] or by her grandfather (again maternal or paternal) (Lev. 18.10).[3] Presumably sexual relations with her father were also prohibited, for although not specifically mentioned in the law codes, such relations would be central to the system of incest taboo which was developing and could in any case be inferred from Lev. 18.6-7.[4] The Tannaim extended the number of kin relationships within which marriage involved incest, ranking them as 'seconds' (שׁניות) or subordinates to be forbidden as a safeguard against possible infringement of the

---

1   The law of Leviticus was an extension of the earlier law which allowed marriage between maternal siblings (Gen. 20.12; 2 Sam. 13.13). Paternal half-sister prohibition was of special concern to Ezekiel (22.11), and his concern shows that the practice continued.

2   We might note that Moses and Aaron were both born of such a union (Exod. 6.20; Num. 26.59), but this was of course before the Levitic legislation. Most of the laws in the Code of Holiness are developments upon the earlier system which had, to judge by the biblical narratives, allowed half-sibling, nephew-aunt, and on one occasion (Gen. 19.31-38) father-daughter unions. For these shifts see Archer, *op. cit.*

3   The other incestuous relations itemized in Lev. 18 and 20 belong to the category of incestuous adultery (that is, group-wife prohibitions) or pertain to polygamy and are therefore not our concern here. For a full analysis of the incest laws in Leviticus, their function and origin, see Stephen F. Bigger, 'The Family Laws of Leviticus 18 in their Setting', *JBL* 98 (1979), pp. 187-203. Also Robin Fox, *Kinship and Marriage*. For a siting of these laws in the wider context of historical shifts in Jewish social structure and the changing position of women, see Archer, *op. cit.*

4   Another interpretation is, however, possible. All the laws of incest are taken from the male viewpoint, and all the women forbidden to them are under the authority of another man, whether as wife or daughter. (The only exception to this is the ruling against marrying a woman and her daughter at the same time, which was designed to prevent domestic tension.) It is therefore perhaps significant that while express provision was made regarding the incest between a son and his mother, no mention was made until the time of the Tannaim (*Makk.* 3.1) regarding sexual relations between a daughter and her father—because she was under the authority of no other male?

biblical degrees (*Yeb*. 21a-22a). Most of this tannaitic legislation was concerned with extending the group-wife prohibitions (that is, the degrees of incestuous adultery), and consequently has no place in our present discussion. We need only
mention the extension of Lev. 18.10 to include a woman and
her great-grandfather (paternal and maternal) among the
prohibited degrees of kinship (*Yeb*. 21a). Finally, mention
should also be made of the way in which the Qumran exegetes
extended the law of Lev. 18.13 (aunt-nephew incest) to
include niece-uncle incest. The *Damascus Document* records
their views on the subject:

> And each man marries the daughter of his brother or sister,
> whereas Moses said, 'You shall not approach your mother's
> sister; she is your mother's near kin' (Lev. 18.13). But
> although the laws against incest are written for men, they
> also apply to women. When, therefore, a brother's daughter
> uncovers the nakedness of her father's brother, she is (also
> his) near kin.[1]

As far as we know, however, the authors of the *Damascus
Document* were the only members of the Jewish community
who considered such unions incestuous. Indeed, as the
opening words reveal, the Jews of Hellenistic Palestine did
contract niece-uncle marriages and presumably regarded
them as permissible. The fact that Jews in the main did not
deem these unions incestuous or prohibited is demonstrated by
the way in which traditional exegesis translated the
apparently incestuous union of Abraham and Sarah (see Gen.
12.13 and 20.12 in the light of Lev. 18.9, and above p. 132, nn. 2
and 3) into the acceptable kinship terms of marriage between
an uncle and a niece (*Ant*. 1.151; *Ps. Jon.* on Gen. 11.29;
20.12).[2]

In defining the forbidden degrees of kinship, the biblical legislators were once again primarily concerned with the question of purity, for, as was the case with intermarriage, incest
in their eyes brough pollution to the individual and the

---

1 CD 5, English translation, Vermes, *op. cit.*, pp. 101-102.
2 These authors rendered the word 'sister' (Sarah's relation to Abraham) in the
   wider sense of 'niece', and so described her as the daughter of Haran, Abraham's
   brother. On this see G. Vermes, 'The Qumran Interpretation of Scripture in its
   Historical Setting', *ALUOS* 6 (1966-68), p. 88, also in *Post-Biblical Jewish Studies*,
   pp. 40-41 and *Scripture and Tradition*, p. 75.

community at large. So the holy people were warned: 'Defile not yourselves in any of these things (אל תטמאו בכל אלה)... that the land vomit not you out also when you defile it, as it vomited out the nation that was before you' (Lev. 18.24, 28).

But although purity was the stated context for the promulgation of the incest laws, the prohibition on sexual relations between blood-relatives had a more practical content in that it ensured the practice of exogamy and through exogamy the development of necessary affinal kinship links. This was particularly important when the extended family system gave way to the nuclear family (see above, p. 85).[1] As Levi Strauss wrote, 'Exogamy provides the only means of maintaining the group as a group, of avoiding the indefinite fission and segmentation which the practice of consanguinous marriages would bring about'.[2] Philo recognized this all-important aspect of the incest taboo in his discussion of brother-sister marriage (*Spec. Leg.* 3.22f.). According to him, Moses forbade such marriages on the grounds that they outraged family decency and prevented alliances with less closely related families. As Philo wrote:

> Why hamper the fellow feeling and inter-communion of men with men by compressing within the narrow space of each separate house the great and goodly plant which might extend and spread itself over continents and islands and the whole inhabited world? For intermarriages with outsiders create new kinships not a wit inferior to blood relations (*Spec. Leg.* 3.25).

The biblical legislators did not prescribe any particular penalty for the crime of incest but simply declared that those guilty of such 'abominations' would be 'cut off from among their people' (Lev. 18.29). The Tannaim, however, classified the offences of incest according to their degree of seriousness and decreed some punishable by stoning (*Sanh.* 7.4), some by burning (*Sanh.* 9.1; cf. *Ket.* 3.2), and others by flogging (*Makk.* 3.1). Incest between a woman and her father or step-father, her grandfather or step-grandfather was punished by burn-

1 In this context, note the date of the Levitical extension of the incest laws, *viz.*, exilic.
2 C. Lévi-Strauss, 'The Principles of Kinship', in J. Goody (ed.), *Kinship*, p. 48.

ing,[1] while that between a woman and her brother or her nephew met with a flogging.[2] Marriage with a man who lay within the forbidden secondary grades of kinship (as enjoined by the sages, see *Yeb.* 21a) resulted in the woman losing the right to claim her *kethubah* (*Ket.* 11.6). Finally, any children who were born of an incestuous union were considered bastards in rabbinic law (*Kidd.* 3.12; *Yeb.* 4.13; see p. 131, n. 1 above).

Although for the sake of completeness the various categories of secondary kinship have been included in this survey of the incest laws, in all probability most Jews in Graeco-Roman Palestine would have been familiar only with the basic biblical prohibitions. The general ignorance regarding the post-biblical extensions is demonstrated by the non-rabbinic writers of the period who, in their discussions about incest, neither referred to nor evinced knowledge of any law beyond those in the Bible.[3] That serious account was taken of the (biblical) incest laws is demonstrated by a piece of advice which was offered by Josephus to all young men who desired to take a woman in marriage. He instructed them to follow the normal procedure and first approach the father of the prospective bride, and he specifically characterized the father as one 'who is authorized to give away the hand of one who is not ineligible on account of nearness of kin' (*Con. Ap.* 2.199).

Again within the Jewish nation, the woman had to take into consideration other forbidden unions of a non-incestuous nature. Palestinian society was divided into a number of rigidly defined groups, membership of which was determined by the individual's parentage. While marriage between cer-

---

1 The inclusion of step-father and step-grandfather highlights the social construction of the incest taboo: it is not based on biology or 'nature' so much as on the structural/cultural needs of society. This fact supports the argument already made that the extensions of the incest laws had close connection with the rise of the nuclear family and the need to legislate for the new system.

2 According to *Ket.* 3.1, brother-sister and nephew-aunt connections were punished by a fine only. This mishnah, however, was concerned with the crime of seduction (in this case of a blood relative) rather than simply with incest, and so a fine was levied from the seducer. The Gemara further explains the apparent contradiction by saying that *Makk.* 3.1 referred to a *bogereth* (through whom no fine may be incurred) and *Ket.* 3.1 to a *na'arah* (to whom a fine is payable) (*Ket.* 31b-32b).

3 See Philo, *Spec. Leg.* 3.12-29; Ps. Phocylides, ll. 182-83; Josephus, *Ant.* 3.274.

tain groups was permitted, alliance with others was prohibited, and the laws which governed both membership and intermarriage were again founded upon that concept of purity which developed in the post-exilic period. These clearly defined social groups appear for the first time in the biblical record of those who returned with Ezra from Babylon, where they are listed in the following order: Israelites, priests, levites, singers, porters, *nethinim*,[1] Solomon's servants, and finally, those of impaired Israelite stock (that is, those who 'could not tell their father's houses and their seed') and those of impaired priestly stock (who could not trace their genealogies and were therefore deemed polluted) (Ezr. 2.2-62 = Neh. 7.6-64). In the centuries which separated Ezra (fifth century BCE) and the Tannaim (first–second centuries CE), various revisions of the biblical list had to be made as a result of the changed composition of Jewish society. The Mishnah's record of the social divisions which existed in Hellenistic Palestine reflects this changed composition by its omission of such groups as the Temple servants; its insertions of new categories, for example, proselytes; and its general revision of the biblical order in consequence of the improved status of certain groups (thus, for example, priests moved to the head of the list). The Tannaim recast the biblical account in the following way:

> Ten families came up from Babylon: The priestly, levitic and Israelitish stocks, the impaired priestly stocks,[2] the proselyte, the freedman, bastard and *nathin* stocks,[3] and the

---

1   Lit. 'men who are given': Temple servants given by David for the service of the Levites (Ezr. 8.20), probably originally of slave stock. On the history of the Nethinim, see Grant and Rowley, *Dictionary of the Bible*, pp. 697-98, and Schürer, *op. cit.*, II, pp. 290-91.
2   Those born of unions forbidden to priests in Lev. 21.1f.
3   The descendants of the Temple slaves.

shetuki and *asufi* stocks[1] (*Kidd.* 4.1).[2]

The basic law regarding marriage between these groups was:

> The priestly, levitic, impaired priestly stocks may inter-
> marry; the levitic, Israelitish, impaired priestly stocks,
> proselytes and freedmen stocks may intermarry; the prose-
> lytes, freedman, bastard, *nathin, shetuki* and *asufi* stocks
> may all intermarry (*ibid.*).[3]

We shall now examine the question of permitted/prohibited
unions within the Jewish nation in greater detail and from the
woman's point of view, starting with the marriage of a
woman of priestly descent.

The rules which governed the marriage of a priest's
daughter were far less strict than those which regulated the
marriage of a priest. In fact, they varied little from those
which pertained to all women of pure Israelite stock. Far
greater care was taken to maintain the purity of the priest in
consequence of his role as custodian of the nation's religion
and cult, and the fact that his male offspring inherited the
priestly office—so long as the mother was of a social status
appropriate to her priestly husband (see below for the way in
which children's status was dictated by that of the inferior
parent).[4] Thus, while she was allowed to marry a proselyte, a
freed slave and a priest of impaired stock (*Kidd.* 4.7, 71a,
unions which were permitted but which entailed loss of

---

1   *Kidd.* 4.2, 'And who is deemed of *shetuki* stock? Any that knows his mother but
    does not know his father. And *asufi* stock? Any that was picked up from the street
    and knows neither his father or his mother.' As with all the internal social divi-
    sions, the question was not the transmission of Jewishness but rather the legiti-
    macy of the parents (which then determined the status of the offspring). Thus in
    the instance of *shetuki*, the mother could avert the suspicion of *mamzerut*
    (bastardy) being cast on the child by declaring that the father was a legitimate Jew
    or gentile. In the latter case, the child took its status from its mother and was a Jew
    of her social ranking (*Kidd.* 74a; see p. 131 n. 1 above). Note the importance of
    establishing/knowing paternity in all these rulings.
2   Cf. *Kidd.* 69a-b for an explanation of these classes based on the descriptions in
    Ezra.
3   But see *Kidd.* 4.3 for the view that assured stock may not marry doubtful stock,
    and doubtful stock may not marry with doubtful stock.
4   Cf. Ezekiel's characterization of the priests as ones who 'shall teach my people the
    difference between the holy and the common and cause them to discern between
    the unclean and the clean' (44.22). Also Philo: 'The rights and duties of the priest-
    hood are of a special kind, and the office demands an even tenor of blamelessness
    from birth to death' (*Spec. Leg.* 1.102).

priestly privilege both for her and the children, see below), he was allowed to marry only Israelites of unblemished ancestry and the daughters of priests or Levites (*Kidd.* 3.12). She was not, however, allowed to marry a bastard or a *nathin* (*Yeb.* 8.3).

A priest's daughter was allowed to marry a priest as long as she was not a harlot or 'profaned' (Lev. 21.7).[1] The prohibition on harlots applied to the woman if she had engaged in illicit sexual relations at any time in her life for 'a harlot is profane in body and soul, even if she has discarded her trade and assumed a decent and chaste demeanour' (*Spec. Leg.* 1.102). Philo equated her permanent loss of privilege with the case of priests who were barred from holding office on account of some natural or inflicted physical defect:

> It would be foolish if, while the bodily scars which wounds leave behind them, marks of misfortune and not of depravity preclude one from the priesthood, the women who have sold their personal charms not only under compulsion but some-times by free and deliberate choice, should, just because of a belated and reluctant repentance, pass straight from their lovers to wedlock with priests and exchange the stews for a lodging in holy ground (*Spec. Leg.* 1.103).

Similarly, a woman who had been taken captive in war was forbidden to a priest, for it was assumed that she would have suffered sexual connections at the hands of her captors and so was placed on the same level as the harlot (*Ket.* 2.9; *Yeb.* 6.5; cf. *Ant.* 13.288f.; *Sukk.* 4.9). A woman who was sterile was also not allowed to marry a priest (*Yeb.* 6.5).

Only a virgin of unblemished ancestry was permitted to marry a high priest (Lev. 21.13-15), for 'the view of the law was that the greater sanctity and purity required of the latter in all other matters should be extended to his choice of marriage partner' (*Spec. Leg.* 1.109). According to Philo, this

---

1 The biblical terms חלל זונה were later interpreted to refer respectively to a proselyte, a freed woman, a seduced woman and the daughter of an illicit priestly marriage (*Yeb.* 6.5; *Sifra Lev.* 2.7; 47b). It is probable, however, that most interpreted the terms at face value to mean prostitute and a woman who had been seduced or in any other way lost her virginity. See, for example, Jos. *Ant.* 3.276; 4.245. According to Ezekiel, she also had to be a virgin (44.22), but in the Torah this was only required of those taken in marriage by high priests (Lev. 21.13-14).

ruling not only barred the non-virgin from marriage with a high priest but also the woman who had been betrothed to another 'even though her body [was] that of a maid intact' (*Spec. Leg.* 1.107). The Tannaim further restricted the concept of 'virgin' to girls who were between the ages of twelve and twelve and a half years (*Yeb.* 6.4).

It is interesting to note that Philo saw two reasons for the ruling that only virgins were permitted to join with high priests. While his first reason, that 'the holy seed may pass into pure and untrodden soil', was simply a restatement of the biblical concern for purity, his second had no scriptural authority and throws an interesting light on the whole ideology behind virgin-marriages. He wrote that,

> by mating with souls entirely innocent and unperverted, they [that is, successive high priests] may find it easy to mould the characters and dispositions of their wives, for the minds of virgins are easily influenced and attracted to virtue and very ready to be taught. But she who has had experience of another husband is naturally less amenable to instruction (*Spec. Leg.* 1.105-106).

A woman of impaired priestly stock (see below) was not allowed to marry a high priest or even a common priest (*Kidd.* 4.6), and in this respect was deemed of lower status than the Israelite woman. The rules which governed the prohibited/permitted unions of the latter were the same as those which applied to the woman of unimpaired priestly stock.

We shall now look briefly at those women of non-priestly and non-Israelite stock. A freedwoman and a female proselyte were forbidden to marry priests,[1] but they could join with Levites and Israelites (*Kidd.* 4.1; cf. 4.7; *Bikk.* 1.5). Those with grave 'social' blemishes, such as the daughters of an incestuous or adulterous union, could only marry men of similar impure ancestry, proselytes, or freed slaves (*Kidd.* 3.12; 4.1; *Yeb.* 2.4; 8.3; 9.2-3; *Makk.* 3.1). The same ruling applied to those who were foundlings or fatherless and could not establish their ancestry. These were also barred from marriage

---

1 The former was assumed to have had sexual connections with her master while the latter was always considered by the rabbis to have led a loose life prior to her conversion. See above, p. 137 n. 4.

with legitimate Israelites on the grounds that they might, without being aware of it, enter into an incestuous union with a relative and so unwittingly pollute the holy seed (*Kidd.* 73a).

These then, in brief, were the rules which governed the question of marriage between the various categories of people who comprised Jewish society in the days of the Tannaim. If the rules were broken serious consequences ensued, both for the individuals concerned and for their descendants. Thus, women of pure ancestry who polluted themselves by marriage with members of low status groups were punished by loss of privilege and their children were forced to assume the lower status of their fathers. Woman who suffered grave 'social' blemishes and who attempted to marry into higher status groups were punished by flagellation and their unions were deemed mere concubinage.[1] We shall pause to look in slightly greater detail at the consequences of prohibited intermarriage.

> Wherein does a priest differ from a woman from the priestly stock?... She may impair her priestly rights but he cannot impair his priestly rights [by marrying one of impaired stock] (*Sot.* 3.7).

Thus, if a priest entered into a forbidden union, only his children were affected (children followed the status of the inferior parent, *Kidd.* 3.12). His right to function as a priest was unimpaired.[2] Such, however, was not the case for a woman of priestly stock. If she married a man who was not eligible for marriage into the priestly caste, she immediately forfeited her right to eat of the Heave-Offering (Lev. 22.12; *Yeb.* 7.1f.). This loss of priestly privilege applied even if she married an Israelite, even though such a union was not technically forbidden (*Ter.* 7.2). The reason for the difference between the man and the woman was that the latter had only an indirect claim to the privileges of the priesthood through her father or her husband. (Hence she was always described as the wife or daughter of a priest, whereas he was simply a priest.) Should her connection with a priestly male be severed—in this

---

1 In the rabbinic sense of the word. See p. 130 n. 2 above.
2 Such was the case only with a common priest. A high priest could impair his rights by marrying an unfit woman. See *Ant.* 13.288f.; *Kidd.* 66a; *Sukk.* 4.9.

instance by marriage with a non-priest—she lost her right to eat of the Heave-Offering.[1] She could regain the right if her marriage ended in divorce or widowhood, for she could then return to her father's house and re-establish her priestly connections. She could only do this, however, if the marriage had produced no offspring (Lev. 22.13). If there were children, 'the mother must take her place with her children. For sons and daughters belong to the house of the male parent and carry with them into it the mother also' (*Spec. Leg.* 1.130; cf. *Nidd.* 5.3).[2]

If a woman of impure descent married a priest, her sons and their male descendents were forever forbidden to hold priestly office (*Kidd.* 4.1, 77a-b), and her daughters were not allowed to marry priests (*Kidd.* 4.6). In all cases of valid but sinful marriage (for example, that of an Israelite woman with a bastard or *nathin*), the children followed the status of the inferior parent (*Kidd.* 3.12).[3] Where the union was mere concubinage (as, for example, between a bond-woman and an Israelite), the offspring followed the mother (*ibid.*).

All these laws were designed to preserve the purity of the higher social castes. The fact that the promise of messianic salvation was only held out to Israelites of unblemished ancestry (*Kidd.* 70b) meant that those who were privileged to belong to these groups would not lightly consider intermarriage with lower-status individuals. They would also be eager to preserve their purity for reasons of a more practical nature: only families who maintained an unblemished ancestry were entitled to the full civil rights enjoyed by all legitimate Israelites.[4] Families of pure descent therefore had much to lose by marriage into the lower social groups. To avoid all dan-

---

1 Cf. *Ter.* 8a, 'If a [priest's] wife [non-priestly, but entitled to heave offering through her husband] was eating heave offering and they came and said to her, "Thy husband is dead", or "He has divorced thee"; and so too with a [priest's] slave [Lev. 22.11], if he was eating heave offering and they came and said to him, "Thy master is dead", or "He has sold thee to an Israelite" . . . they had to stop eating forthwith'.

2 Cf. *Yeb.* 7.5 where a priest's daughter who has been violated is only deprived of her right to eat of the Heave Offering if she was rendered pregnant.

3 According to *Makk.* 3.1 the individuals who entered into such forbidden unions were also to be punished by flagellation.

4 For details of these civil rights, see Jeremias, *Jerusalem in the Time of Jesus*, pp. 206f.

ger of contracting such polluting unions, the genealogies of prospective sons-in-law and daughters-in-law were carefully examined before marriage (*Kidd.* 71b). Each individual was expected to know at least his immediate ancestors and the tribe to which he belonged. Thus, for example the apostle Paul was able to give his social status as 'an Israelite, a descendant of Abraham, a member of the tribe of Benjamin' (Rom. 11.1; cf. Phil. 3.5). Some individuals could trace their line of descent back through several generations as, for example, Tobit who styled himself as 'the son of Tobiel, the son of Hananiel, the son of Aduel, the son of Gabael, the son of Raphael, the son of Raguel, of the seed of Asiel, of the tribe of Naphtali' (Tob. 1.1). Women were also required to know their pedigree. Thus the heroine of the book of Judith was described as 'the daughter of Merari, the son of Ox, the son of Joseph, the son of Oziel, the son of Elkiah, the son of Ananias,... [through nine more generations]' (Jdt. 8.1) and as belonging to the tribe of Simeon (9.2). More simply, the prophetess Anna was described by the Evangelist as 'the daughter of Phanuel, of the tribe of Asher' (Lk. 2.36).

As we have already noted, particular care was taken to preserve the purity of priests. Before a woman could be taken in marriage by a priest she had to have her pedigree investigated to ensure that 'her parents and grandparents and ancestors are equally pure, highly distinguished for the excellence of their conduct and lineage' (*Spec. Leg.* 1.101). If she claimed to be a woman of priestly stock, then her husband-to-be was obliged to trace her family back to her great-great-grandparents, on both her mother's and father's side (*Kidd.* 4.4). If she were of Israelite or levitic stock, he had to trace her descent back one more generation (*ibid.*). There was, however, no need to investigate her pedigree if her father was known to have ministered at the Temple or held any public office (*Kidd.* 4.5).[1] According to Josephus, the details of her ancestry were to be found in a special archive which contained a record of all the priestly genealogies (*Con. Ap.* 1.30f.; cf. *Vita* 1-6). This archive was apparently kept at the Temple in Jerusalem

---

1 For a man to qualify for any of these offices, the family's purity would already have been established (cf. *Kidd.* 4.5).

(*Sifre Num. Korah* 116 on 18.7).[1]

In addition to the priestly archive, there would also seem to have been some written records kept of the genealogies of lay families for in the Mishnah we read of the existence of a 'family register at Jerusalem' (*Yeb.* 4.13) whose exclusive concern, according to later traditions, lay with non-priestly families (*y. Taan.* 4.2; 68a). The Christian writer Julius Africanus also referred to written lay genealogies which, he claimed, were destroyed by Herod in an attempt to hide his non-Israelite origins.[2] Even if we assume that these records only covered a small proportion of the population (it would have been a tremendous undertaking to register the genealogical details of every individual in the country), they would at least have provided the means of checking the genealogical claims of some of the leading lay families in Graeco-Roman Palestine.

Thus far we have seen the way in which men investigated the pedigree of their prospective brides—but did women (or their fathers) check the ancestry of their husbands-to-be? According to the Talmud, only men were obliged to make an investigation (*Kidd.* 76a), for the responsibility of ensuring the legitimacy of the proposed union, according to the rabbis, rested on their shoulders. It would, however, seem extremely unlikely that no check was made of the man's pedigree, especially in the case of the marriage of a priest's daughter or, indeed, of any woman of pure stock. To render meaningful the complex of laws which we have examined, a two-way investigation would have had to have been conducted. Evidence for the practice of examining the pedigree of the man as well as of the woman is furnished by the Mishnah:

> [If he said, 'Be thou betrothed to me] on the condition that I am a priest', and he was found to be a levite; or 'that I am a levite', and he was found to be a priest; or 'that I am a *nathin*', and he was found to be a bastard, or 'that I am a bastard', and he was found to be a *nathin*,... in all such

1 'Thus they said that there was a place behind the temple curtain where they checked priestly genealogies.' In *Con. Ap.* 1.33, Josephus speaks of the way in which diaspora Jews sent to Jerusalem for genealogical details. See *Kidd.* 4.5 which mentions 'the old archives at Sepphoris'.
2 *Letters to Aristides*, preserved in Eusebius, *HE* 1.7.13f.

cases... her betrothal is not valid. And so too if it was she
that deceived him (*Kidd.* 2.3).

Thus far in our survey of 'Whom to Marry?' we have seen
that the Jewish woman was not allowed to marry gentiles,
near kinsmen, or members of certain social groups, dependent
upon her own status. We may now turn to the second stage of
our examination and consider those marriage partners who
were permitted to the woman but not particularly favoured by
her, for although, as was stated earlier, a woman would do
anything rather than remain unmarried, certain considerations of a non-legalistic nature were, where possible, taken
into account when choosing her husband.

At the head of the list of ill-favoured partners came those
men who plied dishonourable or suspect trades. First among
these were publicans, tax-collectors, usurers and gamblers, all
of whom were despised by society at large (cf. Mt. 9.10; 11.19;
18.17; 21.31f.; Mk 2.15f.; Lk. 7.34; 15.1f.; 18.11; 19.7), to such
an extent that they were deprived of the basic civil rights to
which even bastards had access (*Sanh.* 3.3, 25b). It is doubtful
whether any upright Jewish family would ever consider marriage with this group of social outcasts. Another category of
professionals to whom social and legal stigma attached were
goldsmiths, flaxcombers, pedlars, weavers, tailors, barbers,
launderers, bloodletters and bath attendants, all of whom were
suspected (in rabbinic eyes at least) of immorality because
their work involved direct dealings with women (*Kidd.* 82a-b).
None of these was permitted to hold public office. Although
these men were not held in the same disdain as publicans and
tax-collectors, it is unlikely that they would have been considered particularly suitable marriage partners for Jewish
women of any social standing. In addition to these there were
trades which were considered repugnant but not dishonourable. Dung collectors, copper smelters and tanners fell into this
category, and the prospect of marriage with any of these
would have held little appeal for a Jewish woman. In fact, the
rabbis deemed these occupations to be so repugnant that they
granted the right of compulsory divorce to any woman who
had the misfortune to be married to either a dung collector, a
copper smelter or a tanner. All she had to say was, 'I thought I

could endure it, but now I cannot endure it' (*Ket.* 7.10).[1]
Finally, there were trades which were characterized in the
Mishnah as 'the crafts of robbers' (*Kidd.* 4.14). These included
ass and camel drivers, sailors, shopkeepers, physicians and
butchers, and marriage with any of these would have been
regarded as a poor alliance by the upper stratum of Jewish
society.

Consideration must also have been taken as to the man's
state of physical and mental health. If he had a serious defor-
mity or was stricken with some unsightly or contagious dis-
ease or was an 'imbecile' (a term used frequently in the Mishnah, presumably with reference to a variety of mental disor-
ders), he was unlikely to be considered the ideal husband.
According to the Mishnah, any man who was afflicted with
boils or polypi was 1, arded with particular distaste by the
woman (*Ket.* 7.10). With regard to the prospective husband's
general physical features we have no information, for
although the sources abound with descriptions of the beauty to
be desired in a woman (see Chapter 3 §C), they are silent as to
the features to be looked for in a man. The only opinion the
rabbis had on the subject was that a woman should not marry
a man who was of the same height and colour complexion as
herself (*Ber.* 45b), an opinion which doubtless had little bearing on the practical reality of choosing a husband. Similarly in
our male written and oriented sources, there is no attention
given as to the desired character traits in a husband, though
there are some statements to that effect regarding women.

The rabbis were very much opposed to marriage being
contracted between a young woman and an old man on the
grounds that a union of dissimilar ages created strife in the
home (*Yeb.* 44a, 101b). They also feared that since a girl could
not willingly accept one who was much older than herself, she
might be led into committing adultery (*Sanh.* 76a-b). Such
statements, however, while doubtless reflecting genuine rabbinic concern, may also have had little bearing on reality
where women could be used as alliance pawns and betrothed
at the wish of their fathers.

---

1 See below, however, p. 220, for the way in which the husband had still to be the one
who issued the *get*: a court might command him to divorce his wife, but it could not
force him so to do.

The rabbis were also opposed to individuals of disparate social backgrounds and wealth being married to one another as this too would create friction (*Kidd.* 49a, 70a; cf. *Con. Ap.* 2.199), but on this subject Pseudo-Phocylides wryly commented that 'a woman [does not] reject a bad man when he is rich' (l. 204). He did, however, advise men not to

> bring... as a wife into your home a bad and wealthy woman.
> You will be a slave of your wife because of the baneful dowry
> (ll. 199-200).

Finally, women in the rabbinic texts were urged never to contemplate marriage with an *'am ha-'aretz* (*Pes.* 49b). All of these negative considerations were intended to guide the woman towards finding a well-matched partner, and on this Ben Sira wrote:

> Three things hath my soul desired,
> And they are lovely in the sight of God and men:
> The concord of brethren and the friendship of neighbours,
> And a husband and wife suited to each other (25.1).

We may now turn to the final part of our survey and examine those unions which were not only permitted but also regarded with favour by society. There would seem to have been a particularly positive attitude toward non-incestuous endogamy, that is, marriage within the kin and tribal group which did not offend the levitical laws. Thus, for example, a part of Judith's virtue lay in the fact that she had married a man who was 'of her tribe and of her family' (Jdt. 8.2). The somewhat self-righteous Tobit included in his catalogue of virtuous deeds the fact that, 'when I became a man, I took a wife of the seed of our own family' (Tob. 1.9), and he advised his son to do similarly:

> take first a wife of the seed of thy father, take not a strange
> wife, which is not of thy father's tribe... Noah, Abraham,
> Isaac, Jacob, our fathers of old time, remember, my child,
> that they all took wives of their kinsmen and were blessed
> with children... Scorn not in thy heart thy brethren and the
> sons and daughters of thy people so as not to take one of them
> (4.12-13).

Within this framework of preferred endogamy, the marriage of closely related (though not incestuously prohibited) individuals was especially encouraged. We have already seen the way in which the Jews of Hellenistic Palestine engaged in uncle-niece marriage (p. 133). A more favoured union would, however, seem to have been that of first-cousin marriage. An indication of this preference is to be found in the book of *Jubilees*, whose author rewrote the biblical genealogies of the Patriarchs' ancestors almost without exception in terms of first-cousin marriage, a fact which he emphasized by the repeated formula of 'N. took to himself a wife, and her name was N., the daughter of his father's brother' (4.15). His obsession with fathers' brothers also suggests that marriages between the children of two sisters and cross cousins were not viewed with the same degree of favour as marriages between the children of two brothers.[1] Another indication of the very positive attitude toward cousin marriage is to be found in the book of Tobit, which tells the story of the seven successive husbands of Sarah who were fated to die on their wedding night, because, unbeknown to them, there existed one who had a prior claim to Sarah's hand in marriage: her cousin Tobias. According to this writer, therefore, cousin marriage was not simply a matter of preference. The words which Sarah's father, Raguel, addressed to Tobias make this fact clear:

> there is no man whom it appertaineth to take Sarah my daughter except thee, brother... I have not power to give her to another man than thee, because thou art my nearest kin... She is given to thee according to the decree of the book of Moses, and from heaven it hath been decreed that she is given to thee; take thy sister[2] (7.10f.; cf. 13.15).

The reasoning behind the practice of granting near kinsmen priority over other suitors was the desire to keep all prop-

---

1 The same phenomenon was noted by Hilma Granqvist in her survey of marriage conditions in the Palestinian village of Artas (*Marriage Conditions in a Palestinian Village*, pp. 74f.). She observed that where the relationship was reckoned with a woman as the connecting link, whether a man's bride is the daughter of his mother's sister, his mother's brother or his father's sister, then that union was not looked upon with so much favour. Compare this with the early biblical period when a key link in marriage arrangements was often a mother's brother. For the history and significance of the shift towards father's brother's daughter, and of mother's houses to father's houses, see Archer, *op. cit.*, p. 4.

2 For the term 'sister' being the usual form of address to a wife, see below.

erty within the family group.[1] When a woman married, she
and her dowry passed into her husband's household, and
marriage with a relative was an obvious means of ensuring
that this property was not removed from the family group.
Thus Philo recommended that husbands be,

> if possible, of the same family as the girl's, or if that cannot
> be, at any rate of the same ward[2] and tribe, in order that the
> portions assigned as dowry should not be alienated by inter-
> marriage with other tribes, but should retain the place given
> to them in the allotments originally made on the basis of
> tribes (*Spec. Leg.* 2.126).

The need to retain property within the family group was felt
so strongly by the author of the book of Tobit that he considered the marriage of closely related kin to be compulsory.
According to him, the failure of a father to marry his
daughter to a kinsman rendered him liable to death 'according to the book of Moses' (6.13). For this view, however, he had
no biblical or rabbinical authority. The Tannaim never considered such marriages obligatory.[3]

The advantage to the woman of marrying a kinsman was
that she enjoyed greater security than would otherwise have
been the case had she been married into an alien family group,
removed from the immediate protection of her father's house.
She would also have a wider community of interests with a
kinsman than with a stranger. Finally, we might note that
present-day Fellahin consider cousin-marriage to be especially advantageous by virtue of the fact that a cousin cannot
curse her husband's relatives because they are also her relatives[4]—a fact which may also have been taken into account by
the Jews of Hellenistic Palestine.

Although it is impossible to gauge how common the

---

1 We should be careful to distinguish between this case of near-kin marriage and
   the endogamy which was enforced in the case of a daughter inheriting property in
   the absence of male heirs (Num. 36.6f.). Here we are dealing with property in a
   father's lifetime, and the endogamy was preferred, not enforced.
2 In the Loeb edition of the *Special Laws*, Colson writes: 'This is a case in which
   Philo seems to adapt the law to contemporary conditions. We do not hear of δῆμοι
   in old Israel, but apparently a classification into φυλαί and δῆμοι was in force in
   Alexandria.'
3 For this, see Belkin, *op. cit.*, pp. 215f.
4 See Granqvist, *op. cit.*, pp. 68-69.

instances of near-kin marriage were, it is interesting to note
that the usual form of address between spouses was that of
'brother' to the husband and 'sister' to the wife (1 Kgs 13.30;
Songs 4.9, 10; 5.1; *Jub.* 27.14-17; Tob. 7.11, 15; 8.21; Esth. 15.9
[Additions to Esth. (D) v. 9]; *Gen. Apoc.* 2.9, 13; note also its use
in one of the Elephantine marriage contracts, *K.* 7.3-5). These
terms were normally reserved for members of the same clan,
who were conscious of the blood-bond which united them
(Gen. 13.8; 14.4; Lev. 21.10; Deut. 2.4, 8; 23.8; 1 Sam. 20.29).

To conclude our survey of those unions which were both
permitted and favoured, we shall look at the way in which
individuals preferred to marry within their own social groups
despite the fact that the laws which regulated intermarriage
allowed them greater mobility. The considerations which
encouraged caste endogamy were somewhat different to
those which lay behind the desire for near-kin marriage, and
so deserve a separate examination.

The tendency toward endogamous marriages was especially marked in priestly circles in consequence of this group's
desire for absolute purity. Thus, the biblical injunction, 'Do not
profane thy daughter to cause her to be a whore' (Lev. 19.29),
was interpreted by some to refer to a priest giving his daughter in marriage to a levite or an Israelite (*Sanh.* 76a). It would
seem to have been the custom—though not the rule—for
women of priestly stock (particularly those who were a part of
the priestly aristocracy of Jerusalem) to marry priests (cf.
Yeb. 62b). This was especially true of the daughters of high
priestly families (cf. *Pes.* 57a).[1] It is probable that the lay
nobility also practised some kind of caste endogamy, for they
jealously guarded their privileged position and in consequence
doubtless only married their daughters to fellow aristocrats.
Mention must also be made of such groups as the Pharisees
and Sadducees who, in consequence of their peculiar
community rules, would not have favoured marriages with
outsiders. In addition to considerations as to purity or
privilege, the simple question of suitability often determined
whether or not an individual married outside of his or her

---

1 For examples of caste endogamy among priestly and high priestly families, see
   Stern, 'Aspects of Jewish Society', in *Compendia Rerum Iudaicarum ad Novum
   Testamentum*, II, pp. 582f., and Jeremias, *op. cit.*, pp. 154f., 218f.

own social group. It has already been noted that the rabbis frowned upon alliances between individuals of disparate social backgrounds on the grounds that such unions created domestic strife. They therefore urged women not to contemplate marriage with a member of a higher caste, but to be content with a partner who was of the same social rank. The rabbis encouraged caste endogamy by ruling that

> in an advantage of birth [for example, if he says 'On condition that I am a *mamzer*', and is found to be a *nathin*], all agree that she is not betrothed. What is the reason? 'I do not want a shoe too large for my foot' (*Kidd.* 49a).

Finally, in addition to considerations as to social background, the favoured marriage partner was also expected to be a man of some learning. We have already learnt in a previous section of the great importance which was attached to education by the Jews of Graeco-Roman Palestine and of the ever widening gulf which existed between the educated Torah-observing citizen and the *'am ha'aretz*. In consequence of this, it was not considered fit for a woman of any standing to marry an ignoramus. Thus, even Ben Sira, who had scant regard for daughters and who viewed their marriage as merely the end to a father's troubles, advised that she be married to an educated man:

> Marry thy daughter and sorrow will depart,
> But bestow upon her a man of understanding (7.25).

To conclude: the desire for racial and religious purity was the explicit motivation for most of the Hebrew legislation on marriage. This desire created rigid divisions in Jewish society of which people were very aware. To marry beneath one's station not only affected the individual, but also affected the whole family unit. In consequence of this, the Talmud declared that

> He who takes a wife who is not fitting for him, the Writ stigmatizes him as though he ploughed the whole world with salt (*Kidd.* 70a).

According to the rabbis, all unfit marriages were registered in a heavenly book by God and the prophet Elijah:

> Elijah writes and the Holy One, blessed be he, attests: 'Woe to

him who disqualifies his seed, blemishes his family and him
who takes to wife one who is not fit for him, Elijah binds and
the Holy One, blessed be He, flagellates' (*ibid.*).

Thus it was that when the virgins of Israel went forth to dance
in the vineyards, they were represented as having cried out to
the men looking on:

Young man, lift up thine eyes and see what thou wouldst
choose for thyself. Set not thine eyes on beauty, but set thine
eyes on family (*Taan.* 4.8).[1]

B. *Betrothal*

A man may betroth a woman either by his own act or by that
of his agent; and a woman may become betrothed either by
her own act or by that of an agent. A man may give his
daughter in betrothal while she is still in her girlhood [while
still a *na'arah*] either by his own act or that of his agent
(*Kidd.* 2.1).

Thus did the Tannaim state the legal competence of the parties concerned to initiate a contract of betrothal—a contract
which by the late Hellenistic period was considered a necessary preliminary to marriage proper. Of interest to us in the
present discussion of the first marriage of a virgin (which, as
we shall see, would usually have taken place before the girl
reached the age of twelve and a half) is the mishnah's last
statement regarding the betrothal of a minor. As the mishnah
states—and as was demonstrated earlier in this book—a
minor was not permitted by law to contract her own betrothal.
That power rested with her father in consequence of the
absolute authority vested in him as *pater familias* (see above,
pp. 49ff.). Only a *bogereth* was permitted control over her own
betrothal. The full implication of this ruling will be realized as
we examine the age at which women in Graeco-Roman
Palestine were usually married.

Among the peoples of the ancient Near East, marriage for
both men and women occurred at an early age, and in this the

1 This custom had in fact ceased by the period under consideration (see Chapter 1
§E, especially p. 120 n. 5). Nevertheless, the sentiment in the mishnah's record of
the event is pertinent.

Jews were no exception (cf. Sir. 7.25; *T. Levi* 9.10). The opti-
mum age advised for men by the Tannaim was eighteen
(*Aboth* 5.21) or at most twenty years (*Kidd.* 29b).[1] No specific
age is mentioned for women, but it may be assumed that they
married when much younger, for the Talmud frequently
refers to girls of pre-menstrual age already living with their
husbands (e.g. *Nidd.* 1.4; 10.1, 64b; *Ket.* 6a-b). That the norm
was for girls to marry about the time of puberty is further
demonstrated by a ruling of the Essenes which expressly forbade cohabitation until after a girl had menstruated at least
three times and so proved that she was ready for and capable
of conception (*BJ* 2.161). We might also note the words used by
the righteous mother in *4 Maccabees* in respect of her
marriage, that 'I lived with husband *all the days of my youth*'
(18.9).

This custom of early marriage for women has persisted
down to the twentieth century among oriental peasant communities. Thus Granqvist, in her survey of the marriage conditions in the Palestinian village of Artas, conducted in the
1920s, recorded the way in which brides were often too small
to lean over household ovens, or too small to ride on the horses
traditionally used for the wedding procession. She also
observed the way in which children were sometimes born to
women who had not yet seen their first menstrual blood.[2] We
may well imagine that such was often the case in Graeco-
Roman Palestine also.

The reason why women were married at such a young age
lay in the advantage it had to offer to men. A young bride
benefited her husband for a longer period of time than would
an older woman, both in respect of her labour and of child-
bearing—a consideration neatly captured for us in the following Fellahin saying:

> The little one will be mature when the older one is crippled
> with age... How clever is he who takes young brides. He has
> got the better of the merchants.[3]

---

1 Advice attributed in the Talmud to Sages who lived c. 70 CE. Cf. *Compendia*, II,
   p. 755.
2 Granqvist, *op. cit.*, pp. 33f., especially p. 38 n. 1.
3 Quoted by Granqvist, p. 43.

Given the desire for young brides, early marriage was also something to be recommended from the father's point of view. If a daughter was allowed to pass her early teens without having secured a husband, the task of arranging a good match for her would be rendered far more difficult. Another consideration was the preservation of a daughter's purity—a duty which, as we have seen, was regarded as the father's responsibility (see above, pp. 25ff., 111ff.). Marriage at about the age of puberty was considered the most obvious and efficacious way of ensuring that a girl was a virgin when she went to her husband—a fact which benefited both him and her father (and satisfied concerns regarding paternity). Thus the Talmud declared:

> He who... arranges their marriage [that is, his children's] just before they attain puberty, of him the Bible says, 'You shall know that your tent is safe' (Job 5.24) (*Yeb.* 62b).

Having seen that early marriage was the norm, we may now return to our original mishnah and appreciate that of the betrothal arrangements listed there, only the last one would in fact have had any reality for the majority of women in Graeco-Roman Palestine (at least in so far as first marriage was concerned). That such indeed was the case is clearly demonstrated by the advice which Philo had to offer regarding the preliminary steps to be taken by a man who wished to marry. He wrote:

> If indeed you have any legitimate feelings of love in your soul for the maiden, go to her parents if they are alive, and if they are not, go to her brothers or her guardians[1] or to any other persons who are in charge of her, and revealing to them your affection toward her... ask her in marriage and implore them not to consider you unworthy (*Spec. Leg.* 3.65-71).

Josephus also assumed that the normal procedure was for a man to approach a girl's father rather than the girl herself (*Con. Ap.* 2.200), and the book of Tobit nicely depicts the non-

---

1 Philo's mention of an *epitropos* is an addition to Tannaitic law and is presumably a reflection of his own environment. In the halakhah it was only the father or, in the event of his death, the mother or brothers who could give a girl in marriage. See Belkin, *op. cit.*, p. 22.

involvement of women in the negotiation of their own
betrothal and marriage (7.8-9; cf. *Jub.* 30.7; Deut. 22.16).
Finally, we might note *en passant* the opening formula which
was employed in each of the four marriage contracts from the
Jewish colony of Elephantine in Upper Egypt.[1] With slight
variations the introductory phrase is 'I [the groom] have come
to your house that you might give me your daughter N. in
marriage'.[2] Thus we see that a woman's betrothal was normally controlled and arranged by someone other than herself.
We may, however, ask whether her consent was necessary to
make the contract legally binding. It would appear that even
this was not required, for the Mishnah states that a girl
(unlike a boy) could be betrothed from the day that she was
born (*Kidd.* 3.5). Not surprisingly, the various marriage contracts which are preserved from Elephantine and, more
importantly, the Judaean Desert, contain no expression of the
bride's consent (excepting P. *Mur.* 21—see below, p. 188), but
simply record the groom's declaration that 'She is my wife
and I her husband from this day for ever', a clause which
immediately followed the introductory formula mentioned
above and one which underlined the woman's passivity.[3] We
might also note the way in which only men were obliged to
make the required oral declarations of intent ('Behold thou art
consecrated unto me') at the betrothal ceremony (*Kidd.* 5b-
6a). The bride-to-be remained silent while her father
responded along the lines of, 'Today you shall be my son-in-
law' (cf. 1 Sam. 18.21). From a legal standpoint, therefore,
only the assent of the prospective husband and the person
having *potestas* over the bride were necessary to create a valid
deed of betrothal or marriage (*B.B.* 10.4). It is true that,

1 A Jewish military colony was established at Elephantine in the sixth century BCE
and continued in existence through to the fourth century. It left to us a body of
Aramaic papyri and ostraca which tell of the community's internal organization,
family relations, law, and religious and business practices. For a brief history of
the colony and a bibliography of the main collections of the documents, see conveniently Schürer, *op. cit.*, III.i, pp. 38-40.
2 *C.* 15.3; *K.* 2.3; *K.* 7.3. While the Elephantine community obviously cannot be
taken as representative of Jewish practice in Hellenistic Palestine, and indeed
the documents from that community evince considerable differences in practice,
it is interesting to note here the similarity in custom regarding betrothal and the
fundamental of *patria potestas*.
3 *C.* 15.4; *K.* 2.3-4; *K.* 7.4; *DJD*, II, 21.7.

presumably from a humanitarian point of view, later thinkers did urge that consideration be taken of the girl's wishes, encouraging the postponement of betrothal arrangements until such time as she was capable of saying, 'I want so-and-so' (*Kidd.* 41a; cf. 2b, 44a; *B.B.* 48b). In a sense, however, such an arrangement was nothing more than a formality in a society which was strictly patriarchal and one in which marriage was viewed primarily in terms of family interests rather than the individual. As Granqvist writes:

> So long as the forms of society remain unchanged, so long will the demand for the woman's consent to her own marriage be purely formal—without any real import. When a woman in the last minute is asked as to her will she is already prepared by her people who have talked to her on the subject until she feels there is nothing else for her to do but to bow to the inevitable—to Fate. A woman has no external power. What could she do against her family? She is completely in their hands. If she does not wish to be expelled from society she cannot, nor will she, break with them who are and will remain all her life her natural protectors, her father and brothers.[1]

It is in the light of these remarks that the oft-quoted 'consent' of Rebecca to her marriage with Isaac is to be viewed.[2]

We may now turn to the means by which betrothal was effected. *Kidd.* 1.1 states that: 'A woman is acquired in three ways: by money, by deed, and/or (ו) by intercourse'.[3] A problem immediately presents itself with this mishnah. Does it mean that a woman was acquired by any one of the three elements listed, that is, 'by money, deed *or* intercourse', or should it be interpreted as meaning that she could only be acquired by a combination of all three, that is, 'by money, deed *and* intercourse'? It is likely that its original meaning was the latter, for

---

1 *Op. cit.*, pp. 56-57.

2 Gen. 24.56, 'And they [Laban and Bethuel] called Rebekah and said unto her, "Wilt thou go with this man?" and she said, "I will go"'. Significantly, this report of Rebekah's 'consent' comes after the account of the actual marriage arrangements as finalized between Laban, Bethuel, and Abraham's servant ('Behold, Rebekah is before thee, take her and go, and let her be thy master's son's wife', v. 51). According to the context of the passage, it is moreover possible that Rebekah was simply consenting to a change in travel plans.

3 האב זכאי בבת בקדושיה. בכסף בשטר. Cf. *Ket.* 4.4, האשה נקנית בשלש דרכים בכסף בשטר ובביאה ובביאה.

the book of Tobit speaks of the way in which all three together constituted the marriage of Sarah and Tobias (7.13-15; 8.1).[1] In support of this interpretation Epstein points to the parallel formula of 'by money, by deed and by usucaption' employed in the Mishnah to describe the manner in which realty was conveyed. At least two of these elements were required to make such a transaction valid (*Kidd.* 26a; see further the conveyance of property recorded by Jeremiah which involved all three elements, Jer. 32.9-10). Basing himself upon this parallel, Epstein concluded that a combination of money, writ and use was necessary to conclude a legal conveyance, whether it be of realty or of a wife.[2] While the formulae may be parallel, we should note that Epstein is incorrect in his labelling of marriage as a legal conveyance of women. Women could not be bought and sold like real estate. The money element in *Kidd.* 1.1 and that of the mishnahs dealing with property served very different functions. The former was a compensation payment (see below) and the latter was a purchase price, carrying with it full rights of ownership. This fact does not, however, invalidate Epstein's basic argument that all three elements were necessary for both marriage and property conveyance.

Such, however, could only have been the original meaning of *Kidd.* 1.1. Later halakhists unanimously read it as, '[a woman] is acquired *either* by money, *or* by deed, *or* by intercourse' (t. *Kidd.* 1.2; y. *Kidd.* 58b). The reason for this difference between the earlier and the later halakhah was due to the way in which the character of marriage changed in the course of the period under consideration. In its original meaning, *Kidd.* 1.1 (a mishnah of some antiquity as is evident from the way in which it was treated as a text for discussion by the Shammaites and Hillelites) referred to a period when little distinction was made between betrothal and full marriage, and when there was often only a negligible time-

---

1 Belkin (*op. cit.*, p. 242 n. 82) argues that this was a special case due to its being an instance of agnatic marriage. I see no reason why the procedure should be different for the marriage of near kin than for any other union (excepting the levirate where special rules applied), especially given the fact that near kin marriage, as we have seen (above, pp. 146ff.) may well have been the norm.

2 *The Jewish Marriage Contract*, pp. 11-12. We might also note that the Karaites had a tradition that all three elements together constituted marriage.

lapse between the two ceremonies. (Thus, for example, Tob. 7.10–8.9 records the way in which Sarah's marriage to Tobias was both arranged and consummated the same day.) For those occasions when there was to be a time-lapse, the custom had arisen of writing a *shetar*, that is, a simple betrothal deed whereby the man protected his claim to the woman. The writing of a *shetar* gradually became standard procedure for all betrothals and came to be viewed as a necessary instrument of cohabitation by which a father granted his future son-in-law the right to sexual relations with his daughter in exchange for monies received (that is, the bride-price).[1] The transaction was concluded by the act of intercourse. Three elements, therefore, constituted the legal acquisition of a wife. Such at least was the understanding of the authors of our mishnah who, in response to the period's lack of meaningful differentiation between betrothal and marriage, treated them as a single transaction and so lumped the elements of money, deed and intercourse together under the general heading of 'the acquisition of a woman'.[2]

In the course of time, however, as Jewish society developed different moral and social profiles, the act and state of betrothal and of marriage received sharper definition and were rendered more separate. In the first place it was decreed that a definite period of time should elapse between betrothals and the wedding ceremony. In the case of a virgin, she was granted a full twelve months 'after the husband has demanded her... wherein to provide for herself' (*Ket.* 5.2). During this time the couple were not permitted sexual relations (*Eduy.* 4.7; *Gitt.* 8.9) despite the fact that the bride-price continued to be paid at the time of betrothal (see below). The girl remained in her father's house and under his control until her wedding day. The actual ceremonies of betrothal and marriage became more elaborate and formalized, and society

---

1 Cf. Tob. 7.14 where Raguel wrote an 'instrument of cohabitation' for Tobias and so gave him his daughter Sarah to wife 'according to the decree of the law of Moses'. Consummation of the union followed immediately. This document was probably an elaboration of the earlier *shetar* but served the same function of granting and protecting the rights of the groom. For the fact that the bride-price also had the function of a compensation payment, see below pp. 164-65.

2 Compare the wording of this old mishnah with, for example, that of *Ket.* 4.4 (quoted above, p. 155 n. 3).

signalled the difference between the two contracts by the
introduction of a חופה (*chupah*) into the wedding ceremony
which symbolized the final passage of the woman into her
husband's control (see below).[1] Only after the חופה ceremony
were the couple deemed properly man and wife (*Ket.* 56a). In
line with these various developments, the Tannaim frequently
employed a new term for 'betrothal', replacing the scriptural
word *erusin* with *kiddushin* which meant 'sanctification'.[2]
They similarly stressed the new distinction between betrothal
and marriage by substituting the term האשה מתקדשת ('a woman
becomes sanctified, betrothed') for the older formula of האשה
נקנית ('a woman is acquired'). One final development was the
introduction of a written marriage contract, the כתובה
(*kethubah*). This document, which was required for all lawful
unions, recorded the various financial obligations which a
man undertook in respect of his wife and their children (see
next section). Although not effective until after their marriage, it was nevertheless drawn up at the time of betrothal in
consequence of the older practice of writing the *shetar* at that
time and because it contained the necessary statement of
intent which could replace the older deed.[3]

It was in the light of these various developments that later
halakhists were obliged to reinterpret the older tradition contained in *Kidd.* 1.1. No longer could it be read in its original
meaning, for intercourse as a means of betrothal or
acquisition was no longer applicable, and the *kethubah* had
effectively replaced the *shetar*. As the mishnah could not
simply be discarded, however, the rabbis decided to place the
three elements in the context of alternatives. Although
appearing to give equal sanction to each of the three elements,
its reformulation was in fact but a technical or legalistic
compromise, for in practice only the first of the three, that is,
money, had any real application. Intercourse and deed, as

1 For the way in which the חופה was in fact a nuptial chamber and not a canopy as is
   normally assumed, see Chapter 2 §D.
2 For the significance of their selection of this word, see B. Cohen, 'On the theme of
   betrothal in Jewish and Roman Law', *AAJR* 18 (1948-49), p. 77 and the same
   author's *Jewish and Roman Law, A Comparative Study*, pp. 289-90. For the meaning of *erusin* and *arusah*, see Neufeld, *Ancient Hebrew Marriage Laws*, p. 142
   n. 3.
3 Cf. *DJD*, II, 20.3; 21.8; 115.3 (Appendix I).

means of betrothal, were neither morally nor socially
endorsed (though they did remain legal). For a considerable
part of our period, therefore, the usual form of betrothal was
by money—either in earlier days as a direct financial
transaction or later, as we shall see, as a kind of deferred
payment for which the *kethubah* stood guarantee.

In the early biblical period the amount paid as bride-price or
mohar by a man to his future father-in-law[1] would appear to
have been a matter for negotiation (see for example Gen.
34.12). Apart from money, the *mohar* could consist of payment in kind or services rendered as agreed between the parties. Thus David secured Michal by furnishing Saul with the
hundred Philistines' foreskins which the king had demanded
as the price of his daughter (1 Sam. 18.25; 2 Sam. 3.14);
Othniel acquired Achsah by rising to Caleb's challenge of 'He
that smiteth Kiriath-Sepher and taketh it, to him will I give
my daughter to wife' (Josh. 15.16); while Jacob laboured seven
years to obtain the hand of Rachael (Gen. 29.27). By the seventh century, however, it would seem that the *mohar* had
assumed a more definite and uniform character, at least in
respect of the price demanded for virgins.[2] This may be
inferred from Deut. 22.29 which declared that a man guilty of
the seduction or rape of an unbetrothed virgin must marry his
victim and pay her father the sum of fifty shekels (lit. 'fifty of
silver', חמשים כסף). That this figure was in fact the girl's bride-
price may be seen from the context of the passage itself and
from the earlier ruling of Exod. 22.15-16 (to which Deut. 22.29
was a supplement—see above, pp. 51-54) which demanded
that the man pay monies of unspecified amount 'according to
the price of virgins' (כמהר הבתולה). The Deuteronomic legislators simply updated the Covenant Code's ruling by setting
an actual figure on the מהר בתולה—a figure which presumably
was in accordance with the custom of the day. It would seem,

---

1 Or brother-in-law where earlier institutions lingered. See Archer, 'The Virgin
and the Harlot in the Writings of Formative Judaism', *History Workshop Journal* 24 (1987), p. 4, and above Chapter 1 (p. 21 n. 3).
2 With regard to the bride-price of non-virgins, the Bible offers little information.
It is likely that widows and divorcees did receive a *mohar* (see, e.g. Hos. 3.2), but
we remain in the dark as to the amount, though probably it was less than for a virgin. Such at least was the case in the later period (cf. *Ket.* 1.2).

therefore, that by the seventh century the bride-price of a virgin was reckoned at a fixed minimum of fifty silver shekels.[1] The amount could, of course, be greater than this, depending upon the social and economic standing of the families concerned and the personal qualities of the bride-to-be. This amount apparently remained the minimum requirement for a virgin's *mohar* throughout the subsequent centuries, for, in line with the Deuteronomic figure, the Tannaim set the virgin's price at 200 *zuzin* (*Ket.* 1.2; 4 *zuzin* = 1 sacred shekel) with the postscript that 'if a man is minded to add thereto, even 100 *minas*, he may do so' (*Ket.* 5.1).[2] There was, however, one significant difference between the Tannaitic statement and the earlier legislation: where the Bible had employed the term *mohar* to designate the bride-price, the Mishnah now used the word *kethubah*, a word which literally meant 'written instrument' but which had specific application to the marriage deed which, as was noted above, originated in the post-biblical period.[3] To understand the reasons for this change in terminology it will be necessary to quote at length a passage from the Talmud:

> Rab Judah says in olden times they would write 200 *zuzin* for a virgin and one hundred for a widow (clause A), but they would grow old and would not marry wives (B). Whereupon Simeon ben Shetah came and instituted that all the husband's property should be lien for her *kethubah* (C). The following Tannaitic tradition supports it. In olden times, they would write 200 *zuzin* for a virgin and 100 for a widow (A), but they would grow old and would not marry wives (B). Whereupon it was instituted that it should be kept in her father's house (D). Yet if he became wroth with her, he could

1 Further proof for this may be found in Deut. 22.19 which prescribed a hundred shekel fine, that is, double the price of virginity, for the man who falsely accused his wife of being a non-virgin at marriage. (Note that a double penalty for a thief was not uncommon in ancient law; cf. Exod. 22.3-8.)

2 He may not, however, assign less than 200 *zuzin*, for such, according to R. Meir, was accounted fornication. The Tannaim also set a minimum figure of one *mina* (half the virgin's price) on the price of a widow. That these sums were actually employed is evidenced by the deeds from the Judaean desert (20.5; 115.5) and by a contract of remarriage from the Babatha archive (Yadin, 'Expedition D', *IEJ* 12 [1962], p. 245). See further below, §C, for details regarding the Babatha archive and the Judaean Desert deeds.

3 For an examination of the *kethubah*'s date of origin, see next section.

say to her, Go to thy *kethubah*. It was therefore further
ordained that it should be put in the house of her father-in-
law. Rich women would make of it gold and silver baskets,
poor ones would make of it brass grape containers (E). Still,
in a fit of anger, he would say to her, Take thy *kethubah* and
go. Thereupon came Simeon ben Shetah and instituted that
he write her, 'All my property be security for the payment of
her (thy) *kethubah*' (C) (*Ket.* 82b).

The Palestinian Talmud has a somewhat modified account
of the same tradition, and again deserves to be quoted in full:

> In early times her *kethubah* remained with her parents and
> he found it easy to divorce her (A). So they decreed that the
> *kethubah* remain with her husband, yet he could easily
> divorce her (B); so they decreed that a man should buy with
> his wife's *kethubah* cups and bowls and pots (C) ... and they
> later decreed that a man should do business with his wife's
> *kethubah*, for, as he uses his wife's *kethubah* in business
> and loses it, he will find it difficult to divorce her (D). And
> this is what Simeon ben Shetah instituted ..., that a man put
> his wife's *kethubah* into his business (y. *Ket.* 8.11, 32b).

Finally, the Tosefta provides a brief summary of the tradition:

> In olden times when her *kethubah* was at her father's
> house, it was easy for him to divorce her (A). Therefore did
> Simeon ben Shetah institute that her *kethubah* be with her
> husband and that he write 'All my property be lien and
> guarantee for the money of thy *kethubah*' (B) (t. *Ket.* 12.1).

Taken together, these three texts yield a reasonably detailed
account of the transition from bride-price proper to *kethubah*,
and indicate that the reasons for this transition were both economic and moral. Four stages led up to the enactment of
Simon ben Shetah (leading Pharisee at the time of Alexander
Jannaeus and Queen Alexandra Salome; fl. 90–70 BCE). In the
first stage the bride-price was paid directly to the girl's father
and remained in his possession. The only difference between
this and the biblical practice was that the transaction was
recorded in the marriage contract (*babli*, A). In the next stage
the bride-price was still paid to the girl's father but this time
he did not actually possess it. He merely held the money as
trustee for the bride (*babli*, D; *yerushalmi*, A; *tosefta*, A). Thus
the husband did not completely lose sight of his money, for

ultimately he or his children, as heirs to the bride, would get it back. This change in practice was intended to provide an inducement to men to marry—apparently the outright loss of the bride-price had been causing them to think twice about entering into marriage (*babli*, B). The next stage, which was designed as a further inducement, allowed the man himself to act as trustee of his wife's *mohar* (*babli*, E; *yerushalmi*, C). However, while this meant that the bride-price remained in his home rather than being transferred to his father-in-law, the change again only availed him in the long term. In the fourth stage the man was provided with a more immediate incentive for making the initial outlay in that he was permitted usufruct of his wife's *mohar* during her lifetime (*yerushalmi*, D). While these various developments presumably did much to encourage marriage, they failed to solve the basic problem faced by most prospective husbands: how to raise the minimum but considerable amount demanded as the price of a virgin. In other words, the young suitor still had to have 200 *zuzin* in his possession before he approached the girl's father—a fact which forced many to delay their marriage indefinitely (*babli*, B). The final stage in the transition from *mohar* to *kethubah* was designed to combat this problem. By the enactment of Simeon ben Shetah, men were released from the obligation of furnishing a payment prior to marriage. They simply had to promise delivery of the *mohar* at some future date, and that promise was substantiated by a lien clause in the marriage contract (*babli*, C; *tosefta*, B).

Apart from economic motives, these various changes were prompted, according to the Tannaim, by a desire to render divorce more difficult. Under the original system, when the *mohar* passed completely out of the husband's hands, a man had nothing (financially) to lose if he divorced his wife, and so he could quite readily contemplate such action. Gradually, however, in consequence of the changes traced above, it became more and more to his advantage not to divorce her. Such was especially the case following the enactment of Simeon ben Shetah, when the 200 *zuzin* was only paid to the woman (or her father) in the event of the couple's separation. In the last stage of the development, therefore, the *mohar* in effect became a divorce penalty, and as such was presumably a real deterrent to hasty divorce (given that the woman was blameless and entitled to a financial settlement, see below).[1] We should note, however, that despite the *mohar's* changed character, it was nevertheless still regarded as a bride-price, albeit in deferred form. This fact is indicated by the way in which the Sages explicitly equated the talmudic 200 *zuzin* with the biblical מהר בתולה, bride-price of virgins (see, for example, *Ket.* 10a). Finally, the change in the title of the bride-price from *mohar* to *kethubah* was simply due to the fact that the sum was now registered in a special clause inserted in the marriage deed or *kethubah*. Any one of the clauses in the contract could be referred to separately as 'kethubah',[2] and this was especially true of the one which guaranteed payment of the bride-price. Thus the term 'kethubah', with no further qualification, was commonly used as synonymous with 'mohar'.[3]

By the first century BCE, therefore, it was customary for no bride-price money to change hands, but for the sum to be registered in the *kethubah* and only paid in the event of divorce. In consequence of this development, however, and in order to retain the original character of betrothal/marriage which demanded some actual and immediate transfer of goods or payment in exchange for the woman, there was instituted the practice of paying a small sum at the time of betrothal. The sum was of nominal value: according to the School of Shammai, a *denar* or a *denar's* worth; according to the School of Hillel, the lower amount of a *perutah* or a *perutah's* worth (*Kidd.* 1.1; *Eduy.* 4.7). Presentation of this amount by the groom together with a formal declaration of intent ('Be thou

---

1 See, for example, the report of *Gitt.* 57a about a man who wanted to divorce his wife 'but hesitated because she had a big marriage settlement'. R. Meir prohibited any man to keep his wife without a *kethubah* 'even for one hour, the reason being that it should not be an easy matter in the eyes of the husband to divorce a wife' (*B.K.* 89b; cf. *Ket.* 57a; *Yeb.*89a). Later thinkers saw another motive for the change in that it gave the woman a stronger financial position for remarriage (*Ket.* 39b, 84a, 97b; *Gitt.* 49b).

2 Thus, for example, we have *kethubath b'nan nukban* which guaranteed support to daughters born of the union; *kethubah b'nin dikrin* which gave certain guarantees to sons regarding succession to their parents' property, etc. See next section.

3 Thus we read in *DJD*, II, 21.13, 'The male children which thou shall have by me shall inherit thy *kethubah*'. See also the various Talmudic passages cited in this discussion of *mohar/kethubah*.

betrothed to me with this') were necessary to effect a valid contract of betrothal (*Kidd.* 2.1). Unlike the *kethubah*, of course, payment of the כסף קדושין (money of sanctification) could not be deferred or pledged. In the event of the first marriage of a virgin, the money would normally pass to the bride's father since he enjoyed the right to his minor children's earnings (see above, p.55) and she, as we have seen, would usually be less than 12 years old.

The apparent similarity between the formula of *Kidd.* 1.1 and that used to describe the acquisition of slaves or real estate, and the fact that Jewish society demanded the payment of a bride-price for its womenfolk, have led many scholars to conclude that Jewish marriage was in essence a financial transaction for the transfer of ownership over a woman, that is, purchase marriage. This view is, I believe, erroneous. Certainly money had to pass hands to validate a marriage, but this is not to say that the man was actually *buying* himself a wife or that he was her *owner*. The fact that the girl never lost her ties with her father's house;[1] that her father furnished a dowry; that gifts in general were exchanged between the families; that the husband did not have the right to dispose of his wife in the way that he could real estate, etc., all show that it was not a case of outright purchase. By no means did a man *own* his wife.[2] It has frequently been argued that the *mohar* was the price of the girl's virginity, or a compensation payment for the loss of her virginity. Undoubtedly, one consideration in the bride-price was virginity, a highly prized

1 Women were usually identified as 'daughter of N.' rather than 'the wife of N.'; on widowhood or divorce they normally returned to their father's house, and during marriage it was their right to visit the parental home. See also Granqvist, *op. cit.*, pp.57, 146, regarding the way in which present-day Fellahin, even when married, continue to regard fathers and brothers as their natural protectors, an aspect encouraged by the marriage of near kin. Note also that Robin Blackburn in his survey of slavery through the ages ('Defining Slavery: Its Special Features and Social Role', in Archer (ed.), *Slavery and Other Forms of Unfree Labour*, pp.262-79) sees the primary distinction between (free) women and slaves as being the systematic *negation* of the latter's family and kinship: women, who were not owned and had a different function and status within society, did not suffer the same fate (pp.266-67).

2 For definitions of ownership, see Blackburn, *op. cit.*; Ste Croix in Archer, *op. cit.*, p.22.

'commodity' among most peoples[1] and something which a
girl, or rather her father (see Chapter 1 §A, B) had to 'sell'. But
the fact that actual and statutory non-virgins[2] were also
accorded a bride-price, albeit of lower amount, demonstrates
that the payment had also another function, and that was the
recognition that one family was losing and another gaining an
individual's labour. Originally, therefore, in the period before
the various economic difficulties outlined above forced the
transition from *mohar* to *kethubah*, compensation was paid,
and paid to the family who lost out, not the individual. The
bride-price was thus a compensation payment to the girl's
family and not the purchase price of the girl herself. Intrinsic
to the concept of compensation, of course, was the recognition
of the woman's value. Thus present day Fellahin women
regard the absence of a bride-price among westerners as a
grave insult to women. Their attitude nicely shows that way
in which the system of bride-price payment was viewed by the
people rather than by the historian.[3] It should be said, however, that while this may have been the popular understanding of the bride-price, it remained the case that the
mohar reflected patriarchal concerns and that the contract
was essentially an inter-male transaction, concerned on one
level at least with inter-male respect and alliance, with the
woman being merely a pawn.

Just as a man had a financial obligation toward the girl's
family, so did the girl's father have the duty of ensuring that
'men should eagerly desire her [lit. 'spring upon her']' (*Kidd.*
30b), i.e. marry her and thereby extend the alliance network

1 Cf. Westermark, *The History of Human Marriage*, I, p. 371; II, pp. 383f. See
   above, pp. 51f, 106ff.
2 To the first class belong widows and divorcees who had had intercourse with their
   husbands; to the second class belonged widows and divorcees who having entered
   the nuptial chamber, had had no contact with their husbands plus the proselyte, the
   freed captive woman, and the slaves who had been freed after the age of 3 years
   and 1 day (*Ket.* 11a).
3 A different perspective to the usual western attitude on the whole issue of bride-
   price/bride purchase was presented to Granqvist in the course of her survey of
   marriage conditions in Palestine. She wrote that, 'In Jerusalem I once discussed
   this matter with an educated Arab and he said: "The Arabs again say that Euro-
   pean women buy themselves husbands, and only if the Westerners agree to call
   the dowry a form of bride-groom purchase can the Arabs agree to see bride purchase in the giving of a bride-price"' (*op. cit.*, p. 134).

(see above, previous section). The custom of providing a dowry would seem to have been as ancient as that of paying a bride-price, and as was the case with the latter, it was originally of non-uniform character and unspecified amount. Thus, for example, Laban furnished his daughters each with a female slave (Gen. 29.24, 29); Caleb gave his daughter a 'field of Springs' (Judg. 1.15); while from the post-biblical period we learn of how Sarah took into her marriage with Tobias half her father's possessions (Tob. 10.10). No indication is given in the biblical and intertestamental literature as to whether there was any social expectation or demand regarding the amount of dowry. Although biblical law contained no stipulation about dowries (indeed, there is not even a word in the Old Testament for 'dowry'),[1] the Tannaim did decree that a man could not assign his daughter less than fifty *zuzin* (*Ket.* 6.5). However, whilst the halakhah prescribed a minimum amount, it did not attempt to standardize dowries. The absence of an upper limit meant that dowries could often reach enormous proportions, at least among wealthy circles (see *Ket.* 54a-b, 66a-b; *B.M.* 104b; *Yeb.* 67a), acting as powerful magnets to prospective suitors regardless of the personal qualities of the girl in question and regardless of the affection which might or might not exist between the couple. The obvious dangers of such a state of affairs to the institution and sanctity of marriage, and to notions of male power and prerogative/respect, were recognized by a number of writers from our period. Thus Pseudo-Phocylides most forcefully urged men not to 'Bring... as wife into your home a bad and wealthy woman. [For] you will be a slave of your wife because of the baneful dowry' (ll. 199-200), and Ben Sira similarly advised men,

> Fall not because of the beauty of a woman
> And be not ensnared for the sake of what she possesseth,
> For hard slavery and a disgrace it is

---

1. Though see the use of ברכה in Josh. 15.18-19, and שלחים in 1 Kgs 9.16. The Tannaim again coined no special term to denote dowry, commonly using the circumlocution 'things that come in with her from her father's house to her husband's house' (see, for example, *Ket.* 47a). For discussion on the terminology employed in Scripture and Talmud, see Cohen, *Jewish and Roman Law*, p. 353; Epstein, *The Jewish Marriage Contract*, p. 89; Neufeld, *Ancient Hebrew Marriage Laws*, pp. 110-11.

[If] a wife support her husband (25.21-22; cf. 7.19).

Josephus believed that the Law itself commanded men not to be influenced by a woman's dowry (*Con. Ap.* 2.200) and the Tannaim, while not regulating the amount of dowry, declared that 'He who takes a wife for the sake of money will have unworthy children' (*Kidd.* 70a). It was not until the time of the Amoraim that an attempt was made at setting an upper limit. Feeling that excessive dowries deprived sons of their rightful inheritance, they ruled that a father should not give more than ten per cent of his possessions as dowry to a daughter (*Ket.* 53a).

While wealthy families might compete with each other over the amount of dowry which they could bestow upon their daughters, poorer folk still had the obligation of furnishing the minimum sum required by law and for many this was an onerous duty. In recognition of this fact Philo urged the rich to 'help parents without the means to marry their daughters and provide them with an ample dowry' (*Fug.* 29).

If a father died before his daughter's marriage, then she was entitled to receive her dowry from his estate (see above, p.69), and if there was more than one daughter, then, as was the case with their maintenance, the elder was not entitled to take a larger amount at the expense of her sisters (*B.B.* 8.8).[1] Should the estate be insufficient to furnish a suitable dowry, then the girl was assigned not less than fifty *zuzin* from the poor funds, and

> ... if there was more in the poor funds, they should provide
> for her according to the honour due her (*Ket.* 6.5).

Society's concern to see that all women were adequately provided for is further attested by a special ruling contained in the *Damascus Document*. Members of the sect which adhered to that Rule set up a special fund from their earnings out of which 'the virgin with no kin, and the maid for whom no man cares' were to receive aid.[2]

Prior to the innovation of a written marriage deed, the

---

1 The idea was that the dowry was a substitute for succession. See Epstein, *op. cit.*, pp. 90f.
2 CD 13, G. Vermes, *op. cit.*, p. 116.

dowry would seem to have been an outright gift to the woman by her father. It remained her private possession and could not be used by the husband without her express permission. With the introduction of the *kethubah*, however, the dowry was entered in the contract and a distinction was made between the 'property of iron sheep' (נכסי צאן ברזל) and the 'property of plucking' (נכסי מלוג). Goods in the first category were conveyed to the groom under the terms of tenancy, and in the Assuan Elephantine papyri were indicated by the phrase כל זי הנעלת בידה, 'all that she brought in her hand' (*K*. 2.8, 10; *K*. 7.22; *C*. 15.24-25, 27-28). Those in the second category formed the woman's private estate, and in the Elephantine papyri were described as נכסיה וקנינה, 'her property and possession' (*C*. 15.21-22). We shall reserve more detailed discussion of the woman's property rights within marriage and the distinction between *son barzel* and *melog* for the next chapter.

Once the negotiations for the bride-price and dowry amounts had been completed to the satisfaction of both parties, the betrothal ceremony was held. This was a public celebration intended to act as a testimony to the fact of betrothal, for even when written contracts were in use, the personal statement of individuals was still considered of paramount importance. The ceremony took the form of a special betrothal meal (סעודת ארוסין) and was held in the home of the bride's father (*Pes.* 3.7). It took place in the evening and was obviously a festive occasion, for the Talmud describes the signs of a betrothal as 'lights burning,... couches spread, and people [continuously] entering and leaving [the house of the bride]' (*Gitt.* 89a). In the course of the celebration the groom was required to make a public and formal declaration of intent, 'Be thou betrothed unto me' (*Kidd.* 19a; cf. 5b-6a). He then ritually presented the signed and witnessed marriage contract to his bride, together with the symbolic coin of the כסף קדושין. The celebrations were concluded with special betrothal blessings which recalled the Law's injunctions against forbidden unions (see previous section) and reminded the couple that they were not yet fully man and wife:

> Blessed art thou, O Lord our God, King of the Universe, who has sanctified us by His commandments and has commanded us concerning the forbidden relations, and has for-

bidden unto us the betrothed, and has allowed unto us the wedded [only] through the *chupah* and sanctification (*Ket.* 7b).[1]

The relationship established by the act of *kiddushin* was in many ways analogous to that of the Greek ἐγγύησις, having the character of *matrimonium ratum sed non consummatum*.[2] Like nuptials it could be terminated only by the death of one of the parties or by formal divorce (*Ket.* 1.2; 4.4; *Gitt.* 8.9; *Yeb.* 4.9; 6.4; *Eduy.* 4.7; *Mt.* 1.19). The Mishnah frequently refers to women being divorced or widowed who had yet to enter the חופה (*chupah*) (*Yeb.* 6.4; *Ket.* 3.3; 6.1; 11.2 etc.). Should she be divorced, the betrothed woman was entitled to receive the monies of her *kethubah* (*Ket.* 6.1; 53a, 89b; *Yeb.* 29b, 43b).[3] While not permitted sex with her 'husband', the betrothed woman could be guilty of adultery with others for by *kiddushin* she became 'sanctified' to one man (*Sot.* 2.5; *Kidd.* 2b). In this event, like a fully married woman, she met with the death penalty (Deut. 22.24; *Ket.* 9a, 44b-46a).[4] Similarly, if someone other than her betrothed had sexual relations with her, they were punished accordingly (*Sanh.* 7.4, 9; *Con. Ap.* 2.201; *Spec. Leg.* 3.72f.; Deut. 22.23f. See above, p. 51). In many respects, therefore, the betrothed woman was deemed to be a full wife in the eyes of the Law.

Apart from these various rulings, however, there were certain considerable differences between betrothal and matrimony. As has already been mentioned, the couple were not permitted sexual intimacy. Thus Mary who was betrothed to Joseph, when informed by Gabriel that she was to conceive a child, responded, 'How can this be, since I have no husband?' (Lk. 1.27). If during the period of betrothal a woman did bear a child, then it was deemed to be a ממזר (*mamzer*, 'bastard') or, according to another view, of doubtful legitimacy (שתוקי, *shetuki*, *Yeb.* 69b, see above pp. 137ff.). So Joseph, on learning

---

1 חופה וקדושין together constituted the full marriage. See above, p. 158.

2 Cf. Cohen, *Jewish and Roman Law*, p. 293 and 'On the Theme of Betrothal in Jewish and Roman Law', *AAJR* 18 (1948-49), p. 81; Neufeld, *op. cit.*, p. 144.

3 The *kethubah* passed to her father if she was not yet of age. He also received her *get* (*Ket.* 4.2, 4; see Chapter 1 §B).

4 She was not, however, subjected to the ordeal of bitter waters undergone by suspected adulteresses (*Sot.* 4.1).

that Mary was with child, 'being a just man and unwilling to put her to shame, resolved to divorce her quietly' (Mt. 1.18-19).

It would seem, however, that custom did vary from region to region. In Judaea a betrothed couple were apparently allowed to meet without chaperones or witnesses. If this happened, however, a virginity suit could not subsequently be lodged against the woman (*Ket.* 1.5; Deut. 22.13f.). According to one Tanna, if a Judaean bride was widowed before entering into full marriage, then she was required to wait three months before remarrying in order for the groom to be certain that she was not already pregnant by her previous fiancé (*Yeb.* 4.10). The Talmud makes it clear, however, that these rules applied only to the southern region of Palestine, the implication being that practice in Galilee was much stricter—a fact borne out by the Gospel narratives.[1] The Amoraim later tried to explain these regional differences by saying that it was customary in Judaea to include the special nuptial blessings which sanctioned cohabitation (see below, §D) in the betrothal ceremony. In the Galilee, these prayers were reserved for the חופה ceremony (*Ket.* 7a-b).[2]

During the betrothal period the woman remained in her father's house, receiving maintenance from him, and subject to his authority (*Ket.* 4.4). The only share her future husband had in this authority was the power to join with his father-in-law in annulling her vows (see above, p. 49). If the twelve months allotted for the betrothal period elapsed without a marriage having taken place (through the man's fault), then the duty to maintain the woman passed to the groom (*Ket.* 2a-b). According to an earlier law, the woman could from this moment on even eat of *terumah* if her betrothed was a priest (*Ket.* 5.2-3; Lev. 22.12-13). Finally, if a woman died while still in a state of betrothal, her husband was not subject to the religious duty of mourning her. He did not inherit her dowry and

---

1 See also y. *Ket.* 25c which records how women of prominent Judaean families were often already pregnant when they entered the חופה.
2 Belkin (*op. cit.*, p. 246) believes that the Judaean custom of pre-marital relations resulted from the persecutions suffered under Antiochus Epiphanes when *ius primae noctis* was in force. He bases himself upon y. *Ket.* 25c, a passage which is normally understood to refer to the persecutions under Hadrian.

if a priest, was not permitted to defile himself by attending her funeral (*Ket.* 53a; cf. Lev. 21.1f.). If he died, then she similarly was not required to enter into mourning, and if his death occurred during one of the festivals she was not allowed to defile herself by attending his corpse (*Ket.* 53a). We shall reserve discussion on the property rights of betrothed/married women for the next chapter.

C. *The Marriage Contract*

As was seen in the previous section, by the time of the Tannaim it was customary for a written marriage contract to accompany all lawful unions, *kethubah*-less marriages being regarded as no marriage at all, or stigmatized as mere concubinage (in the rabbinic sense of the word, *B.K.* 89a; *Gitt.* 57a; y. *Ket.* 29d; y. *Sanh.* 21a). It is unclear when the written instrument was actually introduced. There is no mention of it in the Bible, but the Deuteronomic legislation about written bills of divorce has encouraged many scholars to assume a similar early date for the use of written marriage contracts. Thus, for example, Epstein writes,

> On the basis of this passage (that is, Deut. 24.1-3) the probability is very strong and the logic compelling that in Deuteronomic days the writ was already employed in Israel both for the dissolution as well as for the contraction of marriage. That one writ and not the other was adopted by the Jews is very unlikely.[1]

In support of his argument, the same author assumes a kinship between written deeds of sale (known to have been in existence from the time of Jeremiah—Jer. 32.8-12) and the marriage contract:

> there is little difference between the conveyance of a field and the conveyance of a daughter in marriage. Marriage represents purchase... Hence one concludes with a fair degree of confidence that in Jeremiah's time (sixth century BC) not only was the deed of realty known, but even the marriage writ was in vogue.[2]

---

1 *The Jewish Marriage Contract*, p. 29.
2 *Ibid.*, p. 30. Cf. Burrows, *The Basis of Israelite Marriage*, p. 31: 'The Old Testament nowhere mentions such a document, but where bills of divorce (Deut. 24.1-4) and written deeds in real estate (Jer. 32.10f.) were used, written marriage contracts would hardly be unknown'.

The discovery of marriage contracts from the fifth century Jewish military colony at Elephantine has encouraged the view that such deeds must also have been known in Judaea from an early period. Moving to a somewhat later date, many scholars have treated the 'instrument of cohabitation' referred to in Tobit (7.4) as some kind of proto-*kethubah*. However, while these various arguments may seem attractive, they are basically insubstantial and certainly inconclusive. The facts are that the Bible, while referring to marriage on many occasions, makes absolutely no mention, in that context, of a written deed. To argue from this silence and on the basis of bills of divorce for the contract's existence is not very convincing. The need to provide the woman with written proof of divorce was felt at an early date in consequence of the fact that adultery was a crime punishable by death. The same urgency did not attach to the drawing up of a marriage contract. With regard to the supposed affinity between deeds of sale and deeds of marriage, it should be remembered that women could not in fact be bought and sold like real estate (see above, pp. 164-65), a fact which undermines the basis of Epstein's other argument. Similarly, the marriage contracts from Elephantine, while of great interest in themselves, furnish no real proof for the existence of similar deeds within Judaea. Their origin is probably to be seen in terms of Egyptian practice, and as such their history and development must be regarded as independent of any (alleged) Judaean innovation.[1] Finally, the 'instrument of cohabitation' recorded in Tobit was probably some form of *shetar* rather than a marriage contract proper (see above, p. 157, particularly n. 1).

Given the silence of our sources, therefore, nothing definitive may be said regarding the origins of the written marriage contract (though the likelihood is that it was of post-biblical origin). All that may be stated with absolute certainty is that the contract was in regular use by the time of the Tannaim, for references to it in the Mishnah are descriptive of custom

---

1 For the way in which the Elephantine deeds evolved from Egyptian practice, see Yaron, 'Aramaic Marriage Contracts from Elephantine', *JJS* 3 (1958), pp. 37-38 and *The Law of the Aramaic Papyri*, p. 49.

rather than innovation.[1] (In this respect, we might also note that the Tannaim were themselves divided as to the historical origin of the *kethubah*, some seeing it as deriving from biblical days [y. *Yeb.* 14d; y. *Ket.* 36b], others considering it a rabbinic institution [*Ket.* 10a, 56a, 110a].) Whatever the truth may be regarding the contract's history, for the purposes of the present survey it is sufficient to know that at least for the latter half of the period under consideration, the *kethubah* was an established fact of life.

From the middle of the first century BCE, that is, from the time of Simeon ben Shetah, the *kethubah* functioned as a record of and guarantee for the various financial obligations which a man undertook in respect of his wife and children, both during his lifetime and subsequent to his death. Its primary character was that of providing (or promising) the woman financial protection against the vicissitudes of widowhood or divorce. Essentially, therefore, it was regarded as her contract, and thus only one deed was drawn up, which remained in her possession. In this section we shall examine the several obligations/promises contained in the contract. Our analysis will concentrate upon the marriage deeds discovered at Wadi Muabba'at in the Judaean desert, with supplementary information from descriptions of the *kethubah* clauses contained in the Mishnah. No attention will be paid to the Elephantine marriage contracts for those, while in a far better state of preservation than the Judaean documents, pertain to a different time and place and therefore may not with justification be used in any detailed survey of the contracts of Graeco-Roman Palestine. Most unfortunately, no analysis of the documents contained in the so-called Babatha archive from the Engedi region will be possible because at the time of writing and some thirty-five years on from their discovery these deeds remain unpublished and therefore

---

1 The statement in *Shabb.* 14b that 'Simon ben Shetah instituted (יפן) a woman's *kethubah*' is not necessarily to be understood as his having introduced the marriage contract. It could refer to the marriage settlement (see above, p. 163 for the way in which 'kethubah' was frequently used as synonymous with 'mohar') and to a new stipulation which was to be inserted in the pre-existing contract. Note also that the word יפן can be translated 'to put straight', 'to improve'. On this, see Neufeld, *Ancient Hebrew Marriage Laws*, p. 158.

unavailable to the wider scholarly world. This forced omission is particularly regrettable as it is known from preliminary reports that the archive contains thirty-five well-preserved documents dating from 93/94 to 132 CE and dealing with various law suits and matters of property to do with the Jewish woman Babatha and her family.[1] Of these documents, two are marriage deeds—one a contract of Babatha's second marriage (date damaged, but probably deriving from shortly after May 124), and the other the *kethubah* of her step-daughter Shelmazion (written in Greek and dated 118 CE). Of the former Yadin most tantalizingly wrote, 'This *ketubah*, which is complementary to the two *ketuboth* published by Milik [*DJD* II, *P. Mur.* 20, 21], is important on account of its early date and the legal formulas employed in it. Though not preserved in its entirety, it is in far better condition than those found in Murabba'at, and indeed enables us to correct some of Milik's conjectured restorations' ('Expedition D', p. 244). However, given the unavailability of these documents, the present analysis will have to rely on the aforementioned Murabba'at contracts, with just the occasional cross-reference to the Engedi *kethuboth* when secondary comment by Yadin and others permits.

Four *kethuboth* were discovered at Murabba'at, two written in Aramaic (P. *Mur.* 20 and 21) and two in Greek (P. *Mur.* 115 and 116).[2] All four date from the first to second centuries CE, and vary as to their state of preservation.[3] Best preserved is the text of P. *Mur.* 115, but as this is a deed of remarriage, with its own special and peculiar provisions, it is of somewhat

1 See Yadin, *Bar-Kokhba*, Ch. 16, and 'Expedition D', *IEJ* 12 (1962), pp. 235-48; Polotsky, 'The Greek Papyri from the Cave of Letters' in the same *IEJ* volume, pp. 258-62. The cache includes deeds regarding the custody of Babatha's son by her first husband; marriage contracts; documents to do with the property of her daughter Shelmazion; claims made against Babatha in connection with property which she gained possession of following the death of her father; and deeds of gift, sale and purchase of various items of family property—all of which would be extremely illuminating if we had them. Of the deeds Yadin wrote, 'From the Aramaic, Nabatean and Greek documents it is possible to reconstruct in detail the life story of Babatha and her family' ('Expedition D', p. 247).

2 Whilst the Mishnah's *kethubah* clause formula is always given in Aramaic, these documents support the Talmudic statement that language does not affect the legality/validity of a contract (see *Gitt.* 9.9; t. *B.B.* 11.4, 8). In the Murabba'at deeds, the same legal terms are used interchangeably in either language.

3 For text and translation, see Appendix I. For purposes of comparison, and also to provide a full *kethubah* text, a medieval marriage contract is also given.

less use in this survey of first marriage than the other three contracts. Of those contracts, P. *Mur.* 20 in a sense provides the fullest text in that no one line (excepting that which would have contained the witnesses' names) appears to be missing. While there may be no significant omission in that respect, the contract is defective in that only the right-hand side is preserved. What remains, however, has few lacunae and permits a certain reading of the opening formula of each line. P. *Mur.* 21 furnishes a reasonably full text, though the opening lines are extremely fragmentary and the body of the deed has a number of small lacunae and doubtful readings of some individual letters. P. *Mur.* 116 consists of two fragments, of which only fragment A is sufficient to permit any meaningful reading. It consists of thirteen lines, none of which are complete and all of which contain many letters whose reading would be uncertain were it not for context and for comparison with the formulae of the other contracts. (Regarding the question of comparison, it is interesting to note that the Murabbaʿat deeds, while not identical, do form a reasonably homogeneous whole in respect to issues treated and clause order, a fact which indicates that there was a fairly high level of standardization in the format of the *kethubah* by the second century CE.) We shall now turn to examining the contents of the deeds.

Before entering upon the itemization of the various obligations and following the required statement of date, place and parties necessary for all legally valid deeds, the contracts record a declaration of intent by the husband: 'You shall be my wife according to the law of Moses' (20.3).[1] There is no reciprocal declaration by the woman, for the *kethubah* was drawn up entirely from the man's standpoint. It was a record of his

---

1 On the basis of later *kethuboth* and Talmudic formula the full text could have read 'You shall be my wife according to the law of Moses and Israel'. See *DJD*, II, p. 112. (P. *Mur.* 115, the document of remarriage, simply refers to the man taking the woman as his 'legitimate wife' (εἰς γυναῖκα γαμετή, l. 5). The opening lines of P. *Mur.* 21 and 116 are missing.) Alternatively, the opening sentence could be restored 'according to the law of Moses and the Jews' in line with the text of the Babatha *kethubah* (Yadin, 'Expedition D', p. 245). Yadin suggests that this was more likely to have been the formula in the years preceding Bar Kokhba, and in support of this view cites *Ket.* 4.8, 'When you enter my house you will be mine for wifehood according to the law of Moses and the Jews' (cf. *Ket.* 7.6). According to Yadin, it was only later that the formula 'Moses and Israel' was introduced.

intent, duties and obligations, and as such any statement by
the woman would be seen as misplaced and redundant.[1]

Following the declaration of intent, it seems likely that the
contracts contained a promise by the husband to maintain his
wife during their life together. Unfortunately, the opening
sections of P. *Mur.* 21 and 116 are not extant, and in P. *Mur.*
20 there is a lacuna immediately after the groom's declaration. However, later *kethuboth* read: 'Be thou my wife
according to the Law of Moses and Israel, and I will work for
thee, honour, support and maintain thee in accordance with
the custom of Jewish husbands who work for their wives, honour, support and maintain them in truth' (see the text from
Maimonides, p. 296 below). While there is not space for this
full formula in our contracts, it seems likely that some
statement to that effect would have been contained for there is
a marked similarity between the two groups of documents,
the later *kethuboth* evolving directly from the earlier deeds
which, as has been noted, had already acquired a high level of
standardization by the second century.[2] Further support for
the view that the missing clause was indeed a maintenance
clause is the fact that the lacuna in P. *Mur.* 20 is immediately
followed by the words ועלם מן נכסי ('Always, from my property',
l. 4). With the insertion of a simple maintenance formula,
therefore, the full text of this clause may well have read: 'You
shall be my wife according to the law of M[oses and Israel, and
me, I will feed and clothe you, from today for] always, from
my property' (ll. 3-4).[3] In a sense, such a statement was

1 The omission of a similar statement of intent by the woman also underlines her
general passivity where the arrangement of marriage is concerned; see above,
pp. 153-55.

2 See also the formula recorded by R. Hai Gaon:
ואנה במימרא דשמיא אפלה ואוקיר ואזין ואפרנס ואכלכל ואכסי יתיכי כאורח גברין יהודאין דפלחין ומוקרין חנין
ומפ דנסין ומכלכלין ית נשידזן בקשטא.

3 See also Epstein, *op. cit.*, pp. 159-60: 'The Talmud does not cite a kethubah clause
stipulating the husband's alimentation obligation. Yet it is not to be assumed that
the Talmudic kethubah had no such clause... Rather must it be taken as an
insignificant omission, for in the levirate kethubah of Talmudic days we do read
the clause: "I so and so, take unto myself so and so as my levirate bride to support
and maintain her properly" (*Yeb.* 52b). The inference from this is apparent, that
the ordinary kethubah also had an alimentation clause. But its format is not
known to us.' (The selection here of the format 'feed and clothe' is based upon the
wording of *Ket.* 47b which sees the provision of food and raiment as fundamental
to the husband's maintenance obligation—see next Chapter.)

something of a nicety or flourish, for the law in any case demanded that a man support his wife in return for her handiwork and use of her property (*Ket.* 4.4, 47b; *Gitt.* 1.6; see above, pp. 60, 63).[1] The insertion of a clause to that effect in the *kethubah* meant that the man was simply reiterating in contractual form his legal obligation. As shall be seen in the course of this survey, most of the promises recorded in the Murabba'at deeds were in fact simple reiterations of rabbinic conditions (תנאי בית דין), the fulfilment of which was binding upon the groom regardless of whether or not they were entered in the marriage contract (see above, p. 67).

The next clause in our contracts was a record of the amount of *mohar* owed to the woman. As was seen in the previous section, by the enactment of Simeon ben Shetah, men were released from the obligation of paying the bride-price prior to marriage: they simply had to promise its delivery at some future date, and that promise was guaranteed by a lien clause written into the marriage contract (see above, pp. 160ff.). Additional to the lien clause was a statement recording the amount of *mohar*, and a remnant of this clause is to be found in l. 5 of P. *Mur.* 20 and possibly also in P. *Mur.* 115, ll. 5-6.[2]

The contracts follow the *mohar* clause with a promise by the groom to pay his wife the sum of her *kethubah* in the event of divorce,[3] the term 'kethubah' being used here as

---

1 For details of the amount and type of maintenance owed to the wife, and reasons for the husband's obligation, see Chapter 3 §A.

2 This clause is not preserved in P. *Mur.* 21 and 116 due to the fragmentary nature of the opening section of those deeds; P. *Mur.* 115, the Greek contract of remarriage, refers to a sum of 200 *denars*, a figure which in fact tallies with the amount prescribed by the Tannaim as the minimum requirement for a virgin's *mohar*. It is not therefore certain whether the figure in this instance actually refers to a *mohar*, and additionally so as the clause in question (ll. 5-6) is poorly preserved and the word used to designate the sum is προίξ, 'dowry' (see *DJD* II, p. 252). However, given the context and the clause's position in the contract (cf. the medieval *kethubah*), it is possible that this is the record of the bride price. Cf. P. *Mur.* 116 where the word φερνή is used with undoubted reference to the *kethubah* (below, p. 183), and the discussion below regarding the contracts' non-itemization of the dowry.

3 This clause is partially preserved in both P. *Mur.* 20 (l. 6) and P. *Mur.* 21 (ll. 9-10), though only the latter has preserved the word 'kethubah'. Following the clause order of these two contracts it is likely that P. *Mur.* 115 recorded the divorce provision at l. 7, though the deed at this point is too fragmentary to state this with certainty. The opening section of P. *Mur.* 116 is not extant. This clause did not have application if the woman was divorced on account of an offence on her part; see below pp. 180-81.

synonymous with 'mohar'[1] and thus having application to the amount specified in the preceding clause. Once again, the inclusion of this clause was in a sense redundant, for the furnishing of a divorce settlement by the groom (or rather his deferred payment of the bride-price) was a stipulation of rabbinic law. Thus the Mishnah states:

> If the husband has not written out a *ketubah* (here = marriage contract) for his wife, she may still claim 200 *denars* if she was a virgin at marriage or one *mina* if she was a widow, since this is a condition enjoined by the court (תנאי בית דין) (*Ket*. 4.7).

According to our contracts, however, payment of the *kethubah* was not the groom's only obligation. He was also duty bound to return the woman's dowry. Thus P. *Mur*. 21, ll.9-10, with some restoration, reads: If I di[vorce you...] I will return [to you the money of your] *kethubah* and everything that is [yours that is with] me'.[2] Although the text is corrupt, sufficient text remains for us to be certain that two separate and distinct payments are referred to here. That the latter half of the clause was indeed concerned with dowry repayment (and that therefore the suggested restoration is possible) finds support in a divorce deed which was also discovered at Wadi Murabba'at. In this deed the man, presumably in fulfilment of his earlier *kethubah* promise, declared that he was both returning his wife's dowry and reimbursing her for any damage caused to those goods in the course of their marriage.[3]

Given that the husband was obliged to refund the dowry to its full value, it is surprising that our contracts, while specifying the amount he owed as *kethubah* payment, contain no record of the items which comprised the woman's dowry—an omission which is in sharp contrast to both the Elephantine

---

1   See above, p. 163, for the way in which the two terms were used interchangeably from the time of Simeon ben Shetah.

2   There is space for a similar restoration in the relevant line of P. *Mur*. 20. For that document the editors of *DJD* II suggest: 'Au cas où tu di[vorcerais, je te rendrai l'argent de ta dot (here, as elsewhere in the translation and notes, the editors make careless use of the word 'dot'; it should be 'kethubah') et tout ce que tu auras chez moi.]'.

3   P. *Mur*. 19, ll. 8-10, 21-23. See the notes to these lines in *DJD*, II, p. 108.

papyri and the medieval *kethuboth*. We know from the Mishnah that the goods which a woman brought in with her at marriage were divided into the 'property of iron sheep' (נכסי צאן ברזל) and the 'property of plucking' (נכסי מלוג), those in the first category being conveyed to the groom under terms of tenancy and those in the second category forming her private estate. Over the latter, the husband enjoyed the right of usufruct and any depreciation in value was not his responsibility, the goods being returned to the woman in whatever condition they stood at the time of his death or the couple's divorce.[1] Over the former, the husband had rights of tenancy and while he as tenant enjoyed any increase in the property's value, he was also liable for any damage or loss incurred, and so in the event of divorce had to make full restitution of the original amount to his wife.[2] Thus, as an instance of property brought into marriage by a woman, the Mishnah states:

> *Melog* slaves are such that, if they die, the woman suffers the loss, and if their value increases, the wife enjoys the increase... the husband is responsible for their maintenance... *Son barzel* slaves are such that if they die, the loss is suffered by the husband, and if their value increases, the husband enjoys the increase... his obligation is to restore them in full... (*Yeb.* 7.1).

From the Mishnah's description and from the declaration in ll.8-10 of *P. Mur.* 19, it is evident that the man's *kethubah* promise to return 'everything [that is yours with] me' applied to the woman's *son barzel* goods: dowry could not be made up

1 Regarding the term 'property of plucking', see *EJ*, VI, col. 187: '*Nikhsei Melog* is a term derived from the word *meligah*, e.g. *meligat ha-rosh*, i.e. plucking of hair from the head which remains intact. Similarly *melog* property is property of which the principal remains in the wife's ownership but the fruits thereof are taken by the husband so that he has no responsibility or right in respect of the principal, both its loss and gain being only hers and upon dissolution of the marriage such property returns to the wife as it stands.'

2 *EJ*, VI, col. 186: '*Nikhsei Zon Barzel* is a term derived from the name of a transaction in which one party entrusts property on certain terms to another, the latter undertaking responsibility therefor as he would for iron, i.e. for return of the capital value of the property as at the time of his receipt thereof, even if it should suffer loss or depreciation; since generally small cattle was the subject matter of such transactions, they came to be described by the above term (*B.M.* 69b and Rashi thereto).'

of *melog* property.[1]

The fact that the man was obliged to pay his wife's *kethubah* and return her dowry afforded the woman greater security on two levels. First, the necessity of payment tended to guard against the dangers of arbitrary divorce (see above, p. 162)—a point of some significance to the woman in a society which accorded men absolute and unilateral powers of divorce.[2] Secondly, if the deterrent failed and the woman were divorced, she would at least depart her husband's house with some financial security and would thus be in a stronger position for remarriage (cf. *Ket.* 39b, 84a, 97b; *Gitt.* 49b). It should be emphasized, however, that the *kethubah* was only paid if the woman was divorced through no fault or failing of her own. Obviously, one guilty of adultery or proven antenuptial incontinence forfeited any claim to the settlement, but the same loss of rights also applied to the woman who had committed wrongs of a far less serious character. According to *Ket.* 7.6,

> These are they that are put away without their *kethubah*: a wife that transgresses the Law of Moses and Jewish custom. What [conduct is such that transgresses] the law of Moses? If she gives her husband untithed food, or has connection with him in her uncleanness, or does not set apart Dough-Offering, or utters a vow and does not fulfil it. And what [conduct is such that transgresses] Jewish custom? If she goes out with her hair unbound, or spins in the street, or speaks with any man.

---

1 See previous section for the way in which this division in the woman's property was designated in the Elephantine deeds by the terms כל די הנעלת בידה (our document's clause) and נכסיה ופצה. For further details of *son barzel* and *melog*, and for the way in which women in fact gradually lost everything, excepting the title to property brought into marriage, see below pp. 229ff.

2 Thus *Yeb.* 14.1, 'The man that divorces is not like to the woman that is divorced; for a woman is put away with her consent or without it, but a husband can put away his wife only with his own consent'. Only rarely was the woman permitted to take any initiative in divorce proceedings, and then she had to apply to a court which chose whether or not to force her husband to give her a bill of divorce (*Ket.* 7.9-10; *Yeb.* 112a; *Ned.* 90b). The initiative of Salome, wife of Costobarus, as reported by Josephus in *Ant.* 15.258-59, was undoubtedly exceptional and contrary to the law. For an outline of the historical foundation of the unilateral character of Jewish divorce, see Epstein, *op. cit.*, p. 200. Regarding the man's legal entitlement to divorce his wife for any reason, however trivial, see *Gitt.* 9.10.

To this list R. Tarfon added the woman who was considered to be a scold (his definition of a scold being 'whosoever speaks inside her house so that her neighbours hear her voice'), whilst Abba Saul included one who cursed her husband's parents (*ibid.*). Another category of women who forfeited their claim consisted of those who prior to marriage had subjected themselves to vows about which they subsequently failed to inform their husbands, or who had physical defects which they had similarly kept secret (*Ket.* 7.7-9). Women who in the course of marriage proved to be barren (as opposed to those who informed their husbands of their sterility prior to the union) could also be put away without their *kethubah* (*Gitt.* 4.8; *Ket.* 11.6). Thus it is evident that while the institution of *kethubah* payment afforded the woman some protection against arbitrary divorce, there were still many ways open to a man which could release him from his obligation and so deprive the divorcee of her financial security.[1]

Following the divorce clause, three of our four contracts then treat of the maintenance of daughters from the union (P. *Mur.* 21.10-12; 115.9-10; 116.4). In P. *Mur.* 20 the insertion of this clause is delayed until after the question of the woman's death has been treated (ll. 8-9). The position of this clause in the contracts would indicate that it dealt with the daughter's maintenance during their father's lifetime and not, as is commonly understood, with the maintenance which was their legal due subsequent to his death (*Ket.* 4.6, 11). For an analysis of this clause, see above, pp. 65ff.

Next in the contracts comes provision for the event of the demise of one or other spouse. In P. *Mur.* 20, 21, and 116 the question of the woman's death is treated before that of the man's (20.7-8; 21.12-14; 116.4-6), while in the deed of remarriage this order is reversed (115.12-13). No significance need be attached to this change in order, however, for the contents of the clauses are the same in all four contracts. The contracts' concern in treating the death of the woman was to state who inherited her *kethubah*. In a sense the statement was once again something of a nicety, for rabbinic law clearly stipulated that male children were to succeed to their mother's

---

1 For further details regarding divorce, see pp. 217-20 below.

kethubah, even in the event of her predeceasing her husband (*Ket.* 4.10). In the marriage deed the man contractually reiterated this law, declaring, 'If you go to the house of eternity bef[ore me,] the sons which you [shall have] by me [will inherit] the money of your *kethubah* and [all] of yours [that is with me and that is written] above, inside and outside' (21.12-14). It is apparent from this and the other contracts that the sons inherited both the woman's *kethubah* and the goods which she had brought in with her to the marriage. The fact that the clause in P. *Mur.* 115 and 116, in line with the wording of *Ket.* 4.6, concludes with reference to the sons' share in the paternal inheritance indicates that their succession to their mother's property also did not come into effect until after their father's death. While the man had no claim to his wife's property if there were sons from their marriage, he did enjoy rights of tenancy during his lifetime, the goods only reverting to the woman's heirs at his death. Children of any subsequent union had no share in the original wife's *kethubah*; sons divided the estate of their common father but only inherited the *kethubah* of their respective mothers. If there were no sons, the woman's property passed to the husband fully, and at his death the usual order of inheritance was followed (*B.B.* 8.1-2).

The contracts then go on to consider the question of the husband's death and the maintenance which was the woman's due should she be left a widow. According to the Mishnah:

> [If he had not written for her,] 'Thou shall dwell in my house and receive maintenance from my goods so long as thou remainest a widow in my house', he is still liable [thereto], since this is a condition enjoined by the court (*Ket.* 4.12).

A clause to that effect is found in varying states of preservation in all the contracts.[1] Implicit in the mishnah was

---

1 P. *Mur.* 115, ll. 11-12: extremely fragmentary, but what remains undoubtedly refers to the widow's maintenance; P. *Mur.* 20, ll. 9-11: lengthy lacunae due to the missing right hand margin, but from the surviving text and on the basis of *Ket.* 4.12 the editors of *DJD*, II suggest the following restoration:

או הן אנא לבח [או דך אהרך מקדמכי אנתי חהוא יתבה...] ומחזנה ומכסיא [כל ימין ביחהן די בניא...

.די] ארמלו זי לכ <י> מן בת [די ועד למחוחכי...]

The restoration of this text is facilitated by P. *Mur.* 21.14-16 where the maintenance clause is in a reasonable state of preservation. P. *Mur.* 116, ll. 8-11: some small lacunae and doubtful letters, but nevertheless a clear, detailed statement of the provisions for widowhood. Only the concluding line of the clause is fragmentary in this document.

the understanding that the woman could chose to leave her dead husband's home. If she did so choose, she forfeited her claim to maintenance but was entitled to receive the sum of her *kethubah* from the heirs. The widow's freedom in this respect is made explicit in P. *Mur.* 116:

> If Aurelios happens to die before Salome,
> Salome will be nourished and clothed with the help of the Fortune of Aurelios all the time that she wishes to remain a widow.
> But if she wishes
> To go out after his death or if she send to his place...[1]
> [She will recover the 'dowry' [2] (φερνή) of] 200 denars (ll. 8-12).

According to this contract and according to the law, therefore, it was the woman's decision whether to stay or leave: she was legally entitled to demand either maintenance or *kethubah* payment from the heirs. It would seem, however, that in certain parts of Palestine action could be taken which differed from this and which in fact deprived the widow of this independence. Such may be inferred from *Ket.* 4.12 which, after stating the maintenance clause quoted above, continues:

> Thus used the people of Jerusalem to write; and the people of Galilee used to write after the same fashion as the people of Jerusalem. But the people of Judaea used to write, '... until such time as the heirs are minded to give thee thy *kethubah*'; therefore, if the heirs were so minded they could pay her her *kethubah* and let her go (פוטרין אותה).

The strength of this mishnah is that the heirs, if they chose, could force the woman to take her *kethubah* and so drive her off the paternal estate.[3] It is couched in terms of their decision

---

1 'or if she sends to his place': the woman was entitled to claim her *kethubah* up to twenty five years after leaving her husband's home. See below, p. 186.
2 'Dowry': suggested restoration and translation by the editors of *DJD*, II on the basis of l. 6 of the contract—the *kethubah* clause—which uses the word φερνή. See p. 177 n. 2 above for the way in which the word must refer to the *kethubah* payment and so would be better not translated 'dot' as by Milik.
3 The force of the expression פוטרין אותה is somewhat hidden by Danby's translation 'let her go'. The essential meaning of פטר is 'to send off', 'to dismiss'. See Jastrow, p. 1157.

rather than the widow's choice, and in such form could be
entered in the marriage contract.[1] If this course of action were
taken, especially with regard to a woman who by virtue of her
age or other considerations had little prospect of remarriage,
then the widow's plight could be dire. There was also the possibility that she might have difficulty persuading the heirs to
fulfil their *kethubah* obligations and so might not even secure
the settlement which was her legal due (see Lk. 18.1f.; 1 Tim.
5.3, 8). That the lot of the widow was frequently not a happy
one is amply testified by the repeated appeal by writers of the
period to show her mercy and charity.

In theory the payment of the woman's *kethubah*, whether
following divorce or widowhood, was guaranteed by a lien
clause inserted in the marriage contract (see above, pp. 160ff.).
According to the Tannaim, the formula of the lien clause was:
'All my goods are surety for thy *kethubah*', though the mort-
gaging of the groom's property as security for the settlement
was a statutory obligation regardless of whether or not it was
contractually promised (*Ket.* 4.7). This simple formula would
seem to have been elaborated upon in the Murabba'at documents, presumably with the intent of furnishing the woman
greater security for her claim to the *kethubah*. By the mishnaic formula, as the date of the marriage deed was also the
date for the lien, the lien was only effective against property
held by the husband at that time and not against property
bought by him subsequent to the drawing up of the contract.
To provide greater security, in our deeds a revised formula
was employed which included all future possessions in the lien
(P. *Mur.* 115.17; 20.12; clause not extant in P. *Mur.* 21 and
116). This revision was in keeping with the later Amoraic
stipulation that the groom should place as surety for the
money he owed 'property that I did acquire or that I shall
acquire' (*B.B.* 44b; *Ket.* 82b). The fact that all of a married
man's property was permanently mortgaged for the security
of his wife's *kethubah* rendered the conveyancing of real
estate something of a problem, for property could not be sold

---

1   The wording of Babatha's *kethubah* follows Judaean custom rather than that of
Galilee and Jerusalem. According to Yadin ('Expedition D', p. 245) it reads:

ואם אנה[א]והך ל[וב]ל[ת] עלם קרמך חה[רי]ן [יתבא] ומחזון (!) מן ביתי ומן נכסי ער זמן די יצבון ל[רח]י
למנתן לך דמי כתבתך

without the woman renouncing any future claim to it. If she did not expressly waive her rights, the buyer had no security that she would not at a later date reclaim his acquisition in payment for her *kethubah*. It was necessary, therefore, for the vendor to include in the deed of sale a declaration by his wife renouncing her claim to the goods. Such a declaration is found in P. *Mur*. 30.25-28, a deed of sale of land by one Dositheios in 134 CE.[1]

In the main, payment of the *kethubah* was settled privately between the parties concerned. Only in the event of a husband being absent, or when the woman experienced difficulties with the heirs, or was claiming payment on property sold by the husband, did she have to work through a court. If a divorcee received her money directly, then a deed of quittance was drawn up to protect the husband from the possibility of her representing her claim to the settlement (*Ket*. 9.9). If the settlement was made through a court, she was required to take an oath that she had not already been paid (*Ket*. 89b-90a). The same was required of a widow. When working through a court, a divorcee was obliged to present her bill of divorce as proof of her entitlement to the *kethubah* (*Ket*. 9.9). Only when oppressive edicts forbad the observance of Jewish rites, as for example after the Bar Kochba revolt, was this requirement waived. Under normal conditions, if she claimed that she had lost the *get* it was necessary for witnesses to testify to that effect (*Ket*. 16a-b). It was usual for the woman to present her marriage contract when claiming her *kethubah*. If a divorcee, for whatever reason, could not do this, she was still entitled to receive the full settlement because her bill of divorce was obvious proof of her having been married (and therefore entitled to *kethubah* payment) (*Ket*. 9.9). In the case of a widow, however, whose only proof of marriage was the marriage contract, non-presentation of the deed meant loss of the full set-

---

1 It is possible that P. *Mur*. 29, another deed of sale, also contained such a declaration, for as in P. *Mur*. 30, a woman's name is found as the second signature to the document. Unfortunately, little has survived of the body of the deed. On this see Yaron, 'The Murabba'at Documents', *JJS* 11 (1960), p. 162. For an example of the reality of a husband's property standing guarantee for the *kethubah*, see Yadin, *Bar-kokhba*, p. 247, regarding a document from the Babatha archive where it is stated that Babatha is owner of her dead husband's palm groves 'in lieu of [her] bride-money and due'.

tlement and payment only of the minimum amount of the *mohar* (*Ket.* 4.7). With the *kethubah* in her possession the woman could collect the amount owed her many years after her divorce or her husband's death. Only in the case of a widow who had left her husband's home without claiming her money was a statute of limitation imposed. Then, if the settlement had not been claimed after a twenty-five year period, the *kethubah* was cancelled on the assumption that the woman had waived her rights. This, however, only applied to the *kethubah*: the dowry was never cancelled until paid (*Ket.* 104a-b). In the event of there being co-wives, the first wife had prior claim on any property left by the dead husband in consequence of the ruling that a lien of earlier date superseded a lien of later date (*Ket.* 93b). In the unlikely event of them all being divorced on the same day, her *kethubah* payment again took precedence, for as the Mishnah states:

> If they were all put away on the same day, whosoever preceded her fellow even by one hour acquires [first] right. Thus in Jerusalem they used to declare in writing the hour of the divorce. If they were all put away in the same hour and there was property worth only one *mina*, they share equally (*Ket.* 10.5).

Finally, if a woman was widowed and there were no heirs, she was entitled to sell her husband's property as payment for her *kethubah* without a court order, provided that she had proved her claim to the settlement (*Ket.* 11.2). She was, however, obliged to call in a committee of three laymen to appraise the value of the property (*Ket.* 97a-b; 98a; *B.M.* 32b). Although all the husband's property stood surety for the *kethubah*, we might note that according to the Tannaim:

> Compensation for damage is paid out of the best land, a creditor out of medium land, and a wife's *kethubah* out of the poorest land (*Gitt.* 5.1).[1]

Only at a much later date was this ruling amended in favour of the woman, with medieval *kethuboth* declaring that the groom would

---

1   R. Meir differed from the general consensus and recommended that the *kethubah* be paid out of medium land (*ibid.*).

take upon myself and my heirs after me the responsibility of
this marriage contract, of the dowry and of the additional
sum, so that all this shall be paid from the best part of my
property, real and personal, that I now possess or may hereafter acquire.

As has been seen in the course of this survey, most of the
clauses contained in the Murabba'at deeds were in fact simply
reiterations of rabbinic law. Only one of these rabbinic conditions was not included and that was the husband's duty to
ransom his wife,[1] but as the Mishnah states:

> If he had not written for her, 'If thou art taken captive I will
> redeem thee and take thee again as my wife', or, if she was
> the wife of a priest, '[I will redeem thee and] will bring thee
> back in thine own city',[2] he is still liable [so to do] since this
> is a condition enjoined by the court (*Ket.* 4.8).[3]

In later years, this clause was intentionally omitted 'so as to
avoid the mention of bad luck'.[4] Such may well have been the
case with our deeds.

Although the *kethubah* was drawn up at the time of the
couple's betrothal, most of its clauses did not come into effect
until after the nuptials had taken place (see above, p. 158).
Thus, for example, if the woman died whilst still only
betrothed, her fiancé had no right of succession to her property
(*Ket.* 80b; *Yeb.* 38a). Equally, he had no obligation to maintain
her during the betrothal period (*Ket.* 4.4-5; 5.2-3; 2a-b). The
only clause which did apply from the moment of betrothal was
the woman's claim to her *kethubah* should she be divorced or
widowed (*Ket.* 5.1; 11.2). This was in consequence of the fact
that betrothal, like full marriage, could only be terminated by
the death of one of the parties or by formal divorce (see above,

---

1 Possibly also the clause which treated maintenance of daughters after their
  father's death. On this, see above, pp. 64ff.
2 Since, by being taken captive, she became unfit to remain a priest's wife and so
  must return to her father's house. See above, p. 138.
3 Friedman, *Geniza Studies*, p. 71, believes that the ransom clause was in fact contained in P. *Mur.* 20 (and possibly also in 21). On the basis of *Ket.* 4.9 (חיב נשבית
  לפצותה), instead of restoring ... חבן[חשם אם at l. 6, he suggests ... תבין[חשם אם. His
  reconstruction is, however, extremely unlikely, for it was far more important that
  provision for divorce be made than that a ransom clause be included in the marriage contract. His reconstruction would leave no room for the divorce formula.
4 Cf. Friedman, *op. cit.*, pp. 57f., and *PAAJR* 37 (1969), p. 30 n. 2.

p. 169).

As was mentioned earlier, the *kethubah* was drawn up
entirely from the man's point of view. Being a record of his
intent, duties, and obligations there was no necessity for the
woman to make any statement. Her consent to the contents of
the deed could be assumed without any written declaration to
that effect, for according to the Talmud, silence was regarded
as voluntary consent (*Yeb.* 87b; *B.M.* 37b). It is therefore surprising that in P. *Mur.* 21 a special clause was inserted which
expressly recorded the woman's agreement to 'that which is
written above'.[1] This clause is not found in the other
Murabba'at deeds, and it could be that special considerations—now lost to us—prompted its inclusion in this
document. Later (mediaeval) *kethuboth* do not record the
woman's consent, and from all that we have learnt about the
contract and the woman's role generally in the marriage
arrangements, it would seem that this was something
unusual. On the basis of the limited evidence at our disposal,
however, it is not possible to gauge definitively the extent to
which the inclusion of such a clause was exceptional or not.

The Murabba'at deeds conclude with a promise by the
groom to replace the document should it ever be lost or
destroyed.[2] As was noted earlier, the *kethubah* was essentially
the woman's document (and her security), only one deed
being drawn up and that remaining in her possession. The
inclusion of this final clause underlines the tremendous
importance of the contract to the wife.[3]

1 Line 18. The clause is very fragmentary, but sufficient remains for us to
conclude that it did treat the woman's consent.
2 P. *Mur.* 20.13-14; 21.19-20; clause not extant in 115 and 116.
3 Further evidence for the obvious importance of the marriage deed for the woman
is provided by the Babatha archive. Of the 35 documents in that cache, most were
discovered bound in batches according to subject matter. Just a few were found
individually wrapped, each one in its own sacking. Of this latter group Yadin
wrote, 'These documents were of special importance to the women of the family
and had been wrapped up in this way to enable them to have them in their own personal keeping. This is evident from the contents of three of these documents. Document 6 is a deed of gift whereby Babatha's father made over all his property to her
mother; No. 7 is the *kethubah* of Babatha's second marriage; and No. 16 is the
marriage deed of Shelmazion' ('Expedition D', p. 236).

D. *The Marriage Ceremony*

As was demonstrated earlier in this chapter (above, pp. 157-58), during the latter part of the period under consideration, the transition from unmarried to married state was effected by two distinct ceremonies, those of *kiddushin / erusin* (betrothal) and *nissu'in* (taking in marriage). In consequence of the way in which the former constituted a legally binding contract (see above, pp. 169f.), the celebration of *nissu'in*, by which the couple became fully man and wife, contained no further formal declaration regarding the commitment to communal life. It consisted simply of the ceremonial transfer of the betrothed woman to her husband's house for the consummation of the marriage. A popular expression for the act of marriage, therefore, was simply כנס (lit. 'take home') rather than *nissu'in*.[1] In this section we shall examine the various rituals which constituted the marriage ceremony and marked the woman's passage from one man's authority to another.

According to the Talmud, the wedding of a virgin was meant to take place on only one day of the week: Wednesday (*Ket.* 1.1). Various reasons were put forward by the Sages to explain this ruling. According to the Mishnah the choice of that particular day was dictated by a desire for prompt action regarding complaints of non-virginity (cf. Deut. 22.13f.):

> A virgin should be married on a Wednesday and a widow on a Thursday, for in towns the court sits twice in the week, on Mondays and on Thursdays so that if the husband would lodge a virginity suit he may go forthwith in the morning to the court (*Ket.* 1.1).

The artificiality of this reasoning, however, is self-evident: why restrict the celebration of marriage to a Wednesday if the courts also sat on Mondays? As later commentators to this mishnah themselves correctly noted:

> Well, let her be married on the first day of the week, so that if he had a claim to her virginity he could go early [on the morning of the second day of the week] to the court of justice

---

1 Thus Admon, a civil law judge in Jerusalem from the latter days of the Second Temple, quotes the popular expression for marriage and divorce as כנס או פטר או כנס (*Ket.* 13.5). See Jastrow, p. 649.

(*Ket*. 2a).

Having recognized the fundamental flaw of the Tannaim's line of argument, these later thinkers strove to find a different explanation for the custom of virgins marrying only on Wednesdays, and suggested that it was to give the groom sufficient time to make the necessary wedding preparations:

> The Sages watched over the interests of the daughters of Israel so that [the bridegroom] should prepare for the [wedding] feast three days, [namely] on the first day in the week, and on the fourth he marries her (*Ket*. 2a).

Again, however, as an explanation of the custom this was (and is) by no means satisfactory. Indeed, the manifest artificiality and high degree of rationalization evident in both explanations would indicate that a very different reason lay behind the selection of Wednesday for marriage. Possibly the true origin of the custom may be discovered from a passage in the Jerusalem Talmud, where it is stated that מפני הכשפים ('on account of sorceries') no wedding may ever take place on a Monday (y. *Ket*. 1.1, 1a). The reason given for this particular prohibition would suggest that superstitious motives similarly lay behind the recommendation that virgins marry on a Wednesday. In other words, of the seven days in the week, Wednesday was considered to be singularly free from supernatural threat and therefore especially auspicious for the start of married life. As we shall see in the course of this survey, a great many of the rituals performed in the course of the wedding celebrations had their origin in superstitious belief and practice.

In common with other peoples in the ancient world, the Jews had a profound belief in the existence of evil spirits or demons. The belief was that these spirits, though unseen, were omnipresent and were the cause of all the inexplicable experiences of human existence. While posing a constant threat to human wellbeing, they were held to be particularly active and malevolent at such critical moments of life as birth, marriage and death, that is, at times of transition from one state to another.[1] Particular danger attached to the bride and groom,

---

1   For the danger which surrounded a person at birth, see Chapter 1 §B. For the belief in general, see J. Morgenstern, *Rites of Birth, Marriage, Death and Kindred Occasions among the Semites*, and J. Trachtenberg, *Jewish Magic and Superstition*.

for in addition to their vulnerability on passing from the unmarried to the married state, they were susceptible on account of the demons' jealousy of all human happiness. On the threshold of marriage they became the objects of the envy of the spirits and consequently were especially liable to be harmed by them. Thus in the *Testament of Solomon* the demon Asmodeus is given the following words to say:

> My business is to plot against the newly wedded, so that they may not know each other. And I sever them utterly by many calamities; and I waste away the beauty of virgins and estrange their hearts (22-23).

As shall be shown in more detail below, there was also the belief that the spirits had a right to the first act of sexual intercourse with a virgin. In popular imagination, therefore, the occasion of that first intercourse was held to be fraught with danger, both to the woman, over whom the demon had dominion, and to the man, who was usurping the spirit's prior claim. That the most critical period in a person's life was indeed thought to occur at the time of marriage is further demonstrated by the following statement of Rab Judah: 'Three persons require guarding [from evil spirits], namely, a sick person, a bridegroom and a bride' (*Ber.* 54b).

The power of the evil spirits over the bride and groom was believed to endure for precisely seven days, the number seven being considered a particularly unlucky, ill-omened number by the ancient Semites.[1] Throughout this time various rites were performed, all of which acknowledged in one way or another the prior right of the demons over the bride and the consequent threat to the groom. The rites were obviously intended to protect the couple from harm and were, as we shall see, either directly aimed at warding off attack, or designed to deceive the spirits into indifference, or placatory in character. At the close of the seven-day period, these various exercises came to a natural end: the couple were henceforth considered fully married and able to go about the activities of

---

1 See Morgenstern, *op. cit.*, pp. 24ff.; and Ch. 1 §B in the context of birth ritual, and Ch. 4 in the context of death ritual.

ordinary, profane existence without fear of the spirits which had posed such a threat during the time of instability and change.

From this brief outline of the various superstitious beliefs and practices which accompanied marriage in the ancient Semitic world, it becomes even more likely that Wednesday was originally chosen to start the seven-day festive period because of some peculiarly auspicious character which attached to it—a character now lost to the modern mind and apparently also to the Sages of our period who, as we have seen, struggled to find an explanation for the selection.[1] Although little value can thus be attached to the Sages' statements, their concern to provide explanations does indicate that the custom was for virgins to marry on the fourth day of the week. The only time when this practice was revised was 'from the time of danger and onwards [when] the people made it a custom to marry on the third day and the Sages did not interfere' (*Ket.* 3b). The danger that the Jews were here seeking to avoid was the imposition by the Romans of *ius primae noctis*. Such at least is the explicit meaning of the Talmud which refers both to Roman officials and to a statement by Rabbah that 'a maid that gets married on the fourth day [of the week] shall have the first sexual intercourse with the prefect'. To allay any superstitious fears about marrying on a Tuesday, the religious leaders declared, on the basis of Gen. 1.22, that that day augured well for a couple's fertility (y. *Ket.* 1.1, 1a). It is apparent, however, that Wednesday continued to be the most popular day for marriage, for as the Talmud states, if a Roman prefect or general was passing through a town and did not stop, then any wedding which had been arranged for a Tuesday was delayed until the fourth day of the following week (*Ket.* 3b).

The bride's day of transfer began at her father's house with personal preparations for her procession to the groom's home

---

1 It is possible that the Sages were in fact consciously striving to underplay the people's belief in demons, and for this reason made no mention of the real explanation. In the light of Rab Judah's comment, however, regarding the need to protect bride and groom (above, p. 191), this seems unlikely. It could simply be that the particular details as to the original choice of that day were now lost and so the Sages sought other explanations.

and the subsequent celebrations. In Ezekiel we are given the following description of how the bride Jerusalem was prepared for her wedding to Yahweh:

> Then washed I thee with water... and anointed thee with oil. I clothed thee also with richly woven cloth and shod thee with seal skin, and I wound fine linen about thy head and covered thee with silk. I decked thee also with ornaments, and I put bracelets upon thy hands and a chain on thy neck. And I put a ring upon thy nose and earrings in thine ears, and a beautiful crown upon thy head (16.8f.).

Before meeting with Boaz, Ruth similarly washed and anointed herself and donned her best attire (Ruth 3.3; cf. Isa. 2.32; 61.10). The custom of preparing the bride in this manner continued throughout the period, many passages in the intertestamental literature making reference to her jewels, garlands, and perfumed hair (for example, *2 Bar.* 10.13; *3 Macc.* 4.6). That such preparations were regarded as an essential part of the wedding celebrations and continued to be so to the close of our period is evidenced by a tale of R. Tarfon who, on witnessing the procession of a poorly attired bride, ordered that she be brought into his house to be 'bathed, anointed and adorned' as befitted all women on such occasions (*Aboth de R. Nathan* 41, 67a).[1]

One distinctive feature of the bride's dress was an elaborate crown. This was made out of salt and brimstone with myrtle and roses and intertwined with gold thread (*Sot.* 49a).[2] A similar crown was worn by the groom (*Sot.* 9.14; *Gitt.* 7a; cf. Songs 3.11). The most important element of the crown was the salt which, it was believed, had the property of repelling attacks from demons and averting the evil eye.[3] Myrtle may have

---

1 Regarding the acceptibility of this material as a source for our period, see Schürer, *op. cit.*, I, p. 80: '*Aboth de-Rabbi Nathan* [is] an expansion of the Mishnah tractate Aboth, with supplementary accounts from the lives of the rabbis and other haggadic material. It has survived in two recensions and first received its present form in the post-Talmudic period. But since the teachers whom it quotes all belong to the age of Mishnah, the tractate may be considered as Tannaitic in substance.' R. Tarfon was a contemporary of Akiba who flourished c. 110-35 CE.

2 According to Rashi, the crown was cut out of a block of salt and then figures were traced upon it with brimstone. The gold was apparently sometimes used to make a design in the form of the city of Jerusalem (*Shabb.* 59a).

3 See Morgenstern, *op. cit.*, pp. 196-98 n. 27; also above pp. 38ff. for its use in birth ritual.

been included as a symbol of prosperity, for among present-day Fellahin the bride is always decorated with green twigs in order that 'her entrance may be blessed and her heels may be green'.[1] The roses and gold were presumably for perfume and decoration. The use of such crowns continued until the destruction of the Temple. Then, as *Sot.* 9.14 reports:

> During the war with Vespasian [emperor, 69-79 CE] they [that is, the rabbis] decreed against the crowns of the bride-grooms and against the [wedding] drum. During the war of Quietus[2] they decreed against the crowns worn by brides...

The reason given by the rabbis for this prohibition was that,

> When the mitre is worn by the high priest, ordinary persons can wear the crown, but when the mitre has been removed from the head of the high priest, the crown must be removed from the head of ordinary persons (*Gitt.* 71a).[3]

Prior to the bride's departure, it would seem that a feast was held at her father's house. Unfortunately we have little information about this event for the sources concentrate almost exclusively upon the wedding celebrations which took place at the home of the groom later the same day. Though no details are available, however, the fact that such a feast was held may be deduced from the following mishnah whose aim was to prevent accidental breach of the law which prohibited slaughter of a female animal and its young both on the same day (Lev. 22.28):

---

1 Fellahin saying quoted by Granqvist in *Marriage Conditions in a Palestinian Village*, II, p. 66. Cf. Jaussen, *Coûtumes Palestiniennes*, I, p. 79: 'en Orient la verdure est toujours l'emblème de la prospérité'.

2 See note to Soncino Mishnah: 'The text has Titus; but Neubauer's *Medieval Jewish Chronicles*, II, p. 66 has the correct reading'. Quietus was a Roman general of Moorish origin who distinguished himself in the wars during Trajan's reign and was one of the principal commanders in the Parthian campaign. Among his activities in Mesopotamia was the subduing of Jews hostile to Rome. In 117 CE he was appointed governor of Judaea where he apparently continued his activities against the Jews. Such at least is suggested by the rabbinic tradition regarding a 'War of Quietus', but details are not available to us.

3 It is possible, however, that among certain circles the use of the crown for brides continued, for in *Gitt.* 7a the following baraitha is found: 'Rabina discovered Mar son of R. Ashi weaving a garland for his daughter. He said to him, Sir, do you not hold with the interpretation... "Remove the mitre and take off the crown?"—He replied: The men [have to follow] the example of the high priest, but not the women.'

if a dealer sold the dam to the bridegroom and the daughter
to the bride, it is needful to tell the matter [to both parties]
since it is known that they will both slaughter [their beast]
the same day (*Hull.* 5.3).

Further evidence is adduced by A. Büchler who notes the way
in which t. *Meg.* 4.15 refers to three feasts in connection with
marriage, the first at betrothal, the second at the wedding and
the third being held at the בית המשתה (house of eating/drink-
ing).[1] Commenting on this passage, Büchler writes:

> As the last is the designation for the feast given by the father
> of the bridegroom on the day of the marriage, the second, the
> feast of נישואין [*nissu'in*, i.e. the start of the ceremonial home-
> taking] is, evidently, the feast arranged by the father of the
> bride at his house, before she leaves to proceed to her hus-
> band's home.[2]

We have no information as to whether the bride herself was
present at this feast. It is possible that it was celebrated only by
the men of the household, together with their male guests,
while she was being prepared by the womenfolk. It is also
likely that this feast at the start of the *nissu'in* ceremonial was
less significant than that held later the same day at the bride's
new home, for the Gemara to *Hull.* 5.3 contains the following
comment:

> Why does he [R. Judah] particularly state THE DAM TO THE
> BRIDEGROOM and THE YOUNG TO THE BRIDE?—He inciden-
> tally tells us that it is the proper thing for the bridegroom's
> family to make greater festivities than the bride's family'
> (*Hull.* 83a).

At her departure the bride received words of advice and
blessings from her family. Particular emphasis was placed
upon expressing the hope that she be the mother of many children. Thus, in the earlier biblical period Laban and Bethuel
say to Rebekah, 'be thou the mother of thousands of ten thou-

1 'This was the custom of the societies in Jerusalem: some of the members went to a
feast of betrothal, others to a feast of marriage, others to a circumcision, others to
the collection of bones for the final burial [see pp. 255-57 for details of this
practice], others לבית המשתה, and others again to the house of mourning.'
2 A. Büchler, 'The Induction of the Bride and the Bridegroom into the חופה in the
First and Second Centuries in Palestine', in *Livre d'hommage à la mémoire du
Dr. Samuel Poznanski*, p. 108.

sands, and let thy seed possess the gate of those that hate them' (Gen. 24.60), whilst in the later intertestamental book of Tobit, Raguel and Edna both express the hope that they may see children of Sarah before their death (10.11-12; cf. Ruth 4.11-12). The fact that the woman was passing into the authority and protection of a new family group was also underlined, as was the family's desire that she do nothing to sully their good reputation. Thus Raguel advises Sarah:

> Go unto thy father-in-law, because henceforth they are thy parents as they who begat thee; farewell, daughter. May I hear good report of thee so long as I live (Tob. 10.12).

After the benedictions the bride started her journey to her new home. The procession to the groom's house was a joyous occasion, the young woman being accompanied by flute players, trumpeters and drummers (*B.M.* 6.1; *Sot.* 9.14; *Ket.* 17a).[1] As many people as possible joined her on her journey, since it was considered a *mitzvah* to 'gladden' her heart (*Ber.* 6b). Indeed, so important was this *mitzvah* (which, incidentally, was regarded as equal to making a thanksgiving offering), that it was permitted to abandon the study of Torah in order to swell the ranks of a procession rather than let the bride be accompanied by too few people (*Ket.* 17a). And according to the Sages, the definition of insufficient numbers was twelve thousand men and six thousand trumpeters! Dances and juggling tricks were performed before the bride, sometimes with an excessive degree of hilarity which was thought unbecoming in certain circles. Thus, for example, Rav Aha was rebuked by his colleagues for having danced with the bride upon his shoulder (*Ket.* 17a). In addition to the dances, songs of praise were sung extolling the woman's beauty and virtue. An example of such a song is found in the Babylonian Talmud:

> Thus they sing before the bride in the West [that is, in Palestine]: No powder and no paint and no waving [of the hair] and still a graceful gazelle (*Ket.* 17a).

---

1   The evidence for this part of the wedding celebrations comes principally from rabbinic sources but obviously reflects older and continuing practices: the mishnayoth are old and the material subject to discussion by Shammai and Hillel (first century BCE—first century CE), founders of schools named after them. For indicators as to the wedding ceremonial and procession in the Bible see, for example Isa. 49.18; 61.10; Jer. 2.32; 7.34; 16.9; 25.10; Ps. 45.8-15.

It is apparent that the joyfulness of the occasion often encouraged excesses among the singers also, for the schools of Shammai and Hillel had a longstanding dispute about the dangers of exaggerating the bride's attributes, the former maintaining that there should be no superfluous praise and the latter arguing that all compliments were permitted (*ibid.*).

In the course of the procession, dried corn and nuts were scattered in front of the bride and goblets of tithed wine were passed before her (*Ket.* 16b-17a; *Ber.* 50b). It is likely that such action had its origin in the desire to avert evil, the grain, nuts and wine being originally intended as offerings to the demons to bribe them not to harm the bride.[1] In its secondary character, it symbolized prosperity and abundance, as did the myrtle twigs which were waved at the bride throughout her procession (*Ket.* 17a).[2] The bride herself travelled, with her hair unbound, in a special litter, הינומא, which was also decorated with myrtle (*Ket.* 2.1, 17b).[3]

The scattering of foodstuffs, the marriage song and dance, the bridal litter, and the woman's unbound hair were all the distinctive marks of a virgin's wedding, the weddings of widows and divorcees being celebrated on a much less grand scale. These various rituals served a practical purpose: should the woman at some later date loose her marriage contract which contained record of the amount of *kethubah* owed her, she could call upon those who had witnessed her bridal procession to give testimony of the fact that she had been a virgin at marriage and was therefore entitled to the larger sum of two hundred *zuzin* in the event of widowhood or divorce (*Ket.* 2.1, 16b).

On the bride's arrival at her husband's house, the groom came out with his relatives and friends to greet her. So in 1 Maccabees we read,

> the children of Ambri were making a great marriage and were bringing the bride from Nadabath with a great train, a daughter of one of the great nobles of Canaan..., a great ado and much baggage; and the bridegroom came forth and his

---

1 See Westermark, *History of Human Marriage*, II, p. 484; J.Z. Lauterbach, 'The Ceremony of Breaking a Glass at Weddings', *HUCA* 2 (1925), pp. 358-59.

2 See above, pp. 193-94 and p. 194 n. 1.

3 The use of the litter also stopped at times of persecution (*Sot.* 9.14).

friends and his brethren to meet them [that is the bridal pro-
cession] with timbrels and minstrels (9.37-39).[1]

This formal welcome of the bride by the groom and his family
constituted the important part of the wedding ceremony, for,
as was noted earlier, the celebration of *nissu'in* consisted
essentially of the induction of the woman into her new home.
The importance which society attached to the groom greeting
his bride in person is demonstrated in the book of Tobit. There,
due to unusual circumstances, Tobias and Sarah had jour-
neyed together to Tobias' family home, having already consummated their union at Sarah's house. On reaching the
gates of the city, however, Tobias' companion Raphael urged
him to 'run forward before thy wife and prepare the house
while they are coming' (11.3). Tobias was thus able to join his
father in formally welcoming the bride to her new home
(11.16).

After the bride had been greeted by her new family, she was
escorted to a specially prepared wedding chamber, the חופה, by
some of those who had accompanied her on the procession,
while the groom joined his wedding guests for a banquet.[2]
That the bride herself was not present at this feast is
demonstrated by the description of the wedding celebrations in
Tobit:

> And Raguel called Edna, his wife, and said unto her, Sister,
> prepare the other chamber and bring her [that is, Sarah] in
> thither. And she went and spread the bed in the chamber as
> he bade her, and brought her thither... And when they [that
> is, the wedding guests] had finished eating and drinking,
> they desired to sleep, and they led the young man [that is,
> Tobias] away and brought him into the chamber (7.15–8.1).

Further evidence for the absence of the bride is to be found in
the various talmudic passages which, when speaking of the
preparations for the banquet, employ the formula 'N. made a
wedding feast for his son' (for example, *Shev.* 7.4; *Kerith.* 3.7;
Ber. 30b; *Taan.* 14b; cf. Mt. 22.2f.). No mention is ever made of
the bride. Similarly, in discussions about the banquet's seating

---

1 Although this refers to a non-Jewish clan, the story can doubtless be taken to
   reflect general local custom.
2 In Judaea the groom was permitted to spend a little time alone with his bride on
   her arrival, not to consummate the union but simply to get to know her a little. He
   then went to the feast (*Ket.* 12a).

arrangements, no word is said about placing the bride (*Mo'ed Katan* 28b; cf. Lk. 5.34; Mt. 9.14-15). We might also note that the ritual benedictions which were recited in the course of the meal are simply termed 'the blessing of the bridegrooms' (*Ket.* 7b). The bride remained in the חופה, probably with women friends in attendance, making final preparations for the moment when 'as a youthful wife she will receive him' (Sir. 15.2).

The feast itself was a sumptuous affair prepared and financed by the groom's family. Whole beasts were purchased and slaughtered for the occasion (*Kerith.* 3.7; *Shev.* 7.4; Tob. 8.19; Mt. 22.4) which was attended by a great many guests (t. *B.M.* 8.28; Mt. 22.10) who were expected to wear their most festive garb (Mt. 22.11). Wine flowed freely, for, as the Sages themselves declared, 'without wine, there is no joy' (*Pes.* 109a; cf. Jn 2.3f.) and there was general merrymaking in the form of songs and story telling (cf. Judg. 14.10f.; *Sot.* 9.11). Certain protocol was observed regarding the seating arrangements (Lk. 14.8-11), with the groom in the place of honour at the head of the gathering (*Mo'ed Katan* 28b), ready to receive the special blessings which were pronounced in the course of the meal (*Meg.* 4.3; *Ket.* 7b-8a).[1] Organization of the feast was placed in the hands of a steward specially appointed for the occasion (Jn 2.8; Sir. 32.1-2).

At a particular point in the celebrations, the groom's father ritually smashed a cup before his guests. Thus in the Talmud we read:

> Mar the son of Rabina made the wedding feast for his son. When he noticed that the rabbis were very gay, he brought a precious cup worth 400 *zuzin* and broke it before them and they immediately became sad. R. Ashi made the wedding feast for his son. When he noticed that the rabbis were very gay, he brought a cup of white glass and broke it before them and immediately they became sad (*Ber.* 30b-31a).

This is the first mention we have of the custom of breaking a glass at weddings, a custom which has remained a feature of Jewish marriage ceremonies through the ages,[2] and it comes

---

1 Cf. *DJD*, VII, pp. 80ff.
2 Though nowadays it is the groom himself who performs the ritual.

to us from a relatively late Talmudic account, at least in so far as our period is concerned. It is evident, however, that the action of Mar and Ashi, both of whom were fourth-century Babylonian Amoraim, was neither strange nor unprecedented, for the Talmud makes no attempt to explain their behaviour. The custom may therefore be read back in time. According to the baraitha, it was prompted by a desire to curb the wedding guests' excessive hilarity; later commentators explained the need for this in terms of the duty to mourn the destruction of Jerusalem, even on happy occasions. It is likely, however, that in its original meaning the ceremony derived from superstitious belief. We have already noted the way in which demons were believed to be at their most dangerous during times of human happiness. To avoid provoking their envy, it was considered necessary to deceive them into believing that the people were in fact sad, and this was the purpose of breaking the glass.[1] The act broke the spell of revelry, reminded the guests of their danger, and caused them to appear sad for the moment. An aspect of the ceremony's purpose which is not suggested in the baraitha but which is nonetheless very probable is that the noise of the shattering glass was thought to frighten away from the gathering any hovering spirits. A more direct attack upon the demons was designed at a later date when the glass was thrown at the wedding hall's northern wall, evil spirits being believed to lurk around walls and to come from the north (cf. *Hull.* 105b), and one post-talmudic feature of the ritual was to smash the vessel with its contents, the wine thus spilled acting as an offering to the demons.

At the close of the feast the groom was escorted by the wedding guests to the חופה (*chupah*). We might note, *en passant*, that the חופה to which the groom was escorted and within which his bride waited, was not some form of bridal tent-bed as some scholars, influenced by the later use of symbolic wedding canopies (also called חופות), have asserted. It would seem

---

1 If this was the meaning of the ceremony, then the silence of the Talmud on the subject becomes more understandable in that, while the rabbis could not suppress popular superstitious practice, it is possible they would not emphasize the importance demons had in popular imagination. See Lauterbach, *op. cit.*, pp. 353-54, 363f. Cf., however, p.192 n. 1 above.

from the various Talmudic descriptions of its construction to
have been an actual room, either within the groom's family
home and specially designated for the couple's use, or a separate structure, perhaps a temporary wooden building.[1] The
fact that the bride, who remained within the חופה throughout
the wedding week, was visited by relatives and friends during
that seven-day period (see below), is further proof that the חופה
was a room rather than a curtained bed: had it been the latter,
she would not have been able to accommodate her guests.[2]

Prior to the couple consummating their union, it would
seem that one final ritual, again of a protective nature, was
performed. As was noted earlier, the occasion of the first sexual intercourse was believed to be attended by all manner of
demonic beings who, it was held, hankered after the virgin
and her hymeneal blood.[3] Immediate danger did not, however,
attach to the woman herself: she was simply a vehicle for possession through which the spirits could attack the groom in
order to prevent him usurping their prior claim. Thus, in the
book of Tobit,[4] Sarah outlives her seven husbands, each of
whom is killed by the demon Asmodeus 'before they had been
with her as is appointed for women' (3.7-8), and as Tobias, the
eighth possible victim, comments:

> And now I for my part I fear—for her he harmeth not,
> but the man who would come in unto her, him he slayeth...
> (6.15).[5]

The superstition that women were particularly susceptible
to demonic possession (and therefore a source of danger to
their menfolk) had its rationalization in the belief that the

---

1 Cf. *Gitt.* 57a which records how in Judaea it was customary to plant a cedar tree at
   the birth of a son and an acacia tree for a daughter, the branches of which were
   later used for the construction of the children's חופה.
2 See Büchler, *op. cit.*, pp. 83f.
3 For this belief, see Morgenstern, *op. cit.*, p. 182.
4 Probably written in the third century BCE and possibly originating in Palestine.
   See Introduction.
5 The book combines concern for near-kin endogamy (see above, pp. 146ff.) with
   the motif of demonic possession. Thus, each of the seven husbands is killed on
   account of distance of blood kinship to Sarah, but significantly the means of dis-
   patch is at the hands of Asmodeus on the wedding night. Even Tobias, who was the
   most eligible of Sarah's suitors (her cousin), remains fearful of the demons and,
   as we shall see, takes measures to protect himself.

spirits, being bodiless entities and therefore imperfect, were in
a constant state of agitation to acquire corporeal existence, and
could only attain that goal by working up through the hierarchy of creation. So, 'just as woman, in herself imperfect, seeks
perfection through union with man, so the demons seek to
unite themselves primarily with woman who represents the
next degree of creation above them' (the legend being that the
demons came into existence on the eve of the Sabbath).[1] Any
man who attempted to 'possess' a woman first thus ran the
grave risk of incurring the demons' wrath as their designs on
the virgin were thwarted. Underlying this entire belief-sys-
tem of women as models for demonic possession—and one of
the prime constituents of that culturally constructed fear of
women already discussed—was the Jews' suspicion of
'female' blood, both menstrual and that consequent upon first
intercourse (see above, pp. 36-38). Unable to explain or control
these flows of blood, they regarded women as suspect beings,
who, during their times of 'impurity', were doubtless under
the control of evil spirits. To protect themselves from danger,
they hedged women's movements with restrictive laws and
forbade association between the sexes during the period of
bleeding and for seven (!) days thereafter (Lev. 15.19f.).[2] It
was, however, obviously impossible to avoid contact with
hymeneal blood, though the necessity of such contact did not
reduce the attendant danger. For a man to approach a virgin,
therefore, was an extremely risky business, for the likelihood
was that she was under the control of a jealous demon because
(i) being on the threshold of a change in state she was particularly susceptible to evil influence; (ii) the spirits desired corporeal existence and the way to that existence was through a
woman as yet unpossessed by man, and (iii) the demons had

1 Trachtenberg, *op. cit.*, p. 50. For women being regarded as inferior, lower on the
   order of creation, and closer to the world of nature, see below and Archer, 'Bound
   by Blood . . . ' and 'In Thy Blood, Live . . . '
2 This was one of the many aspects surrounding the laws of ritual cleanness (see
   above) and could in fact have been a belief generated by those laws—though here
   one gets wrapped into strands of circularity. The association of the blood with
   demonic possession is clearly seen by the legislators' choice of a seven-day period
   of impurity, seven being the number most commonly associated with the power of
   evil and the spiritual world. Morgenstern (p. 116) points to the present-day belief
   that a man will get leprosy if he consorts with an 'unclean' woman.

prior claim to and control of her hymeneal blood.

When the groom came to the חופה for the consummation of his marriage, therefore, he was obliged to adopt counter-offensive tactics to exorcise the demon from his bride before he himself was attacked. Magic was employed for this purpose:

> As regards the heart and liver of the fish, make thou a smoke before a man or a woman who hath an attack of the demon or an evil spirit; and every attack will flee from him, and they shall never more find an abode with him (Tob. 6.7-8; cf. 6.17-18).

On entering his bridal-chamber, Tobias pursued precisely this course of action and so safeguarded himself from the fate suffered by Sarah's previous husbands:

> And when they had finished eating and drinking... they led the young man away and brought him into the chamber. And Tobias... took the liver of the fish and the heart... and put them on the ashes of the incense. And the smell of the fish baffled the demon and he ran away into the upper part of Egypt... And they went forth and shut the door of the chamber... And they slept the night (8.1-9).

The Talmud has nothing to say about this practice, probably because the religious leaders of the time wished to play down the people's belief in evil spirits and their attachment to the magical arts, such superstitions being incompatible with the true worship of Yahweh. Philo, however, does make reference to the offering of 'bridal sacrifices' (*Spec. Leg.* 3.79), and it is interesting to note that among twentieth-century Bedouin and Fellahin it remained the custom for the groom to make a sacrifice of redemption before his bride in order to free her from the possessive power of evil spirits.[1]

Once the groom had entered the חופה the wedding guests retired. They did not stay overnight, but returned to their own homes, so removing themselves from the source of danger. Only the שושבינין (*shoshbinim*) remained whose duties were to guard the house and be on hand to check the tokens of virginity.[2] The שושבינין were specially appointed friends of the couple

1 See Morgenstern, *op. cit.*, pp. 112-15.
2 The שושבינין stayed with the couple throughout the wedding week, their other duties being to rejoice with the bride and groom (*B.B.* 145a; Jn 3.29) and to give presents (*B.B.* 9.4, 144b). Their services and gifts were reciprocated on the occasion of their own marriages (*ibid.*).

and, at least in Judaea, were two in number.[1] They were
chiefly employed to testify, in case of need, to the virginity of
the bride and to ensure that no trickery was resorted to by
either party. Thus they examined the couple before they
entered the bridal-chamber and after the consummation kept
the evidence of the bride's virginity, that is, the stained sheet,
in their possession to prevent the groom destroying the
'tokens' and lodging a false virginity suit (*Ket.* 6b, 12a). It is
commonly assumed that both were men, שושבינין usually being
translated as 'groomsmen'. However, a few considerations
would indicate that in fact the duties were performed by a
man and a woman.

First, the Talmud explicitly states that the practice was to
put up two שושבינין, 'one for him and one for her'. Given the
nature of their duties, and the general concern regarding segregation of the sexes, it is unlikely that a man would have
attended on the bride. Secondly, another talmudic passage
makes clear reference to a female שושבין:

> R. Bibi visited R. Joseph. Having dined he said to them [the
> servants] 'Remove the ladder from under Bibi'.[2] But Rabbah
> said: If her husband is in town, we have no fear on account
> of privacy?—R. Bibi was different [that is, the usual rules did
> not apply], because she was his best friend and intimate with
> him.
>
> (... שאני רב ביבי דשושבינתיה הואי וג׳סא ביה)

Third, the fact that one of the express functions of the attendants was to sleep in the same house as the newly married
couple (*Ket.* 12a; y. *Ket.* 1, 25a) is a further indicator of their
being a man and a woman. As man and woman they could
have been used to deceive the evil spirits into thinking that
they were in fact the bride and groom. Thus the demons
would vainly direct their evil machinations against the

---

1 *Ket.* 12a. The Talmud points to a difference in custom between Judaea and
   Galilee but does not define that difference. It is therefore unclear whether the
   practice in Galilee was to employ only one שושבן or possibly none at all. See, however, *Ket.* 1.5.
2 They were in an upper chamber and then R. Joseph and his wife descended, leaving R. Bibi above. The removal of the ladder was to ensure that Bibi did not associate in an improper way with Joseph's wife.

shoshbinim while the bride and groom consummated their union in safety.[1] This desire to deceive the unsuspecting spirits is possibly the origin of the role of the best man and matron (or maid) of honour in modern Christian ceremonies.

At some point subsequent to her arrival at the groom's house the bride donned a veil. This may be deduced from three facts. First, as we have seen, one distinctive feature of a virgin's wedding was that she travelled from her father's house with her hair unbound. Had she been veiled at this point—and here it should be remembered that the veil was essentially a head covering and not a face covering[2]—the witnesses in a *kethubah* claim would not have been able to testify to her unbound hair (that is, to the fact that hers was a first marriage and she was entitled to the higher bride-price for virgins). Secondly, in *3 Maccabees* we are given a description of the forcible eviction of newly-wedded women from their bridal-chambers under the persecutions of Ptolemy Philopator.[3] Explicit reference is made to the fact that the brides were 'carried away unveiled', the implication being that they had been veiled within their bridal chambers (4.6-9). Third, the act of veiling was commonly a part of the marriage ceremonial, being a visible means to mark the woman's transition from the unmarried to the married state (cf. Gen. 24.65; Ruth 3.9; Ezek. 16.8).[4] It served as a symbol of the man's possession of the woman, and she wore it throughout her married life.[5] It is not clear, however, at precisely what point

1 Morgenstern, *op. cit.*, pp. 243-44, n. 59, suggests that the bridal pair actually slept elsewhere, 'probably in a place not generally known', and derives this idea from the modern Bedouin practice of the bride and groom removing themselves to a 'remote and previously unappointed spot'. It is, however, unlikely that Morgenstern is correct for the Talmud explicitly says that the שושבינין used to sleep in the house in which the bridegroom and the bride slept (*Ket.* 12a). Removal to a different place would also make nonsense of all the passages which discuss the character and function of the חופה, and the entrance of the bridal couple therein.
2 See Epstein, *Sex Laws and Customs in Judaism*, pp. 42-43, and below pp. 247-48.
3 See p. 120 n. 1 above.
4 That unmarried women did not wear veils may be assumed from *Ned.* 30b which says that children did not cover their heads (note that women were usually married by the age of twelve). Also, the fact that young girls had no public life but were kept secluded within their fathers' homes rendered the wearing of a veil meaningless (see above, Chapter 1 §E).
5 Thus according to the Talmud, 'common law marriage' among the Noahides was considered dissolved when the husband removed the covering from his wife's head (*Ber.* 21a). See Morgenstern, *op. cit.*, pp. 99-100, on the cutting off or covering of the hair amongst various Semitic peoples at the transition from virginity to the married state. Regarding the Jews he writes that concealing the hair was a substitute for an earlier custom of cutting off the bride's hair, this having acted as a

in the marriage ceremonial the woman assumed her veil. Possibly she was veiled by the groom when he came out to meet her and the bridal procession, or by her female friends within the חופה prior to his arrival for the consummation.

For the rest of the wedding week the bride remained within the חופה while her husband continued the celebrations with his guests, only joining her at night (cf. *Ket.* 7b).[1] During this time it would seem that she received visits from relatives and friends. Such at least is suggested by a statement of R. Meir: 'During the ninety years of her barren state, Sarah was as a bride in her marriage chamber, and noble ladies came to greet her' (*Gen. Rab.* 45.4).[2]

The reason for the bride's confinement to the חופה was two-fold. First, women in general were accorded no public social role and so only the husband could properly take his place in the wedding celebrations (see next chapter). Second, it was deemed advisable to isolate the bride, who was a potential source of demon possession, away from the guests during the period of danger. At the end of the seven-day transitional period she left the chamber, resumed her normal duties, and re-entered ordinary, profane existence a married woman.

redemptive taboo-rite at the moment of the girl losing her virginity and moving into a profane state. The significance of the veil for the married woman will be treated more fully in the next chapter.

1   Thus Joel 2.16, 'Let the bridegroom go forth from his chamber and the bride from out of her pavillion', and 1 Macc. 1.27, 'She that sat in the bridal chamber mourned'.

2   It is in the context of these visits that the Talmud's statement about the bride being visible during the wedding is to be understood (*Ket.* 17a). The passage is normally taken to show that she was present at the feasts. *Gen. Rab.* was probably compiled in the sixth century CE in Palestine (possibly earlier), while Meir was a third generation Tanna who flourished c. 130-160 CE.

Chapter 3

LIFE AS A WIFE AND MOTHER

A. *Subordinate to Husband—Domestic Duties*
Maintenance—Property Rights

In Chapter 1 we examined the way in which the life of the minor was firmly controlled by her father in consequence of the authority vested in him as *pater familias*. In this section we shall attempt a similar survey of the power exercised over the married woman by her husband. We shall then consider the various tasks which she as wife and mother was obliged to perform, tasks which underlined her position of subordination within the houshold. The second half of this section will be devoted to a detailed examination of the maintenance which was her legal due throughout married life, and will conclude with an analysis of her property rights, most of which were forfeited in return for the support received from her husband.

At the age of twelve and a half the Jewish woman was released from the all-embracing control of *patria potestas*. The custom of early marriage, however, precluded her enjoying her newly found freedom,[1] for society accorded the husband a similar degree of authority as that possessed by the father. The fact that, under normal circumstances, the woman passed straight from one male authority to another is clearly indicated by *Ket.* 4.5, which states: 'She continues within the control of the father until she enters into the control

---

1 In the technical sense at least. In reality, it is hard to imagine how this newly found freedom would have manifested itself or been experienced: the difficulties of functioning within such a male-oriented society must have been immense for the adult unmarried woman, and in all likelihood she would have been obliged to turn for protection to her male kith and kin. For the young girl who had passed the age of 12 and a half without having secured a husband, the probability was that she would stay under the authority of her father until a marriage was arranged (see pp. 45f. above).

of the husband at marriage'. The custom of early marriage thus rendered her passage to adulthood, in respect to independent action, something of an empty technicality. The moment of her removal from paternal control into the authority of her husband came at her entry into the חופה (*Ket.* 48a-b).

As will be seen in the course of this survey, the rights of a husband over his wife were nearly as extensive as those of a father over his daughter. However, while it is in some degree comprehensible that a parent should be given authority over children as yet incapable of taking responsibility for their actions, we may ask why it was that the adult woman was similarly denied freedom of action. Why was she, the married woman, placed in the same category as minors and, like them, subject to the all-embracing power of the head of the household? The answer to this, of course, lies with the rigidly patriarchal structure of Jewish society, a structure which placed women in a secondary and subordinate position at all periods of their lives.[1]

The patriarchal ordering of Jewish life was both expressed and reinforced by the teachings of the nation's religion—itself a cult which centred upon a single male deity and one which was directed exclusively by men.[2] In other words, the authority which men assumed over women was, by our period, viewed in terms of a divine ordering of the universe: woman, created after man and out of him, was by nature inferior, and as the one responsible for man's first fall was deemed to be in need of constant control and supervision. Thus, for example, Josephus declared on the basis of Gen. 3.16:

> The woman, says the Law, is in all things inferior to the
> man. Let her accordingly be submissive, not for her

---

1 Thus it was that differentiation according to gender was also made with respect to the upbringing of children, as was demonstrated in Chapter 1.
2 And here it should be remembered that religious law and tradition dominated life in Hellenistic Palestine. Thus Josephus coined the word 'theocracy' to describe the nation's state of polity, and emphatically declared that 'Religion governs all our actions and occupations and speech' (*Con. Ap.* 11.164f.). For the rise and impact of this religious system, see Archer, 'The Role of Jewish Women in the Religion, Ritual and Cult of Graeco-Roman Palestine', in Cameron and Kuhrt, *Images of Women in Antiquity*, pp. 273-87.

humiliation, but that she may be directed; for the authority
has been given by God to man (*Con. Ap.* 2.201).

Philo, again categorizing the consequences of the Fall, wrote:

> In the next place she tasted deprivation of liberty and the
> authority of the husband at her side, whose command she
> must perforce obey (*Op. Mun.* 167).

Such then was the powerful base-line rationale for the Jews'
rigid patriarchy, the Creation/Fall motif being one of many
related themes to be reiterated and elaborated upon by writers
of our period.[1]

Having placed woman in a position of subordination to and
dependence upon men, the next step was for society to view
women as inherently incapable of taking responsibility for
their actions. Thus, in the *Letter of Aristeas*, when the question
was posed as to how a man could live amicably with his wife,
the answer was

> by recognising that womankind are by nature headstrong
> and energetic in the pursuit of their own desires, and subject
> to sudden changes of opinion through fallacious reasoning,
> and their nature is essentially weak. It is necessary to deal
> wisely with them and not to provoke strife (250-51).

Only men were blessed with the faculty of rational thought;
only they could act from the standpoint of sound, independent
judgment. According to Philo, women operated solely according to the 'rule of custom' (τὸ ἔθος),[2] and a favourite theme of
his was to contrast the 'weak feminine passion of sense perception' with 'manly reasoning schooled in fortitude'.[3] So it
was with some amazement, when speaking of Julia Augustus'
donation to the Temple at Jerusalem, that he wrote:

> What made her do this, as there was no image there? For the
> judgements of women as a rule are weaker and do not
> apprehend any mental conception apart from that which

---

1 For the development of these themes, and their use to define non-ambiguous male-
female social roles and promote the smooth running of patriarchal interests and
power, see Archer, 'The Virgin and the Harlot in the Writings of Formative
Judaism', *History Workshop Journal* 24 (1987), pp. 1-16.
2 *Ebr.* 54-55.
3 *Leg. All.* 3.11; cf. e.g. *ibid.* 2.19f.; 3.49-50.

their senses perceive... (*Leg.* 319-320).

The notion that women were by their very nature light-minded and irresponsible was obviously fostered by the gulf which existed between them and men in respect to intellectual attainment: excluded from the nation's programme of formal education, their ignorance was interpreted in terms of innate inferiority (a belief which could possibly have been furthered encouraged by the contact Hellenistic Palestine had with the Greek world).[1]

Inherent to the system of thought were various apparent tensions and contradictions which, while never resolved (or even addressed or recognized), further compounded the view of women as inferior beings. On the one hand, as we have seen (above, pp. 25ff., 104ff.), women were believed to have a natural propensity for evil and to be 'headstrong in the pursuit of their own desires', and on the other they were regarded as passive creatures incapable of independent action. In either case they were deemed to require male direction throughout their lives.[2] For Philo there was an obvious corollary between the inferior functioning of the senses and innate passivity. Working again from the biblical creation narrative, he wrote:

> 'He [God], took one of his sides': of the many faculties of the Mind [that is, Adam], He took one, the faculty of perception ... 'He built it to be woman': proving by this that the most proper and exact name for sense perception is 'woman'. For just as the man shows himself in activity and the woman in passivity, so the province of the mind is activity and that of the perceptive sense passivity, as in woman (*Leg. All.* 2.19f., 38).

To be male, rational, and active was obviously a state superior to that of women who, in consequence of their assumed (and enforced) passivity, were regarded as in constant need of guidance. Thus,

---

1 See Chapter 1 §D.

2 Such conflicts were part and parcel of the culturally constructed fear of women discussed elsewhere in this volume. By definition patriarchy always has one fundamental, though necessary, flaw, and that is the existence of women who must always represent a threat to the existing order and be seen as in need of control at every level.

virtue is male, since it causes movements and affects conditions and suggest noble conceptions of noble deeds and words,

while to be female was to be

moved and trained and helped, and in general [to belong] to the passive category, which passivity is its sole means of preservation (*Abr.* 102).

Such then was the philosophy. On a practical level, we have already seen the way in which women's designated role was that of closeted homemaker, a role which came about for a variety of reasons, not least of which was the emergence of the nuclear family which combined with other factors to produce a sharp and rigid differentiation of function according to gender (see above, pp. 85ff.). This move toward the nuclear family did little to enhance the position of women. As Rosaldo observes:

A woman's status will be lowest in those societies where there is a firm differentiation between domestic and public spheres of activity and where women are isolated from one another and placed under a single man's authority, in the home.[1]

At all times, therefore, women were to be subject to the authority of men. While the weight of the law worked to enforce this position of subordination, there was also the constant exhortation by writers of our period to women not to forget their divinely appointed position of subservience. Thus, for example, Eph. 5.21f. urged

Wives, be subject to your husbands... For the husband is the head of the wife... As the church is subject to Christ, so let wives also be subject in everything to their husbands... and let the wife see that she respects her husband (cf. 1 Cor. 11.3f.; 1 Tim. 2.8f.; Col. 3.18).[2]

---

1 Michelle Zimbalist Rosaldo and Louise Lamphere, eds., *Woman, Culture and Society*, p. 56.
2 See the Introduction for the use of NT material as a source of information for Jewish custom in Graeco-Roman Palestine. In addition to the direct exhortation, there was also the development in our period of sharply defined and polarized images of women in the literature (evil and ensnaring woman *vs* good and subservient wife) which also encouraged the sexes to stay in their socially appointed

In the eyes of a society structured along rigidly patriarchal lines, therefore, the worst crime which a woman could commit was that of acting independently of male control. Thus, in the Jewish *Sibylline Oracles*, Cleopatra was described with horror as 'an untamable woman' (5.18) and Ben Sira unequivocally declared that 'A headstrong woman will be regarded as a dog' (Sir. 26.25). In essence, therefore, the attitude within Graeco-Roman Palestine toward the married woman was as follows:

> The woman that honoureth her own husband appeareth wise at all, But she that dishonoureth [her husband] is known to all as one that is godless in [her] pride (Sir. 26.26).

The outward sign of the woman's subordination to one man was the veil. As was seen in the previous section, the act of veiling formed a part of the marriage ceremonial and marked by visible means the woman's transition from the unmarried to the married state (above, p. 205).[1] It served as a symbol of her possession by her husband, and had to be worn whenever she was in mixed company or went out in public (see below). Apart from signalling to other men that she was a married woman and therefore unapproachable, the veil signified the authority which society vested in the husband. Thus, in 1 Cor. 11.6f. we read:

> For a man ought not to cover his head since he is the image and glory of God, but woman is the glory of man. For man was not made from woman, but woman from man. Neither was man created for woman, but woman for man. That is why a woman ought to have a veil (ἡ ἐξουσία, 'authority') on her head, because of the angels.[2]

---

roles. On this see further below and Archer, 'The Virgin and the Harlot...'

1 Though they were similarly under the authority of one man, no symbol of subordination was required of young girls in consequence of their secluded life style. As will be seen in the next section, married women were permitted to be socially more active than young girls who were kept confined in the home.

2 The context of the passage is that of women praying in public. The writer is here combining two arguments regarding the use of the veil: on the one hand, it marked the woman's subordination (as the first part makes clear), and on the other, it served as protection against demonic beings, regarding whose influence women were deemed particularly susceptible (hence the reference to 'angels'). The veil was an 'authority' on both counts.

Women who were not under the control of any man, for
example, widows and prostitutes, were not expected to cover
their heads.[1] Similarly a married woman who defied her husband was stripped of this symbol of his authority. So in the case
of one suspected of adultery, the first act performed by the
priest officiating at the 'trial' was the ritual of uncovering the
sotah's head.[2] Thus Philo wrote regarding the procedure for
the trial:

> The priest... removes her kerchief in order that she may be
> judged with her head bared and stripped of the symbol of
> modesty regularly worn by women who are wholly innocent
> (*Spec. Leg.* 3.56).

and similarly Josephus:

> As for the woman, one of the priests stations her at the gates
> which face the Temple and after removing the veil from her
> head, inscribes the name of God upon a skin... (*Ant.*
> 3.270).[3]

And in the previous section we noted the way in which, in the
case of 'common-law marriage', a woman could be released
from her husband's authority by the simple procedure of his
removing her veil, thereby dissolving the union (above, p. 205
n. 5). The significance which society attached to the veiling of
married women is perhaps most clearly seen in *Ket.* 7.6 which
lists seven offences for which a woman could be divorced with

---

1 See, for example, Gen. 38.19; Jdt. 10.3; 1Q4.184, l. 19 (Vermes, *The Dead Sea
Scrolls in English*, p. 256). The wearing of a veil by Tamar in Gen. 38.15 was
simply to hide her identity. Cf. Jastrow, 'An Assyrian Law Code', *JAOS* 41 (1921),
pp. 1-59 for the practice of slaves and prostitutes going unveiled.

2 Num. 5.18: פרע .והעמיד הכהן את האשה לפני יהוה ופרע את ראש האשה can also mean 'to
dishevel'. However, early sources prefer the translation 'uncover'. See LXX *ad
loc.*, ὁ ἱερεύς... ἀποκαλύψει τὴν κεφαλὴν τῆς γυναικός.

3 As the quotes show, the veil also served as a symbol of modesty, but this was a secondary characteristic/development to the subordination element and will be
treated more fully below. Had it been intended primarily for purposes of modesty
we would with justification have expected it to be a face covering, but such apparently was not the case. On this see p. 205 above and note the argument of Morgenstern regarding the veil being a substitute for what was originally an actual
sacrifice of hair at the time of marriage (*op. cit.*, p. 99). See also the story of Qim-
hit, mother of seven sons, who apparently always wore her veil even in the
privacy of the home and boasted 'May [this and that] befall me if the beams of my
house have ever seen *the hair of my head*' (y. *Meg.* 72a; y. *Hor.* 47d; y. *Yom.* 38d).

complete loss of her *kethubah* rights. One of those seven was to go out in public with an uncovered head. Indeed, so serious was this act of defiance that the Shammaites, who recognized no cause for divorce other than adultery (see below), saw it as legitimate grounds for divorce, regarding the deed as equal to unfaithfulness by the wife (y. *Sot.* 16b).

The woman's position of subordination within marriage was originally clearly stated by the terms chosen to denote 'husband' and 'wife'. The word for the former was בעל, meaning 'one who owns or has mastery',[1] while that used for 'wife' was the passive form of the same root, בעולה, 'one who is owned or subject to the authority of another', or simply אשה, 'woman'. An argument for women's position along etymological lines may not in itself be pressed too far in consequence of the way in which words gradually lose or change their original distinctive meaning through common usage, but we should note that the principle was constantly reinforced during our period by the mode of address which society required of the wife when speaking to her husband. So, for example, the author of *Vita Adae et Evae* has Eve prefacing each sentence to Adam with 'My Lord', and in a fragment from Qumran, Bitenosh addresses Lamech with the words, 'O my brother and my lord'.[2] The object of the exercise was clearly stated by St Peter in his first epistle. Urging the women of his own time to model themselves on the quiet, chaste behaviour of the holy women of the Old Testament, he wrote: 'Likewise you wives, be submissive to your husbands... as Sarah obeyed Abraham, calling him lord' (1 Pet. 3.1f.).

While strictly speaking the בעל was not the woman's 'owner' (see above, pp. 164-66), he was without doubt her 'lord and master', and his mastery frequently manifested itself in ways which verged upon the proprietary. This is perhaps most clearly seen in the laws of adultery and in the rules about penalties and damages. Regarding the former, the usual patriarchal attitude prevailed in that the man was never deemed guilty (in the eyes of the law at least) except when he

---

1   It also means one who 'possesses' in a sexual sense.
2   1QapGen (proper) Col. Frag. 2, 11, 9, 13. For use of 'brother' as a mode of address, see above, p. 149.

transgressed the rights of some other man to a woman. He could not commit adultery against his own wife and was permitted association with adult, unmarried women. A wife, on the other hand, whilst unable to charge her husband with adultery, was immediately condemned if she entered into any liaison with another man, married or unmarried (see, for example, Lev. 20.10f.; Num. 5.12ff.; Deut. 22.22; 23.1). Thus Ben Sira declared that it was a sin 'To gaze upon a woman that hath a husband (γυναικὸς ὑπάνδρου)' (41.21c), whilst the book of *Ahikar* succinctly defined both the parameters of adultery in Jewish society and the sentiment of property-protection in the following piece of advice: 'My son, commit not adultery with the wife of thy neighbour, lest others should commit adultery with thy wife' (Syr. A. 2.6; Armen. 2.39).[1] In the legal texts which treat of adultery, the marital status of the woman is always given while that of the man remains unknown and is irrelevant. She is always described as 'a woman being under her husband' (אשה בעלת־בעל; אשה תחת איש: see, for example, Num. 5.19, 20, 29; Deut. 22.22), and her crime is against his authority.[2]

Regarding the penalties incurred for damages inflicted on a woman (by someone other than the husband) the law again placed her in a category similar to that of goods possessed. Thus, regarding compensation for 'indignity and blemish' the Mishnah ruled that

> If it was done to a hidden part [in her body] two thirds [of the compensation] falls to her and one third to him; if in a manifest part, two thirds falls to him and one third to her (*Ket.* 6.1).

The wife did not, however, keep her part of the compensation. In recognition of the fact that the husband had suffered damage to his 'property', the law decreed that he should receive the fullest possible recompense and therefore ruled that 'His

1 For the circulation and use of this book in Jewish society, see p. 23 n. 2 above.
2 Note that although adultery had been a crime since the earliest times, it received greater attention in the exilic and post-exilic writings as concerns regarding paternity and the appropriate transmission of property shifted and intensified according to the new societal structure and the rise of the nuclear family; see above, pp. 26, 85, 104ff.

share is given to him forthwith; but with hers land is bought
and he has the use of it' (*Ket.* 6.1).[1] So, although it was the
woman who had sustained the injuries, compensation was
paid to the husband on the basis that 'one's wife is [like] one's
own body' (*Ket.* 66a).[2] There was no parallel ruling for injury
to the man.[3] The other ruling to do with damages centred
upon assault which caused a pregnant women to miscarry
(Exod. 21.22-23). Here again compensation for loss was paid
by the assailant to the husband:

> They [the judges] assess how much the woman was worth
> before she brought forth and how much after... and he pays
> it to the husband, or, if she has no husband, to his heirs. But
> if she was a freedwoman or a proselyte no penalty is
> incurred (*B.K.* 5.4).[4]

The proprietary element in these damages suits is highlighted
by the final clause of the mishnah which addresses the
instance of assault on a manumitted slave or a proselyte
whose husband, also a proselyte, is no longer alive. No monies

---

1 In addition to this specific reason why the husband was the one to receive full compensation, the ruling was also in keeping with the general appropriation of the
   wife's property which occurred and was legislated for in the course of our period
   (see further below). For the type of damages here referred to, the liability of the
   guilty party, and the means by which compensation was calculated, see *B.K.* 8.1;
   Ket. 3.7.
2 Hence note the 'hidden' and 'manifest' differentiation in the mishnah: if the
   injury was to an exposed part of the body he gets more 'since he not only shares her
   indignity and degradation but, in addition, must also put up with a woman who
   has become disfigured' (notes, Soncino Talmud, *Ket.* i, p. 398).
3 As a point of comparison, cf. Exod. 21.32, 'If the ox gore a bondman or a bond-
   woman, he [the owner] shall give unto their master thirty shekels of silver...'
   See above, pp. 56f. for the similar right possessed by the father in respect of his
   minor daughter.
4 Josephus, *Ant.* 4.278, and possibly also Philo, *Spec. Leg.* 3.108 (though see *Fug.*
   137), has the assailant paying a double fine, one for having diminished the
   population and the other for 'outrage' (Philo's term, ὕβρις; reason unspecified in
   Josephus) which was given to the husband. Neither author names the recipient of
   the first fine, though Goodenough suggests on the basis of the Ptolemaic procedure
   for βία that it was paid to the court or some charitable institution (*Jurisprudence*,
   113f.). In the unlikely event that it was paid to the woman, she would not directly
   benefit for the law would grant right of usufruct to her husband as in damages for
   'indignity and blemish'. Cf. *CPJ*, I, no. 133 for a complaint by a Jew from the
   Fayûm in the mid-second century BCE regarding an assault on his pregnant
   wife.

exchange hands because the woman has neither husband, owner, nor heirs.

Just as adultery was in a sense a one-way affair, so was divorce, though in a different direction. Only the man had the power to divorce, or as the Mishnah puts it:

> The man that divorces is not like to the woman that is divorced; for a woman is put away with her consent or without it, but a husband can put away his wife only with his own consent (*Yeb.* 14.1).

The fact that the woman had neither the right to protest nor the right to initiate divorce proceedings on her own account was due in general to her position of permanent subordination to the wishes of men and in particular to the facts that (i) while her husband could engage in polygamy, she was required to be monogamous (and hence had to be released before she could engage in relationships with other men), and (ii) she was the one who was 'taken' in marriage; just as she had no power to institute the union, so she had no legal right to dissolve it. These several points are nicely put by Epstein, whom I will take the liberty of quoting at length:

> The woman cannot divorce her husband according to Jewish law. This arises from two historical foundations. Divorce in its original form was driving out of the house. The husband is the owner of the house; it is he who brings his wife to his home, it is therefore he who drives her out of his house. The wife cannot drive the husband from the house which is not hers but his. Even when divorce became a social formality by decree or writ it was still impossible to give the wife the power or right to give her husband a bill of divorcement. For one reason because of the more ancient tradition, and for another reason because the bill of divorcement was primarily intended to free the one who was divorced to marry another. Since only the woman is restricted against marrying another before she is freed from her husband, she is the only one who can be divorced.[1]

---

1 *The Jewish Marriage Contract*, p. 200. Note that throughout the passage Epstein assumes the operation of a nuclear family with the woman transferred at marriage to the husband's home and placed under his sole authority. It should be remembered, however, that for the earlier Biblical period when different social institutions lingered (above, p. 21 n. 3) and the extended family was operative,

Although under the Deuteronomic reform the husband was required to provide his wife with a bill of divorce as proof of their separation and her ability to marry another without fear of charges of adultery (Deut. 24.1-3),[1] he was not obliged to furnish grounds for the divorce. No limitation was placed upon his unilateral power and he could dismiss his wife for any reason whatsoever.[2] He had no need to go to a court to show cause for his action but could simply 'put her away privily' as Joseph was minded to do regarding Mary in the New Testament (Mt. 1.19).[3] It is true that, following the exile, various voices were raised about the moral propriety of arbitrary divorce (for example, Prov. 5.15-19; Eccl. 9.9; Mal. 2.14-16), culminating in the rabbinic sentiment that 'If a man divorces his first wife, even the altar sheds tears' (*Gitt.* 90b). It should also be noted that, in the eyes of the Tannaim, one of the reasons for the introduction of deferred bride-price payment (above, p. 162) was the desire to render divorce more difficult.[4]

---

such was not always the case: e.g., Jacob lived at his wives' family home, Moses with his father-in-law, and Samson travelled to the woman of Timnah (Gen. 29.10ff.; 30.25ff.; 31.1ff.; Exod. 3.1f.; Judg. 14.1ff.). In the latter case there was some confusion as to whether the woman had actually been 'divorced' (divorce was not formally instituted until Deuteronomy). This however does not invalidate Epstein's argument as it applies to our period.

1 See pp. 171-73 above for the way in which the divorce deed was introduced before the marriage contract, a fact which underlines the function, character and significance of divorce.

2 Biblical law restricted divorce on two counts only: if a husband lodged a false virginity suit against his wife he was not allowed to divorce her, and if a man raped a girl he was obliged to marry his victim (subject to her father's wishes, see p. 51 above) and was not permitted subsequently to put her away. In either instance, however, if he did act contrary to the law, his divorce was not invalid. Cf. *Ant.* 4.8; *Ket.* 39a. Rabbinic law denied him the right of divorce if his wife was in captivity or was a minor too young to understand and take care of her *get* (*Ket.* 4.9). He also could not instigate divorce if he was insane (*Ket.* 14.1; *Gitt.* 7.1, 67b) or issue a *get* if she was insane (*Yeb.* 113b).

3 Only in instances when the husband's reason for divorce, if proven true, would exempt him from the obligation of *kethubah* payment (see above, p. 180), did he need to present his case to a court. In Joseph's case, had he acted on his intent and proceeded in public, not only would he not have had to pay the *kethubah*, but he could also have charged Mary with adultery.

4 We might also note the Talmudic account of how members of the priestly class, who were regarded as hot-tempered and therefore hasty to divorce, used a peculiar form of *get* which was 'folded' and required three signatures—this to delay the process and give the husband a chance for second thoughts (*B.B.* 160f.).

It is likely, however, that such sentiment was confined to a small section of the population (hence, perhaps, all the admonitions). Judging, for example, by Josephus' extremely brief and detached account of his own divorce,[1]*Vita, 426* the majority opinion followed the old school of thought. Certainly any change in moral consciousness had no impact on the legal situation. In the first century the Shammaites attempted to restrict the man's power of divorce to charges of adultery, but such was the strength of the ancient view that the normally more progressive school of Hillel came out in opposition and declared that:

> [He may divorce her] even if she spoiled a dish for him, for it is written, 'Because he has found in her indecency in ANYTHING' (Deut. 24.1) (*Gitt.* 9.10).

and R. Akiba (fl. c. 110–135 CE) lent his authority to the argument by adding:

> Even if he found another fairer than her, for it is written, 'And it shall be if she finds no favour in his eyes...' (Deut. 24.1) (*ibid.*).

It is apparent from Philo (*Spec. Leg.* 3.30), Josephus (*Ant.* 4.253), and other writers of our period that the reality was that of Akiba and the Hillelites. Society in the main would not brook a diminishment of the husband's power, and the general feeling, simply expressed by Ben Sira, was:

> If she go not as thou wouldst have her
> Cut her off from thy flesh (25.26).

Once 'cut off' from her husband's flesh, the woman was released from the bondage of his authority. The terminology employed in divorce bills to effect this independence, considered alongside the formula of writs of emancipation, says much for the way in which wives, in legal jargon at least, were viewed in terms analogous to those of goods possessed (though

---

1 'At this period I divorced my wife, being displeased at her behaviour. She had borne me three children, of whom two died' (*Vita*, 426). This is sandwiched between Josephus' account of the siege of Jerusalem and that of his treatment by the Roman emperors. In total he devotes three sentences out of the entire *Life* to what he terms his 'domestic history' (ταῦτα μέν μοι τὰ κατὰ τὸν οἶκον).

not technically in that category). Significantly the two deeds
are treated in the same mishnah, *Gitt.* 9.3. The necessary
statement of a bill of divorce was 'Lo, thou art free to marry
any man' (*Gitt.* 9.3; cf. *DJD*, II, 19.5-7). By this statement,
according to *Kidd.* 1.1, the woman 'acquires herself' (קונה את
עצמה).These two elements of (active) release from bondage by
the master and (passive) acquisition of self-determination by
the woman were similarly found in writs of emancipation:
'Lo, thou art a freedwoman; Lo, thou belongest to thyself'
(*Gitt.* 9.3).

Before leaving the question of divorce, it should be noted that
in certain instances a wife was entitled in rabbinic law to
claim a divorce. Such was the case if, for example, her
husband pursued a particularly repugnant profession or had
serious physical defects (see above, pp. 144-45). Then she was
permitted to say 'I thought that I could endure it, but now I
cannot endure it' (*Ket.* 7.9-10). Divorce could also be claimed if
her husband placed her under intolerable vows, restricted her
attendance at legitimate social functions, forced her removal
to a new town, cut off her support, refused to have sex or was
incapable of fulfilling his conjugal duties (*Ket.* 5.5; 7.2-5; 61b,
63a, 71b, 72a, 77ab; *Yeb.* 65b; *Ned.* 11.12). The differences
between her rights and those of the man, however, were
enormous. First, unlike him, she had to present sufficient
cause for her claim for separation. Second, she had to be
aware/informed of the grounds on which she was entitled to
sue for divorce. Third, she herself could not divorce: the union
could only be dissolved by the husband issuing a bill of divorce.
She therefore had to work through a court which considered
her case and at its discretion decided whether or not to
instruct the husband to release her. Finally, even if the court
did decide in her favour, the husband could still refuse her the
necessary document of release. About this the wife and the
court could do nothing, not even if the husband were insane.
Only he had the power actually to effect a divorce and he had
to be of sound mind when delivering the *get* for the separation
to be valid (*Yeb.* 112b; *Gitt.* 67b, 88b). No other could be
instructed or empowered to do the act on his behalf (*Yeb.*
112b).

Turning now to other manifestations of the power of the

husband, we shall first look at the authority given him in respect of his wife's vows. Just as the vows of a minor daughter were controlled by her father (above, pp. 47ff.), so those of a married woman could be annulled by her husband, if he acted on the day on which the oath was uttered (Num. 30.7f.).[1] To appreciate the significance of this aspect of his power, we should remember the enormous importance which was attached by society to the spoken word, both with regard to testimony and promise. To utter a vow,[2] that is, a promise to God to perform or abstain from something, was a matter of serious consequence, a fact reflected by the Talmud's dedication of an entire tractate of eleven chapters and ninety-one folios to this subject (plus a separate tractate treating the Nazirite vow). Indeed the sanctity of the word was so highly regarded that Deut. 23.24 ('that which is gone out of thy mouth thou shalt observe and do') was interpreted as meaning that the mere utterance of the lips was equivalent to a vow,[3] even though the precise formula had not been spoken (*Ned.* 7a). It was this that the husband (and the father) had the power of veto over. In biblical law, no provision was made for the absolution of an individual from vows he/she had taken: the only exception was the voiding of the vow of an unmarried girl by her father or of the married woman by her husband.

According to Philo, it was perfectly reasonable that men should be empowered 'to judge for their wives whether the oath was to hold good or to be cancelled', for women, being naturally light-minded creatures and incapable of appreciating the import of their vows, were liable to 'often, through want of sense, swear what would not be to their husband's advantage' (*Spec. Leg.* 2.24). In giving this as the reason for

1   It is significant that this legislation makes its first appearance in the P strand of the Bible, i.e. its context is the development of the nuclear family and the other societal shifts discussed above. On this see further Archer, 'The Virgin and the Harlot...'. For the importance of vows in Jewish society and religion, see *EJ*, XVI, cols. 227-28.

2   Heb. נדר (*neder*), which was different from the oath (*shevu'ah*) and free-will offering (*nedavah*).

3   Later the custom arose of adding to any such statement the disclaimer 'without it being a vow'.

the biblical ruling, Philo was doubtless simply articulating the belief and attitude held generally by the Jews of the period. So, while virgins were to be controlled 'on account of their youth', wives were to be controlled 'through want of sense'. And the Alexandrian's final piece of advice, addressed to those 'who have none to intervene on their behalf', that is, orphans (= fatherless), widows and divorcees, was that they 'should be slow to swear, for their oaths stand beyond repeal, the inevitable result of their lack of protectors' (*Spec. Leg.* 2.25).[1]

There was, however, one difference between the authority which a father had over his minor daughter's vows and that possessed by a husband in respect to his wife. Whereas the former had absolute power to revoke vows, no attention being paid to their particular nature, the latter could only annul oaths which were regarded as 'afflicting the soul' (Num. 30.14). Talmudic examples of the types of vows which afflicted the soul were if the woman said, '*Konan* forever be to me the fruits of the world if I wash!' or 'if I adorn myself!' (*Ned.* 11.1; cf. *Ket.* 71a). The husband was also permitted to revoke his wife's vow to become a Nazirite (*Naz.* 4.1-5; 9.1; *Ned.* 11.9).[2] Finally, although according to biblical law he was only empowered to cancel vows on the day they were made, later custom apparently allowed him the right to annul all oaths which his wife may have taken upon herself prior to their marriage (see above, p. 50 n. 1). Thus, in the Mishnah we read that:

> Among the disciples of the Sages, before the daughter of one of them left his control, the custom was for him to say to her, 'Let every vow which thou hast vowed in my house be

---

1   According to Num. 30.7f., the authority to disallow vows only applied 'between a man and his wife, between a father and his daughter, being in her youth, in her father's hands'. Hence it did not apply to orphans or to 'the vow of a widow or of her that is divorced when even everything wherewith she hath bound her soul shall stand against her' (v. 10).

2   מיר, from the root נזר, to separate, dedicate oneself. The Nazirite was a person who for any number of different reasons (e.g. the fulfilment of a wish) vowed for a specific period to abstain from partaking of grapes or any of their products, cutting his/her hair, and touching a corpse. See Num. 6.1-21 and the whole of the mishnaic tractate *Nazirim*. Biblical examples of Nazirites are Samson and Samuel (Judg. 13.7; 1 Sam. 1.21, 28), while for the later period we have Agrippa's sister Berenice (*BJ* 2.313-14) and the convert Helena of Adiabene (*Naz.* 3.6).

revoked'. So, too, the husband, before she entered into his control, used to say to her, 'Let every vow that thou didst vow before thou camest into my control be revoked' (*Ned.* 10.4).

He could only take such action, however, during the period of betrothal when the woman was not yet fully his wife. After marriage, the biblical ruling had to be adhered to. According to the Gemara, the motivation for such blanket dismissal was that 'I do not want a wife that is in the habit of making vows' (*Ket.* 73b). And not only could the husband annul vows, he also had the power to impose them (see e.g. *Ket.* 72a). However, just as he could only revoke oaths which were considered to 'afflict the soul', so, on the other side of the coin, he could not place his wife under vows which were intolerable to her. If he did so, she was entitled to claim a divorce.[1]

With regard to the upbringing of children from the union the woman again occupied a position of secondary importance, for within the home the voice of authority was exclusively that of her husband, the *pater familias*. So, for example, in answer to the question 'How does a man differ from a woman?', the Tannaim replied,

> He may impose the Nazirite vow on his son, but she may not...; a man may sell his daughter, but a woman may not...; a man may give his daughter in betrothal, but a woman may not... (*Sot.* 3.8).[2]

Similarly, only a father could perform the various religious duties required by law of a parent toward his children, for example, circumcision and redemption of the first-born (*Kidd.* 1.7, 29a; *Naz.* 29a);[3] only he was responsible for their educa-

---

1 An example provided by the Talmud of a vow which would be intolerable to his wife was if he made her promise not to lend utensils to her neighbours. Such action would give her a bad name and so would 'afflict her soul' (*Ket.* 72a).

2 Regarding the last point, a widow could arrange a betrothal but in this she worked together with her male relatives and her daughter could exercise the right of refusal. In other words, the mother's power was not absolute. See above, p. 51.

3 *4 Macc.* 4.25 reports that during the exceptional circumstances of Antiochus Epiphanes' persecution women did circumcise their sons (cf. 1 Macc. 1.61; 2 Macc. 6.10). From a later period, however, the rabbis categorically denied women the right to do this (despite the fact that the first recorded circumcision in Hebrew history was performed by the woman Zipporah) and declared that if a father died, then it was up to the Beth Din or the child himself on reaching adulthood to

tion (see above, pp. 87ff.); only he was charged with disciplining and rearing them (see, for example, Sir. 30.1-13; 42.9-14). Obviously women were intimately involved with the upbringing of children but theirs was not the authority or religious duty. In the legal and literary texts only men are enjoined and there is no mention of maternal duties other than, for example, the obligation to breastfeed (see below, p. 227). In one instance alone was the mother's voice reckoned equal to his, and that was the case of a 'stubborn and rebellious son', characteristics which, according to biblical law, were deserving of death (Deut. 21.18f.):

> If his father was willing [to accuse him] but his mother was not willing, or if his father was not willing but his mother was willing, he cannot be condemned as a stubborn and rebellious son, but only if they both were willing (*Sanh.* 8.4).

The relative positions of the parents *vis-à-vis* their children is perhaps most clearly seen by two facts. First, in the eyes of the law and of society generally, the definition of an orphan (יתום) was not one who had lost both parents but simply one who was fatherless.[1] Second, the oft-repeated biblical injunction to 'honour thy father and thy mother', which in its bald form might have suggested a certain equality at least in one respect, was in fact qualified by later thinkers in order to reaffirm the all-important position of the father within the family unit.[2] Thus in *Kidd.* 31a we read:

> If my father orders, 'Give me a drink of water' and my mother does likewise, which takes preference?

The answer to this was:

> Leave your mother's honour and fulfil the honour due to your father... for both you and your mother are bound to honour your father (cf. *Kerith.* 6.9).

---

arrange for a circumcision (*Kidd.* 29a-b). For the history and significance of women's total exclusion from this male-oriented rite, see Chapter 1 §B above and Archer, 'Bound by Blood...'.

1 See above, p. 65 n. 1.
2 See above for the way in which the command was also used to reinforce the woman's role as homemaker.

The mother's position of secondary importance both in relation to the upbringing of her children and in relation to her husband, regarding whom she occupied a place similar to that of her children, is nicely summed up by the following mishnah:

> All obligations of a father toward his son enjoined in the law are incumbent on men but not on women, and all the obligations of a son toward his father [honour and fear] enjoined in the law are incumbent both on men and on women (*Kidd.* 1.7).

The subordinate, almost servile position of the woman was reinforced by the various duties of a personal nature that she was obliged to perform for her husband. These included making ready his bed, filling his cup, and washing his face, hands and feet (*Ket.* 4b, 61a). If she refused to render these private services she was treated as a *moredeth*, 'rebel', and was liable to a fine (*Ket.* 63a). Finally, we might note that, according to *Hor.* 3.7, should a couple find themselves in a situation of mortal danger, the ruling was that the man 'must be saved alive sooner than the woman'; should property be lost, then his 'must be restored sooner than hers'; and 'when both stand in danger of defilement, the man must be freed before the woman' (the latter ruling presumably in consequence of the fact that only he was permitted an active role in the nation's cultic affairs which demanded a state of ritual purity). In only one instance was the woman placed before the man, and that was out of consideration for modesty and physical purity: 'A woman's nakedness must be covered sooner than a man's and she must be brought out of captivity sooner than he'.

All in all, therefore, the lot of the married woman was not dissimilar to that of the minor daughter. Both were denied the right to act independently; both were subject to the all-embracing authority of a male overlord. In only one respect was the wife's situation significantly different: she could not be sold into servitude in payment for her husband's debts. This was due to the fact that, unlike a minor daughter, she was an adult and one who was never considered totally a member of her husband's family group. She was, as it were, but an adopted member by marriage, and retained close ties with her own family, her blood relatives (see above, p. 164 and n. 1). Her husband, therefore, was denied the right possessed by a father of disposing of her in this manner.

We shall now consider the types of duties which the woman was expected to perform within marriage generally. As has been demonstrated many times in this volume, her sphere of activity was purely domestic. In the words of Philo:

> Market places and council halls and law courts and gatherings and meetings where a large number of people are assembled, and open air life with full scope for discussion and action—all these are suitable for men both in war and peace. The women are best suited to the indoor life which never strays from the house...

or again,

> Organized communities are of two sorts, the greater which we call cities and the smaller which we call households. Both of these have their governors; the government of the greater is assigned to men under the name of statesmanship, that of the lesser, known as household management to women. A woman should then not be a busybody, meddling with matters outside her household concerns... (*Spec. Leg.* 3.169f.).

A wife, therefore, was confined to domestic matters, the management of which was in a sense regarded as her sole *raison d'être*. Thus, Ben Sira stated that 'the beauty of a good wife is in the ordering of his [her husband's] house' (26.16; cf. *Ant.* 11.50), and declared that the man who was without a wife was as one 'that hath no nest', a wanderer and homeless (36.25-26). So strong was the notion of women as homemakers that the word בית, 'house', was frequently used synonymously for אשה, 'woman' (e.g. *Yoma* 1.1; 13a; *Shabb.* 118b; see above p. 124).

The various tasks which she had to perform included cleaning (see for example, *Kel.* 8.11); laundering (e.g. *Ket.* 5.5; *B.B.* 57b); preparing and cooking the household's food (e.g. *Ket.* 5.5; *Toh.* 2.1; *Mak.* 5.11); fetching water (e.g. *Nidd.* 48b); grinding flour and baking bread (e.g. *Ket.* 5.5; *Ohol.* 5.4; 12.4), a job which was commonly done at night in preparation for the following day; spinning yarn, again a task that had frequently to be done at night after the day's other activities had been attended to (Prov. 31.18-19; *Sot.* 6.1); and making clothes (e.g. Prov. 31.21-22; *Ned.* 7.8). The one domestic chore which was not her responsibility was purchasing goods from the public market. This task devolved upon her husband (*A.Z.* 38a-b), presumably out of consideration for her modesty and the fact that she was not expected to move in the male public arena. That this was the reason and that women in reality were not usually to be found frequenting market places is evidenced both by the passage quoted above and by the following extract also from Philo:

> She [the manageress of the house] should not show herself off like a vagrant in the streets before the eyes of other men, except when she has to go to the Temple and even then she should take pains to go, not when the market is full, but when most people have gone home... (*Spec. Leg.* 3.171).[1]

In addition to these specific duties the woman also had the general burdens of motherhood, that is, the care of young children, and the nursing of infants. The law obliged her to breast-feed her children for a period of twenty-four months and if she refused to do so, gave the husband the right to compel her (*Ket.* 5.5, 59b, 60a).[2] Finally, she was also required to attend on her husband's 'guests and occasional visitors' (*Ket.* 61a; cf. *B.M.* 87a; *Ber.* 10a). That this was considered to be exclusively a task for women—or at least not one that men would willingly perform—is nicely highlighted in Luke's account of a visit by Jesus to the house of Simon:

> And he [Jesus] arose and left the synagogue and entered Simon's house. Now Simon's mother-in-law was ill with a high fever, and they besought him for her. And he stood over her and rebuked the fever, and it left her. And immediately

---

1 Prov. 31.14, 'She is like the merchant ships; she bringeth her food from afar', was written in a period when the morbidity about free mingling of the sexes, so characteristic of the late Second Temple period, had not fully developed. The line could also be viewed merely as a hyperbolic flourish in keeping with the extravagant style of the passage as a whole.

2 This was the minimum period. In 2 Macc. 7.27 the righteous mother boasted that her children were not weaned until the age of three. See also *Jub.* 17.1.

she rose and served them (Lk. 5.38-39).

It was possible for the wife to delegate some of her labours to any bondwomen that she had brought in with her at marriage, or to employ through her husband the outside service of hired women (see below), but this only applied to general domestic duties. She could not delegate responsibility for the services of personal attention which she owed her husband, and was never permitted to throw off so much work as to make her idle, for 'idleness leads to unchastity' (*Ket.* 5.5; 61a). Such delegation, however, could only have occurred in wealthier households or in instances where the woman had a father willing and able to include servants in her dowry. Presumably if there were female relatives living in the house (such as unmarried female dependents of her husband; daughters; or other wives, in those rare instances of polygamous marriage) she would have had some help with the domestic chores.[1] For the majority of women, however, no additional assistance would have been available and their days within the home would have been long and exhausting. So, in Proverbs 31, the virtuous wife and mother was portrayed as one who

> looketh well to the ways of her household
> And eateth not the bread of idleness (v. 27)

and her daily round of activity given as:

> She seeketh wool and flax
> And worketh willingly with her hands...
> She riseth also while it is yet night,
> And giveth food to her houshold...
> With the fruit of her hands she planteth a vineyard...[2]
> Her lamp goeth not out by night.
> She layeth her hands to the distaff,
> And her hands hold the spindle... (vv. 13ff.).

And whilst she was 'girding her loins with strength and

1　On this, note the reference in the Gospel quotation above regarding Simon's mother-in-law, and see below regarding the existence of women's quarters.

2　It was customary for women in rural areas to assist their husbands in the fields, especially during the seasons of fruit collecting and harvest (see e.g. *Yeb.* 15.2, 116b). Such work was of course additional to their domestic duties.

making strong her arms' (v. 17), her husband was presented as one who

> ... is known in the gates,
> When he sitteth among the elders of the land (v. 23).[1]

In addition to her strictly domestic duties the wife was also obliged to 'work for hire in the tasks of women' (Tob. 2.11). This waged labour was conducted from the home (*ibid.*) and consisted principally of spinning wool and making garments to sell (Prov. 31.12; *B.K.* 10.9). If she lived in Judaea, she was required by law to produce a minimum of five *selas* weight of work (or ten *selas* weight of wool) for her husband, and if in the Galilee, double that amount (*Ket.* 5.9). She did not keep the earnings from her work but passed them directly onto her husband in return for the maintenance which she received and as a general supplement to the family income. The reasons for her not being permitted to keep the monies which accrued from her labour will now be discussed in context of the next stage of our examination, that of her property rights within marriage generally.

As was noted in the previous chapter, a woman brought two types of property in with her at marriage, one which was her private estate (*melog*) and one which formed her dowry and was transferred under terms of tenancy to her husband (*son barzel*) (see above pp. 179ff.). When the distinction between the two types of property first arose, the woman had exclusive powers of disposal over her *melog* goods, her husband only being permitted the right of usufruct over the *son barzel* (see above pp. 167-68). However, just as the character of the dowry gradually changed from being an outright gift to the woman

---

1 This is the only verse in Prov. 31 which addresses the man's social role and significantly it concludes the so-called Paean of Praise for the Virtuous Woman (from which the title of the present book is drawn) contained in that chapter (vv. 10-31). While most men would obviously not have been 'sitting among the elders of the land' or at least would not have been doing so exclusively but would have been pursuing their own work in the trades, agriculture, etc., the choice and starkness of the image reveals much regarding societal ordering, the sexual division of labour and the authority/decision-making vested in the male. It is almost as if the author in his textual layout were consciously presenting the woman as the busy private back-up to the man's public activities.

into a marriage portion virtually appropriated by the husband
during the time of their communal life (a development
encouraged by the institution of the lien clause in their marriage contract), so greater freedom was gradually accorded
him regarding her other goods also.

The first restriction placed upon the woman's historic right
to dispose of her private possessions as she saw fit came
towards the end of the period under consideration when it was
decreed that any property acquired by her subsequent to
marriage (e.g. through inheritance) and then sold could be
reclaimed by her husband from the purchaser (*Ket.* 8.1). The
ruling had no foundation in biblical law but derived solely
from a desire to extend the husband's privileges in respect to
his wife's property. The rationalization for the enactment was
that since the wife had acquired the property at a time when
she herself was 'owned', her husband was perforce part-
owner (*ibid.*). Later it was additionally reasoned that she
should not have absolute powers of disposal for this would be to
disregard his right of succession to the property (*Ket.* 50a).
Effectively, therefore, the woman was denied the right to sell
off her private estate, for although technically her sale was
valid it was unlikely that she would find a buyer willing to risk
losing his purchase at some later date.[1]

The School of Hillel attempted to extend the law to embrace
goods which were acquired during the period of betrothal,
arguing that 'Since [the betrothed husband] gets possession of
the woman, does he not get possession of her goods also?' (*Ket.*
8.1). Initially this attempt failed, for as Rabban Gamaliel himself was forced to admit: 'We are at a loss [to find reason for
giving him right] over her new possessions [that is, those
acquired after marriage], and would you even burden us with
the old also!' (*ibid.*). At the start of the Amoraic period, however, the law was amended in favour of the Hillelites, despite
the difficulties expressed by Rabban Gamaliel (*Ket.* 78b).

The rabbis also granted the husband the right of usufruct of

---

1 Compare this with the conveyancing of the man's property which stood as guarantee for the eventual payment of the woman's *kethubah* (above, pp. 184-85). In that
instance her consent was required to assure the purchaser that the goods would not
subsequently be reclaimed.

his wife's *melog*.[1] So, for example, in a mishnah which also
gives indication of the type of goods being discussed, we read:

> If she inherited money, land should be bought therewith and
> the husband has the use of it. [If she inherited produce]...
> the Sages say: What is unreaped falls to him and what is
> reaped falls to the wife, and with it land is bought and the
> husband has the use of it... If she inherited old bondmen
> and bondwomen they should be sold and land bought with
> their price and the husband has the use of it... If she inher-
> ited old olive trees and vines they should be sold as wood and
> land bought with their price and the husband has the use of
> it... (*Ket.* 8.3, 5).

This again was contrary to earlier law, and meant that during
their married life he enjoyed the use of both her private estate
and her marriage portion. There was, however, one significant difference between his uses of the two types of property.
Unable completely to ignore the fact that historically the
dowry (later *son barzel*) was a gift to the woman, the law
obliged the husband to make full restitution of the original
amount to his wife, reimbursing her for any damage caused to
the goods during the time they were at his disposal. Regarding
her *melog* property, however, no such consideration pertained. Any depreciation in value was not his responsibility
and goods in that category were returned to the woman in
whatever condition they stood at the time of his death or the
couple's divorce (*Yeb.* 7.1).

Thus, while the woman legally retained title to both her
melog and *son barzel* goods, she was effectively a stranger to
them throughout her married life, relinquishing everything
except the title of ownership to her husband the moment she
entered the חופה.[2] As Epstein somewhat colourfully remarks,

> What is his is his and what is hers is also his. Her *mohar*

1 The husband's right of usufruct was another reason for the rabbinic prohibition on
women selling their *melog*.
2 *B.B.* 3.3, 'A husband cannot secure title by uscupation to the property of his wife'.
Evidence for the fact that she retained title was (i) the goods had to be returned to
her, and (ii) while the husband enjoyed usufruct, he could not sell any of the property without her consent (*B.B.* 50a; *B.K.* 89a; *Yeb.* 66b; *Gitt.* 55b, etc). For details
about what constituted fruit and capital in Tannaitic *halakhah*, see Epstein, *op.
cit.*, pp. 117f.

and *mattan* are his, her *son barzel* and *melog* are his, her
earnings and what she may find in the street are also his.
The household articles, even the crumbs of bread on the
table, are his. Should she invite a guest to the house and feed
him, she would be stealing from her husband (*Gitt.* 62a).[1]

On several occasions the Talmud poses the question: 'How
can a woman have anything: whatever is hers belongs to her
husband?' (for example, *Sanh.* 71a; *Naz.* 24b). From the survey so far it would certainly seem that the woman was unable
to hold property independently of her husband. However,
prompted by the Talmud's question, we may pause to ask
whether she was as penniless (for all practical purposes) as
the sources thus far examined would have us believe. Certain
facts as yet not considered would indicate that this was not
strictly speaking the case. Within the Tannaitic writings there
are several rules which imply that the wife did have independent property of her own over which she had rights of
disposal, in contradiction to the principle that what a woman
acquires belongs to her husband (מה שקנתה אשה קנה בעלה). So, for
example, in *Naz.* 4.4 we read that

> If a woman vowed to become a Nazirite and had set apart
> her cattle [for the offering], and her husband then revoked
> her vow, if her cattle were his, they may go forth and pasture
> with the flock; but if they were hers... they must be con-
> sumed on the same day [as a sin-offering, a whole-offering,
> and a peace-offering]...

Similarly, and according to the same mishnah:

> If she has money set aside yet unassigned [to each of the
> three offerings] it falls [to the Temple treasury] as a free-will
> offering...

According to *Shek.* 1.5, if a woman paid the half-shekel contribution to the Temple, although not obliged so to do, her money
was to be accepted,[2] and *Kidd.* 24a ruled that a woman could

---

1 *Op. cit.*, p. 113.
2 Only men were under a religious duty to pay the annual half-shekel tax (Exod.
   30.14-15; cf. Neh. 10.32; *Spec. Leg.* 1.76-78). Money thus raised was used to defray
   the cost of the offerings sacrificed for the entire community, plus other expenses.
   The tax was levied on everyone over the age of twenty, excepting women and
   slaves.

redeem the second tithes without giving an additional fifth, if
she was redeeming them with her own money (cf. t. *Masser
Sheni* 4.4). Various sources speak of women giving alms to the
poor who came to their home (Prov. 31.20; *Taan.* 23b; y. *Hor.* 3,
48a).[1]

There is also evidence in documentary form of married
women holding and disposing of property in their own right.
Unfortunately all of this material comes from Egypt, nothing
of a similar type deriving—or surviving—from Palestine
itself (excepting the Babatha archive which as yet remains
unpublished; see pp. 173-74 above). Nevertheless, the picture
presented by the documents is of interest to us in that it may
well, given the Tannaitic evidence already examined, have
had application within Palestine too.

In the deeds women figure prominently as holders of real
estate and capital. For the purposes of the present argument,
however, care must be taken to note the marital status of the
parties concerned, for divorcees and widows were obviously
not bound by the same constraints as itemized above.
Unfortunately, only a few of the documents explicitly state
whether the woman concerned was married; the majority
give no indication as to marital status. So, while it is probable
that at least some of the women in the latter group were in
fact married, to reduce speculation we shall refer only to the
activities of those in the former, smaller body of deeds. Within
that group there is (i) a census return from the beginning of
the second century CE in which a Jewess (married to one
Agathonikos) registered her ownership of 'part of a house in
the quarter of Apollonios Hierax' (*CPJ*, II, no. 430); (ii) an
application for a lease, again in the second century C E
addressed to two women (one of whose husbands is named)
who owned land in the Hermoupolite district. The deed makes
clear that it was the women who were the lessors and that it

1 Though this last point does not necessarily indicate independent property: alms-
giving was an expected and integral part of the social fabric and the woman may
simply have been acting with her husband's permission and handing over items
or money of household concern for which she had day-to-day responsibility but
which were her husband's property (though cf. below). In all likelihood the
amounts involved in such doorstep charity were small.

was they who were to receive the rent agreed upon (*CPJ*, III, 453); (iii) an agreement from the first century BCE concerning repayment of a loan to a credit society. One of the debtors listed is a Jewess by the name of Marion, married to one Lysimachos (*CPJ*, II, 149).[1]

In both the Tannaitic writings, therefore, and the documentary material, there is evidence that the married woman could hold and dispose of property and money independently of her husband. But how could this be if he had a claim to everything that she possessed? The fact was that the law did give her exclusive rights over certain specific categories of property. These were the following: If her husband presented her with a gift of real estate, the law decreed that gift to be absolute and denied him his customary right to the fruits (*B.B.* 51b).[2] He was similarly denied the right of usufruct if his wife received a gift from her father with the express stipulation that

> This money is given thee as a gift on the condition that thy husband shall have no right over it and that thou deal with it at thine own pleasure (*Ned.* 11.8).

The same ruling applied to a gift from a stranger (*Naz.* 24b;

---

1 Women in the larger group of documents about whose marital status we cannot be certain (they are referred to simply as 'N. daughter of N.', the usual form of identification for women; see above, p. 164 n. 1) included a householder (*CPJ*, II, 426); a vineyard owner (*CPJ*, I, 41); owners of land and cattle (*CPJ*, I, 28, 47); and possessors of capital (*CPJ*, II, 424; III, 462). It is possible that *CPJ*, II, 430 cited here in the main text could be simply registration of a woman's title to property (something which as we have seen she never lost); equally, however, it could be evidence for property over which she has the right of disposal. As the deed itself cannot clarify the point, it has been included in the main argument.

2 This type of direct transference of property during the husband's lifetime was something different from the other form of gift, that in contemplation of death, which carried with it various provisions and conditions. See Yaron, *Gifts in Contemplation of Death in Jewish and Roman Law*. The only extant deed of gift from Mishnaic times, which is unfortunately as yet unpublished, comes from the Babatha archive and according to Yadin provides vital information 'about several important aspects of the matter dealt with which are not clearly explained in the Talmudic sources' ('Expedition D', p. 242). The deed treats the gift 'in perpetuity' by one Simeon of all his possessions to his wife Miriam, and he reserves for himself the right of usufruct, possession, payment of debts, and the right to dwell in the sworn over properties during his lifetime. See Yadin, *op. cit.*, pp. 241-44 and *Bar Kokhba*, pp. 236-37.

Sanh. 71a). Property which had been inherited before she was betrothed was also hers to dispose of freely (*Ket.* 8.1). Finally, and on a less grand scale, it would also seem that the woman could keep anything that she might be able to save or make from her housekeeping. These various, and possibly often significant, caveats to the general rule that all goods in marriage were held in one way or another by the husband were summed up by the rabbis when discussing the mishnah with which we started this examination (*Naz.* 4.4, above p. 232). Pondering how the female Nazirite could have an animal of her own to dedicate as part of the vow, they asked: 'Where did she get it from seeing that it has been affirmed that whatsoever a woman acquires becomes her husband's?' The reply was: 'She saved it out of her housekeeping money [lit. 'scraped it off her dough']'. Another possibility is that it was given to her by a third person with the proviso that her husband have no control over it. Alternatively, it was suggested that the husband had transferred an animal to her and 'on transference it becomes her own property' (*Naz.* 24a-b).

Aside from these specific categories, however, the general rule stood and the wife did not have the right to dispose of her own property within marriage, a fact highlighted by both the raising and the phraseology of the opening question to the Gemara quoted above. In this respect the adult Jewish woman was technically at least in a worse position than the minor daughter, for regarding the latter the mishnah clearly stated that the father 'has not the use of her property [that is, inherited movables] during her lifetime' (*Ket.* 4.4, the reason being that he had no duty to provide maintenance [see above, pp. 60ff.]). A husband, however, was legally obliged to support his wife, and it was in consequence of this that his powers in respect of the woman's property exceeded those of her father (*Ket.* 4.4).[1]

As will be shown in more detail below, a husband's duties toward his wife were three-fold. He had to provide her with

1 In reality a minor was unlikely to have had either personal or practical advantage from her legal competence in this respect. It remained the case, however, that in the eyes of the law she had this right and so was in a different position to the adult woman for the reasons itemized.

maintenance during their life together, furnish a ransom in the event of her being taken captive, and ensure that monies were available for her to be given a decent burial. According to the final halakhah, the correspondence between these duties and his use of her property was as follows:

> Maintenance was provided for a wife in return for her handiwork [that is, the earnings from her waged labour]; her ransom in return for usufruct [of her *melog*]; and her burial in return for the *kethubah* [that is, her *son barzel*, *mattan* and *mohar*] (*Ket.* 47b).

However, while it was logical that there should have been some law of correspondence or rule of reciprocity, it is evident that this breakdown was somewhat strained and artificial. Such is indicated by the Talmud's own record of disagreements among the rabbis prior to the final halakhah being reached, by the fact that earlier discussion did not include the woman's *melog* goods, and by the fact that a father was also entitled to a minor's earnings and handiwork but under no obligation to ransom or bury his daughter. What we have in this rule of correspondence is an attempt to rationalize the husband's claim to virtually everything that the woman possessed. As we have seen, the rabbis were constantly extending the husband's rights over his wife's property and sought to find justification for their action. Sometimes they experienced difficulty in this (as was demonstrated by the dispute over property acquired during the betrothal period). In this ruling they forced the notion of exchange to the husband's advantage and granted him right to all his wife's property, goods and earnings (excepting those few categories itemized above) in return for the maintenance which was her legal due.

The maintenance which the woman was entitled to receive consisted principally of food and clothing. The minimum weekly food allowance stipulated by the Mishnah was two *kabs* of wheat or four *kabs* of barley, half a *kab* of pulse, half a *log* of oil and a *kab* of dried figs (*Ket.* 5.8). Sometimes an allowance of wine was added if she was 'a woman accustomed to drink', but this was of limited amount for it was assumed that alcohol would encourage her natural promiscuity or, to use the words of one Tanna,

One cup [of wine] is becoming to a woman; two are degrading; [with] three she solicits publicly; [but if she has] four she solicits even an ass in the street and cares not (*Ket.* 65a).

With regard to the clothing she was to receive the Mishanah ruled that the husband had to provide her with

a cap for her head and a girdle for her loins and shoes at each of the three feasts [that is, Passover, Pentecost and Tabernacles] and clothing to the value of fifty *zuzin* every year. They may not give her new clothes for summer or worn-out clothes for winter; but he should give her clothes to the value of fifty *zuzin* for winter and she may clothe herself with the rags thereof in the summertime; and the discarded garments belong to her (*Ket.* 5.8).

She was also to be provided with a bed and a bed-cover, or at least with a rush mat (*ibid.*). Such then was the minimum maintenance requirement laid down by the law, but how it translated in reality is a matter open to speculation. The general rule or rabbinic hope, however, was that 'His wife ascends with him but does not descend with him' (*Ket.* 48a, 61a). In other words, if she came from a home richer than that of her husband he was required to maintain the standard of living to which she was accustomed; if she came from a poorer family, he was obliged to maintain her according to his own status.[1] At later date cosmetics and perfume were included in the basic allowance (*Ket.* 48a, 66b). If the husband failed to meet his maintenance obligation through prolonged absence overseas (without having appointed an agent to manage his affairs) or severe illness (for example, insanity), the court took possession of his estate and provided his wife with food and clothing (*Ket.* 48a). If he was guilty of voluntary non-support, then she was entitled to claim a divorce with full *kethubah* payment (*Ket.* 7.1, 71a), for as *Gitt.* 1.6 declared:

if a man is minded not to provide for his slave, this is his right; but if he is minded not to provide for his wife, this is not his right.[2]

1 Cf. pp. 145, 150 above where we saw that the rabbis in fact encouraged people to marry within their own social and economic stratum.
2 Though see p. 220 above for the difficulties facing a woman in gaining a divorce through the courts.

238   *Her Price is Beyond Rubies*

The husband was also obliged to pay any medical expenses which his wife incurred. In the Mishnah this duty was treated separately from the maintenance obligation on the basis that whereas it was possible to gauge the amount needed to keep a wife fed and clothed, it was not possible to estimate how much a husband might have to spend to cure his wife. Although payment for medical treatment was a condition of marriage therefore, out of consideration for the fact that a man might be faced with economically ruinous bills, the law did permit him to release himself from this obligation by the simple expedient of divorcing his wife, after which she had no claim upon his estate or recourse to a court. The ruling was:

> If she received injury he is liable for her healing; but if he said, 'Lo, here is her bill of divorce and her *kethubah*: let her heal herself' he has the right [so to do] (*Ket.* 4.9).[1]

The two other duties which a husband was obliged to perform in return for the use of his wife's property were those of ransom and burial. The former was a condition enjoined by the court, which meant that its fulfilment was absolutely binding upon the husband and not something to be escaped from by divorce (*Ket.* 4.9) (see Chapter 2 §C). He was obliged to redeem her and, if an Israelite, take her again as wife, or if a priest, return her to her father's house (see p. 138). With regard to burial, he was obliged to provide a funeral procession comprising not less than two flute players and one wailing woman (*Ket.* 4.4). This was the minimum requirement. The general Talmudic ruling was that he should arrange a funeral such as befitted the dignity of his or her status, whichever was the higher, for as was the case with maintenance, 'She rises with him but does not go down with him, even after her death' (*Ket.* 48a).[2]

Such, then, were the conditions of life for the married woman. With regard to the authority which was exercised over her by the husband, her position was analogous to that of the minor daughter, for both were subject to the wishes of the

---

1 For the distinction in law between material support and medical aid, and details of what the latter comprised, see Epstein, *op. cit.*, pp. 162f.
2 For details of the funeral arrangements and mourning ritual, see Ch. 4.

pater familias and both were bound to honour and obey him. In legal terms the wife's position differed from that of a daughter in only a few respects: she could not be sold into servitude; honour (albeit of a qualified nature) was accorded her; and maintenance was her legal due (though in return for this she forfeited most of her property rights). She was also able to act independently in some spheres (for example, conveyancing of property given to her), and unlike a daughter presumably had some power on a day-to-day basis within the home, the management of which was her stated *raison d'être*. As will be seen in the next section, the wife's lifestyle was also less physically restricted than that of a daughter. In the main, however, she still occupied a position of subordination to and dependence upon the male, and this continuity from childhood to adulthood is nicely encapsulated by Philo who declared that 'for the purpose of giving protection the husband is to the wife what the parents are to the maiden' (*Spec. Leg.* 4.178).

Following on from Philo's words, however, it should be remembered that while marriage was the only future and security for the adult woman, a wife could never experience a sense of real security. As we have seen, she could be dismissed from the marital home at any time and for any reason. She would then share the plight of the widow obliged to return to the familial home or attempting to move in a patriarchal society without the protection of a man.

B. *Seclusion*

Earlier in this work (Chapter 1 §A) it was demonstrated that in the course of the period under consideration a complex of restrictive rules was brought to bear upon the freedom of movement and general conduct of women at all periods of their lives—these restrictions being the result of the post-exilic community's obsession with ritual purity and of their increased morbidity where sex relations were concerned. It was noted, however, that the various codes of social conduct did not have equal application to all women at all periods of their lives. Differentiation was made according to age and marital status (above, pp. 101-102), far greater freedom being accorded to married women than those yet to enter the bridal chamber, who, as we have seen, were strictly confined within the home. The purpose of this section is to examine the rules which applied to married women, and the extent to which they were permitted contact with men and allowed general freedom of movement beyond the home.

Of the many new ideas which emerged in the post-exilic period, perhaps the one with the most far-reaching consequence for the adult woman's freedom was that of the Evil Woman, of wickedness personified in the female form (see above, pp. 104-105). As was demonstrated earlier, this concept—itself the result of a complex of ideas—quickly made inroads into the popular imagination, and by the Hellenistic period belief in the essential evil of woman was a fundamental of Jewish religious thought. Woman was seen as a temptress, a tool in Satan's hands to lure men away from the path of righteousness. This she did by enticing men into liaisons which directly contravened the day's standards of sex morality. Thus the author of the *Testament of Reuben* wrote:

> evil are women... they use wiles by outward attractions, that they may draw him to themselves. And whom they cannot bewitch by outward attractions, him they overcome by craft... women are overcome by the spirit of fornication more than men, and in their heart they plot against men; and by means of their adornment they deceive first their minds, and by a glance of the eye instil the poison, and then through the accomplished act they take them captive. For a woman cannot force a man openly, but by a harlot's bearing she beguiles him (5.1-3).

The author of the *Testament of Judah* expressed the fear which men felt when faced with this mysterious and uncontrollable female power:

> And the angel of God showed me that forever do women bear rule over king and beggar alike. And from the king they take away his glory, and from the valiant man his might, and from the beggar even that little which is the stay of his poverty (15.5-6).

The reason why association with women had such disastrous consequences was due to the belief that

> if men... see a woman who is comely in favour and beauty,

they let all those things go, and gape after her, and even with
open mouth fix their eyes fast on her (1 Esdras 4.18).[1]

Thus Ben Sira warned men:

> Give not thyself unto a woman
> So as to let her trample down thy manhood...
> Give not water an outlet
> Nor to a wicked women power (9.2; 25.13).[2]

Simply issuing words of warning, however, was not sufficient to protect men from the dangers of womankind. Because
they were deemed helpless in the face of such sexual allurement and women were considered incapable of controlling
their lust for pleasure (cf. Sir. 26.11-12), care had to be taken
to ensure that the sexes did not in fact associate too freely. So
the author of the *Testament of Reuben* wrote:

> if you wish to be pure in mind, guard your senses from every
> woman. And command the women likewise not to associate
> with men, that they also may be pure in mind. For constant
> meetings, even though the ungodly deed be not wrought, are
> to them an irremedial disease and to us a destruction of
> Beliar and an eternal reproach (6.1-3).[3]

In order to promote the desired standard of behaviour, a
code of social conduct had to be formulated and imposed. As
was noted in Chapter 1, a controlling factor in the formulation
of any code of sex morality and conduct is the position of
women within a given society. When the need is felt in a patriarchy to place limits upon the free mingling of the sexes, it is
the woman who suffers restrictions on her freedom of move-

---

1 For this development and the way in which a notion of *sexual* woman was pivotal
   to the whole post-exilic system, see Archer, 'The Virgin and the Harlot in the
   Writings of Formative Judaism', *History Workshop Journal* 24 (1987), pp. 1-16.
2 Note the powerful 'double standard' at work in these texts. Note also the way in
   which on the one hand women are perceived as weak and powerless, yet on the
   other are seen as having strength over men: men purport to be rational and powerful, yet they are powerless in the face of female snares (see pp. 105, 210). What we
   have here, once again, is both that culturally constructed fear of women from the
   centre, and the notion (reality?) of power from the margins. On women always
   representing a threat to patriarchy, see p. 210 n. 2.
3 Cf. *Ned*. 20a: 'do not converse much with women, as this will ultimately lead you
   to unchastity'; *Aboth* 1.5, 'He that talks much with womankind brings evil upon
   himself and neglects the study of the law and at the last will inherit Gehenna'.

ment and not the man whose sphere of activity is situated
firmly in the public arena. While this in general held true for
both married and unmarried women in Graeco-Roman
Palestine, the nature of the advice offered in the sources thus
far presented would indicate that adult women were in fact
visible in public places. If not, then the words of warning to
men to avoid their snares would have been redundant. The
difference in attitude regarding the freedom of movement of
the two categories of women is nicely highlighted by Ben Sira.
Regarding young girls, his advice was strict confinement
within the home:

> Over thy daughter keep a strict watch...
> In the place where she lodgeth let there be no lattice
> Or spot overlooking the entrance roundabout.
> Let her not show her beauty to any male,
> And among wives let her not converse (42.11-12).[1]

With respect to married women, however, all he could urge
was:

> With a married woman sit not at table,
> And mingle not wine in her company,
> Lest thou incline thine heart toward her
> And in thy blood descendest to the Pit (9.9).[2]

In other words and as we shall shortly see in more detail,
married women, unlike virgins, were to be found in areas frequented by men. This, of course, is not to say that they were
accorded absolute freedom of movement. In the main they
were expected to lead a life of modest retirement, removed
from the gaze of men and the dangers of possible intimacy.
Thus Philo, basing himself on the notion that 'women are best
suited to the indoor life', wrote that 'A woman should not be a

---

1 Cf. Ps.-Phocylides, ll. 215-16: 'Guard a virgin in firmly locked rooms, and let
   her not be seen before the house before her wedding day'. For this strict
   confinement of daughters, see Chapter 1 §E.
2 Cf. Sir. 9.8; 19.2; 41.21c; *T. Reub.* 3.10. See Charles, notes to the quoted passage:
   ' "And in thy blood"... The reference is to the vengeance of the husband who
   slays the adulterer... "The Pit" = Sheol, as often elsewhere'. We should note,
   however, that although women could be present at banquets (as the quotation from
   Sir. shows), in the main they ate apart from their husbands and male guests. See
   above, p. 115.

busybody, meddling with matters outside her household concerns, but should seek a life of seclusion', which never strays from the house (*Spec. Leg.* 3.169f.). However, while seclusion was always the ideal, in practical terms married women were granted a limited amount of freedom. This we shall now examine.

According to rabbinic teaching, a married woman was allowed to leave the confines of her home to attend certain specific social functions, of which the two principal ones were weddings and funerals.[1] Of these two, attendances at funerals was considered to be particularly important, for if she was not seen to mourn others publicly then 'Tomorrow she might die and no creature would mourn for her' (*Ket.* 72a).[2] In the opinion of the rabbis, no husband had the right to deny his wife access to such functions. To do so was to 'close all doors against her', whereupon she would be entitled to claim a divorce with full payment of the *kethubah* (*Ket.* 7.5). He could only restrict her freedom in this respect if he felt that the feasting place was frequented by dissolute men (*ibid.*).

With regard to the mingling of the sexes at such occasions it would seem that there was no fixed rule of segregation, though that may well have been the custom. We have already seen how the tendency in wedding celebrations was to have men and women feasting separately (though a passage in the Gospel of John [2.1; cf. Lk. 7.11; *Mo'ed Katan* 3.8, 9] could be taken as showing that they might celebrate together when gathered *en masse* for such a public occasion. Alternatively it could reflect the type of regional variation noted elsewhere in this volume in other contexts. Given the lack of detail in the

---

1 Indeed, these are the only functions which are mentioned in the Talmud in connection with women. Talmudic descriptions of other public occasions such as the circumcision of a son or redemption of the first-born give the impression that only men were present—a state of affairs which we would expect given the specific and exclusive male character of these events. A woman had no religious or social role on these occasions. See Chapter 1 §B

2 Cf. *Ket.* 72a, 'if a man mourns for other people, others will also mourn for him; if he buries other people, others will also bury him; if he lifts up his voice to lament for others, others will lift up their voices to lament for him . . . ' In addition to this aspect, there was also the fact that historically women were especially associated with ceremonies for the dead and with the ritual of mourning. On this, see Ch. 4.

Gospel account, it could be that the guests in any case gathered spontaneously into discrete groups, but we have no means of ascertaining this.) With regard to funerals, a late Tannaitic text suggests that women in the mourners' procession should walk ahead of the coffin and men at the rear (or vice versa), and in another late Tannaitic text reference is made to men and women gathering in separate parts of a house of feasting, but such segregation (at least with regard to these two very public functions) was probably only a rabbinic ideal and not a rule imposed in reality (*Sanh.* 20a; *Kidd.* 81a).

Another social liberty which it was considered reasonable to grant the woman was that of visiting her parents. Denial of this right by the husband again resulted in the woman having a claim to divorce through the courts (*Ket.* 71b-72a). She was not, however, expected to visit her parents too frequently for that would have been to manifest irresponsibility with respect to her own domestic duties. She was advised to go once or twice a year around the time of a high holiday (*Ket.* 70a-71b). It must be said regarding this piece of advice, however, that once again we are relying on rabbinic evidence in the absence of any other. The statement may therefore again represent a rabbinic ideal, and while reflecting a general sentiment or attitude, it may not be a rigid rule for actual behaviour. Additionally we should note that the Talmud assumes some geographic distance between a married daughter and her parents. This may not always have been the case in the marriage arrangements of Graeco-Roman Palestine, and may therefore indicate the late date of this passage. As the original ruling about grounds for divorce shows, and as was observed earlier in this survey, close ties were expected between a daughter and her parents, but we cannot gauge how this translated in reality. Much would have depended on the wishes of the parties concerned—particularly those of the husband—and the geographic distance between a wife and her parental home.

Attendance at synagogue and the Temple was similarly not to be restricted (*Ant.* 4.209), though it should be remembered that the practicalities of running a home and caring for children frequently rendered the bestowal of the legal right meaningless, as did the fact that the woman had no immediate or active involvement in the ceremonial and indeed no *mitzvah* to fulfil with regard to attendance (see above, pp. 90ff.). According to Philo she was to make her trips to the synagogue after market hours when the streets were quiet:

> She should not show herself off like a vagrant in the streets before the eyes of other men... she should take pains to go, not when the market is full, but when most people have gone home, and so like a freeborn lady worthy of the name, with everything quiet around her, make her oblations and offer her prayers... (*Spec. Leg.* 3.171).

She was also not to be prevented from going to the bathhouse so long as the trips there were not made at an unreasonable time of the day (y. *Ket.* 31b).[1]

That married women did in fact move about in the public domain is further demonstrated by the various rules which the Tannaim formulated regarding the public social conduct of the sexes. No greeting was ever to be exchanged between a man and a woman in public, not even through the agency of a third party (*B.M.* 87a; *Kidd.* 70b). A man was always to walk ahead of a woman in order to prevent his indulging in lascivious thoughts through observation of the female form. If one did find himself walking behind a woman, the law obliged him either to turn in another direction or hurry to get ahead, or to fall back to such a distance that scrutiny of her figure was no longer possible. The prohibition on walking behind a woman applied even to the married couple, for otherwise people might suspect that the husband was following a stranger to some illicit rendezvous. In sum, the view of the Talmud on this subject was 'It is better to walk behind a lion than behind a woman' (*Erub.* 18b; *Kidd.* 81a; *Ber.* 61a). Finally, when a man saw a woman in the street he was immediately to avert his gaze, the reason being that 'The heart and the eye are two

---

1 For ritual purification following menstruation the woman was required to immerse herself totally in the living water of the *mikveh*. Immersion was also required following corpse contact, sex, and other instances of ritual impurity laid down in the Torah (see *JE*, I, p. 69 and *EJ*, XIII, cols. 1405-1406). It is apparent that the rules of *niddah* had dimensions and purposes other than the cultic from the fact that, significantly, only they (and the immersion for proselytes) stayed in force following 70 CE when all the other laws of impurity went into abeyance.

agents of sin; the eye sees and the heart desires' (quoted in Epstein, *op. cit.*, p. 117). Ben Sira urged:

> Hide thine eye from a lovely woman
> And gaze not upon beauty which is not thine;
> By the comeliness of a woman, many have been ruined,
> And this way passion flameth like fire (9.8; cf. 41.21c; *T. Reub.* 3.10).

The New Testament, rather more didactically, declared that 'Whosoever looketh on a woman to lust after her hath committed adultery with her in his heart' (Mt. 5.28).[1]

Women, too, had to observe certain standards of public modesty. Above all, they were to do nothing which would attract undue attention to themselves. They were encouraged whenever possible to go about their business at quiet times of the day when men would be occupied elsewhere. So, as we have seen, Philo urged women to make their visits to the synagogue after the markets had closed for the day. They were not to dawdle in the streets but were to go directly to their destination. Women who did loiter in public places were assumed to be harlots (Prov. 7.10f.; Sir. 9.6-7; *Sac.* 21f.; 4Q184.17-18).[2] When out in public they were expected to keep their eyes averted and to dress in a manner becoming to decent women. To gaze about the street was to invite immediate suspicion for, as Ben Sira wrote,

> The whoredom of a woman is in the lifting up of her eyes,
> And she shall be known by her eyelids (26.9).

Similarly, one of the central characteristics of 'the seductress' according to the author of 4Q184 was that 'She will never rest from whoring, her eyes glance hither and thither. She lifts up her eyelids naughtily, to stare at a virtuous one',[3] while the *Testament of Reuben* stated that the fatal act was virtually

---

1 That these last two quotations applied specifically to married women is clear both from the wording and the nature of the warnings. They reveal, as we have seen elsewhere in this survey, that the basic reason for the taboo on looking at such women was the breach of another man's authority. A different morality presumably applied with respect to unmarried adult women, but we have little information regarding that category.

2 See p. 119 above and Archer, *op. cit.*

3 4Q184.18-19; trans. Vermes, *The Dead Sea Scrolls in English*, p. 256.

accomplished once the eye instilled the poison (5.1-4). The use
of cosmetics and jewellery was also regarded with suspicion,
for these were viewed as beautifying agents which had no
other purpose but to arouse the passions of men.[1] Decent
women were required to 'adorn themselves in modest apparel
with shamefacedness and sobriety, not with braided hair or
gold or pearls or costly array' (1 Tim. 2.9; cf. 1 Pet. 3.3; *T. Reub.*
5.1-4).

In general, the type of modesty expected of women when
moving in public may be inferred from the period's numerous
diatribes against the unseemly behaviour of harlots who spent
their time and energy frequenting 'the broad places of the
city', luring men into immoral liaisons. One particularly
expansive example from this mound of invective is to be found
in Philo, who characterized Pleasure (= strumpet) in the following way:

> the lascivious roll of her eyes is a bait to entice the souls of
> the young; her look speaks of boldness and shamelessness;
> her neck is held high; she assumes a stature that Nature
> has not given her; she grins and giggles; her hair is dressed
> in curious and elaborate plaits; under her eyes are pencil
> lines; her eyebrows are smothered in paint...; her flush is
> artificial; her costly raiment is broidered lavishly with flow-
> ers; bracelets and necklaces and every other feminine orna-
> ment wrought of gold and jewels hang around her; her
> breath is laden with fragrant scents; a strumpet of the
> streets, she takes the market place for her home (*Sac.* 21f.).

One standard requirement of dress for married women was
the veil. This was essentially the symbol of the husband's
authority (see pp. 205, 212 above). As such, and by a logical
extension of meaning, it came to be regarded as the chief
token of the woman's 'modesty', that is, her unavailability to
others—a fact which highlights, in this context at least, the

---

1 See *1 Enoch* 8.1-2, 'And Azazel... made known to them [men] the metals (of the
earth) and the art of working them, and bracelets and ornaments, and the use of
antimony and the beautifying of the eyelids, and all kinds of costly stones, and
all colouring trickeries. And there arose much godlessness, and they committed
fornication, and they were led astray, and became corrupt in all their ways'. Cf.
Ahikar 2.5; *T. Reub.* 5.1f. where women 'by means of their adornment deceive
[men's] minds'.

real character and function of so-called modesty and moral behaviour (cf. p. 26 n. 1 above). The veil, which covered the head,[1] was a sign of demure behaviour, bareheadedness being interpreted as haughty, arrogant and provocative, that is, contrary to the behaviour demanded of a woman subject to the authority of her husband.[2] Thus, as we have seen in the trial of a woman suspected of adultery, one of the first rituals performed by the officiating priest to mark the fact that the woman's decency was in question was the removal of her veil.[3] The significance which the veil had as a symbol of authority and of her decorous behaviour is most clearly seen in *Ket.* 7.6 which lists seven offences for which a woman could be divorced with complete loss of her *kethubah* rights. One of those seven was to go out in public with an uncovered head.[4]

Finally, the most important rule of conduct for women when moving in public was that they should never, under any circumstances, speak to a man. To do so was to invite instant divorce with total loss of *kethubah* payment (*Ket.* 7.6).

Within the home married women were again visible to men other than their husbands, for although they had separate quarters (see above, pp. 114f.), they were not confined to them as was the case for virgins. As was seen in the last section, they were required to attend on their husbands' 'guests and occasional visitors' (*Ket.* 61a; cf. *B.M.* 87a; *Ber.* 10a), and such guests would without doubt have been male.[5] They also came

---

1 Contrary to common assumption the veil did not cover the face but only the head (see p. 205 above). Had it covered the face then the various warnings to men not to gaze upon a woman's beauty would have been meaningless. Note also that Josephus records as a peculiar law among the Persians that they forbade their wives to be seen by strangers (*Ant.* 11.191). See *Ket.* 72a-b where the rabbis, while advocating the traditional use of the veil, agreed that it was in accordance with the Torah if the woman's head was covered by her work basket when she was out in public. It was not until the time of the Amoraim that veiling the face, as an extreme of modesty, became more general. For the custom in that period see the comment of R. Dimi in *Erub.* 100b that the woman in Palestine is 'veiled like a mourner and banished from people' (mourners were required to cover their faces).

2 For this development, see Epstein, *Sex Laws and Customs in Judaism*, pp. 38ff.

3 *Num.* 5.18; *Spec. Leg.* 3.56; above p. 213.

4 See above, pp. 212-13, for the way in which the Shammaites regarded such action as equal to unfaithfulness by the wife.

5 Apart from serving visitors, wives did not participate in social functions which

into contact with men when selling the products of their waged labour from the home (see above, pp. 229), when purchasing goods from itinerant pedlars (*B.K.* 82a-b; *B.B.* 22a), and when distributing alms to beggars who called at the house (Prov. 31.20; *Toh.* 7.9). In rural areas they assisted their husbands in agricultural work (*Yeb.* 15.2; *Eduy.* 1.11; *B.M.* 7.6) and could be seen carrying water jars to and from the village well (Jn 4.7f.).[1] The only rule of conduct (apart from general modest behaviour) which pertained within the home was that should a married woman have cause to meet with a man in her husband's absence, then a chaperone was required to be present. This rule applied even to male relatives (excepting sons) (*Kidd.* 80a-81a; *Sanh.* 21a-b; t. *Kidd.* 5.10).

Thus we see that married women, unlike virgins, were visible in public places and did have contact with men. However, it must be stressed that the extent of any woman's freedom of movement was totally dependent upon the wishes of her husband. Whilst the religious leaders of the time might sanction visits to the synagogue or attendance at weddings, and declare any denial of such legitimate freedom reprehensible, they could not actually impose their opinions upon the authority of the husband. Similarly, if a woman's lifestyle became so restricted as to entitle her to claim a divorce, although a court might decide in her favour, it could not force the husband to issue the *get* which was necessary for her release (see above, p. 220). The following report by R. Meir illustrates the way in which women were subject to the whims of their husbands:

> As men differ in their treatment of their food, so they differ in their treatment of their wives. Some men, if a fly falls in their cup, will put it aside and not drink it. This corresponds to the way of Papus B. Judah who used, when he went out, to

took place within the home (see above, p. 115). The only time when they did sit with male guests was on the occasion of a religious feast such as Passover (see *Pes.* 7.13). In the main they ate in their own quarters, often only joining their husbands for a communal meal once a week (see *Ket.* 5.9).

1 Such, however, was only the case in rural areas. In towns water was stored in a cistern in the courtyard, and according to *Aboth de Rabbi Nathan* (A), 20 the custom was that 'men draw the water and women serve it'. For the difference in lifestyle, see *Nidd.* 48b which refers to townswomen taking baths and wearing scarves and to village women grinding corn and carrying water jars.

lock his wife indoors. Another man, if a fly falls into his cup, will throw away the fly and then drink from the cup. This corresponds to the way of most men who do not mind their wives talking with their brothers and relatives. Another man, again, if a fly falls into his soup, will squash it and eat it. This corresponds to the way of a bad man who sees his wife go out with hair unfastened and spins cloth in the street with her armpits uncovered and bathe with men... Such a one it is a religious duty to divorce (*Gitt.* 90a-b).

Finally, it should be remembered that even if a husband did grant his wife a reasonable amount of freedom, the principle of domestic seclusion remained the ideal, for

If God had meant women to rove, He would have created her out of Adam's foot instead of from his rib (*Gen. Rab.* 18.2).

Chapter 4

DEATH

In this chapter we turn to the subject of death, both the woman's own death and the attention paid her in that event, and also her role as a mourner in the event of someone else's demise. This examination of the rituals surrounding death and burial may be seen not only as the logical conclusion to a survey of the 'average' Jewish woman's life, but also as a useful tool for exploring further her status and position as cross-culturally funerary practices tend to reflect and restate the patterns and preoccupations of life, the divisions within any given society, and the former social role or function of the deceased. The concern of this chapter, therefore, is to examine the funerary practices of Graeco-Roman Palestine to see what they reveal of society's ordering and with an eye open as to whether any differentiation was made in the rituals performed consequent upon the sex of the deceased. The chapter will fall into three parts. First, in order to contextualize the discussion *vis-à-vis* women, a general description of Jewish burial practices and mourning rituals will be given. Then we shall review, again in general terms, the woman's position in life, the roles she was accorded and the attitudes which society manifested towards her. Having reminded ourselves of the woman's position in life, we shall in the third section turn to those questions which are the principal concern of this concluding chapter, that is, the possibility and the implications of gender differentiation in death and mourning customs.

To turn firstly then to the burial practices:[1] the mode of

---

1 Owing to limitations of space the following survey of tomb history will be both general and in consequence somewhat simplistic. For ease of discussion the material will be presented in terms of a clear-cut, lineal development in tomb type and history from one period to the next, despite the fact that there was much chronological overlapping and variety. Additionally most of the evidence will be taken from the environs of Jerusalem, Jericho, and the necropolis of Beth Shearim (see p. 255 n. 1

burial among the Jews was interment and not cremation, a
custom based in rabbinic understanding upon the prescription
of Gen. 3.19 of 'dust thou art and to dust thou shalt return',
and one noted by Tacitus in his *Histories*, 'They [the Jews]
bury rather than burn their dead' (5.5).[1] In biblical times[2]
bodies were simply laid to rest in rock caverns or in the earth
without the use of coffins.[3] The caverns, natural or hewn out

below), a fact which may pose questions as to the overall representativeness
(though note the comment of Amos Kloner from his survey of burial in Jerusalem:
'If the caves are an indication of social status, we can conclude that ossuaries [see
below] were used by all levels of society' [*The Necropolis of Jerusalem in the
Second Temple Period*, p. xiii]). There is also the fact that much of the
archaeological research is still in an ongoing state, and its details are beyond the
scope of this survey. With these caveats in mind, however, a broad and central
trend in Hebrew/Jewish burial practices is discernible, and it is that trend which
is here presented. For more detailed discussion of the material secondary literature will be referenced throughout.

1 The only exception to this would be when a person was burned to death by way of
execution, as was the case for a priest's daughter who 'played the harlot' (Lev. 21.9;
Ant. 4.248; see above p. 109 n. 2 and Chapter 2 §A). For the early biblical period
Segal ('Popular Religion in Ancient Israel', *JJS* 27 [1976], pp. 1-22) maintains that
'cremation was restricted to criminals, and possibly to enemies' (p. 3) but this is a
rather sweeping statement. For 'criminals' he cites Gen. 38.34 (Tamar) and for
'enemies' 1 Sam. 31.12 (Saul), which conflicts with the evidence of 1 Chron. 10.12.

2 The expression 'biblical times' of course covers a huge period of time and is moreover largely outside our immediate concern. For a more detailed breakdown of
the period and the tomb types of which we have remains, see Rahmani, 'Ancient
Jerusalem's Funerary Customs and Tombs, Part Two', *BA* 44 (1981), pp. 229-35,
who divides the evidence into Early Middle and Late Canaanite (third to second
millennium BCE) and Israelite I and II (fourteenth to seventh century BCE); and
Rodgers who focuses on the latter (Iron Age) material in *Palestinian Burial
Practices from 1200—600 BCE*. Throughout this survey of tomb types I am grateful
to Fanny Vitto, Wolfson College, Oxford, for her very useful comments.

3 See, for example, 2 Sam. 3.31 for the typical use of a bier. Joseph's coffin (אֲרוֹן, Gen.
50.26) is to be understood in terms of Egyptian practice. From the literary evidence
it would seem that the use of a bier and winding cloth remained the norm through
much of the later Graeco-Roman period (see, e.g., Mt. 27.57ff.; Mk 15.46; Lk. 7.11-
17; 24.12; Jn 19.40), though note the evidence provided by Hachlili and Killebrew
regarding wooden coffins at Jericho around the turn of the era which they argue
would have been the norm elsewhere in the country ('Jewish Funerary Customs
during the Second Temple Period, in the Light of the Excavations at the Jericho
Necropolis', *PEQ* 115 [1983], pp. 115-16, 126). The archaeological evidence for this
is, however, inconclusive given the organic decay of the material: see Rahmani,
'Ancient Jerusalem... Part Three', *BA* 45 (1981), p. 44 and *ibid.*, for an explanation regarding the unusual discovery of coffins in the Dead Sea region. Only in
rabbinic times did the custom of burying in coffins come into general use, though
here note the story of R. Judah ha-Nasi ordering holes to be drilled in the base of
his coffin so that his body might touch the soil (y. *Kil.* 9.4, 32b). For an analysis of
the various Talmudic names for coffins and instructions for interment of persons

of the rock, were usually simple structures, occasionally with
clay-levelled ledges on which the body plus various grave
goods (see below) were placed, or, for the later period, benches
with shallow depressions and carved head rests.[1] There was
also sometimes a repository pit for the transference of bones
(see below).

With the Graeco-Roman period, however, certain developments occurred and there emerged a type of tomb, again
hewn out of the living rock, whose pattern, with some modifi-
cations, was to survive the next few centuries. This was the
chamber tomb which had around its walls individual burial
recesses of the *kokh*, or later the *loculus*, type.[2] The *kohk*
recess was a narrow shaft running perpendicularly back
from the chamber wall into which the body was inserted head
first and the opening then sealed with a close fitting stone,[3]
while the *loculus* was a niche in the form of a shelf which ran
lengthways with the wall of the chamber onto which the body
was placed, with or without a sarcophagus.[4] Unlike the earlier
period when entrance to the cavern was often marked and
obtained by a vertical shaft leading down to the chamber, the
tombs of the later Graeco-Roman period had surface-level

of different status, see Bender, 'Beliefs, Rites and Customs of the Jews connected
with Death, Burial and Mourning', *JQR* 7 (1895), p. 267.

1 See Rahmani, 'Ancient Jerusalem... Part Two', p. 234; Vincent, *Underground
   Jerusalem*, pp. 24-29; Avigad, 'Architectural Observations on some Rock Cut
   Tombs', *PEQ* 79 (1947), pp. 112-15; Ussishkin, 'The Necropolis from the Time of
   the Kingdom of Judah at Silwan, Jerusalem', *BA* 33 (1970), pp. 34-46; Barkai,
   Kloner, Mazar, 'The Northern Cemetery of Jerusalem in the First Temple
   Times', *Qadmoniot* 8 (1975), pp. 71-76 (Heb.; Eng. summary in *IEJ* 26 [1976],
   pp. 55-57).
2 *Kokhim* made their first appearance in Jerusalem in the second century BCE and
   thereafter were the most common form of burial in the Hellenistic and early
   Roman period. *Loculi*, or arcosolia, were first employed in the first century CE
   and continued in frequent use after 70 CE. For theories regarding the origin in
   Palestine of these recess type tombs (which were widespread in the semitic world
   during the Hellenistic to Roman period), see Hachlili and Killebrew, *op. cit.*,
   p. 110, and Kloner, *op. cit.*, pp. 228-31.
3 For details of the dimensions of the *kokhim* as revealed by archaeological
   excavation (which corresponds to the measurements laid down by the Mishnah,
   B.B. 6.8), see Kloner, *op. cit.*, p. ix.
4 At the Jericho necropolis coffins were used within the *kokhim*: see Hachlili and
   Killebrew, *op. cit.*, and n. 2 above. Regarding the use of sarcophagi, Kloner
   reports from his survey of Jerusalem tombs that their use was very rare in the
   Second Temple period.

courtyards (of varying dimensions) backing directly onto the cave entrance. Following a burial this was sealed with a close fitting stone, or very occasionally a hinged door.[1]

The tombs themselves were usually quite simple affairs, though occasionally—and despite the statements of Josephus (*Con. Ap.* 2.205)—ones of a more grand design were erected or hewn. These were marked by a surface level monument most commonly in the form of a portico with two or more columns supporting a lintel or pediment above which was sometimes a gable.[2] The entrance courtyards to these monumental tombs were larger and often had benches around the sides.[3]

The number of chambers in each rock-hewn tomb was usually one or two, though this could vary, as could the actual dimensions of the chamber despite the very precise (?idealized) regulations of the Mishnah regarding central spaces, vaulting, and so on (*B.B.* 8.8, 100b-102b). The size of the tombs, plus other archaeological and literary evidence, makes it clear that each tomb was designed to hold the remains of members of the same family, usually over several generations.[4] The only exception to this was the vast complex of interlocking chambers at the necropolis of Beth Shearim which served as a burial place for prominent Jews from various diaspora com-

---

1 See Kloner, *op. cit.*, p. viii; Rahmani, 'Ancient Jerusalem... Part Three', p. 44.
2 See the description in 1 Macc. 13.25-30 of the elaborate Maccabaean tomb at Modin. For details of the various monumental tombs found around Jerusalem and dated to the first century BCE-first century CE, see Rahmani, 'Ancient Jerusalem... Part Three', pp. 46-49; Goodenough, *Jewish Symbols in the Graeco-Roman Period*, I, p. 79. For the one monumental tomb discovered at Jericho, see Hachlili and Killebrew, *op. cit.*, p. 112.
3 See Kloner, *op. cit.*, pp. 210, 244; Hachlili and Killebrew, pp. 112-13.
4 A point to which we shall return. Burial with one's kith and kin was also characteristic of the biblical period: see e.g. Gen. 25.8; 49.29; 2 Sam. 19.38; 21.12-14; and Rahmani, 'Ancient Jerusalem... Part One', *BA* 44 (1981), p. 174 and 'Part Two', p. 234. For Second Temple times, see Tob. 4.4; *Apoc. Mos.* 42.5f.; Jdt. 16.23; *Jub.* 35.20; 1 Macc. 13.25-30; and later *Sem.* 13.8; 14.2; also Hachlili, 'The Goliath Family in Jericho: Funerary Inscriptions from a First-Century AD Jewish Monumental Tomb', *BASOR* 235 (1979), pp. 31-65, and 'A Jerusalem Family in Jericho', *BASOR* 230 (1978), pp. 45-56; Rahmani, 'Jewish Rock Cut Tombs in Jerusalem', *Atiqot* 3 (1961), pp. 116-17; Strange, 'Late Hellenistic and Herodian Ossuary Tombs at French Hill, Jerusalem', *BASOR* 219 (1975), p. 63; Hachlili and Killebrew, *op. cit.*, pp. 125-26.

munities and parts of Palestine.[1] The more usual type of rock-cut, *loculi* or *kokhim*-lined single chamber family tomb remained the characteristic feature of Jewish burial in the Graeco-Roman period.[2]

As regards use of the tomb and disposal of the body, in the early period the dead were simply laid out on the floor of the cavern or on a slightly elevated platform until such time as the grave was needed for a new burial.[3] Then their bones were collected and placed at the back of the central area in order to create the necessary space for the new interments, or, at a somewhat later date, removed to a communal charnel pit designed for the same purpose.[4] For the first half of the Graeco-Roman period the same procedure was followed, the bones being removed from their bench or (from the second century BCE) *kokh* and heaped in a corner of the chamber or in a special charnel within the tomb. With the first century BCE, however, a change in practice occurred and small boxes or 'ossuaries' came to be used for holding the bones of individuals or close relatives once the initial process of decomposition had been completed. Although this new practice did not do away with the older custom completely, it does seem to have been both popular and common, ossuaries having been found in all types of graves both elaborate and simple, and appar-

---

1 See e.g. y. *M.K.* 3, 5a: 'people are brought here from many places like Upper Caesarea for burial in Beth Shearim'. Tomb inscriptions reveal the burial of people from Antioch, Tyre, Sidon, Beirut, Byblos, Palmyra, Messene, and Himyar. The cemetery of Beth Shearim was famous from the time of Judah ha-Nasi. For a history of the necropolis and description of the site, see conveniently *Encyclopaedia of Archaeological Excavations in the Holy Land*, ed. M. Avi Yonah, I, pp. 229ff.

2 It should also be remembered that additional to the cavern/chamber interments there would also have been simple burials in the earth, but of these we have no evidence and so they cannot form a part of this analysis. With perhaps some over-statement, Galling in the 1930s calculated that though multitudinous, the rock cut tombs of Jerusalem could only have provided space for about 5% of the burials from that city during the Graeco-Roman period ('Die Nekropole von Jerusalem', *Palästinajahrbuch des Deutschen Evangelischen Instituts für Altertums-wissenschaft des Heiligen Landes zu Jerusalem* 32 (1936), pp. 73-101). Those tombs, however, are representative of all levels of society (see p. 251 n. 1).

3 See p. 252 n. 3, p. 253 n. 1 above.

4 For the early evidence (Bronze Age) see Rahmani, 'Ancient Jerusalem... Part Two'. For the later (Iron Age, especially eighth to seventh centuries BCE) development of repository pits, see *ibid.*, p. 234.

ently used by all levels of society.[1] The custom began in Jerusalem and its immediate environs and then spread to other parts of the country such as Jericho, the Judaean foothills, the coastal plain and Galilee.[2] In Jerusalem ossuaries were used from the time of King Herod until the Bar Kokhba revolt; elsewhere they continued in use to the third or possibly the fourth century CE.[3]

The emergence of the practice of osselegium would seem to be closely associated with changing concepts about life after death and the expiation of sin. In the biblical period the dead were conceived of as simply descending into the darkness of a netherworld (variously called שאול, עפר, בור) where they became 'shadows' or 'weak ones' (רפאים) cut off from the living and from God and fated never to rise again.[4] Such thoughts continued through to the late Hellenistic period and then new ideas in keeping with the eschatological thinking of the time began to emerge alongside the old ones.[5] These revolved around notions of individual physical resurrection and were first expressed by the Hasidim of the Maccabaean period.[6]

---

1 See Kloner, *op. cit.*, pp. xiii-xiv. For mishnaic references to the custom see e.g. *Pes.* 8.8; *M.K.* 1.5; *Sanh.* 6.6.

2 Rahmani, 'Ancient Jerusalem. . .Part Four', *BA* 45 (1982), p. 109.

3 *Ibid.*; Kloner, *op. cit.*, p. xiv; Goodenough, *op. cit.*, pp. 149ff. Kloner, p. ix, suggests that in the century before the introduction of ossuaries small *kokhim* were used for secondary burial or bone collection.

4 Gen. 37.35; Isa. 14.15, 19; 26.14, 19; Pss. 22.30; 30.10; 88.6, 12-13; 115.17; Job 10.21-22; 14.21. The only biblical reference to individual physical resurrection—as distinct from the collective re-establishment of the nation (Isa. 26.19; Ezek. 37.1-4) and aside from the possible ascent of Elijah (2 Kgs 2.11) which cannot be counted in this category—is in Dan. 12.2 which belongs to the Hellenistic period. See *EJ*, V, cols. 1420f. and Rahmani, 'Ancient Jerusalem. . . Part One', pp. 173-74. For a discussion of the way in which body and soul were regarded as a unit, and of the terms 'sheol' and 'being gathered to one's fathers', see Meyers, 'The Theological Implications of an Ancient Jewish Burial Custom', *JQR* 52 (1971), pp. 95ff.

5 The continuation in the Graeco-Roman period of biblical beliefs is evidenced by the continued custom in some circles of bringing food offerings to the grave, either as sacrifices or in the belief that the deceased needed material sustenance on his/her journey to the nether world. See e.g. *Jub.* 22.17; Tob. 4.17; *Epistle of Jeremy* 27, 32 (cf. Deut. 26.14; Ps. 106.28). This practice was condemned by Ben Sira (7.33; 30.18-19) who had an even harsher view of the fate of the dead: 'The expectation of man is decay. . . When a man dieth he inheriteth worm and maggot, lice and creeping things' (7.17; 10.11). For discussion of the food offerings see Rahmani, 'Jewish Rock Cut Tombs', pp. 118-19; Goodenough, *op. cit.*, p. 107.

6 See 2 Macc. 7; 12.41-45; 14.46; cf. Dan. 12.2. For the eschatological expectations of the period and the growth of both individualism and universalism, see Schürer,

They were then accepted by the Pharisees and rapidly made inroads into the popular imagination with the result that by the turn of the eras, outside of Sadducaean circles, a belief in the resurrection or reanimation of the dead, in one form or another, was firmly established.[1] Only the virtuous could expect to be resurrected (*Ant.* 18.15; *BJ* 2.163) and the belief was that the dead person made atonement for his sins during and by the painful process of decomposition (*Sanh.* 6.5-6; *M.K.* 1.5) and then his bones were carefully laid, in their sinless state, in an individual ossuary to await resurrection in the world to come.[2] The gathering and safe-keeping of the complete skeleton was also necessary for the hoped-for awakening.

With regard to preparation of the body prior to primary burial, the corpse was washed and anointed (Mt. 26.12; Mk 14.8; 16.1; Lk. 23.56; 24.1; Jn 19.39-40; Acts 9.37; Jos. *Ant.* 17.199; *BJ* 1.673; *Shabb.* 23.5; *Ber.* 8.6, 53a; *Sem.* 12.9),[3] had its limbs straightened (*Naz.* 9.3, 65a), eyes closed (*Shabb.* 23.5; *Sem.* 1.4; cf. Tob. 6.5; *Ahikar* 1.5), hair cut (*M.K.* 8b, except in the case of an unmarried girl, see below), orifices blocked and mouth bound (*Sem.* 1.2).[4] It was then dressed in a winding

The History of the Jewish People in the Age of Jesus Christ, II, pp. 492-547.

1 *Pss. Sol.* 3.16; 14.22ff.; Jos. *Ant.* 18.14f.; *BJ* 2.163; 3.374f.; *Con. Ap.* 2.218; *2 Bar.* 30.1-5; 50.2; 51.6; *4 Ezr.* 7.32; *1 Enoch* 51.1; *T. Judah* 25.1; *T. Ben.* 10.6-7; *Sanh.* 10.1; *Aboth* 4.22. For the denial of the resurrection by the Sadducees, see Jos. *Ant.* 18.16; *BJ* 2.165. The Essenes taught only the immortality of the soul, *Ant.* 18.18; *BJ* 2.154-58. For details about the spread of the belief and the various forms which it took, see Schürer, *op. cit.*, II, pp. 539-47 and *s.v.*, index.
2 The souls of the just immediately entered into a blessed state, those of the unjust lingered during this time in a place of torment; see Schürer, *op. cit.*, II, pp. 540-46. For the close connection between the emergence of osselegium and the Pharisees, see Rahmani, 'Ancient Jerusalem . . . Part One', pp. 174-76 and 'Jewish Rock Cut Tombs', pp. 116-19 and 'A Jewish Tomb on Shahin Hill', *IEJ* 8 (1958), p. 105. Against this view see Meyers, *op. cit.*, pp. 108ff. and Kloner, *op. cit.*, pp. 111ff. For cross-cultural ideas and practices regarding the transitional period of the corpse see van Gennep, *The Rites of Passage*, pp. 148-49, and for the careful disposal of the skeleton in the box see Hachlili and Killebrew, *op. cit.*, pp. 119-20.
3 A task performed by either men or women in the case of a dead male but only by women for a dead female (*Sem.* 12.10). For details of the cleansing ritual, see *EJ*, XV, cols. 1188-89 and Bender, *op. cit.*, pp. 259f. The various duties here described were performed by relatives and/or friends of the deceased, or at a later date, by members of organized charitable groups (*Hevra Kaddisha*, first referred to in t. *Meg.* 4.15).
4 For a convenient survey of these and other rituals for the dead see Safrai and

sheet or in simple garments (Mt. 27.59; Mk 15.46; Lk. 23.53;
Jn 11.44; 19.40; *Kil.* 9.4; *Sanh.* 6.5; *M.Sh.* 5.12; *M.K.* 8b; *Men.*
41a, etc),[1] and placed on the floor with the feet pointing
towards the door and a lighted candle close to the head (*Shabb.*
151a; *Ber.* 8.6, 53a).[2] Watchers were appointed to stay with
the corpse until such time as all arrangements had been made
and the funeral procession could commence (*Ber.* 3.1, 18a; t.
Shabb. 17.9). This was interpreted by the rabbis as a mark of
respect for the dead, but in fact had probably more to do with
averting the danger of evil spirits and in particular protecting
the living from the ghost of the dead person.[3] Whenever possible burial occurred on the same day as the death,[4] and relatives, friends and professional wailing women (see below)
gathered to process to the graveside (Mt. 9.23; Mk 5.38-39;
M.K. 3.9). The body was carried on a bier (Lk. 7.12-14) and it
was customary to stop seven times en route to the burial place
for public lamentation and praise of the dead to be made (*Ket.*

Stern, *Compendia Rerum Iudaicarum ad Novum Testamentum*, II, pp. 773-87.
Regarding the use of *Semahoth*, often dated to the eighth century CE by modern
scholars, see Zlotnik, *The Tractate 'Mourning'*, pp. 4-8, who argues convincingly
for a third century CE date with many of the traditions contained in the text reaching back to earlier times. Both Meyers (*op. cit.*, p. 101) and Rahmani ('Ancient
Jerusalem . . . Part One', p. 173 and 'Part Three', p. 43) agree with his dating.

1 See Bender, *op. cit.*, p. 261. In some circles lavish garments and funerals were
indulged in, but the sources do not speak favourably of such practices. See Jos.
Ant. 15.60-61; 16.182; *BJ* 1.670-71; *Ket.* 8b; *M.K.* 27b; *T. Judah* 26.3.
2 Bender (*op. cit.*, p. 668) suggests that the positioning of the body and the presence of
the light were to encourage any demons present to flee. Similarly Morgenstern,
Rites of Birth, Marriage, Death and Kindred Occasions among the Semites,
Ch. 14, argues for the close relationship between death rituals and a concept of evil
spirits, or at least a belief in the continued existence in some form or other of the
dead which could threaten the living. See e.g. p. 253 n. 114, where he suggests that
the cutting off of the corpse's hair (see below) and the closing of the orifices were
designed to prevent the soul returning.
3 See Morgenstern, *op. cit.*, Ch. 14 and *EJ*, V, cols. 1425-26. Rahmani ('Ancient
Jerusalem...Part Two', p. 234) argues against Morgenstern's thesis that the ghosts
of the dead were conceived of as dangerous and hostile to be dealt with carefully
for the protection of the living, but in this view I believe him to be mistaken.
4 *Sanh.* 6.5; *B.K.* 82a; t. *Neg.* 6.2; *Sem.* 11.1; cf. Deut. 21.22f.; Josh. 8.29. The reason usually given by scholars for this custom is the rapid decomposition of the
body in the hot climate of Palestine. See, however, Morgenstern (*op. cit.*, pp. 137,
142) who points to the possibility of its also being based on fear of the spirit of the
dead person. It is significant in that context to note the wording of the talmudic
injunction for burial on the same day, 'one should not keep the corpse *through the
night*' (the hours of darkness of course being the time when the spirits had most
power).

2.10; *B.B.* 6.7; *Ohol.* 18.4).[1] After the corpse had been interred,
those attending the funeral formed two ranks through which
the official mourners, that is, the deceased's kin, passed to
receive the mourners' benediction (*Meg.* 4.3; *Sanh.* 2.1, 19a;
M.K. 3.7; *Ber.* 3.2; *Sem.* 10.8; 11.3). The mourners then went
home, pausing another seven (!) times on the way for further
condolences to be offered (*Meg.* 4.3; *B.B.* 100b; *Sem.* 14.11), and
there continued the official period of mourning.

In the Bible the outward signs of mourning were wailing (by
individual mourners and professional keeners, Gen. 23.2;
50.10; 1 Sam. 31.13; 2 Sam. 1.11; 3.31; 11.26; 15.30; 19.1ff.; 1
Kgs 13.30; Isa. 22.12; Amos 5.16; Jer. 6.26, etc.), rending garments (Gen. 37.34; 1 Sam. 4.12; 2 Sam. 1.11; 3.31; 13.19; 2 Kgs
6.30; 19.1; Josh. 7.6; Isa. 37.1; Job 9.20), wearing sackcloth
(Gen. 37.34; 2 Sam. 3.31; 2 Kgs 6.30; 19.1; Isa. 22.12; Amos 8.10;
Jer. 6.26; Lam. 2.10; Ezek. 27.31), casting dust on the head (1
Sam. 4.12; 2 Sam. 13.19; Josh. 7.6; Jer. 6.26; Lam. 2.10; Ezek.
27.30), not wearing ornaments and desisting from music and
dance (Exod. 33.4; Isa. 24.8; Jer. 31.12; Lam. 5.15), refraining
from washing and anointing (2 Sam. 12.20; 14.2), fasting (1
Sam. 31.13; 2 Sam. 1.11; 3.35; cf. Ezr. 10.6; Neh. 1.4), tearing
the hair and making gashes in the skin (Isa. 22.12; Jer. 16.6;
41.5; Amos 8.10; Job 9.20; Ezek. 27.31).

Apart from these last two acts, which were banned as pagan
under the Deuteronomic reform,[2] these mourning rituals
continued unchanged through the Graeco-Roman period (see
e.g. Dan. 10.23; Sir. 38.16-17; *Ned.* 12a; *M.K.* 22b, 25a, 27b;

---

1 This tradition was interpreted by later rabbis as symbolizing the seven times that
the word *hevel* ('vanity') occurs in Eccl. 1.2 (*B.B.* 100b) and corresponding to the
days of the creation of the world and the seven stages of man's life (*Eccl. Rab.*
1.2). However, given what we have already learned (Chapter 1 §B, Chapter 2 §D)
regarding the significance of number seven in Jewish ritual practice, it is more
likely that the custom was based on superstitious belief and the notion of transitional states discussed already in context of birth and marriage. As we shall see
the number seven figured prominently in mourning ritual.

2 Deut. 14.1; cf. Lev. 19.28; 21.5. See Morgenstern, *op. cit.*, pp. 147-48 and elsewhere,
for the way in which Yahwism gradually made inroads into what he terms 'the
cult of the dead', declaring certain acts incompatible with worship of the One True
God while absorbing and recasting others into its own belief system. See *ibid.* for
a cross-cultural analysis of these various rituals in terms of a (temporary)
separation of the bereaved from the larger community; taboo sacrifice; appease-
ment of the dead; and protection for the living.

Sem. passim), the only difference being that the Talmud, unlike the Bible, specified in detail the length of time which was to be given to mourning and within that period distinguished four separate stages of successively lightening mourning duties, the total comprising twelve months (y. *M.K.* 3.7, 83c; *Sem.* 9.10-13).

In the earlier centuries and throughout much of the Graeco-Roman period the tendency would seem to have been to mourn for seven days, with possibly particular lamentation during the first two or four days of bereavement (Gen. 50.10; 1 Sam. 31.13; Jdt. 16.23; Sir. 22.12; *Apoc. Mos.* 43.3; cf. Sir. 38.17; *Vita Adae et Evae* 51.1-2) and occasionally an extended mourning time of thirty days (Deut. 34.8; Num. 20.29; cf. Deut. 21.13). The rabbis formalized these various customs and stipulated that the first three days were to mark the height of mourning (the period defined in various haggadoth as the one of greatest danger for the mourner. See *M.K.* 27b; y. *M.K.* 3.5, 82b; y. *Yeb.* 16.1, 15c); the next few days up to the end of the first week to be less extreme; a thirty-day period following burial to be again more moderated; and—an addition to the biblical practice—a further eleven months of light mourning duties.[1] They also added to the biblical mourning rituals a prohibition on manual work, entering into marriage or using the conjugal bed, and imposed an exemption from many of the positive precepts such as donning *tefillin* and reciting the *shema* (*M.K.* 16b, 20a; *Sem.* 5.1; 6.2, 11; 7.8-9, etc.).

The stipulation that there should be a mourning period totalling twelve months arose at the same time as the emergence of the practice of secondary burial. According to rabbinic belief it took twelve months for the flesh of the deceased to decay and for the process of atonement to be completed (*Shabb.* 152a; *Eduy.* 1.10; cf. *Sanh.* 6.5-6, 47b). Only on the last day of that period did the mourners go and with some limited ritual gather the bones and place them in the ossuary to await resurrection (y. *M.K.* 1.5, 80c; *M.K.* 8a; *Sem.* 12). The mourners themselves then re-entered ordinary

---

1 For details of the mourning period and the rituals which marked each stage, see Zlotnik, *op. cit.*, introduction and notes; *EJ*, XII, cols. 488-89. For the significance of the choice of the three, seven, and thirty day stages, see Morgenstern, *op. cit.*, Ch. 14.

society and resumed their normal duties and lifestyles.[1]

Such then, in brief, were the burial and mourning practices of Graeco-Roman Palestine. Before turning our attention to the question of whether there was any differentiation made between men and women in the performance of these rituals, we shall quickly review the woman's position in life for, as was stated at the outset of this chapter, death rituals tend to reflect and restate the condition and preoccupations of the living. The review will serve both as a useful recapitulation of what we have learned in the course of this survey of the 'average' Jewish woman's life, and provide a necessary context for our final discussion *vis-à-vis* death.

As we have seen, Jewish society was ordered along strictly patriarchal lines with the woman's life being marked by subordination to and dependence upon men at all times. She was declared legally incompetent to shoulder most of the social, legal, and cultic responsibilities and roles which constituted the public functioning of society, and in the main was regarded as an inferior or secondary being whose 'glory' was to work quietly, behind the scenes, in domestic seclusion. Her marginality in society was marked at the start of her life by the absence of any rite of initiation into her tribe or religion. Thus, while for a boy the rite of circumcision served to signal his passage to ordinary, profane existence, his entry into society, and his potential as a full participant in the nation's religion, the eighth day of a girl's life passed without any official recognition. In ritualistic terms she was but a member of society through association with her father or brothers. Similarly, and again unlike a boy, no ceremony surrounded the occasion of her receiving a name—an omission of some significance when we recall the tremendous importance which

1   See Morgenstern, *op. cit.*, pp. 153, 161, 166, for the way in which the close of the year signalled the final departure of the soul of the deceased from this world and the end of fear for the mourners. Also van Gennep, *op. cit.*, pp. 146-47, regarding death rituals cross-culturally: 'the living mourners and the deceased constitute a special group situated between the world of the living and the world of the dead... Mourning... is a transitional period for the survivors, and they enter it through rites of separation and emerge from it through rites of re-integration into society... the transitional period of the living is a counterpart of the transitional period of the deceased, and the termination of the first sometimes coincides with termination of the second'.

attached to name giving in the ancient world and the fact that it was only with the bestowal of a distinguishing title that the infant was accorded status as a full human being and regarded as having an identity of its own. The scene was set early on in her life.

During the years of her minority (i.e. up to the age of twelve and a half) a daughter was totally under the control of her father, bound to honour and obey his every dictate. Should he choose to sell her into servitude, such was his right, though he was not allowed to take such action in respect of a minor son. Up until marriage—a contract which was arranged by her father and future husband and not by her—she remained strictly secluded within the paternal home, removed from the public gaze and the possibility of sin. During this time it would seem that she could be regarded simply as an onerous burden upon the family resources. Such at least was the considered opinion of Ben Sira who stated that a daughter was born to her father's loss, his only consolation to those having sired such offspring being 'Marry thy daughter and sorrow will depart' (7.25).

At marriage, which took place early in her life, the girl was transferred to her husband's house, a practice which again reinforced the impression of marginality in that neither she nor society could ever regard her as being permanently and absolutely based in one family group. Her husband was accorded virtually the same authority over her as had been vested in her father, and she was obliged to work for him and raise his children. While honour was obviously accorded her in her role as mother, it was a qualified or hierarchical honour, for she in turn, like her children, was bound in total obedience to and respect of the head of the household, her husband. Should there be no children her position and status could be tenuous.

Legally, little security was to be found in the marital home, for in the eyes of the law the husband had absolute and unilateral powers of divorce and dismissal could be for the slightest offence. If divorced she was obliged to leave his house and might return to her father, if he (or male kin) were willing, leaving behind any children which she had borne to her husband. In the event of widowhood, the same could happen or she could remain in her dead husband's home being supported by the heirs to her *kethubah*, her children. It is apparent, however, from the numerous references to the plight of the widow that support was not always to be found.

Throughout her life the Jewish woman was expected to be modest and demure in her clothing and behaviour. As far as possible she was not to stray beyond the confines of the home and control of her assumed natural proclivity for sexual misdemeanour was considered the responsibility of men. Her education and training were tailored for a life of domestic duties and she was denied access to what was regarded as the higher realm of learning—a learning which, apart from anything else, opened the doors to positions of civil and religious responsibility. She was accorded no formal means of giving public expression to her piety and had little or no active role to play in the public functioning of the nation's religion and cult.

The patriarchal ordering of Jewish life was both expressed and reinforced by the teachings of the nation's religion, itself a cult which centred upon a single male deity and one which was directed exclusively by men. By the Graeco-Roman period the authority which men assumed over women was viewed in terms of a divine ordering of the universe: woman, created after man and out of him, was by nature inferior, and as the one responsible for man's first fall (or at least as the one from whom temptation came) deemed to be in need of constant control and supervision. Being lower on the order of creation she was considered to be closer to the world of demons and 'nature' than man, operating solely according to the rule of custom and sense perception rather than from the standpoint of sound, independent judgment and rational thought. In addition to being considered lightminded and irresponsible, the woman was also regarded for a large part of her life as a major and dangerous source of pollution to those around her in consequence of the blood of childbirth and of the menstrual cycle. Anyone who did have connection with a menstruant was rendered ritually impure for the same seven-day period as one who contracted uncleanness from a corpse (Lev. 15.19-24; Num. 19.11-22; see below).

Such then were the main features of the woman's life. The essential facts to emerge from this very quick review are her subordination to and dependence upon men; her imposed role of domestic passivity and modest retirement; her marginality, and her uncleanness. The question we now have to ask is, was the pattern of the woman's life symbolically repeated or restated in death? Was there any differentiation made according to gender in the mourning rituals and burial practices of Graeco-Roman Palestine?

The first thing to say is that women were buried and were mourned. According to the Talmud, the same formal mourning period was required equally for a wife or husband, mother or father, sister or brother, daughter or son, and for relatives in the second degree (*M.K.* 20b; *Sem.* 4.1-2). The equality in this respect is normally taken for granted in the secondary literature, but it has some significance when one considers the fact that in many societies a woman's death warranted a shorter period of mourning than that given a man.[1] Indeed, the only differentiation Jewish law made in this respect was to single out both father and mother over and above all other relatives for receipt of the fullest possible mourning, that mourning, with certain differences (see below), to be performed by both sons and daughters. Thus, in *Semahoth* 9 we read:

> One does not bare the shoulder for the dead in general but only for his father and mother...
> For the dead in general one does not bare the chest, but for his father and mother he bares it...
> For the dead in general one rends only the uppermost [garment] but for his father and mother he must rend all...
> For the dead in general one tacks the rent together after seven days and [completely] restitches [the edges] after thirty, but for one's father and mother one never restitches [the edges]... (*Sem.* 9.3f.; cf. y. *M.K.* 3.8, 83d; *M.K.* 22ab)

and so on, many of the mourning duties continuing for the full twelve months and not lessening in intensity in the same way as was the case for other relatives.

This equal emphasis upon both father and mother was in keeping with the general commandment to honour one's parents and in that context the treatment of the subject in the

---

1 See p. 254 n. 4 above.

Talmud need not surprise us. We have seen, however, that the
honour accorded a mother in her lifetime was tempered by
and subject to the absolute authority which society vested in
the head of the household. We may ask whether this state of
affairs was in any way reflected in the funerary practices,
despite the equality so far demonstrated.

At the outset of our discussion—regarding both mothers
and women in other social categories—it is essential to
appreciate not only the existence of an overriding patriarchy
but also the fact that Jewish society's calculation as to who
mourns for whom and for how long was based on the same
sociological kinship ties and hierarchical purity concerns as
examined in Chapter 2 §A. Thus according to the Talmud
formal mourning was required for all kin corresponding to
those for whom a priest was to defile himself (Lev. 21.1ff.).
This meant that the list of relatives mentioned above (*M.K.*
20b; *Sem.* 4.1-2) was qualified to exclude (from the male
viewpoint, the perspective of our texts), mourning a divorced
wife, a betrothed woman, and a married or non-virginal sister
(*ibid.*). Regarding priests the general principle was that they
were permitted to defile themselves 'for anyone who is eligible
[to marry] a High Priest, but may not... for one who is not
eligible [to marry] a High Priest' (*Sem.* 4.7), and High Priests
were never allowed to defile themselves by contact with the
dead, not even for a father or mother (Lev. 21.10-11) though
mourning was permitted (*Sem.* 4.4, 5, 20).

Turning then to the more detailed analysis of mourning and
burial practices for women, we have seen that the custom was
for members of the same family (as defined sociologically
rather than biologically) to be buried in the same tomb. Such is
evidenced in the early period by the narratives of the Old
Testament and by the scriptural euphemism of 'sleeping with
one's fathers' or 'being gathered to one's fathers' (an obviously
patriarchal turn of phrase), and in the later period by the
archaeological evidence of skeletal remains and ossuary
inscriptions which bear witness to several generations of the
same family being buried in the one chamber. At death a man
remained with his blood kin group but a woman, if married,
was buried with the family group to which she had contractual ties, her husband, by Talmudic times, being obliged to

furnish the necessaries for her funeral.[1] So, for example, we read of Judith being buried in the cave of her husband Manasses,[2] and of Tobit commanding his son to bury him well and on the death of his mother to 'bury her by me in one grave' (Jdt. 16.23; Tob. 4.4). While one would not wish to dispute the obvious affection which could exist between a man and a woman—an affection which doubtless encouraged the desire to be buried together—the custom of joint interment, together with the legal situation, had another statement to make, and that was the subsuming of the woman's identity under that of her husband and the family of which he was the head, and a symbolic re-enactment of the authority wielded over her during her lifetime. Thus in the *Vita Adae et Evae*, which claimed to lay down the definitive rules for burial 'until the day of the resurrection', Eve is depicted as setting an example to all women by praying to God that she might be buried alongside her husband in order that in death as in life 'thy handmaid might not be estranged from the body of Adam, for from his members didst thou [God] make me' (42.5). The reason given by the author for Eve's choice of burial partner had little to do with mutual respect or affection.

Archaeological evidence supports this view of the inferior or secondary status of the woman continuing in death. We have seen that it was sometimes the practice in the pre-*kokh* or *loculus* type family tomb to shape troughs and head rests on the benches or floor of the cavern to hold the bodies of those interred (p. 253 above). Regarding one such tomb from the eastern slopes of the Kidron Valley, dated to the eighth or seventh century BCE and containing two resting places of this type, the archaeologist Ussishkin writes:

> It must be assumed that here a man and his wife were interred, and this should explain the following curious fact: in each of the two double troughs the two pillows were not cut at one level, but one is a few inches higher that the other. Furthermore, the bottom of the trough which corresponds to the higher pillow seems to be higher than the other half. Thus it seems that one body, almost certainly that of the husband, was placed higher than that of the wife, so that the

1 *Ket.* 4.4. See p. 238 above.
2 For the particular situation of widows see further below.

woman's inferior status was also demonstrated after death![1]

From the later period ossuaries, sarcophagi, or burial niches of the father founders of a family tomb occupied the main place of the burial chamber and inscriptions tell their own story.[2] So, for example, incised in the rock at the entrance to one of the rooms in Catacomb 12 of the Beth Shearim necropolis which contained six skeletons was the following inscription: 'There are in this apsis grave six belonging to [the man] Aidesios'[3]—a simple and direct statement of the way in which the relative positions of the wife and children in respect of the *pater familias* continued in death.

With regard to ossuary inscriptions—which are relatively rare for the number of boxes excavated and also sketchily executed[4]—the anonymity of the woman, if married, is striking. In cases where the bones of the husband and wife were gathered in the one ossuary,[5] the inscriptional formula tended to be 'N. and his wife', the woman most commonly being unnamed.[6] In instances of separate burial, the inscription for a man consisted of his name and sometimes the patronym, with occasionally a nickname and mention of his profession and place of origin.[7] For a woman the details were much more simple and pivoted around her marital status (which was not

---

1 *Op. cit.*, p. 38; cf. Rahmani, 'Ancient Jerusalem... Part Two', p. 234. According to Ussishkin and others, the tombs of this particular complex are to be attributed to the 'nobles and notables of the kingdom of Judah'. This fact does not, however, invalidate the point here being made regarding women's status at all levels of society: the owners of these tombs could simply afford to make a physical statement of the general attitude.

2 Tombs usually only contained up to three generations of a family. See works cited on p. 254 n. 4. Only sons and their families were buried with their parents; married daughters were buried with their husband's family. See Hachlili, 'The Goliath Family in Jericho', p. 57, and secondary literature cited there.

3 ΕΙΣΙΝ ΕΝ ΤΗ Α/ΨΔΙΚΡΗΠΙ/ΔΕΣΕΞΣ/ΔΙΑΦΕΡΟΥ/ΣΑΙ ΑΙΔΕΣΙΩ.

4 See Rahmani, 'Ancient Jerusalem... Part Four', pp. 111-12, on those found around Jerusalem, and Goodenough, *op. cit.*, I, p. 111.

5 A not uncommon occurrence. Cf. *Sem.* 13.8, 'Whomsoever a person may sleep with when he is living, he may be buried with when he is dead'.

6 For example, [ו]אתתה שמעון (Rahmani, 'Jewish Rock Cut Tombs', p. 107); אליעזר ואשתו (Savignac, *RB* 12 [1904], pp. 262f.); אתת מריה (Sukenik, 'A Jewish Hypogeum near Jerusalem', *JPOS* 8 (1928), p. 118 = Frey, *CIJ*, II, 1356, p. 118; and אנתת אלעזר (Sukenik, *JPOS* 8 [1928], p. 119). See Hachlili, 'The Goliath Family in Jericho', p. 55.

7 Rahmani, 'Ancient Jerusalem... Part Four', pp. 111-12.

stated in the case of a man). Thus, for example, on one ossuary
from the Kidron Valley which contained the bones of a single
female skeleton, the incised inscription quite simply read
'Shalom, Eleazar's wife'.[1] It would seem, therefore, that the
identity of the wife was subsumed under that of her husband.

With regard to the burial of a widow, the heirs to her
kethubah were meant to be responsible for her funeral, those
heirs being either her children or, in the event of her dying
childless, male kin of her husband (*Ket.* 11.1; see Chapter 2
§C). In the first, presumably more common, context it is interesting to note the virtual non-existence of the title 'mother' in
funerary inscriptions. To date we have reference only to one
'Sabatis, Mother of Damon' (Greek ossuary inscription from
the Kidron Valley tombs);[2] another mentioning 'Shlomsion
our mother' (again an ossuary, in Aramaic, from Jerusalem);[3]
another Greek inscription from Jerusalem,[4] and one in
Aramaic from Jericho which refers to a Sholmsion as the
mother of Yehoezer.[5] Regarding the last, Hachlili writes:

> The reference to Shlomasion as the mother of Yehoezer is
> unusual; where women are mentioned in ossuary inscrip-
> tions they are generally listed only as the wife of a male
> member of the family (*op. cit.*, p. 55),

and she explains the occurrence of the title accorded
Shlomasion, who headed three generations of the same family
buried in the Jericho tomb, in the following way:

1 *Ibid.*
2 See Avigad, 'A Depository of Inscribed Ossuaries in the Kidron Valley', *IEJ* 12
   (1962), p. 6.
3 *Idem* and Frey, II, 1363; Avigad, *op. cit.*; Sukenik, 'A Jewish Hypogeum near
   Jerusalem', p. 117.
4 See Hachlili, 'The Goliath Family in Jericho', p. 55.
5 Hachlili, 'The Goliath Family in Jericho', pp. 31-66, especially pp. 55ff. The formula 'X mother of Y' is also found on one epitaph from Beth Shearim but this
   belongs to a much later date (see Avigad, *op. cit.*, p. 6; cf. *IEJ*, V [1955], p. 232). I am
   grateful to Fanny Vitto for informing me that occurrence of the title 'father' is also
   extremely infrequent (see e.g. Frey, II, 1359; Sukenik, 'A Jewish Hypogeum', p.
   116). This, however, does not invalidate the point here being made and is, moreover, to be expected: the fact of having sired offspring was known from the usual
   way of listing individuals as 'N. daughter/son of (male) N.' and if a man had
   any other detail epigraphically recorded it would be his profession or some other
   public activity. Such could not be the case for a woman whose sole *raison d'être*
   was domesticity and motherhood. For the few instances of the title 'mother' outside
   the Jerusalem–Jericho area, see Frey, II, 903, 948.

From the anthropological examination, Yehoezer son of
Eleazar died at the young age of approximately 35, while his
wife Shlomasion died at the approximate age of 60. This may
explain her important status in the family, as having outlived her husband by many years, she was responsible for
raising the children. Thus her name appears in the inscriptions of other family members, instead of her husband's
name (*ibid.*, pp. 57-58).

One must assume that there were other instances of women
like Shlomasion who outlived their husbands, had children,
chose not to (or were unable to) remarry and stayed at their
former husband's home, though of course we have no idea of
their numbers. We have, however, no inscriptional record
similar to that of Shlomsion for those women. The evidence of
the inscriptions shows that by far the most common practice
was to list women as the wife or daughter of some man,
dependent upon their marital status and circumstances at the
time of death. It would seem, therefore, that in the main a
widow readopted her dead husband's name if she was buried
by his kin in his family tomb, her status or position as mother
(if there were children) being elided in favour of a re-record-
ing of her contractual ties and the male line of that family.

Alternatively, the near total absence of inscriptions bearing
the title 'mother' could indicate the fact that heirs sometimes
shunned their responsibility to the woman, a possibility discussed already in Chapter 2 §C, that is, at the death of her
husband they forced her to return to her father's house and
she was then buried in his family tomb with the title 'N.
daughter of N.' That heirs did sometimes fail to fulfil the
duties which the law required of them in respect of a widow—
despite the commandment to honour both father and
mother—is amply testified by the biblical and post-biblical
writings' constant appeal to their readers to show widows
mercy and charity.

On the other hand, a widow could have chosen to forgo the
maintenance which was her due, collected her *kethubah* and
left her dead husband's estate (pp. 177-78 above). If she did not
remarry, she would again look to her father's family for
burial, similarly reassuming the title 'N. daughter of N.' The
scenario of a widow choosing to leave her dead husband's

house with no security for the future arranged is, however, an unlikely one.

The above analysis of the widow's situation and the title accorded her at death is, of course, largely conjecture. The tomb and ossuary inscriptions are not comprehensive and the information on them mainly piecemeal and sketchy. To begin to see any significant pattern regarding the burial of widows much work would have to be done in correlating the evidence of skeletal remains and funerary inscriptions; tracing (if and where possible) the genealogies and kinship networks of the deceased; and making demographic projections for the period and area under consideration—a huge task when one considers the vast amount and nature of the material which exists and which has never been systematically collected and studied, and certainly not studied from this point of view.

With regard to a divorcee the situation was much less ambiguous. On receipt of her *get*, all ties with her husband's family were severed, and so in *Sem.* 4.3 we read that a man

> For his divorced wife, although he had children by her, does not mourn, grieve, or [if a priest] defile himself,

a ruling which also applied to a betrothed woman (cf. *Sanh.* 28b; *Yeb.* 22a, 29b). She presumably returned to her father's house and was buried by him or other male kin in that family tomb, reassuming the title 'N. daughter of N.' Such may well have been the case for the woman Mariah who was buried in the Goliath family tomb. Anthropological evidence shows that she was about forty when she died (an age when she was unlikely not to have had a husband assuming there was no mental or physical deficiency), and the inscription on her ossuary reads 'Mariah, daughter of Nath[an]el, (grand)-daughter of Shlomasion'.[1] She could, of course, have been a widow.[2]

Moving away now from the tomb itself to the rituals of

---

1   Hachlili, *op. cit.*, pp. 53-54, 69. The fact of her tracing her ancestry back to Shlomasion, as we have seen, was very unusual. The more normal formula would have been 'Mariah, daughter of Nathanel, son of Yehoezer'.

2   Note in this context the unusual inscription found on a first-century CE sarcophagus from Jerusalem: 'Miriam, sister of Jehezkiah' (*EJ*, XII, col. 1505). One must assume that Jehezkiah was the founder of the tomb and hence the relationship was stated in this way. This, however, was not the norm.

mourning, we shall see that here too some significant differentiation according to gender was made, despite the impression to the contrary which is given in secondary sources on the subject.[1]

We have seen that it was the practice in Talmudic times for formal public lamentation to be made in the course of the funeral procession. The cortège made seven stops en route to the tomb, those stops in urban communities occurring in the 'broad places' of the city. The bier was laid to the ground and, amid general lamentation, eulogies were delivered over the body of the deceased (cf. *Meg.* 4.3; *Ket.* 2.10; *M.K.* 4.3; *B.B.* 6.7).[2] It seems unlikely that such memorial addresses were given for women—or at least not usually given—and several facts lend support to this surmise. First, the Mishnah categorically states that the bier of a woman was never to be set down on public ground 'out of honour' or 'respect' (מפני הכבוד, *M.K.* 3.8).[3] To have laid her down in the broad places of a city in full view of the public's gaze would have been totally contrary to the pattern of her life and to the rules of a society which demanded modesty at all times, even in death.

Second, and closely associated with the first reason, was the fact that a eulogy or memorial address was by definition a very public affair or statement, drawing upon those characteristics of the deceased which both warranted praise and could be itemized and which were known to the community at large. This latter point was one which was particularly stressed by the rabbis who were concerned lest the eulogy degenerate into a meaningless literary form or be 'woven out of nothing'.[4] So in *Sem.* 3.6 we read:

> In Jerusalem there was a saying, 'Perform actions [which can be lamented] in front of your bier...' and in Judaea there was a saying, 'Perform actions [which can be lamented] behind your bier',[5]

---

1 See e.g. Safrai and Stern, *op. cit.*, pp. 773-87, especially p. 783.
2 The eulogists were normally professionals who received a fee for their work (*M.K.* 1.5; t. *M.K.* 8a). See Safrai and Stern, *op. cit.*, p. 779.
3 אין מניחין את המטה ברחוב, שלא להרגיל את ההספד, ולא של נשים לעולם, מפני הכבוד. Cf. *Sem.* 11.2.
4 See Zlotnik, *op. cit.*, p. 19.
5 In Galilee and Jerusalem eulogists preceded the bier while in Judaea they followed it. Cf. *Shabb.* 153a.

while *Sem*. 3.4 states that the minimum requirement for a memorial address to be given was that the deceased have been known to his neighbours. This ruling may be compared to one about the death and funeral of a child:

> Whenever a child is known to the community, the public takes part in his rites; whenever a child is not known to the community, the public does not take part in his rites (*Sem*. 3.3).

This expression 'known to the community' was later understood as referring to one who was accustomed to leaving the house (Rashi to *M.K.* 24b). Thus though it could be argued that a woman's bier was simply kept raised from the ground while a eulogy was delivered, it seems certain that the facts of her lifestyle—characterized as it was by domestic seclusion and removal from the activities of the public arena and the community at large—neither furnished the material for such an address nor were compatible with that type of occasion.

Third, provsion of a memorial address was not included in the Mishnah's statement of the husband's duties with regard to his wife's funeral. He was required simply to bury her and to provide two flute players and one wailing woman for the funeral procession (*Ket*. 4.4). The later source of *Sem*. 14.7 does say that in places where eulogies were customary for women, the husband should give a speech in memory of his wife, but the tenor of this ruling is one very much of the exception rather than the rule, and may, in any case, have been influenced by extra-Palestinian practice. Moreover, it is noteworthy that this ruling stipulated that the address be made by the woman's husband and not by a member of the larger community or a paid professional.

Fourth and finally, all the examples of funerary eulogies in the Talmud have as their focus only men, and discussion of the subject is similarly nearly always conducted with reference to and in terms of men.[1] On the very rare occasions when women are mentioned, then the advice given by the rabbis is singularly revealing: should an address be delivered for a woman (an act which was not actually prohibited), then

---

1 See the various source references cited in this section and Safrai and Stern, *op. cit.*, pp. 778-79.

praises were to be sung not for her individual qualities but for those of her male relatives. Thus in *Sem*. 3.5 we read:

> In the case of a child... we dwell [in the memorial address] on his own [good] deeds, and if he has no such deeds [by virtue of his age] we dwell on the deeds of his parents... In the case of a bride, we dwell on the honour of her father or father-in-law, because she rises [in esteem] with him.[1]

It would seem, however, that in the main eulogies were not delivered for women. Their works and deeds were not individuated or regarded as having an equal merit to the activities of men in the public arena. The way in which the woman at death remained in a sense marginalized from the concerns of the larger community is further highlighted by the fact that public officials only accompanied the cortège of a man (*Sem*. 11.2).

Before we leave the subject of public funerary orations, slightly more consideration is due to the mishnaic stipulation about never laying a woman's bier on the ground. We have seen that one of the reasons for this ruling may well have been concern for the woman's modesty and the maintenance of a continuity of attitude and practice from life to death. It is likely, however, that the mishnah had another reason behind it in addition to the one already described. According to the school of Shammai all women that died were deemed to have died while they were menstruants (*Nidd*. 10.4), and according to the same mishnah,

> If a man or a woman that had a flux, or a menstruant, or a woman after childbirth, or a leper have died, they convey uncleanness by carrying until the flesh has decayed.[2]

Similarly, from a somewhat later date, we have reported that

> Formerly they were wont to subject to [ritual] ablution all

---

1 Also compare the wording of *Sem*. 11.5 on delivering eulogies for men *versus* bewailing brides.

2 The school of Hillel disagreed with Shammai, stating that 'Only she that dies while she was a menstruant is deemed a menstruant' (*Nidd*. 10.4; cf. *M.K.* 27b-28a where the Nehardeans argued that *M.K.* 3.8 only applied to women who had actually died in childbirth). While we have no way of knowing definitely which ruling was accepted, it has been shown elsewhere in this survey that the attitude of the more traditional school of Shammai frequently prevailed.

> utensils that had been used by [dying] menstruants and the
> living menstruant women felt thereby shamed. They there-
> fore instituted that they should subject utensils used by all
> [dying] women alike, out of deference to the living menstru-
> ants (*M.K.* 27b).

In the light of these texts, it is possible that the woman's body
was not in fact lowered to the ground because she and her bier
would in some sense convey double uncleanness to those gathered at the funeral—a conceptual if not a practical possibility
if we remind ourselves of the biblical ruling about corpse and
menstrual impurity. Regarding the former, Num. 19.11ff.
states:

> He that toucheth the dead... shall be unclean seven days;
> the same shall purify himself therewith on the third day and
> on the seventh day... Whosoever toucheth the dead... and
> purifieth not himself... that soul shall be cut off from
> Israel... When a man dieth in a tent, everyone that cometh
> into the tent and everything that is in the tent shall be
> unclean seven days. And every open vessel which hath no
> covering... is unclean. And whosoever in the open field
> toucheth one that is slain with a sword, or one that dieth of
> himself, or a bone of a man, or a grave, shall be unclean
> seven days... And whatsoever the unclean person toucheth
> shall be unclean; and the soul that toucheth him shall be
> unclean until even.

The ruling for menstrual uncleanness was:

> And if a woman have an issue, and her issue in her flesh be
> blood, she shall be in her impurity seven days; and whoso-
> ever toucheth her shall be unclean until the even. And every-
> thing that she lieth upon in her impurity shall be unclean;
> everything also that she sitteth upon shall be unclean. And
> whosoever toucheth her bed... [or] anything that she sitteth
> upon... shall be unclean until the even... And if any man
> lie with her, and her impurity be upon him, he shall be
> unclean seven days; and every bed whereupon he lieth shall
> be unclean (Lev. 15.19-24).

Given that the need was apparently felt to classify all women
as menstruants when they died, the mishnah's wording of
מפני הכבוד could well be read as referrring both to the honour of
the woman, that is, her modesty, and—perhaps more importantly—to the honour of the community, that is, concern for

its ritual purity in some impossible but emotive sense. Whatever the case may be, it is of significance to note that the woman, in death as in life, was regarded as a source of special uncleanness.[1] The situation at the close of her life may also be compared to what we earlier learned about her entry into this world, that is, the special social taboos and double impurity regulations imposed at the birth of a girl (pp. 36ff. above).

Turning now to the objects which which were buried with a person, we see that here too differentiation was made according to gender. In addition to general items such as lamps, jars, cooking pots, jugs and bottles which were commonly placed in tombs,[2] a woman's grave was often marked (in instances where goods were interred, which was not always the case) by the presence of cosmetics, mirrors, needles and spindle-whorls, that is, things of 'female' concern,[3] while that of a man contained ink pots, writing tablets, ledgers and trading measures.[4] These objects were placed in the grave both as a statement and in honour of the deceased's interests and virtues in life,[5] and in the belief that provision was being made

1 See also *Sem.* 11.1, 'If a man and a woman [died at the same time], they first take out [for burial] the woman because a woman is apt to become disfigured more quickly', a ruling connected by Rashi to *M.K.* 27a and the question of female discharge.
2 See Rahmani, 'Ancient Jerusalem... Part Three', p. 46; Kloner, *op. cit.*, p. xiv; Hachlili and Killebrew, *op. cit.*, pp. 164ff.; Rahmani, 'Jewish Rock Cut Tombs', pp. 97ff.; Strange, *op. cit.*, pp. 62ff. Grave goods are found mainly in context of primary rather than secondary burial. The lamps had both a symbolic and a practical significance in that they could provide light for the dead person's journey to the nether world and be used for visitors to the tomb: see Rahmani,'Ancient Jerusalem... Part Four', p. 234; Goodenough, *op. cit.*, I, p. 148; Safrai and Stern, *op. cit.*, p. 745. The jars and pots, usually of poor quality and/or defective, may have been used for storing water for purification (Hachlili and Killebrew, *op. cit.*, p. 121, and works cited), though the fact that the bases of the pots were sometimes sooty could suggest another function (Rahmani, 'Jewish Rock Cut Tombs', pp. 118-19; Goodenough, *op. cit.*, p. 107; Kloner, *op. cit.*, p. xiv). The jars and bottles probably contained funerary spices and ornaments (Hachlili and Killebrew, *ibid.*).
3 See works cited in n. 2 above, and especially Rahmani, 'Jewish Rock Cut Tombs', pp. 104, 110.
4 See works cited in n. 2 above, and *Sem.* 8.2-7.
5 So, Rahmani notes that in addition to the obvious occupational symbolism of the goods, the presence of spindle-whorls, for example, immediately brings to mind the characterization of the virtuous woman of Prov. 30.19 who 'layeth her hands to the distaff and spindle', while trading measures might, given the ancients' concern with just weights and measures, have been indicative of the deceased's integrity in life ('Jewish Rock Cut Tombs', pp. 97, 104).

for life beyond the grave—a common cross-cultural belief often assumed not to pertain in Judaism but in fact evidenced by the customs of the day and by the popular understanding of such statements as that found in *2 Bar.* 50.2:

> For the earth shall assuredly restore the dead.
> It shall make no change in form
> But as it has received so shall it restore them,[1]

and by such tales as found in *Ber.* 18b about dead women requesting living relatives to send them combs and cosmetics through someone about to die. According to van Gennep in his study of rites of passage in many societies,

> The most widespread idea [concerning worlds beyond the grave] is that of a world analogous to ours, but more pleasant, and of a society organised in the same way as it is here. Thus everyone re-enters again the categories of clan, age-group, or occupation that he (*sic*) had on earth.[2]

From Jewish burial customs it is evident that the belief in Graeco-Roman Palestine was that women (and men) were to occupy the same position in the new world as they had in the old. It is additionally significant to note that grave goods of an obviously personal and gendered type were more commonly buried with women than they were with men[3] and that such goods were strikingly uniform, while those for men, when they occurred, were much more varied and individuated. It would seem, therefore, that in addition to providing for a re-enactment of the deceased's social function in life, the presence and type of grave goods also reflected and restated that social characterization noted elsewhere in this survey, that is, subtle, complex, ambiguous male *vs* stereotyped, clear-cut female.[4]

---

1 Cf. *Sem.* 9.3, 'In the same clothes in which a man descends to sheol will he appear in the age to come'.
2 *Op. cit.*, p. 152.
3 See the predominance of 'female' goods listed for the tomb excavations in the works cited on p. 275 n. 2. Note also the extreme case of the Jericho necropolis where personal goods were only found in the graves of women and children (Hachlili and Killebrew, *op. cit.*, pp. 116, 121).
4 Cf. pp. 210-11, 239ff. above and note the way in which archaeologists can surmise on the basis of grave goods alone that a particular grave had held the remains of a woman but not necessarily do the same if the grave had potentially held the

In line with van Gennep's conclusion that everyone 're-enters again the categories of clan, age-group or occupation', we might also note the ruling that the hair of a dead 'bride', that is, a woman who had died without having ever married, was not cut off as was customary in the preparation of other corpses.[1] She entered the tomb as she would have done her wedding, the only difference (apart from the obvious!) being that in this instance her hair was covered as a sign of mourning.[2]

Finally, mention may be made of two sundry matters which involve gender differentiation. The first concerns grave vestments. We have seen that the custom was to wrap the corpse in a winding sheet or dress it in simple clothes. As the period progressed the latter habit seems to have become the more common one (see e.g. *Sem.* 9.23) and by late Talmudic times regulations regarding the outfit of the dead were laid down.[3] Although strictly speaking outside the period under consideration in this survey, it is of interest to note that included in these regulations was the fact that a man should be buried in his *tallit* (once the fringes had been rendered ritually unfit). As a woman did not wear the prayer shawl in life she did not of course adopt it in death. The only special regulation for her was that she be dressed in an apron (סינור), thus marking again the different social roles for men and women and bringing to a 'natural' conclusion the process of gender differentiation noted thus far.[4]

The second item concerns the actual positioning of the body and its limbs in the tomb. It would seem that the usual practice was to straighten the corpse, place it face upwards in the coffin or on the ledge, with the head to one side and hands close to the

---

remains of a man (see e.g. Rahmani, 'Jewish Rock Cut Tombs', p. 110; Strange, *op. cit.*, p. 63).

1 *Sem.* 8.7; *M.K.* 8b. For possible reasons why the hair of a dead person was normally cut off, see Morgenstern, *op. cit.*, p. 253 n. 114, who suggests, amongst other things, that it was to remove possible hiding places in which the soul might lurk trying to regain entry to its former earthly abode.

2 For the way in which the public sign of a virgin's wedding was the girl's long flowing hair, see p. 197 above.

3 For details see Bender, *op. cit.*, p. 261.

4 *Ibid.*

side of the body.[1] It is possible that a small but significant variation of this practice could have occurred for (some) female burials. Such at least is indicated by the burial, c. 50 CE, of Queen Helene of Adiabene, a zealous convert to Judaism whose body when excavated was discovered to have its two hands not resting by the sides of the corpse but crossed instead over the pubic region.[2] It is to be assumed that this limb positioning was intended as a sign of her eternal continence and modesty.

To turn now from the dead person to the living mourner, we see that here too some differentiation according to gender was made, both with regard to who performed the funeral and graveside rituals and to the duties incumbent upon the bereaved during the various mourning rituals. Concerning the first, the emphasis, as in all other areas of public religious activity, was on the male. In Chapter 1 §A we saw that one of the reasons for a man's strong desire to have sons lay in the comfort such offspring brought regarding his eventual death and burial. The focus on sons in this context rested on the fact that according to law and custom only they (or other males) could perform the various rituals necessary for a man's proper interment; daughters could not fulfil this role. A prayer in the book of *Ahikar* highlights this particular aspect of the desire for sons:

> I ask of thee, O God, that I may have a male child,
> so that when I die he may cast dust on my eyes.[3]

Similarly in Tob. 6.15 we read of the son of Tobit and Anna worrying lest he die before his parents and be unable to bury them, for 'I am my father's only child... and they have no other son to bury them'. As the passage shows, sons were responsible not only for the burial of their father but also for that of their mother. Thus in *4 Maccabees* the righteous woman who witnessed the martyrdoms of her seven sons is

---

1 See Hachlili and Killebrew, *op. cit.*, p. 115; Safrai and Stern, *op. cit.*, pp. 780-81.

2 Goodenough, *op. cit.*, pp. 134-35. For details of her conversion and adherence to halakhic Judaism, and description of the monumental tomb in which she and her son were buried, see *Ant.* 20.24-96; Rahmani, 'Ancient Jerusalem... Part Three', p. 48.

3 1.4-5, see above pp. 17ff., and especially p. 22.

depicted as saying:

> Ah, thrice wretched me, and more than thrice wretched!
> Seven children have I borne and am left childless! In vain
> was I seven times with child, and to no profit was my ten
> months' burden seven times borne and fruitless have been
> my nursings, and sorrowful my sucklings. In vain for you,
> O my sons, did I endure the many pangs of labour, and the
> more difficult cares of your upbringing. Alas, for my sons,
> that some were yet unwed and those that were wedded had
> begotten no children... Ah me, that had many beautiful
> children, and am a widow and desolate in my woe! Neither
> will there be any son to bury me when I am dead! (16.6-11).[1]

Both men and women, therefore, looked to males, and prefer-
ably sons, for the performance of the necessary rituals at
death. Women were not counted as eligible or competent to
discharge these duties.

The various rituals which have been surveyed, therefore,
largely devolved on men. So, for example, the seven stops *en
route* to the tomb for the purpose of formal lamentation and
eulogy only occurred if at least ten men were in attendance at
the funeral, that is, the same number as comprised the quorum for a full synagogue service (*Meg*. 4.3), and, as we have
seen, the eulogies themselves could only be given by a man.
Similarly the mourners' benediction at the graveside and the
mourners' consolation after the interment could only occur if
ten men were present (*ibid.*; cf. *Ber.* 2.7; *Sanh.* 2.1).

The actual burial was also performed by men unless they
wished to avoid incurring ritual impurity from contact with
the corpse and grave in readiness for participation in one of
the major festivals, in which event they enlisted the help of
women. Such was the case for burial described in t. *Ohol.* 3.9
which took place on the eve of Passover. There the women
took care of the interment and tied ropes around the entrance
boulder to the tomb for the men to pull it closed while remaining outside and removed from contact with the grave. As

---

1 Strictly speaking, according to the story, the extreme righteousness of the bereaved
mother in fact lay in her not having uttered these laments: such moanings would
have been the concern of ordinary mortals. The fact that she is depicted as not having said them, however, does not invalidate the sentiment so eloquently expressed
by the author of *4 Macc.* regarding the importance of sons.

women were exempt from the obligation to attend the Temple
or the ceremony of such festivals as Passover, Pentecost and
Tabernacles, it did not matter if they incurred the corpse
uncleanness which would prevent their (passive) involvement
in the feasts. As we have seen, only circumcised men were
bound to fulfil the command to appear.[1]

Similarly only the men of the community were placed
under the command to escort the dead to the grave and provide comfort for the bereaved at the 'house of mourning', a
great *mitzvah* which even interrupted study of the Torah
(*Pe'ah* 1.1; *Sem.* 12.5; *Ket.* 17a; *Ber.* 18a; y. *Bikk.* 3.3, 65c). As
Josephus declared, 'All who pass by when a corpse is buried
must accompany the funeral and join in lamentations' (*Con.
Ap.* 2.205). His use of the word 'all', however, only had application to any male onlookers. Although women were not to be
denied access to the 'house of mourning' (see above, p. 243),
they were, apart from the immediate relatives of the deceased,
under no religious obligation to attend. As *Sem.* 10.8 makes
clear, men fulfilled this duty by virtue of their ability to act as
agents or representatives of the community at large:

> Rabban Gamaliel had a borrowed grave in Jabneh where
> they brought the dead and locked the door behind it. Men
> came, stood in the row and comforted the mourners and the
> public was thereby exempt [from this duty].

As Loewe writes regarding the analogous situation of only
men being able to perform public religious duty in the synagogue:

> the ineligibility of women... [to act]... as leaders in prayer
> for congregations including men [rests] on the principle that
> whereas obligation may be fulfilled by a plurality of those
> liable to it acting cooperatively, one of their number taking
> the lead and the others consciously fulfilling their obligation
> in unison with him, the situation would be quite otherwise
> were the quasi-representative figure not under an obligation
> of precisely analogous quality to that of the remainder of the
> congregation.[2]

1 See above pp. 34, 91, and Archer, 'The Role of Jewish Women in Religion, Ritual
and Cult of Graeco-Roman Palestine', in Cameron and Kuhrt, *Images of Women
in Antiquity*, pp. 277f.
2 *The Position of Women in Judaism*, pp. 44-45.

As we have seen, funerals were very much a matter of community concern. They were not private religious affairs hidden away from the public's gaze but events that everyone felt bound to participate in. Ritualized care for the dead and for the bereaved devolved upon the community, not just upon the deceased's immediate kin, and an appreciation of this fact is very important for our understanding of the gender differentiation at work in the performance of death ritual. Thus, not only was there the obvious elevation within patriarchy of the male over the female, and the fact examined elsewhere in this survey of men being the principal participants in the public religious life of the nation and the ones upon whom the full body of the commandments was incumbent, but flowing from both these points was the fact highlighted by Loewe, that only they in consequence could act as representatives of the community, one man fulfilling the duties of many men. For a combination of these reasons, it was the male mourners who performed the formal religious rituals of death and burial in Graeco-Roman Palestine.[1]

Women were, however, present at funerals and not only in the role of passive, silent bereavement. While men conducted the official prayers, the formal and specific eulogies and benedictions, they engaged in general and very vocal lamentation for the dead. Such lamentation was an expected and integral part of every funeral, and was performed always by women, both the relatives of the deceased and professional keeners whose services were paid for.[2] The fact that women had

1 It should be noted, of course, that implicit in both Loewe's analysis and to the narrative and law of the ancient texts is an understanding and use of the term 'community' and 'public' not as all-embracing and gender-free but as exclusive and gender-blind. The community the texts address is in fact the male community. For an analysis of the gender-blind character and use of 'community' in this and other contexts of Jewish life and law, see Archer, 'Notions of Community and the Exclusion of the Female in Jewish History and Historiography', in Archer and Sorkin (eds.), *Notions of Community and Jewish Identification* (forthcoming).

2 *M.K.* 3.8-9; 28b; *Ket.* 4.4, 46b; *Shabb.* 23.4; *B.M.* 6.1; *Sem.* 14.7; cf. Jer. 9.16; Judg. 11.40; 2 Sam. 14.2; 2 Chron. 35.25 (which exceptionally refers to singing men as well as singing women). Josephus and Matthew mention male keeners (*BJ* 3.437; Mt. 9.23), but this is something unusual: tannaitic literature refers only to female keeners (*mekonenot*). See *EJ*, vol. X, col. 1009; Safrai and Stern, *op. cit.*, pp. 775, 778.

exclusive responsibility for this very important part of the funeral might surprise us given what we know of their non-involvement in public ritual and their lack of visibility in public places. A closer look, however, at the nature and function of the lamentation reveals much about this unusual bestowal of public duty upon women and about the male-female division of labour at funerals.

The women's lamentation consisted of wailing, hand clapping, beating the chest and chanting dirges, the dirges (*kinot*) being either of a traditional repetitive form or spontaneous compositions.[1] The principal features of the lamentation were therefore its loudness, lack of formal structure, and manifest emotionality—all of which set it apart from the other burial rituals. It may be surmised that the wailing and hand clapping were intended, at one level at least, to drive away any lurking spirits (including that of the deceased) which, as has been shown elsewhere, were considered to be particularly threatening at times of vulnerability and transition from one human state to another.[2] The fact that it was women who performed this task may be linked to the belief in their being closer to the world of nature, and hence to the spirit realm and the possibility of demonic possession, than men (see pp. 201ff. above). Their noisy antics were thus intended not only as a device to frighten the demons away but also as a means to actually attract the spirit's attention to themselves, thereby deflecting the spirits from their principal target of the deceased's grieving and therefore vulnerable kith and kin. The process may be compared to what was earlier learned regarding the function of the *shoshbinim* at weddings (pp. 203-204 above). The fact that unlike at weddings it was

1 *M.K.* 28b. For examples of the formal type of *kinot*, see *EJ*, X, col. 1009. In the main, the women's lament consisted of general expressions of grief which were only slightly adjusted to fit each individual deceased, while in contrast the eulogists' laments were composed just for the person being buried. See Safrai and Stern, *op. cit.*, pp. 778-79.

2 Obviously the keening served to mark the ordinary mourning and respect for the dead. The fact, however, that keeners were always brought into the burial ritual, even to the extent of paying them for their services, shows that their noisy lamentation had a deeper purpose—even if that purpose was not recognized or articulated in the sources. Had it been otherwise, then the deceased's next of kin and any men present would have been sufficient for the general mourning.

only women, that is, those closest to the shadowy world of spirits, who fulfilled this role at funerals may be understood in terms of the heightened superstition always present at the life-death transition and the perceived extreme danger of the event and the need to protect by the best possible means those attending the dead (though of course this need was not actually spelled out).[1] Having no active part in the public formal religion of the day, women in any case were generally associated with popular and overtly superstitious magic and practice.[2] Additionally, although an integral part of the funeral by custom, keening was not a religious requirement or *mitzvah* and so it was appropriate that women filled this role. Significantly, unlike men, their action was informal and individualistic. They were not acting in any official sense as agents of the community.

The other reason why women were the ones to perform this task lay with the keeners' need to be both noisy and visibly emotional—matters which were deemed incompatible with society's constructed notions of maleness but totally appropriate to its ideas regarding femaleness.[3] Thus Schechter, writing about women's exclusion from the public ritual of the synagogue and Temple, commented:

> One privilege was left to women—that of weeping... of this privilege they were not deprived, and if they were not allowed to sing any longer, they at least retained the right to weep as much as they pleased... they held public office as mourning women at funerals... Indeed woman became in those times the type of grief and sorrow. She cannot reason, but she feels much more deeply than man.[4]

A somewhat more illuminating analysis of women's involvement in death ritual than Schechter's mere reproduction of the old gender ascriptions is provided by Sally Humphreys in her survey of social life and law in ancient

1 The other reason for the difference was that at weddings the *shoshbinim* were modelling the newly married couple and hence both male and female representation was required: such a need obviously did not pertain at funerals.
2 See, for example, 1 Sam. 28.7f.; Exod. 22.17; *Aboth* 2.7; *Sanh.* 67a; y. *Hag.* 2.2, 77d; *Sanh.* 6.9, 23c. See Archer, 'The Role of Jewish Women...', pp. 283-84.
3 See p. 210 above where Philo's views on 'the weak feminine passion of sense perception' versus 'manly reasoning schooled in fortitude' are discussed.
4 *Studies in Judaism*, I, p. 390.

Greece. She describes the profound conflicting social demands and transitional states which follow a death, and suggests that women's involvement with the dead was due in part to their non-involvement with the living (i.e. the public life of the nation). Although the focus of Humphreys's study is classical Greece, many of the general points which she raises ring true also for the situation in Graeco-Roman Palestine. They may with some justification be translated cross-culturally and, when taken in context of what has already been said here regarding the position of and attitude toward Jewish women, be of use in the present discussion. I take the liberty of quoting her at some length:

> The period immediately preceding and following death is that which faces the bereaved with the most conflicting demands. On the one hand they are expected to share in some sense in the journey of the dead away from society; on the other hand they are involved in an intense social activity of reaffirming relationships, mobilising resources for the entertainment of guests or the destruction of wealth, legitimating an altered social order. Contact with the corpse is often considered polluting, and the mourners, whether for this reason or others, are often required to segregate themselves from normal social intercourse... It is perhaps not surprising in view of these conflicting demands, that many societies assign to women the roles which involve the closest contact with the corpse and the most marked detachment from the rhythms of everyday life, while leaving men to deal with the more public aspects of the funeral. But the situation here is far from simple. The less intense participation of women in public social life, which functionally justifies associating them with the dead rather than the living when a division of labour along these lines is required, may often itself be ideologically justified by ascribing to women qualities for the manifestation of which death offers exceptional opportunities.[1]

Humphreys goes on to discuss the way in which the opposition between men and women in Greece, as in Palestine, was based on the distinction between emotional control and unrestrained emotional displays, the latter being not only non-social but in fact anti-social. In context of our understanding the division of

---

1 *The Family, Women and Death*, p. 150.

labour at Jewish funerals and the assignment of public lamentation to women, her remarks are useful. The principal points to be considered are the interruption of the rhythms of everyday life—men maintained their usual public image but women stepped outside their traditional invisible and silent roles (in this respect at least; in other mourning duties the opposite was the case, see below); women's association with the dead rather than the living, an aspect which has been touched on already; and the ascription of gender characteristics to accommodate and support the social order of the day.[1] Such then was the division of duty at the graveside and in the funeral procession. With regard to the various manifestations of mourning following the interment we see that here too there was some differentiation according to gender, a differentiation which again reflected social order and mores.

First, it should be noted that the texts which deal with mourning ritual (both the primary and very commonly, in unquestioning reflection, the secondary too) not surprisingly address themselves primarily to men. Thus the seemingly neutral term 'mourner' (אבל), when taken in context, is revealed to be gendered and in fact male. So, for example, it is stated in various passages that during the *'aninut* and *shivah* periods (i.e. from the moment of death to the time of burial, from the burial up until the close of the seven days intensive mourning),

> a mourner is forbidden to read the Pentateuch, Prophets and Hagiographa; he is also forbidden to study Mishnah, Talmud, halachoth and haggadoth... he does not put on the tefillin... he is exempt from reading the shema... and [up

1 Later, in diaspora communities, the same assumed gender characteristics which made women in Graeco-Roman Palestine ideal keeners and deflectors of demonic wrath were used to support a different social order. Thus, for example, Rabinowicz wrote of his own community in England in the 1960s: 'There is no *din* governing the attendance of women at funerals. It is a question of local custom at to whether they attend and in Anglo-Jewry women are discouraged from attending. The *Zohar* (*Vayakhal* 196b) strongly disapproves: "For when the women wail in the funeral procession, the Angel of Death descends and places himself among them" ' (*A Guide to Life. Jewish Laws and Customs of Mourning*, p. 52). Other writers speak of women's display of emotion being unseemly to the occasion and distracting to the (male) mourners.

until the burial] from all of the commandments prescribed
in the Torah (*Sem*. 6.1, 3; 10.1; *Ket*. 6b; *M.K*. 15a-b, 23b).

Similarly *Sem*. 10.11 says that

> In the first week a mourner does not enter the synagogue; in
> the second week he enters but does not sit in his [usual]
> place; in the third week he enters and sits in his [usual]
> place but does not speak: in his fourth week he is like any
> other person (cf. *M.K*. 23a).

Various additional matters included being obliged to cover
one's head and to refrain from greeting people in public (*Sem*.
6.1, 2; *M.K*. 15a-b). It is evident from both content and context
that 'mourner' in these texts meant the male mourner. Such
restrictions would have had no application for women who
were in any case as we have seen throughout this study
already either exempt from these positive precepts or bound
by social custom not to engage in public greetings or go out
with uncovered head. These matters were not, therefore, a
part of women's mourning ritual.

The other visible signs of mourning additional to rending
one's garments and not wearing finery were not working; not
preparing one's own food; not cutting the hair or anointing
one's body or washing one's clothes; not wearing leather shoes,
and not sharing the conjugal bed (*M.K*. 15a-b; see above).
Most of these restrictions applied principally to the initial
seven-day mourning period, though some extended beyond
that (see above). Given that these rituals did not have as their
basis the positive, time-bound commandments whose
observance was incumbent only on men, we might expect to
find women sharing equally in them. Such, however, was not
always the case, for although both male and female relatives
of the deceased were bound to observe these rituals, certain
qualifications were added for female mourners. Thus, with
regard to the command to rend one's garments, the ruling of
Sem. 7.8 was that:

> For the dead generally one tacks the rent together after seven
> days and [completely] restitches [the edges] after thirty; but
> for one's father and mother one never restitches [the edges].
> A women tacks the rent together after seven days and
> restitches [the edges] after thirty. R. Judah said: A woman

tacks the rent together immediately and restitches [the
edges] after seven [days].

M.K. 22b makes clear the fact that this ruling of differentiation regarding women was due to considerations of modesty.

With regard to the prohibition on working during the first
seven days of mourning, the ruling of *Sem.* 5.1 would suggest
that this was all-embracing:

> A mourner is forbidden to engage in work throughout the
> seven days of mourning: he, his sons, his daughters, his
> slaves, his bondmaids and his cattle.

Other passages, again taken from the male viewpoint (e.g.
M.K. 20b) add to the list wives and mothers. There was, however, one significant caveat to the definition of work and that
was that 'House cleaning, dishwashing, and bedmaking ought
not to be thought of as work for a mourner' (*Sem.* 11.9). In
other words, tasks traditional to women were deemed permissible during the mourning period. Apart from the obvious
reason for this ruling in respect of keeping the management
of the household ticking over, there was also the fact that such
work was done in the privacy of the home. It did not,
therefore, fall into the category of visible (that is, public) signs
of mourning and in that sense may to some extent be
compared to the ruling that a man might engage in work
after the third day so long as it was done in private and not in
fields or public places of the city (*Sem.* 6.6-7). The significant
difference, however, was that the majority of women's work
was done from the home, and so for the female mourner the
period of intense mourning had little in terms of work to
distinguish it from everyday life. Indeed, by logical extension
of the public-private dynamic of mourning ritual, the rabbis
declared that women might even engage in such activities as
spinning and sewing so long as they avoided the courtyard
and rooftop and stayed indoors where they could not be seen
by their neighbours (*ibid.*).

One task which was not included in the rabbinic list was the
preparation of food. We may assume, however, that women
continued with this duty, with the possible exception of the
very first meal after the burial. By custom, this first meal
formed part of the general consolation for mourners and was

provided by neighbours and friends of the bereaved (*M.K.* 27a-b; *Sanh.* 2.1, 63a; *Sem.* 11.2; 14.14).[1] Such, however, was only the case if the principal mourner (that is, the most immediate relative of the deceased) was a man or a married woman, for the ruling was that

> The mourners' meal should be prepared for a man in mourning, but not for a woman in mourning (*Sem.* 11.2),

meaning that if the woman were not under the protection of a man, the gathering of people to her house would give rise to suspicions of irregular conduct and sexual misdemeanour. Such would apply, for example, to a widow living in her former husband's house who lost a child; or to a childless woman (that is, one without sons) whose husband died; or to a divorcee, an only child, whose father died. The ruling may even have been extended to include married women who lost blood kith and kin (that is, consanguines as oppose to affines, relatives by marriage), for in these instances it could be they and not men who were the principal mourners.[2] For these mourners no 'meal of consolation' was provided, and so they presumably catered for themselves and went without the ritualized introduction to the period of intensive mourning which was accorded all men.

Of the various outer manifestations of grief which were listed at the start of this section, therefore, only the duties not to wash or anoint oneself, wear finery or leather shoes, or engage in sexual intercourse were equally as incumbent on women as they were on men. All the other formal rituals associated with death and burial either had as their focus men, or were exclusionary to women, or had some

---

1 Reference to this practice is made throughout the Bible. See *EJ*, XII, col. 487: 'The comforting of mourners is accomplished by the tenderly spoken word (Isa. 40.1-2), by sitting with the mourner (Job 2.13), by providing him [*sic*] with compensation for his loss (Gen. 24.67; Isa. 60.2-9), and by offering him bread and wine (2 Sam. 3.35; Jer. 16.7). The bread is called "bread of agony" (*lechem onashim*, Ezek. 24.17; cf. *lechem 'onim* in Hos. 9.4), and the wine "the cup of consolation" (Jer. 16.7). The serving of such a meal has been variously explained as an affirmation of the bonds between the survivors, a reaffirmation of life itself after a period of fasting from death to burial, and as an act of conviviality with the soul of the deceased.'

2 Note the continuation of *Sem.* 11.2 where R. Judah gave an exception to the general rule: 'If she has small sons the mourners' meal may be shared with them'.

qualification attached in so far as their observance by female mourners was concerned. In ritualistic terms the period(s) of mourning for women were not nearly as clearly demarcated as they were for male mourners. For men, the rhythms and tasks of everyday life were severely interrupted; for women, apart from the graveside ritual of keening, life continued much as it had before the bereavement.

At the start of this chapter it was stated that cross-culturally funerary practices tend to reflect and restate the patterns and preoccupations of life, the divisions within any given society, and the former social role or function of the deceased. It would seem from our survey that this conclusion is an apt one for Graeco-Roman Jewish society, at least with regard to the primary preoccupations or divisions, that is, the perception and construction of gender and gender roles—matters which have, of course, been the primary focus of our analysis and of the book as a whole. At death, as in life, the woman remained in many senses marginalized from society, that is, from the public functioning male-defined 'community'. As a mourner, her passivity and dependence upon men were underlined, as were other gender ascriptions such as modesty, retirement, emotionality, domesticity, and irrationality. Her only active part in the funeral ritual was in consequence of her 'nature' and assumed closer association with the non-human world. The various differentiations in the rituals/duties to be performed by men and women during the mourning period(s) reflected all the preoccupations and gender-based divisions of labour operative at other times in a person's life. In this fundamental respect the routine was not interrupted and the social order was maintained.

As a dead person, the attention paid to the woman again reflected and reinforced the gendered social order and such concerns of Jewish society as the maintenance of purity, the esteem accorded scholars, the divisions according to 'class' or other groupings, and the sociologically defined family and kinship patterns. At death the woman's life was symbolically re-enacted. The anonymity and privateness of her lifestyle were maintained; her modesty and uncleanness reiterated; her dependence on men and the significance of marital status underlined; her works and deeds unindividuated and removed from the concerns of the public arena; and the general characterization or perception of the female as stereotyped and clear-cut in contrast to the subtle, complex and ambiguous male maintained.

In sum, it is evident that a detailed examination of the funerary rituals and practices of Graeco-Roman Palestine, even taken in isolation from any other information or analysis, reveals much about the preoccupations of Jewish society and the position of and attitude towards its women. Apparently the same gender patterns and roles were to continue in the next world, but discussion of the afterlife must await a second volume of study.

APPENDIX I

Text and Translation of Murabba‘at Documents
(Marriage and Divorce Deeds)

P. Mur. 20

Recto

I

```
[         ]בְ]שבעה לאדר שנת חדה עَשרה
[         ]בר] מנשה מן בני אלישיב [
[         ]את]ְי תהוא לי לאנתה כَדין מَ]ושה
[         ]וَ]לעَלْם מן {נَכֹסֹ} נَכֹסי וعَנَלי
[         ]טֹב טביע כסף זוזין [        5
[         ]וَ]להוא קים אם תש]ן
[         ]ה]ֹן לבית עלמא תהך [מקדמי
[         ]   ]הוראה ואם בנן להَוَין
[         ]לَ]בעלין או הן אנה לבת]ן
[         ]ומתזנה ומכסיא [        10
[         ]ארמלו די לך מן בתَזרי
[         ]אَ]קנא אחראין וعَرَ]נבין
[         ]וקודם ירתיך מן כול]ן
[         ]לכי שטרא כَ]די חיא
```

II

```
[         ]בשבעה [        15
[         ]בחרדונא [
[         ]מן בני אליَنשיב
```

Verso

```
יהודה בר יהَון···[ על נפשה]
```

Recto Col. 1

1. [On] the seventh of Adar, the year ele[ven at Haradona, Yehuda son of Yo...
2. Son of] Manasseh, of the sons of Eliashib [living at Haradona, said to... daughter of...
3. Yo]u shall be my wife according to the law of Mo[ses...

and me I shall feed and clothe you, from today for]
4. Always, from my property and upon [me is the duty of/I am giving you the *mohar* of your virginity...]
5. Of good coinage, the sum of [200] *zuzin*...[
6. And] it shall be valid. And if you are di[vorced from me I will return the money of your *kethubah* and all that you have brought to my house.
7. I]f you go to the house of eternity [before me, sons which you have by me will inherit your *kethubah*...
8. According to] the law. And if there shall be daughters [which you shall have by me, they shall live in my house and shall be maintained from my goods.
9. Until] marriage. Or if I [go] to the house [of eternity before you, you will dwell...]
10. And you will be nourished and clothed [all the days, in the house of our children throughout the time of]
11. Your widowhood, af[ter me (my death) and until your death/you cannot be prevented from living in my house. All the goods that I have and that
12. I shall] acquire are guarantees and sure[ties for your *kethubah*...]
13. And in favour of your heirs against every [counter claim... And at whatever time you ask it of me, I will renew]
14. For you the document as long as I am alive

Recto Col. 2

15. On the seventh [...]
16. At Haradona [...]
17. From the sons of Eliashib [...]
18. Yehuda son of Yo... [for himself] (verso)

P. Mur. 21

Recto

I
[   ] בּ֗דּ / ל oo[שׁנתן]
[   ] לעֿז֗ותו֗ן ברתֿן]
[   ] יֿהב לעוֹתֿ֗נ֗ון]
[   ] oיל הבֿoא[ ]o
[   ] ת מן כל דּ֗י[ ] 5

II

[   ]   [ ]··[   ]   ] בעשרי[ן ואח]ד
[   ]   אנת ת[הו]הן לי לאנתה   [   ] א ע[י°]°
[   ]   [תמן   ]ז   ]°ן לו[ת]°
[   ]   הן] [ה]ן אפֿטֿ[ו]רנך   [   ] ··· [   ]

10 ואתבנו[ך] כסף כ[ח]תבתיך עם כל ע[ו]ליך די ע[מי והן ב[נ]ן יהין לך מן]ין
כנמסא והנ[ן י]הין י[ת]בן ביתי ו[י]היה]מתזנן מן נכסי[ן···עד]
לבעלין [או מ]ן בתר[י עז]מך ··· מזגה[י]ן והן] אנת ל[בית עלמא ת]ה[ך מק]דמ[י]
בנך מני ירתון] כסף כתבתיך ו[כל] ל[י על]י[ך] די עמי ודי כתיב[ממל]א
בבת ובנ[ברא הן] אנה אהך לבית[א]ד[ך מק]ד[ין]מיך אנת תהוה יתבה]

15 ומתזנה]מנכסי[ן] כל ימן ב[יתהון ד]נ[י בנינ]א בת די אר[מ]לו די לך עד]
למתותך וכת]בתיך ת[ן   ] ה]ן] א[ת לך]   ] [ ]ז[[   ] [
ואנ[ה מנחם] בר   ]מע]ן [ ] די מ[ן לענ]ח[ת]ו[ן]ך [ ]° [ת]°°[[   ]°ת[
ואנה לעותתן ברת   ]ען] [די מ]ן לעל[נ]א כתיב]
וב[נ]ז]מן די ת[נ]אמרין לי אח[לֿ]פֿ ל[ו]תך ית ש[נ]טרא]

20 [כד]י] חֿיֿא

Verso

[מנחם   בר···על]ֿ נ]ֿפשה
[···]   בר י[הֿ]וסף ספרֿ[א]
[לעותתן ברת···]ֿ מ]ֿן נֿפֿשה כתב
[···]   בר···]ֿ מן··יה] [[
[···]   ··· בר]ֿ חֿסדיֿ] [   ] 25
[   ]   ··· בר י[ה]ֿוחנֿ]ֿ ע[נ]ד]
[   ]   °[שֿהד]

Recto Col. 1

1. [On the twenty first of the month]... the year... [Mena-
   hem son of...
2. took as wife Le'Juthon, daughter of [...
3. ...[*hb* Le'uth[on/Le'uth[on has given as dowry
4.
5. ...] guarant[ee from all th[at he possesses...]

Recto Col. 2

6. [On the twen[ty fir]st... Menahem, son of... living at...
   said to Le'uthon
7. Daughter of... living at] 'Ain [... you shall] be [my wife]
8.

9. ...I]f I di[vorce you...]
10. I will return [to you the money of] your [ke]*thubah* and everything that is [yours that is with] me. And if [there be] child[ren (daughters) by me]
11. According to the law, th[ey a]re to live [in] my house and [be] nourished fr[om my possessions... until]
12. To marriage [and even a]fter [me (my death) wi]th you until their marriage. [I]f you [go] to [the house of eternity] bef[ore me]
13. The sons which you [shall have] by me [will inherit] the money of your *kethubah* and [all] of you[rs that is with me and that is written] above
14. Inside and out[side. I]f I go to that hou[se] be[fore you, you are to dwell]
15. And be nourished [from my possession] all the days in the house o[f our son]s, the house of your widow[hood until]
16. Your death [and] your [*keth*]*ubah*... is yours [...]
17. And I Menahem [son of...], which is on the part of Le'[u]th[o]n [...
18. And I Le'uth[on daughter of...] that which [is written] above.
19. And at (any) [ti]me that you [ask me I will re]place for you the doc[ument]
20. [As long as] I am alive...

Verso

21. [Menahem son of... for] himself
22. [... son of J]oseph, the scribe
23. [Le'uthon daughter of...] for herself has written
24. [... son of]... from... (witness)
25. [... son of] Hasdai... (witness)
26. [... son of] Yohanan [witness]
27. [... son of...] witness

P. Mur. 115

1 Ἔτους ἑβδόμου Αὐτοκρά[τ]ορος Τραϊανοῦ Ἀδριανοῦ Καίσαρος Σεβαστοῦ ὑ[π]α[τευόντω]ν Μανίου Ἀκ[ιλίου Γλ]αβρίωνος καὶ Βελλικίου Τορκουάτου πρὸ ιδ̄ κ(αλανδῶν) Νοενβρίων

2 Δύστρου ιε̄ ἐν Βαιτοβαισσαιας .ιῳ..κ. τοπαρχείας Ἡρωδείο[υ] Ἐξομολ[ογ]ήσα[το καὶ σ]υνεγράψατο Ἐλεαῖος Σίμωνος τῶν ἀπὸ κ(ώμης) Γαλωδῶν τῆς περὶ Ἀκραβαττῶν

3 οἰκῶν ἐν κώμῃ Βαιτοαρδοις τῆς περὶ Γοφνοῖς πρὸς [Σα]λώμην ['Ι]ωά[νου Γαλγ]ουλὰ προγενομέ[νην] αὐτοῦ Ἐλαίου σύνβιον Ἐπ⟨ε⟩ὶ πρὸ τοῦ συνέβη τῷ αὐτῷ Ἐλαίῳ

Appendix I 295

4 Σίμωνος ἀπαλλαγῆναι καὶ ἀπολύειν Σαλώμην 'Ιωάνου Γαλγουλᾶ τὴ[ν..].[.] κ[..]λ[....].ηναι
 σ[υ]ηβιώσεος χάριν νννεὶ ὁμολογεῖ ὁ αὐτὸς 'Ελαῖος Σίμω[νος
5 ἐξ ἀνανεώσεος καταλλάξαι κ[αὶ] προσλαβέσθαι τὴν αὑτὴν Σαλώ[μην 'Ιω]άη[ο]υ Γ[αλγο]ηλὰ
 εἰ[ς γυναῖ]κα γαμετὴν σὺν προικὶ Ζσ οἳ εἰσιν τύριοι η ἃ ὡμολό[γη-
6 σεν ὁ αὐτὸς 'Ελαῖος Σίμωνος ἠριθμ[ῆσθαι....] ε.[...]ηλε.[.].τ.[..]...[.]...[..].[.....]..[..]
 π[ρογε]γραμμ[ένα] Ζσ εἰς λόγον προικὸς παρὰ Σαλώμης 'Ιωάη[ο]η Γαλγο[υλ]ὰ
 .[...]θ......[.....].[..].[...].
7 ....[.]....[.....].[.....].[....]......[.....].[..]φε[...].[......].[....Σ]αλώ-
 μη ['Ιωά]ηου Γαλγουλὰ κατὰ τοῦ αὐτοῦ 'Ελαίου Σίμωνος [.]ηδρα αη[...
8 καὶ κατὰ τῶν ὑπαρχόντηη αὐτῷ   'Ε[......]ωνου..ου.....[....]......[...]φειαι.[....]
 φ.ακιου αὐτῆς καὶ τέκνωη αὑτῆς οὓς ἔ[χ]ει καὶ ο[ὓς ἂν
9 σχῇ ἀπ' αὐτοῦ υἱοὺς ἢ θυγατέρας οὓς εχ[.....]ει.....[.]....ιος ὡς ..[...]. οὓς ἂν σχῇ ἀπ'
 αὐ[τ]οῦ τραφήσονται καὶ ἀμφιασθήσο[ον]ται ἐκ τ[ῶ]η ὑ[παρ-
10 χόντων τῷ αὐτῷ 'Ελεα[ί]ῳ ηρω.[.......]..[.......]...α.[.   'Εὰν δ]ὲ αὐτὸς 'Ελεαῖος
 [Σίμ]ωνος με[ταλλ]άξε[ι......τὸν] βίον πρότερ[ο]η τῆς αὐτῆ[ς
11 Σαλώμης ἢ ἂν αὐτὴ α.[.].μ.[.]....[.....]...[.].[..............].[...Σαλ]ώμη ἐκ τῶ[ν]
 ὑπαρχόντ[ων....................]ηηᾶσι τὰ προγε-
12 γραμμένα Ζσ τῶν π[ερὶ τ]ῆ[ς προ]ικός   'Ε[ὰν δὲ Σαλώμη 'Ιωάνου Γ]αλγουλὰ μεταλλ[ά]ξ[ε]ι
 αὐτὴ [τὸν βίον πρότ]ερον το[ῦ] αὐ[τ]οῦ 'Ελαίου υἱοὺς
13 οὓς ἂν σχῇ ἀπ' αὐτοῦ κλ.[.......].[...]μησουσι .[.......].....[....]τα τῆς τελευτῆς
 ......[........]ορτερον τοῦ ἰδίου μ[ε]ρους
14 κληρονομίας πατρικ[ῆς..]..[..].[..]. ἀδ[ελ]φ[ῶ]η [......].   'Εὰη ...τ.[...]ιος πᾶθη κληρο-
 νο[.]..[....].[........]...........[..].[.].μα.. προβιβά-
15 σεται δὲ 'Ελαῖος Σίμωνο[ς τ]ὴν αὑτὴν γαμικὴν κο[....].[.]. τῶη οι..η αὐτῶν παραγει....
 [..................]... ταύτης ἀξιοχρέου.
16 τῆς πράξεος γεινομέν[ης] τῇ αὑτῇ Σαλώμη 'Ιάη[ου Γαλγου]λὰ καὶ ἀ[λ]λῳ παητὶ τῷ δι' αὐτῆς
 [ἢ ὑπὲρ αὑτῆς........Σα]λώμης ἐπιφέροντι παρὰ τ[οῦ
17 'Ελεαίου Σίμωνος ἀνδρ[ὸς α]ὑτῆς καὶ ἐκ τῶν ὑπαρχό[ντων αὑ]τῷ [ὧν δ]ὲ ἔχει καὶ ὧν ἂν ἐπ[ι]-
 κτ[ήσηται....................].[.]....τῳ τρόπῳ ᾧ ἂη
18 αἱρῆται ὁ πράσσων κυρίας οὔσης .[.]ς δὲ τῆς ..[...........ἐπ]ιφερομέ[ν]ης κυρίως κα..[

19 "Ετους ἑβδόμου Αὐτοκράτο[ρος] Τραιανοῦ Αδρ[ι]α[νο]ῦ Καίσα[ρος
20 καὶ Βελλ[ικίου] Τορ[κο]ηάτο[υ] π[ρὸ ιδ κ(αλανδῶν)...]τε[.........].[
21 τοπαρχ[είας] 'Ηρωδ[εί]ου   'Ε[ξομολογή]σα[το καὶ συνεγρά]ψα[το
22 Ἀκ[ρα]β[αττω]η οἰκ[ῶ]η ἐν [κ]ώ[μῃ Βαιτο]αρδ[οις τῆς] περὶ [Γοφνοῖς

(Only the principal lacunae in the original Greek document are indicated in the translation.)

1. In the seventh year of the emperor Trajan Hadrian Caesar Augustus, under the consuls Manius Acilius Glabrio and Bellicius Torquatus, the fourteenth before the Calends of November

2. Which is the fifteenth of Dystros at Bethbassi... of the toparchy of Herodion. It has been agreed and concluded by Eleaios son of Simon, of the village of Galoda which is under Aqraba

3. Living in the village of Betharda which is under Gophna, with regard to Salome daughter of John Galgoula, who was once married to the same Eleaios. Then it previously happened that the same Eleaios

4. Son of Simon did divorce and repudiate Salome daughter of John Galgoula [...] for the sake of communal life (?), now the same Eleaios son of Simon is agreed

5. To be reconciled again and retake the same Salome daughter of John Galgoula as legitimate wife with a 'dowry' of 200 *denars*, which make 50 tyrian shekels, amount which

6. The same Eleaios son of Simon recognized (acknowledged) having been counted (to him?) [...] the above written 200 *denars* ... as dowry on the part of Salome daughter of John Galgoula...

7. [...] Salome daughter of John Galgoula against (?) the same son of Simon her husband (?)...

8. And against (?) his goods. If [...] and of the children which she has and which she may have

9. By him, sons and daughters that [...] that she may have by him, they will be nourished and clothed with the help of

10. The goods of the same Eleaios [...] If the same Eleaios son of Simon happens to die before the same

11. Salome or if she [... it will nourish and clothe Sa]lome with the help of the goods [...] the above

12. Mentioned 200 *denars* of that which concerns the dowry. If Salome daughter of John Galgoula happens to die before the same Eleaios, the sons

13. Which she may have by him... will inherit [...] death [...] besides their share

14. Of the paternal inheritance... [with their half-] brothers. If... (prior?) claim(?)

15.

16. Right of execution being to the same Salome daughter of John Galgoula and to any other who will act [in her place]/who presents himself for her [in lieu of her]... Salome (right) on

17. Eleaios son of Simon her husband and on (all) his goods, those which he has and those which he may acquire... (execution) in whatever form.

18. That the executor should choose; this contract being valid [...] presented legally [...]

19.

20. (repeat of opening formula, very fragmentary)

21.

22.

P. Mur. 116

1 .ω[
2 αὐτῷ δ[.]......ạ.[......].[
   .ᵋ ᵒᵖ...
3 ρι τουτων δοσι·γειτνια.[....]υ ουσ...[.]...[
4 ἐὰν δὲ θυγατέρας θρέψῃ [κ]αὶ ἐγδῷ σ.....[Ἐὰν δὲ ἡ Σαλώμη πρὸ τοῦ Αὐρηλίου
5 τὸν βίον μ[ε]ταλλάξει υ[ἱοὺ]ς οὓς ἂν ἔξει ἀπ’ αὐτ[οῦ...   κληρονομήσουσιν
6 τὴν φερνὴν καὶ τὰ πρ[ογε]γραμμένα ...αρ[......].ωγ.[..].[...].[..].[
7 επ....π..........[...] τῆς τοῦ Αὐρηλίου οὐ[σ]ίας πάσạ[ν κλ]ηρονομί-
8 αν μεθ’ ὧν ἂν ἔξωσιν ạ[δ]ελφῶν Ἐὰν δὲ ὁ Αὐρήλιος πρὸ̣ [τ]ῆς Σαλώ-
9 μης τὸν βίον μεταλλάξει [τρ]αφήσηται ἡ Σαλώμη [κ]αὶ ἀμφιασθ[ήσ]εται ἐκ τῆς
10 τοῦ Αὐρηλίου οὐσίας ἐφ’ [ὅσ]ον ἂν θέλῃ χηρεύειν χρόνον Ἐ[ὰν] δὲ βουλη-
11 θῇ με⟨τ⟩ὰ τὴν αὐτοῦ τε[λευ]τὴν ἀπεῖναι ἢ ἐὰν ἀνθ’ ἑαυτῆ[ς] ἀποπέμ-
12 ψῃ[.]......ε..[.].[.]π[......].α[..]..[....].[...].ρạ..δ̣ηγ[ά]ρια δισχείλια
13 γ[   ]η[   ].γε[   ]ε[

1.
2.
3.
4. ...if she (?) nourishes the daughters and gives them in marriage... [If Salome before Aurelios]
5. Happens to die sons which she will have by hi[m...] will inherit
6. The dowry and those written above [...
7. [They will moreover divide] all the inheritance of the fortune of Aurelios
8. With the (half) brothers which they may (?) have. If Aurelios before Salo-
9. me happens to die Salome will be nourished and clothed from the
10. Fortune of Aurelios all the time that she wishes to remain a widow... But if she wishes
11. To leave after his death or if she sends in her place...
12. ...[she will recover the *kethubah* of] 2000 (!) *denars*
13. ...

P. Mur. 19

Recto

I

באחד למרחשׁון שׁנת שׁת במצדא
שׁבק ומתרך מן רעתי יומאֿ דנה אנה {יהוסֿף
בר נ} יהוסֿף בר נקסן מן [ ] זֿה יתב במצדא לכֿי אנֿתי
מרים ברת יהונתן [מ]ן הנֿבלטא יתבא

5 במצדא די הוית אנתי מן קדם דה דׄיׄ אׄת
רשׄא בנפשכי למהך וׄלׄמהׄי אׄנׄת לכול גבר
יהׄודׄי די תצבין וׄבׄ[נׄ]דׄיׄ[נׄ] להׄוׄי לכׄי מני ספר תרׄכׄין
וגט שבקין בדין [ ] [קׄא יהבנא וכול חרׄיׄבׄׄ[ן
ונזקן ו··· [ׄ]]ׄעׄ לכי כדן יהי קׄיׄםׄ

10 ומשלׄםׄ לרבעין וׄבׄזׄ[ׄמ]ן]דׄיׄ תמרין לי אחלף לכׄיׄ
שטרה כדי חׄיׄא

II

בׄאׄ[ןׄ]ד למרחשׄ[ן]ׄןׄ]שׄנׄת שת במצדא
שבׄק ומתרׄך אׄנׄנׄהׄ מן רׄעתי יומא דנה
יהׄוסף בר נׄ[ק]סן]לׄכׄי אנתי מרים (ברת)

15 יהונתן [מׄ]ן [ ] הׄ[ן]ׄבׄלׄטא יתׄבׄא
במצדא די הׄ[נׄ]וׄיׄ[ת אנתי
מן קדמת דנא די אתי רשׄׄ[א
בנׄפשכי למנׄ[ה]ׄך למהׄי אנתא
לכול גבר יהׄודׄי די תצבין

20 בׄדין להׄי לכׄי מני סׄ[נׄ]פׄ[ןׄ]ׄר תרכׄין
וׄגׄׄטׄ שבקין בׄ[ד]ין כוׄ[ן]ׄל]ׄק יהׄבׄנה
וכל חרׄ[נׄ]יׄבׄיׄ[ן] [ונזקן ו···ן]ׄ כׄדן
[יהי קים] [וׄ]ׄמׄש]ׄ[ל]ׄם לרבעין ובזמן
[די תׄ]ׄמׄרׄין לׄיׄ[ן אׄ]ׄחׄלף לכׄי שטרה כדי

25 [חׄיׄ]ׄא

Verso

יהוסף בר נק[ס]ׄן] על נפש[ה]
אליעזר [בר] מׄלכה שהד
יהוסף בר מלכה שהד
אלעזר בר חנה שהד

Recto

1. On the first of Marheshwan, the year six, at Masada
2. I divorce and repudiate of my own free will, today I
3. Joseph, son of Naqsan, from [...]ah, living at Masada, you
4. Miriam, daughter of Jonathan [fro]m Hanablata, living
5. At Masada, who was my wife up to this time, so that you
6. Are free on your part to go and become the wife of any
7. Jewish man that you wish. And here on my part is the bill
   of repudiation

8. And the writ of divorce. Now I give back [the dow]ry. And all the ruined,
9. And damaged (goods) and ... [they will be restored] as is my duty by this/ so let it be determined
10. And I will pay (them) fourfold. And at any ti[me] that you ask it of me, I will replace for you
11. The document as long as I am alive

Verso

26. Joseph, son of Naq[san] for himsel[f]
27. Eliezer, [son of] Malka, witness
28. Joseph, son of Malka, witness
29. Eleazar, son of Hanana, witness

Kethubah: Maimonides—'Yad', Yabam 4.33

On (day of the week), the (day of the month), in the year ... since the creation of the world, the era according to which we are accustomed to reckon here in the city of N., how N. son of N. said to this virgin N. daughter of N., 'Be thou my wife according to the law of Moses and Israel, and I will work for thee, honour, support and maintain thee in accordance with the custom of Jewish husbands who work for their wives, honour, support and maintain them in truth. And I will set aside for thee 200 *zuz*, in lieu of thy virginity, which belong to thee (according to the law of Moses), and thy food, clothing and necessaries, and live with thee in conjugal relations according to universal custom.' And N. this virgin consented and became his wife. The dowry that she brought from her father's house, in silver, gold, valuables, dresses and bedclothes, amounts to ... (100 silver pieces), making in all ... (200 silver pieces). And thus said N. the bridegroom, 'I take upon myself and my heirs after me the responsibility of this marriage contract, of the dowry and of the additional sum, so that all this shall be paid from the best part of my property, real and personal, that I now possess or may hereafter acquire. All my property, even the mantle on my shoulders, shall be mortgaged for the security of this contract and of the dowry and of the addition made thereto.' N. the bridegroom has taken upon himself the responsibility for all the obligations of this *kethubah*, as is customary with other *kethuboth* made for the daughters of Israel in accordance with the institution of our sages—may their memory be for a blessing! It is not to be regarded as an illusory obligation or as a mere form of document. We have followed the legal formality of symbolic delivery between N. son of N., the bridegroom and N. daughter of N., this virgin, and have employed an instrument legally fit for the purpose to strengthen all that is stated above, and everything is valid and established.

N. Witness

N. Bridegroom

N. Witness

APPENDIX II

Selection of Images of Women and Womankind taken from the ancient sources

Part I. What the ancients perceived to be the attributes of the ideal wife.

Part II. What the ancients deemed to be features or characteristics peculiar to women in general

1. *The Ideal Wife*

(i) Submissive and retiring:

> ... young women [are to be trained] to love their husbands and children, to be sensible, chaste, domestic, kind and submissive to their husbands, that the word of God may not be discredited (Tit. 2.4-5).

(ii) Demure behaviour to be reflected in clothing:

> ... women should adorn themselves modestly and sensibly in seemly apparel, not with braided hair or gold or pearls or costly attire... (1 Tim. 2.9).

> ... wives, be submissive to your husbands... let not yours be the outward adorning with braiding of hair, decoration of gold, and wearing of robes, but let it be the hidden person of the heart with the imperishable jewel of a gentle and quiet spirit, which in God's sight is very precious (1 Pet. 3.3-4).

(iii) Physical appearance generally:

> ... splendid and beautiful the form of her face... soft the hair of her head... lovely her eyes...pleasant her nose... lovely her breast... beautiful (in) all her whiteness... lovely

her palms... long and dainty all the fingers of her hands...
(*Gen. Apoc.* 20.2-5).

...a firm tread, a serene countenance, her person and her
modesty alike without false colouring... her carriage unaf-
fected, her movements quiet... her adornment that of good
sense (*Sac.* 26f.).

Ben Sira, in praise of the good wife:

As the lamp shining on the holy candlestick,
So is the beauty of a face on a stately figure.
As the golden pillars upon the silver base,
So are beautiful feet upon firm heels (26.17-18).

(iv) Silence a great virtue:

A silent woman is a gift from the Lord (Sir. 26.14).

As a sandy ascent to the feet of the aged,
So is a woman of tongue to a quiet man (Sir. 25.20)

It is better to dwell in a corner of the housetop
Than in a house in common with a contentious woman
(Prov. 21.9).

(v) Innocence and modesty:

...her moral nature free from guile, her conduct from
stain, her will from craft, her speech from falsehood... in
her company come piety, holiness, truth... self control, tem-
perance, orderliness, continence, meekness, frugality...
modesty, a quiet temper, etc. (*Sac.* 26-27).

Grace upon grace is a shamefast woman,
And there is no price worthy of a continent soul (Sir. 26.15).

(vi) Serving, cherishing, and supporting husband:

As the sun arising in the highest places of the Lord,
So is the beauty of a good wife in the ordering of his house
(Sir. 26.16).

...by extreme labour she nurtures thy son (*Ahikar* 2.71).

Philo, in praise of Sarah:

She showed her wifely love by numberless proofs, by sharing
with him the severance from his kinsfolk, by bearing
without hesitation the departure from her homeland, and

the continual and unceasing wanderings on a foreign soil and privation in famine... Everywhere and always she was at his side... resolved to share alike the good and the ill. She did not, like some other women, run away from mishaps and lie ready to pounce on pieces of good luck, but accepted her portion of both with alacrity as the fit and proper test of a wedded wife (*Abr.* 245-246).

Hands that hang down and palsied knees
(Thus shall it be) with a wife that maketh not happy her husband (Sir. 25.23b).

(vii) Ideal wife is a gift from the Lord:

He that getteth a wife (getteth) the choicest possession,
A helpmeet for him and a pillar of support (*Sir.* 36.24).

A good wife—blessed is her husband,
The number of his days is doubled.
A worthy wife cherisheth her husband,
And he fulfilleth the years of his life in peace.
A good wife is a good gift:
She shall be given to him that feareth God, for his portion.
Whether rich or poor, his heart is cheerful
And his face is merry at all times (Sir. 26.1-4).

2. *Womankind in General*

(i) Divinely ordained inferiority—the Creation myth:

In the first week was Adam created, and the rib—his wife (*Jub.* 3.8).

...man... is the image and glory of God; but woman is the glory of man. For man was not made from woman but woman from man. Neither was man created for woman but woman for man (1 Cor. 11.7-9).

Josephus, on Gen. 3.16:

The woman, says the Law, is in all things inferior to the man... Authority has been given by God to the man (*Con. Ap.* 2.201).

Philo, on Lev. 37.2-8:

...the Law laid down a scale of valuation in which no regard is paid to beauty or stature or anything of the kind, but all are assessed equally, the sole distinction made being between men and women, children and adults... (*Spec. Leg.* 2.32).

(ii) The divine plan regarding the creation of woman backfires:

... He considered well from what part to create her. Said He: 'I will not create her from [Adam's] head, lest she be swelled-headed; nor from the eye, lest she be a coquette; nor from the ear, lest she be an eavesdropper; nor from the mouth, lest she be a gossip; nor from the heart, lest she be prone to jealousy; nor from the hand, lest she be a gadabout; but from the modest part of man, for even when he stands naked that part is covered.' And as He created each limb He ordered her, 'Be a modest woman.' Yet in spite of all this ... she is swelled-headed, as it is written, *They walk with stretched-forth necks* (Isa. 3.16)... she is a coquette, *with wanton eyes* (*ibid.*) she is an eavesdropper, *Now Sarah listened in the tent door* (Gen. 18.10)... she is prone to jealousy, *Rachel envied her sister*(Gen. 30.1)... she is light-fingered, *And Rachel stole the teraphim* (Gen. 31.19)... she is a gadabout, *And Dinah went out* (Gen. 34.1) (*Gen. Rab.* 30.1).

Cf. *Deut. Rab.* 6.11,

And everything that God intended should not be in her is to be found even in the best of women. God said, 'I will not create her from the eye... [continues as above, concluding with] I will not create her from the mouth that she may not be talkative, yet of Miriam, the pious, it is written, *And Miriam spoke*. And see what befell her, REMEMBER WHAT THE LORD THY GOD DID UNTO MIRIAM [punished her with leprosy].

(ii) Woman responsible for bringing sin and death into the world—The Fall:

Since no created thing is constant, and things mortal are necessarily liable to changes and reverses, it could not but be that the first man too should experience some ill-fortune. And woman becomes for him the beginning of blameworthy life. For so long as he was by himself... he went on growing like to the world and like God, and receiving in his soul the impressions made by the nature of each... But when woman too had been made... desire begat bodily pleasure, that pleasure which is the beginning of wrongs and violation of law, the pleasure for the sake of which men bring on themselves the life of mortality and wretchedness in lieu of that of immortality and bliss (*Op. Mun.* 151).

From a woman did sin originate
And because of her we all must die (Sir. 25.13).

(iv) Woman's uncleanness—a constant pollution to man:

Man that is born of a woman
Is of few days and full of trouble...
Who can bring a clean thing out of an unclean? Not one...
What is man, that he should be clean?
And he that is born of woman, that he should be righteous?
    (Job 14.1, 4; 15.14).

(v) The essential evil of women:

Evil are women, my children... (*T. Reub.* 5.1).

... Any wound, only not a heart wound,
Any wickedness, only not the wickedness of a woman! (Sir. 25.13).

(vi) Inherent evil manifests itself in promiscuity:

... women are overcome by the spirit of fornication more than men... (*T. Reub.* 5.3).

As a thirsty traveller that openeth his mouth,
And drinketh of any water that is near,
So she sitteth down at every post,
And openeth her quiver to every arrow (Sir. 26.12).

A woman has more pleasure in one *kab* with lechery than in nine *kabs* with modesty (*Sot.* 3.4).

(vii) The dangers of womankind to man:

... if men... see a woman which is comely in favour and beauty, they let all things go and gape after her... and have all more desire unto her than unto gold or silver or any goodly thing whatsoever... Women have dominion over you,... Yea, a man taketh his sword and goeth forth to make outroads, and to rob and to steal, and to sail upon the sea and upon rivers, and looketh upon a lion, and walketh in the darkness; and when he hath stolen, spoiled and robbed,

> he bringeth it to his love... (1 Esdras 4.18-24).

> The majority of wars, and those the greatest, have arisen through amours and adulteries and the deceits of women... (*Jos.* 56).

> ...forever do women bear rule over king and beggar alike. And from the king they take away his glory, and from the valiant man his might, and from the beggar even that little which is the stay of his poverty (*T. Judah* 15.5-6).

(viii) Women by nature evil, because lower on the hierarchy of creation, closer to the world of demons, and belonging to the inferior category of sense perception:

> Pleasure does not venture to bring her wiles and deceptions to bear on the man, but on the woman, and by her means on him... For in us mind corresponds to man, the senses to women; and pleasure encounters and holds parley with the senses first, and through them cheats with her quakeries the sovereign mind itself... (*Op. Mun.* 165).

> ...the spirit of fornication is seated in the nature and in the senses (*T. Reub.* 3.3).

(ix) Women—inferior, irrational beings:

> ...womankind are subject to sudden changes of opinion through fallacious reasoning (*Letter of Aristeas* 250).

> The judgements of women as a rule are weaker and do not apprehend any mental conception apart from that which their senses perceive... (*Leg.* 320).

> ...the rule of custom is followed by women more than men... (*Ebr.* 54).

> ...two ingredients... constitute our life-principle, the rational and the irrational; the rational which belongs to mind and reason is of the masculine gender, the irrational, the province of sense, is of the feminine. Mind belongs to a genus wholly superior to sense as man is to woman (*Spec. Leg.* 1.201).

(x) Sense perception (woman) = passivity:

> Of the many faculties of the mind [= Adam] He [God] took one, the faculty of perception. 'He built it to be a woman',

proving by this that the most proper and exact name for sense perception is 'woman'. For just as the man shows himself in activity and the woman in passivity, so the province of the mind is activity, and that of the perceptive sense passivity, as in woman (*Leg. All.* 2.38).

... virtue is male, since it causes movement and affects conditions and suggests noble conceptions of noble deeds and words... (*Abr.* 102).

... male is more complete, more dominant than the female, closer akin to causal activity, for the female is incomplete and in subjection and belongs to the category of the passive rather than the active (*Spec. Leg.* 1.200).

(xi) Women—domestic beings:

Organised communities are of two sorts, the greater which we call cities and the smaller which we call households...; the government of the greater is assigned to men under the name of statesmanship, that of the lesser, known as household management, to women (*Spec. Leg.* 3.170).

... men should divide inheritances among themselves, to be taken as the reward for military service and the wars of which they have borne the brunt;... Nature, who grants woman exemption from such conflicts, clearly also refuses them a share in the prizes assigned thereto (*Vit. Mos.* 2.236).

To sow and beget belongs to the man and is his peculiar excellence... Welfare in child-bearing... belongs to women, and the nature of man admits not of it (*Sac.* 101).

(xii) Other miscellaneous 'characteristics' of women:

... women are glutonous (*Toh.* 7.9).

... the more women, the more witchcrafts (*Aboth* 2.7).

... there is no wrath above the wrath of a woman (Sir. 25.15b).

(xiii) No taint of the Female to attach itself to Man; ultimate punishment for misdeeds the absorption of female traits:

So earnestly and carefully does the Law desire to train and exercise the soul to manly courage that it lays down rules even about the kind of garment which should be worn (cf.

Deut. 22.5). It strictly forbids a man to assume a woman's garb, in order that no trace, no merest shadow of the female should attach to him and spoil his masculinity (*Virt.* 18f.).

A sword is upon the Chaldeans, saith the Lord...
And they shall become as women...
The purposes of the Lord are performed against Babylon...
Their might hath failed, they are become as women (Jer. 50.35, 37; 51.29, 30).

(xiv) Conclusion. The world shall cease if ever the 'natural' order is reversed and women hold sway over men:

...at whatsoever time the threatened vengeance of the Almighty God draws near... then the world shall be under the dominion of a woman's hands, obeying her every behest. Then when a widow shall reign over the whole world and cast both gold and silver into the godlike deep, and the brass and iron of shortlived man cast into the sea... then God whose dwelling is in the sky shall roll up the heaven as a book is rolled. And the whole firmament... shall fall on the divine earth and on the sea: and then shall flow a ceaseless cataract of raging fire... and the firmament of heaven and the stars and creation itself it shall cast into one molten mass and clean dissolve (*Sib. Or.* 3.71f.).

BIBLIOGRAPHY OF WORKS CITED

Aberbach, M., 'Educational Institutions and Problems in the Talmudic Age', *HUCA* 36 (1966), 107-20.

Abercrombie, J.R., *Palestinian Burial Practices from 1200 to 600 BCE* (doctoral thesis, University of Pennsylvania, 1979).

Abrahams, I., *Jewish Life in the Middle Ages* (London, 1932).

Archer, L.J., 'The Role of Jewish Women in the Religion, Ritual and Cult of Graeco-Roman Palestine', in *Images of Women in Antiquity*, ed. A. Cameron and A. Kuhrt (London, 1983), 273-87.

—'The "Evil Woman" in Apocryphal and Pseudepigraphical Writings', *Proceedings of the Ninth World Congress of Jewish Studies*, Division A: *The Period of the Bible* (Jerusalem, 1986), 239-46.

—'The Virgin and the Harlot in the Writings of Formative Judaism', *History Workshop: A Journal of Socialist and Feminist Historians* 24 (Autumn 1987), 1-16.

—(ed.), *Slavery and Other Forms of Unfree Labour*, London and New York, 1988.

—'Bound by Blood: Circumcision and Menstrual Taboo in Post Exilic Judaism', in *Women, Theology and Judaeo-Christian Tradition*, ed. J. Martin-Soskice (London, 1989).

—'Notions of Community and the Exclusion of the Female in Jewish History and Historiography', in *Notions of Community and Jewish Identification through the Ages*, ed. L.J. Archer & D. Sorkin (forthcoming).

—' "In Thy Blood Live": Gender and Ritual in Judaeo-Christian Tradition', in *Through the Devil's Gateway*, ed. A. Joseph (in press).

Avigad, N., 'A Depository of Inscribed Ossuaries in the Kidron Valley', *IEJ* 12 (1962), 1-12.

—'Architectural Observations on some Rock-Cut Tombs', *PEQ* 79 (1947), 112-15.

Avi-Yonah, M., 'Synagogue Architecture in the Late Classical Period', in *Jewish Art. An Illustrated History*, ed. C. Roth and B. Narkiss (London, 1971), 65-82.

—(ed.), *Encyclopaedia of Archaeological Excavations in the Holy Land*, vols. I-IV (London, 1975).

Barkai, G., A. Kloner and A. Mazar, 'The Northern Cemetery of Jerusalem in the First Temple Times', *Qadmoniot* 8 (1975), 71-76 (in Hebrew; English summary in *IEJ* 26 [1976], 55-57).

Baumgarten, J.M., 'The Exclusion of the Nethinim and Proselytes in 4 Q Flor.', *RQ* 9 (8/1) (1972), 87-96.

Belkin, S., *Philo and the Oral Law. The Philonic Interpretation of Biblical Law in Relation to the Palestinian Halakah* (Cambridge, 1940).

—'Levirate and Agnate Marriage in Rabbinic and Cognate Literature', *JQR* 60 (1969-70), 275-329.

Bender, A.P., 'Beliefs, Rites and Customs of the Jews connected with Death, Burial and Mourning', *JQR* 6 (1894), 317-47, 664ff. and *JQR* 7 (1895), 101-18, 259-69.

Benoit, P., J.T. Milik and R. de Vaux, *Discoveries in the Judaean Desert,* vol. II, *Les Grottes de Murabba'at* (Oxford, 1961).

Bigger, S.F., 'The Family Laws of Leviticus 18 in their Setting', *JBL* 98 (1979), 187-203.

Birnbaum, S.A., 'The Kephar Behhayu Marriage Deed', *JAOS* 78 (1958), 12-18.

—*The Bar Menasheh Marriage Deed* (Istanbul, 1962).

Blackburn, R., 'Defining Slavery—Its Special Features and Social Role', in *Slavery and Other Forms of Unfree Labour,* ed. L.J. Archer (London/New York, 1988), 262-79.

Bonsirven, J., *On the Ruins of the Temple* (London, 1931).

—*Le Judaïsme palestinien au temps de Jésus Christ,* vols. I-II (Paris, 1935).

Bright, J., *A History of Israel* (London, 1964).

Brooks, B.A., 'Fertility Cult Functionaries in the Old Testament', *JBL* 60 (1941), 227-53.

Brown, F., S.R. Driver & C.A. Briggs, *A Hebrew and English Lexicon of the Old Testament* (Oxford, 1955).

Buchanan, G.W., 'The Role of Purity in the Structure of the Essene Sect', *RQ* 15 (4/3) (1963), 397-406.

Büchler, A., 'The Nicanor Gate and the Brass Gate', *JQR* 11 (1898), 46-63.

—'The Fore-Court of Women and the Brass Gate in the Temple of Jerusalem', *JQR* 10 (1898), 678-718.

—'Learning and Teaching in the Open Air in Palestine', *JQR* 4 (1913-14), 485-91.

—*Types of Jewish Piety from 70 BCE to 70 CE* (London, 1922).

—'The Induction of the Bride and Bridegroom into the Chuppah in the First and Second Centuries in Palestine', in *Livre d'hommage à la mémoire de Dr. Samuel Poznanski* (Warsaw, 1927), 83-97.

—'Family Purity and Family Impurity in Jerusalem before the year 70 CE', in *Studies in Jewish History. The Büchler Memorial Volume* (London, 1956), 64-98.

Burrows, M., *The Basis of Israelite Marriage* (New Haven, 1938).

—'Levirate Marriage in Israel', *JBL* 59 (1940), 23-33.

—'The Ancient Oriental Background of Hebrew Levirate Marriage', *BASOR* 77 (1940), 2-15.

Canaan, T., 'The Child in Palestinian Arab Superstition', *JPOS* 7 (1927), 159-86.

—'The Curse in Palestinian Folk-Lore', *JPOS* 15 (1935), 235-79.

Charles, R.H., *Apocrypha and Pseudepigrapha of the Old Testament,* vols. I-II (Oxford, 1913).

Cohen, B., 'On the Theme of Betrothal in Jewish and Roman Law', *PAAJR* 18 (1948-49), 67-135.

—'Concerning Divorce in Jewish and Roman Law', *PAAJR* 21 (1952), 3-34.

—*Jewish and Roman Law. A Comparative Study* (New York, 1966).

Cohen, Y.A., 'The Shaping of Men's Minds: Adaptations to Imperatives of Culture', in *Anthropological Perspectives on Education*, ed. M.L. Wax, S. Diamond and F.O. Gearing (New York and London, 1973).

Cowley, A., *Aramaic Papyri from the Fifth Century BC* (Oxford, 1923).

Cross, E.B., *The Hebrew Family* (Chicago, 1927).

Danby, H. (trans.), *The Mishnah* (Oxford, 1933).

—(trans.), *The Code of Maimonides*. Bk. 10 *The Book of Cleanness* (New Haven, 1954).

Di Lella, A.A., *The Hebrew Text of Sirach. A Text Critical and Historical Survey* (The Hague, 1966).

Epstein, L.M., *The Jewish Marriage Contract* (New York, 1927).

—*Marriage Laws in the Bible and Talmud* (Cambridge, Mass., 1942).

—*Marriage Laws and Customs in Judaism* (New York, 1948).

—*Sex Laws and Customs in Judaism* (New York, 1967 [1948]).

Finkelstein, L., 'The Origin of the Synagogue', *PAAJR* 1 (1930), 49-59.

Fitzmyer, J.A., 'A Re-Study of an Elephantine Aramaic Marriage Contract, (AP. 15)', in *Near Eastern Studies in Honour of W.F. Albright*, ed. H. Goedicke (Baltimore and London, 1971), 137-68.

—& Harrington, D.J., *A Manual of Palestinian Aramaic Texts* (Rome, 1978).

Fohrer, G., *History of Israelite Religion*, trans. D. Green (London, 1973).

Fox, R., *Kinship and Marriage* (London, 1967).

Frey, J.B., *Corpus Inscriptionum Iudaicarum. Recueil des inscriptions juives qui vont du IIIe siècle avant Jésus Christ au VIIe siècle de notre ère*, vol. II (Rome, 1952).

Friedman, M.A., 'Termination of the Marriage upon the Wife's Request: A Palestinian Ketubba Stipulation', *PAAJR* 37 (1969), 29-55.

—*Geniza Studies in Jewish Marriage Law* (Tel-Aviv, 1974).

—'Israel's Response in Hosea 2.17b "You are my Husband" ', *JBL* 99 (1980), 199-204.

—*Jewish Marriage in Palestine—A Cairo Geniza Study: Marriage Contracts according to the Custom of Eretz Israel*, Vol. I, *The Ketubba Traditions of Eretz Israel;* Vol. II, *The Texts* (Tel-Aviv, 1980-82).

Galling, K., 'Die Nekropole von Jerusalem', *Palästinajahrbuch des Deutschen Evangelischen Instituts für Altertumswissenschaft des Heiligen Landes zu Jerusalem* 32 (1936), 73-101.

Gennep, A. van, *The Rites of Passage*, trans. M.B. Vizadom & G.L. Caffee (London, 1960).

Gifford, E.H. (trans.), Eusebius, *Praeparatio Evangelica* (Oxford, 1903).

Goitein, S.D., *A Mediterranean Society*, Vol. III, *The Family* (Berkeley and Los Angeles, 1978).

Goodblatt, D.M., *Rabbinic Institutions in Sasanian Babylonia* (Leiden, 1975).

—*Schools in Sasanian Babylonia* (Leiden, 1975).

—'The Beruriah Traditions' in *Persons and Institutions in Early Rabbinic Judaism*, ed. W.S. Green (Brown Judaic Studies, 3; Missoula, 1977), 207-35.

Goodenough, E.R., *Jewish Jurisprudence in Egypt* (New Haven, 1929).

—*Jewish Symbols in the Graeco-Roman Period*, Vols. I-XII (New York, 1953–)

Granqvist, H., *Marriage Conditions in a Palestinian Village*, Vols. I-II (Helsingfors, 1931, 1935).

—*Birth and Childhood among the Arabs* (Helsingfors, 1947).

Grant, F.C. & H.H. Rowley, *Dictionary of the Bible* (Edinburgh, 1963).

Gutman, J. (ed.), *Ancient Synagogues. The State of Research* (Brown Judaic Studies 22; Brown University, 1981).

Hachlili, R., 'A Jerusalem Family in Jericho', *BASOR* 230 (1978), 45-56.

—'The Goliath Family in Jericho: Funerary Inscriptions from a First Century AD Jewish Monumental Tomb', *BASOR* 235 (1979), 31-66.

—& Killebrew, A., 'Jewish Funerary Customs during the Second Temple Period in the Light of the Excavations at the Jericho Necropolis', *PEQ* 115 (1983), 109-33.

Haldar, A., *Associations of Cult Prophets among the Ancient Semites* (Uppsala, 1945).

Heinemann, I., *Philons griechische und jüdische Bildung* (Breslau, 1932).

Hoenig, S.B., 'Qumran Rules of Impurities', *RQ* 24 (6/4) (1969), 559-67.

Hollis, F., *The Archaeology of Herod's Temple* (London, 1934).

Horst, P.W. van der, *The Sentences of Pseudo Phocylides* (Leiden, 1978).

Humphreys S.C., *The Family, Women and Death. Comparative Studies* (London, 1983).

Jastrow, M., 'An Assyrian Law Code', *JAOS* 41 (1921), 1-59.

—*A Dictionary of the Targumim, Talmud Babli and Yerushalmi and the Midrashic Literature* (Israel, 1926).

Jaussen, *Coûtumes Palestiniennes* (Paris, 1927).

Jeremias, J., *Jerusalem in the Time of Jesus* (London, 1969).

Kamsler, H.M., 'Hebrew Menstrual Taboos', *Journal of American Folk-Lore* 51 (1940), 76-82.

Kloner, A., 'The Necropolis of Jerusalem in the Second Temple Period' (doctoral thesis, Jerusalem, 1980) (in Hebrew; English summary pp. iv-xix).

Knight, D.A. & G.M. Tucker (eds.), *The Hebrew Bible and its Modern Interpreters* (Philadelphia and Chico, 1985).

Kohler, K., 'The Essenes and the Apocalyptic Literature', *JQR* 11 (1920), 145-68.

Kraeling, E.G.H., *The Brooklyn Museum Aramaic Papyri* (New York, 1953).

Krauss, S., 'Outdoor Teaching in Talmudic Times', *JJS* 1 (1948), 82-84.

Lauterbach, J.Z., 'The Ceremony of Breaking a Glass at Weddings', *HUCA* 2 (1925), 351-80.

Lehmann, M.R., 'Ben Sira and the Qumran Literature', *RQ* 9 (3/1) (1961), 103-16.

—'Studies in the Murabba'at and Nahal Hever Documents', *RQ* 13 (4/1) (1963), 53-81.

Levi, J., *The Hebrew Text of the Book of Ecclesiasticus* (Leiden, 1969).

Lévi-Strauss, C., 'The Principles of Kinship', in *Kinship*, ed. J. Goody (London, 1971).

Liddel, H.G. and R. Scott, *A Greek-English Lexicon* (Oxford, 1953).

Lindblom, J., *Prophecy in Ancient Israel* (Oxford, 1962).

Loewe, R., *The Position of the Woman in Judaism* (London, 1966).

Lowry, S., 'Some Aspects of Normative and Sectarian Interpretation of the Scriptures (The Contribution of the Judaean Scrolls towards Systematization)', *ALUOS* 7 (1966-68), 98-163.

Macdonald E.M., *The Position of Women as Reflected in Semitic Codes of Law* (Toronto, 1931).

Meyers, E.M., 'The Theological Implications of an Ancient Jewish Burial Custom', *JQR* 62/2 (1971), 95-119.

—and J.F. Strange, *Archaeology, the Rabbis and Early Christianity* (London, 1981).

Moehring, H.R., 'Josephus on the Marriage Customs of the Essenes', in *Early Christian Origins. Studies in Honour of Harold R. Willoughby*, ed. A. Wikgren (Chicago, 1961), 120-27.

Montgomery, J.A., 'Ascetic Strains in Early Judaism', *JBL* 51 (1932), 183-213.

Morgenstern, J., 'The Origin of the Synagogue' in *Studi Orientalistici G. Levi della Vida* (Rome, 1956), Vol. II, 192-201.

—*Rites of Birth, Marriage, Death and Kindred Occasions among the Semites* (Cincinnati, 1966).

Morris, N., *The Jewish School* (London, 1937).

Mueller, J.R., 'The Temple Scroll and the Gospel Divorce Texts', *RQ* 38 (10/2) (1980), 247-56.

Muffs, Y., *Studies in the Aramaic Legal Papyri from Elephantine* (Leiden, 1969).

Neufeld, E., *Ancient Hebrew Marriage Laws* (London, 1944).

Neusner, J., *The Idea of Purity in Ancient Judaism*, with critique and commentary by M. Douglas (Leiden, 1973).

Oesterley, W.O.E. & T.H. Robinson, *Hebrew Religion. Its Origin and Development* (London, 1937).

Peritz, I., 'Women in the Ancient Hebrew Cult', *JBL* 17 (1898), 111-47.

Pfeiffer, R.M., *History of New Testament Times with an Introduction to the Apocrypha* (New York, 1949).

—*The Books of the Old Testament* (London, 1957).

Polotsky, H.J., 'The Greek Papyri from the Cave of Letters', *IEJ* 12 (1962), 258-62.

Porten, B., *Archives from Elephantine* (Berkeley, 1968).

Rabinowicz, H.M., *A Guide to Life, Jewish Laws and Customs of Mourning* (London, 1964).

Rahmani, L.Y., 'A Jewish Tomb on Shahin Hill', *IEJ* 8 (1958), 101-105.

—'Jewish Rock Cut Tombs in Jerusalem', *Atiqot 3* (1961), 93-120.

—'Ancient Jerusalem's Funerary Customs and Tombs', Part One, *BA* 44 (1981), 171-77; Part Two, *ibid.*, 229-35; Part Three, *BA* 45 (1981-82), 43-53; Part Four, *ibid.*, 109-19.

Rosaldo, M.Z. & L. Lamphere (eds.), *Women, Culture and Society* (Stanford, 1974).

Safrai, S., 'Elementary Education: Its Religious and Social Significance in the Talmudic Period', *Cahiers d'histoire mondiale* II (1968), 148-68.

—'Was there a Woman's Gallery in the Synagogue of Antiquity?', *Tarbiz* 32 (1969), 329-38 (in Hebrew).

—'The Synagogue', in *Compendia Rerum Iudaicarum ad Novum Testamentum*, vol. II, ed. S. Safrai & M. Stern (Assen, 1976), 908-44.

—'Education and the Study of Torah', in *Compendia Rerum Iudaicarum ad Novum Testamentum*, vol. II, ed. S. Safrai and M. Stern (Assen, 1976), 945-70.

—and M. Stern (eds.), *Compendia Rerum Iudaicarum ad Novum Testamentum*, vol. II (Assen, 1976).

Savignac, R., 'Ossuaries. Tuiles romaines. Varia', *RB* 12 (1904), 262-65.

Schechter, S., *Studies in Judaism*, vol. I (London, 1896).

Schürer, E., *The History of the Jewish People in the Age of Jesus Christ*, revised edition: vols. I and II, ed. G. Vermes, F. Millar and M. Black (Edinburgh 1973, 1979); vols. IIIi and IIIii, ed. G. Vermes, F. Millar and M. Goodman (Edinburgh, 1986, 1987).

Seager, A., 'The Architecture of the Dura and Sardis Synagogues', in *The Synagogue: Studies in Origins, Archaeology and Architecture*, ed. H.M. Orlinsky with prolegomenon by J. Gutman (1975).

Segal, J.B., *The Hebrew Passover from the Earliest Times to AD 70* (London, 1963).

—'Popular Religion in Ancient Israel', *JJS* 27 (1976), 1-22.

—'The Jewish Attitude towards Women', *JJS* 30 (1979), 121-37.

Segal, M.Z., *The Complete Ben Sira* (Jerusalem, 1962); *Sefer Ben Sira Ha-Shalem* (Jerusalem, 1968).

Smith, W. Robertson, *Religion of the Semites* (London, 1894).

Ste Croix, G.E.M. de, 'Slavery and Other Forms of Unfree Labour', in *Slavery and Other Forms of Unfree Labour*, ed. L.J. Archer (London and New York, 1988), 19-32.

Stern, M., 'Aspects of Jewish Society: the Priesthood and other Classes', in *Compendia Rerum Iudaicarum ad Novum Testamentum*, vol. II, ed. S. Safrai & M. Stern (Assen, 1976), 561-630.

—*Greek and Latin Authors on Jews and Judaism*, vols. I-II (Jerusalem, 1976, 1980).

Strange, J.F., 'Late Hellenistic and Herodian Ossuary Tombs at French Hill, Jerusalem', *BASOR* 219 (1975), 39-67.

Swete, M.B., *The Old Testament in Greek according to the Septuagint* (Cambridge, 1887-1894).

Sukenik, E.L., 'A Jewish Hypogeum near Jerusalem', *JPOS* 8 (1928), 113-21.

—*The Ancient Synagogue of Beth Alpha* (Jerusalem, 1932).

—*Ancient Synagogues in Palestine and Greece* (London, 1934).

—*The Ancient Synagogue of El-Hammeh (Hammath by Gadara)* (Jerusalem, 1935).

Tcherikover, V.A. and A. Fuks, *Corpus Papyrorum Judaicarum*, vols. I-III (Cambridge, Mass., 1957-1964).

Torrey, C.C., *Apocryphal Literature. A Brief Introduction* (New Haven, 1963).

Trachtenberg, J., *Jewish Magic and Superstition. A Study in Folk Religion* (Cleveland, 1961).

Urbach, E.E., *The Sages. Their Concepts and Beliefs*, trans. I. Abrahams, vols. I-II (Jerusalem, 1975).

Ussishkin, D., 'The Necropolis from the time of the Kingdom of Judah at Silwan, Jerusalem', *BA* 33 (1970), 34-46.

Vaux, R. de, *Ancient Israel. Its Life and Institutions*, trans. J. Machugh (London, 1961).

Vermes, G., *Scripture and Tradition in Judaism* (Leiden, 1961).

—'The Qumran Interpretation of Scripture in its Historical Setting', *ALUOS* 6 (1966-68), 86-97.

—'Sectarian Matrimonial Halakhah in the Damascus Rule', in *Studies in Jewish Legal History,* ed. B.S. Jackson (London, 1974), 197-202.

—*Post-Biblical Jewish Studies* (Leiden, 1975).

—*The Dead Sea Scrolls in English* (London, 1975).

Vincent, L.H., *Underground Jerusalem* (London, 1911).

Westermark, E., *The History of Human Marriage*, vols. I-III (London, 1921).

Wilson, R.R., *Genealogy and History in the Biblical World* (New Haven, 1977).

Yadin, Y., 'Expedition D', *IEJ* 12 (1962), 235-48.

—*The Ben Sira Scroll from Massada* (Jerusalem, 1965).

—*Bar-Kokhba. The Rediscovery of the Legendary Hero of the Last Jewish Revolt against Imperial Rome* (London, 1971).

—'L'Attitude essénienne envers la polygamie et le divorce', *RB* 79 (1972), 98-100.

Yaron, R. 'Aramaic Marriage Contracts from Elephantine', *JJS* 3 (1958), 1-39.

—*Gifts in Contemplation of Death in Jewish and Roman Law* (Oxford, 1960).

—'The Murabba'at Documents', *JJS* 11 (1960), 157-71.

—*Introduction to the Law of the Aramaic Papyri* (Oxford, 1961).

—'The Restoration of Marriage', *JJS* 17 (1966), 1-12.

—'Mistake-Occasioned Palingamy', in *Studies in Jewish Legal History*, ed. B.S. Jackson (London, 1974), 203-25.

Zeitlin, S., 'The Origin of the Synagogue: A Study in the Development of Jewish Institutions', *PAAJR* 2 (1931), 69-81.

—'The Am-ha aretz: A Study in the Social and Economic Life of the Jews before and after the Destruction of the Second Temple', *JQR* 23 (1932), 45-61.

—'The Origin of the Ketubah. A Study in the Institution of Marriage', *JQR* 24 (1933), 1-7.

—'An Historical Study of the First Canonisation of the Hebrew Liturgy', *JQR* 38 (1948), 289-316.

—'The Offspring of Intermarriage', *JQR* 51 (1960), 135-40.

—'Testamentary Succession: A Study in Tannaitic Jurisprudence', *JQR* Anniversary Volume (1967), 574-81.

Zlotnik, D., *The Tractate Mourning (Semahot)* (New Haven and London, 1966).

INDEXES

INDEX OF MODERN AUTHORS

INDEX OF BIBLICAL REFERENCES

INDEX TO ANCIENT LITERATURE

in the order
Pseudepigrapha (arranged alphabetically)
Qumran (arranged alphabetically)
Midrash
Sifra
Sifre
Targum
Mishnah (arranged alphabetically)
Babylonian Talmud (arranged alphabetically)
Jerusalem Talmud (arranged alphabetically)
Tosefta
Philo
Josephus
Other Jewish Authors
Other Ancient Authors
Papyri

OTHER ANCIENT AUTHORS

JOURNAL FOR THE STUDY OF THE OLD TESTAMENT

Supplement Series